Teaching in Further Education and Skills: Concept to Classroom

Dan Williams
Kayte Haselgrove
Mike Tyler

For the CertEd,
Diploma in Teaching,
LST Apprenticeship,
PGCE / PGDE

The publisher gratefully acknowledges the permission of copyright holders to reproduce copyright material.

p.92 Bildgigant/Shutterstock; p.98 © SylviaDuckworth; p115 (spiral) iStock.com/Shinsuke Kubo, (network) iStock.com/isiddheshm, (web) iStock.com/illust-monster; p.160 iStock.com wongmbatuloyo; p.164 (left) iStock.com/anuwat meereewee, (right) iStock.com/invincible_bulldog; p.206 iStock.com/Khafizh Amrullah; p.220 iStock.com/JDawnInk; p.222 iStock.com/ Yulia Sutyagina

Cover image: © iStock.com/ lioputra

Every effort has been made to trace copyright holders and to obtain their permission for the use of copyright material. The publisher will be glad to make arrangements with any copyright holder it has not been possible to contact.

Copyright © 2025 Dan Williams, Kayte Haselgrove, Mike Tyler

All rights reserved. No part of this publication may be reproduced, distributed, or transmitted in any form or by any means, including photocopying, recording, or other electronic or mechanical methods, without the prior written permission of the publisher, or under licence from the Copyright Licensing Agency. See www.cla.co.uk for more details.

First edition 2025. Impression 10 9 8 7 6 5 4 3 2 1

ISBN 978-1-917048-06-4

Whilst every effort has been made to ensure all information in this book is correct, the publisher shall not be liable for any loss of profit or any other commercial damages, including but not limited to special, incidental, consequential, personal, or other damages, due to any information or advice contained in this book.

Ordering Information

Special discounts are available for class set purchases by colleges and universities. For details, contact the publisher at: orders@eboru.com

Trade orders: copies of this book are available through the normal wholesalers. For any queries please contact: orders@eboru.com

www.eboru.com

Contents

Foreword	vii
Introduction	1
What does it mean to be evidence-informed?	2
The best available evidence from research	2
The teaching context	3
Teacher experience, expertise and professional judgment	4
How to use this textbook	4
Overview of chapters	5
Author profiles	6
Chapter 1 The further education and skills sector	**8**
1.1 Introduction	8
1.2 What is FES and who is it for?	8
1.3 Background to the FE and skills sector	14
1.4 Navigating professional duties and ethical and legal standards	18
Chapter summary	23
References	24
Chapter 2 Professional duties and responsibilities of an FES teacher	**26**
2.1 Introduction	26
2.2 Responsibilities of an FES teacher	26
2.3 The dual professional	30
2.4 Professional standards	34
2.5 Education for sustainable development	36
2.6 Professional flexibility and resilience	39
Chapter summary	41
References	41

Chapter 3 The learning environment — 44

3.1 Introduction — 44
3.2 Setting the scene — 44
3.3 Institutional culture and policy — 45
3.4 Teacher presence and your teaching space — 50
3.5 Establishing professional relationships — 53
3.6 Creating a positive learning environment — 57
3.7 Establishing and maintaining high expectations — 62
3.8 Maintaining high expectations — 64
3.9 Returning to the policy — 66
Chapter summary — 68
References — 68

Chapter 4 Meeting learner needs — 70

4.1 Introduction — 70
4.2 Valuing diversity — 70
4.3 Legal and ethical considerations — 71
4.4 Identifying learner needs — 72
4.5 Promoting equality of opportunity — 88
4.6 Promoting inclusion — 97
4.7 Challenging discrimination and prejudice — 99
Chapter summary — 100

Chapter 5 Curriculum — 104

5.1 Introduction to chapters 5, 6 and 7 — 104
5.2 What is a curriculum? — 104
5.3 Designing a curriculum – models and intentions — 113
5.4 Designing a curriculum – content — 117
5.5 Designing a curriculum – considerations — 122
Summary — 130
References — 130

Chapter 6 Pedagogy — 133

    6.1 Introduction — 133

    6.2 Pedagogy — 133

    6.3 Pedagogical philosophies — 135

    6.4 Theories of learning and their application — 136

    6.5 Heart – affective and social theories of learning — 137

    6.6 Head – cognitive theories of learning — 149

    6.7 Hands – psychomotor theories of learning — 176

    6.8 Subject specialist and 'signature' pedagogies — 190

    Chapter summary — 191

    References — 192

Chapter 7 Assessment — 199

    7.1 Introduction — 199

    7.2 Methods of assessment — 199

    7.3 Initial assessment — 202

    7.4 Formative assessment — 205

    7.5 Summative assessment — 225

    Chapter summary — 230

    References — 232

Chapter 8 Collaborating in FES — 234

    8.1 Introduction — 234

    8.2 Communication — 237

    Chapter summary — 246

    References — 246

Chapter 9 Supporting learners' progression — 247

    9.1 Introduction — 247

    9.2 Purposeful curriculum design — 247

    9.3 Legislative and regulatory requirements — 248

    9.4 Progression pathways — 250

    9.5 Lower-level vocational and foundation learning — 254

9.6 General education (or 'academic' programmes that support progression to higher education) — 257

9.7 Collaborating with other stakeholders to support progression — 258

9.8 Digital tools for career guidance and progression planning — 260

9.9 The role of personal tutoring in supporting progression — 261

9.10 Measuring progression outcomes — 264

Chapter summary — 264

References — 264

Chapter 10 Success in your initial teacher education programme — 267

10.1 Introduction — 267

10.2 Requirements of your ITE programme — 267

10.3 Reflective practice — 270

10.4 Successful observation practice — 274

10.5 Successful professional development portfolios and discussions — 278

10.6 Getting the most from placements or workplace experiences — 281

10.7 Getting the most from your mentors — 282

10.8 Continuing Professional Development CPD — 284

10.9 Academic writing — 285

Chapter summary — 286

References — 287

Index — 289

Foreword

FE colleges are complex learning environments. They are the subjects of government Acts, white and green papers, codes of practice, and policy guidelines. Their curricula are far wider than those in schools, and their teachers often need to be dual-professionals (i.e. competent in both teaching and successful practitioners of their trade). Most of their students range from 16 to 21 and many of them have left school with disappointing academic results, necessitating challenging resits, all the while navigating the responsibilities of entering adulthood and an emerging sense of agency.

With such demands, it's critical that teachers use evidence-informed techniques to best stimulate learning. But that's not as simple – nor desirable – as simply adopting the pedagogy profile of schools. Given the different challenges and demands of FE colleges and their students, intelligent choices need to be made to best address their dynamics of learning.

This book is a wonderfully supportive guide through this network of perspectives and frameworks. It is both comprehensive and yet also very accessible. It shines a lucid light on the myriad demands on teachers. The organisation of the content is really clear, the writing direct and informative, and the ideas inspiring and practical.

Its three authors are highly respected in the sector, with decades of experience across a number of different levels from teacher to manager and from trainer to designer. They share a deep commitment to the success of their colleagues. This book, I believe, will enable that to happen. I recommend it to all.

Oliver Caviglioli

Introduction

This textbook has been developed to support those teaching, and training to teach, in the further education and skills (FES) sector. We have written this in an accessible, easily digestible format and provided a range of activities that can be used to help you connect key evidence-informed concepts to your FES classrooms and subject specialist teaching practice.

While this textbook has applicability to other initial teacher education (ITE) sectors both in the UK and abroad (such as primary and secondary), the focus is primarily on those undertaking one of the following ITE programmes in the FES sector in England:

- Level 5 Learning and Skills Teacher Apprenticeship
- Level 5 Diploma in Teaching (DiT)
- Level 5 Certificate in Education (Cert Ed)
- Level 6 Professional Graduate Certificate in Education (ProfGCE)
- Level 7 Postgraduate Certificate in Education (PGCE)
- Level 7 Postgraduate Diploma in Education (PGDE)

Readers will benefit from a series of chapters built around core aspects of the FES teaching role in alignment with the Department for Education's (DfE) guidance for 'Further education: initial teacher education' (2024) and the Diploma in Teaching (DiT) qualification framework.

Not only does this textbook map and build upon the occupational standards for learning and skills teachers, which underpin all level 5 and above ITE programmes in the FES sector, but these knowledge, skill and behaviour (KSB) standards are collated into nine duties that each chapter addresses. While we have taken care to include all KSBs for each duty, the nature of each chapter leans towards our professional interpretation of the duty in the context of ITE educators.

Chapter	Occupational duty
1. The FE and skills sector	Duty 7 – Work within professional boundaries and legal and ethical standards to set clear expectations for engaging in learning for all learners.
2. Professional duties and responsibilities of an FES teacher	Duty 8 – Undertake relevant roles and duties and model sustainable practices, having regard to professional standards, demonstrating resilience and adaptability when dealing with challenge and change.
3. The learning environment	Duty 1 – Promote a passion for learning and set high expectations of all learners and support their personal and skills development.

Chapter	Occupational duty
4. Meeting learners' needs	Duty 5 – Work in a manner that values diversity and actively promote equality of opportunity and inclusion by responding to the needs of all learners.
5. Curriculum	Duty 4 – Plan, deliver and evaluate effective evidence-informed teaching using assessment, relevant systems and safe use of technology to support learning.
6. Pedagogy*	Duty 3 – Demonstrate, maintain and evidence excellent pedagogy, subject, curriculum and industry knowledge and practice
7. Assessment	Duty 2 – Maintain a focus on outcomes for all learners, so that they recognise the value of their learning and the future opportunities available to them.
8. Collaborating in FES	Duty 6 – Model professional relationships with learners, colleagues and stakeholders that support high-quality education and training.
9. Progression	Duty 9 – Support learners with their next steps for progression and learning by providing appropriate information, advice and guidance.
10. Being successful as a trainee FES teacher	Aligned to the requirements for FES ITE programmes.

*Pedagogy is another word for teaching practice.

What does it mean to be evidence-informed?

Throughout this textbook, we refer to 'evidence-informed' practice in FES and, as such, we should define what it means to be evidence-informed. In the education world, there have been multiple ways of phrasing this idea (such as evidence-based, research-led and evidence-informed), but Duty 4 of the National Occupational Standard uses 'evidence-informed'. We think this is a good choice, as the difference between evidence and research is important. The word 'research' suggests papers and monographs written by researchers and academics in higher education; this may typically include qualitative studies done under laboratory conditions, meta-analyses and the 'gold standard' randomised controlled trials (RCTs). Typically, research findings are published with careful nuance as to their applicability in the 'real world' of the classroom. Sadly, this nuance can easily be lost in translation, and practice can diverge quite substantially from what is supported by the underlying research. These have come to be known as 'lethal mutations.'

The term 'evidence' encapsulates more than just research, and this is why we prefer it. Scutt (2018) has identified three overlapping areas of evidence that can be helpful to an FES practitioner when selecting and deploying an appropriate pedagogy.

The best available evidence from research

We are immediately faced with the challenge of deciding what counts as the 'best' evidence from research. Is some evidence better than other evidence? What are the criteria we could

Figure 0.1 Evidence-informed practice

use to evaluate the robustness of research findings from one paper compared with another? These are important considerations that will help develop your criticality as a consumer of educational research.

It is worth noting the use of the word 'available' in Scutt's representation. Not all research is accessible to FES practitioners; access to academic journals is not routinely provided, and finding the time during a busy teaching workload to read academic research is a real challenge. Research summaries can be very helpful, as can in-house continuous professional development (CPD) sessions run by professional development teams, but this introduces the question of how well those practitioners understand and apply their reading of the research. Again, lethal mutations can easily creep into practice in this way – be careful!

Real-world teaching scenarios are substantially more complex than those in academic research, where variables and conditions are tightly controlled. To be clear, such research is necessary and can be extremely helpful to the practitioner (as we will explore), but research is not enough. Your teaching context and professional expertise have an equally important role to play in guiding how you teach.

The teaching context

There are commonalities between learners across contexts, but as Wiliam (2018) notes, 'nothing works everywhere'. The complexity of each different teaching context should make us wary of grand assertions about 'what works' in education, particularly when these assertions reduce teaching to a set of procedures that can be mechanically implemented. The context in which teachers teach has a key role in directing judgments about effective pedagogy and includes the system, the setting, the group and the individual (Scutt, 2018).

Each teaching setting – whether a general FE college, a sixth form college, a prison or elsewhere – is situated socially, economically and geographically. There will be specific local skills needs and the local demographic will have a role to play in the sociocultural makeup of the learners you teach. Each of your groups will have its own dynamic that will be influenced by a wide range of factors including the group level, its size, levels of group cohesion and the range and compatibility of personalities present in the teaching space. Different groups may require different approaches.

At the individual level, there are Special Education Needs and Disabilities (SEND) and Social Emotional Mental Health (SEMH) considerations as well as how a learner's home life, interests and motivations shape their engagement with their studies, you and the institution.

Teacher experience, expertise and professional judgment

There is only so much that can be learned about teaching without getting in there and doing it. Testing out strategies and methods in the crucible of the classroom, with real learners in front of you, is where the rubber hits the road. You will find – if you haven't already – that some things just do not seem to work for some learners, and you will need to establish why that is. Should you give up on that task, or persist? Over time, you will have more of these experiences to draw on and more of these kinds of decisions to make. How do you give yourself the best chance of making the right call?

It is important to realise that experience alone is unlikely to make you a better teacher or help you make good pedagogical decisions in the moment. Reflecting on your experience and deliberate practice is necessary if you are going to improve your teaching skills and progress from being an experienced teacher to an expert teacher.

If you are currently training to teach, you will have multiple opportunities to be observed and receive feedback from those more knowledgeable than you. Whether you are newly qualified or have been teaching for a while, continue to take opportunities to discuss your practice with those teachers you know to be experts. The goal is not merely to replicate what others have done but to benefit from their expertise as you develop your own evidence-informed practices for your own learners in your own context.

Teacher hunches are seldom uninformed or arbitrary, but to give yourself the best chance of having good hunches you need to balance your intuitions with the two other forms of evidence (research and context) discussed above. In this textbook you will be encouraged to respond to the research evidence presented and think carefully and critically about what insights you may derive for your own practice.

How to use this textbook

We refer to the FES 'teacher' throughout this textbook, but it is important to recognise that this is a catch-all term and does not preclude those that identify as trainers, coaches, facilitators, lecturers or assessors. While each of these roles does differ slightly, there are fundamental responsibilities that require knowledge, skills and behaviours and we hope that through a series of reflective tasks, case studies, tips for teaching and the 'take it further' feature, you can easily relate the key concepts to your classrooms and subject-specialist teaching practices.

We intend for this textbook to be accessible yet challenging to all those undertaking an FES ITE programme or teaching within the sector. It does not have to be read from start to finish, and you can choose selected chapters that focus on selected occupational duties at your convenience. Throughout each chapter, in addition to rich, evidence-informed content you will find a series of themed activities that help you to connect the concepts to your classrooms.

Below are some of the features and their function:

- **Tips for teaching** – provide practical advice for ways to apply the content to your practice in a range of settings (classrooms, workshops and online).

- **Reflective tasks** – provide you with the opportunity to apply your learning of the content to your context.

- **Case studies** – real examples from a range of settings to bring the content to life.

- **Take it further** – ideal for those who wish to think more deeply and critically about the content.

We have drawn on our wealth of experience and kept the writing formal to support your academic work but, at the same time, hope you will find it very easy to read and see that our personalities come through the text. While we have collaborated on each chapter to add expertise and ensure diverse perspectives are considered, each of us have led on particular chapters where our knowledge, skills and experiences are our real strengths, as outlined below.

Overview of chapters

Chapter 1 centres on Duty 7 and intends to provide you with insight into the FE and skills sector. Dan takes us through what the sector is before considering the qualifications that may be undertaken. He then explores legislative and policy regulations that may impact the role of an FES teacher and shows us the historical influence of these on the sector, arguing that frequent political and societal changes have resulted in a low status compared to other education sectors and its international equivalents. Finally, professional boundaries and legal and ethical standards are considered in relation to the FES teacher's role with a range of reflective tasks and case studies to consider.

In chapter 2, Dan builds on chapter 1 by exploring aspects of Duty 8 (the roles and responsibilities of an FES teacher). He shows us how the role extends beyond the key duties of planning, teaching and assessing learners to one that requires FES teachers to manage competing demands, be resilient and adaptable and be cognisant of broader responsibilities in relation to professional standards and local, regional and global challenges through a lens of education for sustainable development (ESD).

Chapter 3 examines the learning environment in respect of Duty 1. Kayte leads us through a range of philosophical and practical strategies to maintain high expectations and a positive learning environment to help learners succeed.

In chapter 4, which is aligned to Duty 5, Kayte takes us on an empowering journey of understanding the diversity of your cohort and provides a range of strategies to promote equality of opportunity and an inclusive learning environment where all can thrive regardless of their background. Through a range of reflecting activities, you will come to realise how the language and actions in your learning environment can make your learners feel welcome, seen and heard, enabling them to make great progress during their learning journey.

Chapters 5, 6 and 7 link closely together. In chapter 5, Mike sets out a range of approaches to devising a curriculum. The chapter opens by asking the question, 'what is a curriculum?' We look at different curriculum models and intentions and how to go about selecting curriculum content, and finish with some practical considerations for bringing the curriculum to life for your learners. Duty 4 focuses on planning, delivery and evaluation of evidence-informed teaching, which informs the narrative of the chapter.

Chapter 6 is the longest chapter in the textbook and is linked to Duty 3. Pedagogy is so key to effective practice in FES that an extensive approach is warranted. Mike walks us through Bloom's three domains of learning (affective, cognitive and psychomotor) and shows how insights from each domain can be leveraged for great teaching and learning right across the FES sector. Mike also shows how the three domains interact and support each other so you can avoid developing a lopsided pedagogy. Repeatedly through the chapter, you will be reminded to take the pedagogical principles on offer and apply them to your subject specialism.

Chapter 7 focuses on assessment, and here Dan takes us through three principles of assessment practice – initial, formative and summative – with a range of reflection tasks and take it further activities to help you to support your learners to recognise the value of their learning in alignment with Duty 2.

In chapter 8, Dan explores Duty 6 and, through a lens of communication, examines the ways in which professional relationships can form and be maintained with a range of stakeholders in the learning process.

Chapter 9 centres on Duty 9, exploring the wide range of progression opportunities available to learners and draws upon the Gatsby benchmarks to support consideration of how to maximise progression through curriculum design and collaboration with learners and other stakeholders. A critical stance is taken on the different progression routes and how these may enable or hinder learners, particularly those from marginalised backgrounds, with reflection activities to help you consider how you can mitigate against some of the barriers for these groups.

Chapter 10, the final chapter, draws on the DfE guidance for FES ITE and our own experiences as leaders of high-quality, sector-leading programmes to bring you a range of ideas for being successful as a trainee FES teacher. We take you through a range of topic areas to prepare you for the challenges you may face while drawing on the best available research to support your evidence-informed practice.

Author profiles

Dan Williams

Dan has worked in the education sector since 2008, starting out as a lecturer in sport at a college in the Midlands before progressing as an advanced practitioner and then teaching and learning coach across two colleges where he supported teacher development across a range of subject specialisms. In 2016, Dan joined the University of Derby in his current role as programme leader for the post-14 FES ITE provision. In this role, he led the provision to an 'outstanding' Ofsted inspection outcome (May 2024), making it the largest and most diverse provider in the country to achieve this accolade.

In addition to his main role, Dan has held positions as trustee and board member for the ETF and as chair of the Society for Education and Training (SET) management board. Dan has published in the field of FES ITE, has a PhD in education and is currently content curator and editor of the ETF's quarterly inTuition journal.

Kayte Haselgrove

Kayte has worked in the FES sector since 2009, starting with a career in tutorial and pastoral care, before moving in to teaching functional skills and GCSE English and leading maths and IT. Kayte has held a number of roles across several general and specialist FE colleges, including advanced practitioner, subject leader, head of department for English and maths and head of teaching and learning and teacher training. Through her business, EduKayte, she has provided professional development at colleges across the country, representing organisations including the Education and Training Foundation. Kayte has been employed as assistant programme lead for the post-14 FE and skills ITE programmes at the University of Derby since 2021, taking a lead on the specialist English pathway and supporting an 'outstanding' Ofsted rating in 2024. Alongside this main role, Kayte is a co-editor, research convenor and co-chair for the Learning and Skills Research Network (LSRN) and Convenor for British Education Research Association (BERA) special interest group for post-compulsory and lifelong learning. Kayte is currently studying for a PhD in education and, as well as being a fellow of the ETF and of the Higher Education Association (HEA), she holds external examiner positions for FES ITE programmes at several universities.

Mike Tyler

Mike began his teaching career as a secondary geography teacher but quickly found himself in the wrong sector. Moving into FES in 2010, he spent 12 years teaching sport at Levels 1–5 at three colleges in the West Midlands, and he completed a masters in sociology of sport in 2020. Mike's roles since 2010 have included delivering cross-college training as a technology enhanced learning champion, quality development manager and professional development manager, as well as BTEC national examiner for sport.

Mike began working in ITE in 2020 teaching on the diploma in education and training before moving to his current post as lecturer in ITE (FE and skills) at the University of Worcester in 2022. As part of this role, Mike has designed the university's diploma in teaching, which is taught at two partner colleges. He is a member of ETF, a fellow of HEA and a BBC Pointless winner!

Chapter 1 The further education and skills sector

Work within professional boundaries, legal and ethical standards to set clear expectations for engaging in learning for all students. (Duty 7)

Knowing yourself is the beginning of all wisdom
Aristotle, (384–322 BCE)

1.1 Introduction

This chapter provides you with a background to the further education and skills (FES) sector and important context for your teaching practices. In understanding the context in which you work and the learners you may teach, this helps you to understand the essential role you have and the responsibilities bestowed upon you. We will examine what the FES sector is before considering the qualifications that may be undertaken. We then explore legislative and policy regulations that may impact the role and pull these together to examine how the FES sector has evolved to its present form, arguing that frequent political and societal changes have led the sector to not really knowing what it is and, consequently, maintaining its low status compared to other education sectors and its international equivalents. We will also consider what this means for teachers working in the sector and how they can navigate their professional boundaries and ethical and legal standards that impact the role.

1.2 What is FES and who is it for?

The FES sector is a section of the education system that is wide-ranging, far-reaching and made of many different types of providers, as shown in figure 1.1 below. General FE colleges are the largest providers of FES, offering a broad range of subjects to learners over the age of 16, with some also offering vocational education to learners aged 14 and over. Independent training providers, sometimes referred to as independent learning providers (ILPs), also form a large portion of the sector, mainly supporting learners that undertake training and development alongside employment. The sector also caters for adult learners, primarily in adult and community education settings. So, the sector caters for a diverse range of learners aged 14 and over and offers different routes towards employment, higher education or lifelong learning.

Each of these providers are funded slightly differently. The Education and Skills Funding Agency (ESFA) is responsible for administering funding to deliver education and skills for 16–19-year-olds, and they use different funding rates based on the learners' backgrounds and size of their study programmes. These funding rules also apply to 14–16-year-olds enrolled in an FES setting and up to 25-year-olds with an educational health care plan (EHCP). For those over the age of 19, the adult skills fund (ASF) supports them to gain skills that lead to meaningful, sustained and relevant employment or further learning that will support that outcome.

Across this broad range of providers are a wide range of curricula that contribute to the programme of study, including academic programmes (such as A-levels), technical programmes (such as T Levels), vocational learning and lifelong learning, all of which bridge the gap between school and higher education or employment, as shown in figure 1.2.

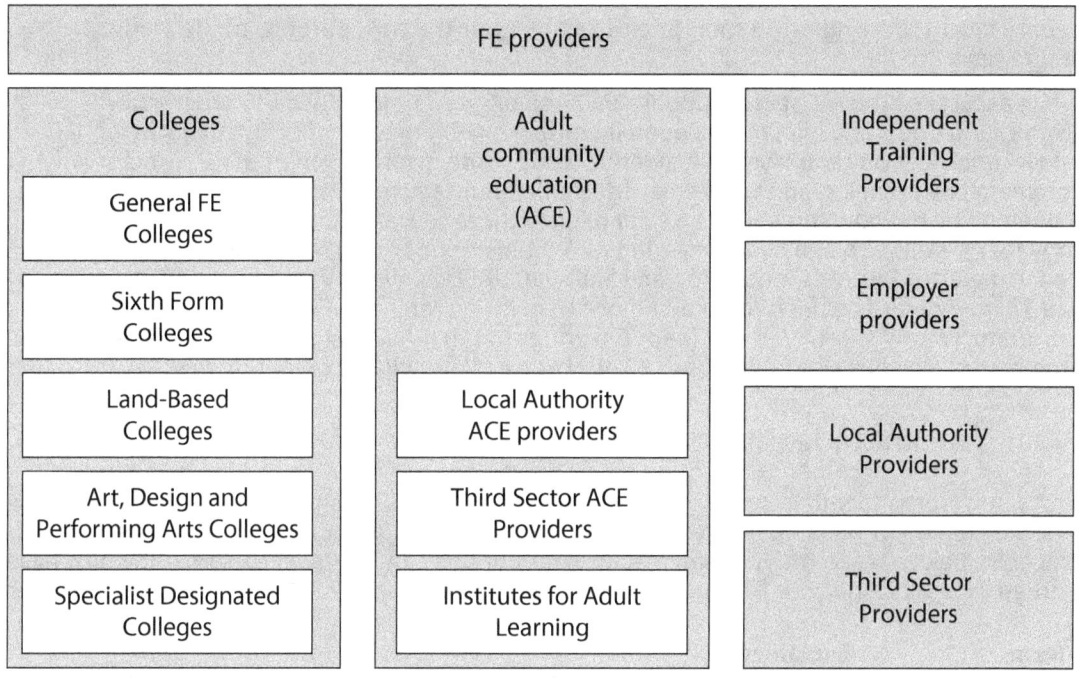

Figure 1.1 *Types of FE and skills provider in England*

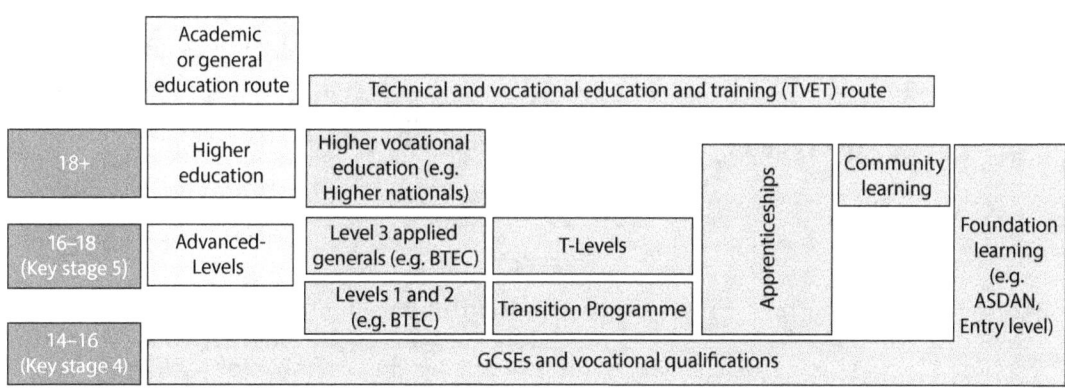

Figure 1.2 *Qualifications available in the FE and skills sector*

In addition to these substantial qualifications, learners' study programmes may also consist of English or maths qualifications, work experience and a non-qualification activity such as enrichment, depending on their prior attainment or the core purpose of the study programme.

While aspects of the FES sector support 'general' or 'academic' education progression, given that schools and higher education institutions (HEI) tend to offer the majority of A-level qualifications and level 4+ academic study respectively, much of the FES sector is dominated by technical and vocational education and training (TVET). England's TVET system is deemed by the government to be a supplier to the labour market through providing the knowledge, skills and behaviours needed for employment or progression in employment (DfE/Department for Business Innovation and Skills, 2016). However, over the past 30 years, it has had 28 major pieces of legislation and more than 30 secretaries of state (Wolf, 2017), and this has led to 'mostly short-lived and inept tinkerings […] that have all failed to solve the central problems of [this] provision' (Hyland, 2014). Let's explore what is meant by this.

What is meant by legislation and policy?

Firstly, it is worth spending some time understanding what is meant by the numerous terms that are created or debated in government and have a huge impact on our day-to-day practices. Below are terms you may read or hear about as an FES teacher, some of which have a greater influence on your role and responsibilities than others.

Term	Explained
Acts	A formal piece of legislation (a law) that has been passed by the UK parliament.
White papers	Policy documents produced by the UK government that outline their proposals for future legislation. White papers serve as a way to present and seek feedback on proposed policies or laws.
Green papers	Consultation documents issued by the government to stimulate discussion and gather feedback on specific policy areas.
Codes of practice	Guidelines and standards for professional conduct within a specific field or industry.
Policies	Formal statements that outline an organisation's rules, principles and procedures. This can be at a government or institutional level.

Reflect

Before we go any further, reflect on your current understanding of any of the terms above that influence the policies and procedures at your organisation or your role and responsibilities as an FES teacher. Try to think of at least one example for each term.

Relevance to FES

Some of you may have identified more examples than those in the table below, but this provides an idea of the wide-ranging legislation and policy that is not only applicable to FES but education more broadly.

Term	Relevant examples
Acts	- **Equality Act 2010** – This act legally protects people from discrimination in the workplace and in wider society under nine protected characteristics. - **Children and Families Act 2014** – This act includes provisions for the support of children and young people with SEND. - **Health and Safety at Work Act 1974 (HASAWA)** – This act provides a legal framework designed to protect the wellbeing of employees, contractors and the general public from risks associated with work activities. - **Data Protection Act 2018** – This act enacts the EU General Data Protection Regulations (GDPR) into UK domestic law, meaning educational institutions must handle personal data lawfully, transparently and securely. It gives individuals greater control over their personal information, including rights to access, rectify and erase data. - **The Safeguarding Children and Young People Act 2023** – This act strengthens legal protections for children and vulnerable young people by establishing more robust reporting requirements, mandatory training standards for professionals working with minors and clearer accountability frameworks for organisations. - **The Counter-Terrorism and Security Act 2015** – This act places a legal duty on specified authorities, including schools and colleges, known as the 'Prevent duty.' This requires educational institutions to have 'due regard to the need to prevent people from being drawn into terrorism.'
White papers	**Skills for jobs: lifelong learning for opportunity and growth (2021)** – This paper outlines a detailed plan to reform post-16 education and training through enhancing skills development, boosting productivity and supporting economic growth.
Green papers	**SEND review: right support, right place, right time (2022)** – This paper proposed a new national SEND and alternative provision system with nationally consistent standards across education, health and care.
Codes of practice	**SEND code of practice: 0 to 25 years (2014)** – This code provides statutory guidance for supporting children and young people aged 0 to 25 with SEND in England.
Policies	**Post-16 Skills Plan** (DfE/Department for Business Innovation and Skills, 2016), which was developed by the Conservative government at the time to reform the TVET system, resulting in technical level (T Level) qualifications. These are aligned to 15 pathways identified as priority areas for boosting economic growth.

As you can see, there are a range of examples that have an impact on your role. However, simply reciting them and their year of production is not something that will offer much value to your practice. You need to understand the extent to which they influence your role and the consequences of this, particularly in the context you are teaching in.

For example, the Equality Act 2010 forms an integral part of your practice as everything you do in your role, from interviewing applicants, planning and teaching your sessions and assessing the learners must adhere to principles in the act, enabling everyone, regardless of background, to have a fair opportunity to learn and progress on your programme. The Health and Safety at Work etc. Act 1974 is particularly crucial for those learning in a workplace or simulated workplace environment, and it is essential that key responsibilities are understood in relation to this act to support safe learning. For example, if using equipment that may cause an injury, appropriate risk assessments should be carried out and all learners should wear the correct personal protective equipment (PPE) and act in accordance with safe working practices. In respect to white or green papers, these are helpful to provide context to what informs the curricula at your institution, such as the introduction of T Levels as a result of the Skills Plan (2016). They may also be drawn upon to support any curriculum enhancements to better meet learners' needs.

Reflect

Select at least three of the above examples in the table and reflect on how your organisational and subject specialist teaching practices are informed by each.

Take it further...

Think about how each of the above have influenced the formulation of the local organisational policies e.g., GDPR (2018) may have led to your FES provider to have its own policy for data handling, obtaining appropriate consent, reporting breaches, and they may also have a designated Data Protection Officer.

In addition to the various legislative and policy factors that impact the role of an FES teacher, there are also numerous organisations or bodies that either produce policies or help to enact them on behalf of the government. It is important to have an awareness of these and consider the impact on your professional duties.

Organisation or body	Roles and responsibilities
The Department for Education (DfE) The government department responsible for children's services and education in England.	Responsible for education, children's services, higher and further education policy, apprenticeships and wider skills in England. Develops education policy, allocates funding to schools and colleges, sets the national curriculum, establishes assessment frameworks and monitors educational standards.

Organisation or body	Roles and responsibilities
Skills England, formerly Institute for Apprenticeships and Technical Education (IfATE) The government body responsible for developing and maintaining high-quality apprenticeships and technical education in England.	Ensures technical education provides clear progression pathways and meets the skills needs of employers and the wider economy. Oversees the development, approval and quality assurance of apprenticeships and technical qualifications in England.
Ofsted The Office for Standards in Education, Children's Services and Skills. Ofsted is a non-ministerial department of the UK government responsible for inspecting and regulating services that provide education, training and care for learners of all ages in England.	Ofsted aims to raise standards in education and children's social care through inspecting a wide range of educational institutions, including state-funded schools, academies, some independent schools, colleges and apprenticeship providers. It reports on its findings to inform parents, carers, policymakers and the public about the quality and effectiveness of these services.
Regulatory bodies - Ofqual in England - Qualifications Wales - CCEA in Northern Ireland - SQA in Scotland All four bodies operate independently of the UK government and are responsible for regulating qualifications within their respective regions.	They ensure that qualifications meet specific standards and are reliable indicators of learners' knowledge and skills. All play a crucial role in maintaining and monitoring the quality of education and assessments. This includes setting standards, accrediting qualifications and ensuring compliance with these standards.
Awarding organisations Awarding organisations (also known as awarding bodies) are entities responsible for designing, developing, delivering and awarding qualifications. Examples include City and Guilds, Pearson/Edexcel, OCR, AQA, NCFE and WJEC.	In designing, developing and delivering qualifications, they ensure that specific standards are met and that qualifications are recognised as credible and valid. They operate rigorous quality assurance processes that are essential to maintain the integrity and reliability of the qualifications.
Education and Training Foundation (ETF) The expert body for professional development and standards in FES and training in England.	They provide a wide range of professional development programs and resources to help educators enhance their skills and knowledge. They develop and maintain professional standards for teachers, trainers and leaders in the FES sector. They conduct research to inform policy and practice, promoting innovation in teaching and learning and advocates for the FE and skills sector, representing its interests to policymakers and stakeholders.

> **REFLECT**
>
> Based on the table above, identify the key organisations that impact your role in your own context. For example, who is the awarding organisation for the curriculum you teach?

Take it further...

Research each of the organisations in the table above and write a short reflection on the links between each organisation and some of the key legislation and organisational policies. For example, you could look at Ofsted's inspection framework and find that there is a big focus on support for disadvantaged and vulnerable children and learners, including those with SEND. This ensures that providers are adhering to key legislation such as the Equality Act 2010, Children and Families Act 2014 and the SEND Code of Practice, and you may have a specific policy in your organisation related to equal opportunities and support for those with particular needs.

1.3 Background to the FE and skills sector

This section identifies key milestones in the history of FE and skills to understand the impact that society, the economy and political decisions have had on the sector. Throughout this section, we shall critically examine the complex FES context and reflect on what this means for us, the curriculum and the learners that study it.

The FES sector has witnessed more change and development than any other education sector in the UK. Despite offering something for everyone, it continues to have a low status compared to European countries such as France and Germany where it is held in much higher regard (Winch, 2018). In the UK, FES and TVET institutions continue to be positioned as a second-choice option providing vocational or remedial ('second chance') academic programmes, with many of the young people undertaking these programmes coming from poorer or minority backgrounds (Atkins, 2013). This, in part, stems from the school system, where children are allocated their pathway for life based on early assessments in reading, writing and arithmetic and grouped based on ability. Higher achievers, usually from more privileged backgrounds, are ushered along a path of academic study to A-levels and more prestigious universities, while others are destined for lower-skilled, lower-paid futures through a path of study geared towards preparation for employment.

When researching the backgrounds of FES learners, Thompson (2009) suggests that 'middle-class failure' is as common as working-class disadvantage when considering prior attainment. Without delving too far into the stratification of different social groups, Thompson's work highlights that there are a large number of learners in FES that may be from wealthier, middle-class backgrounds who have relatively more privileges and opportunities compared to those from poorer groups. This, he argues, is because they have failed on the traditional academic pathway and have opted to enter FES for a second chance at reaching their aspirations – what he calls middle-class failures. This begs the question as to why FES was a second choice in the first place and the messages this sends to those where FES is the only choice. To understand why FES has a low status, we have to take a look back at the development of the sector.

The history of FES

Distinct separations between technical and general education have existed since the establishment of the tripartite education system (grammar, technical and comprehensive) following the 1944 Education Act (Crowther, 1959). These institutions divided young people by their 'academic' abilities, with those deemed of higher intelligence being ushered into grammar schools and on to higher education, those more 'practically inclined' being positioned in technical institutions and into employment and everyone else attending comprehensive schools with a less clear progression pathway. Alongside this, the act also placed a statutory duty on local education authorities (LEAs) to provide provision for FES, which led to a growth in the number of colleges specialising in technical, arts and commercial fields (Simmons, 2016).

Labour governments in the 1960s and 70s

Due to an economic crisis and high levels of youth unemployment, full-time participation in FES increased throughout the 1960s and 70s. While apprenticeships became more formalised as a result of the Industrial Training Act 1964 and increased in popularity, they only supported about 15% of school leavers and aimed at higher technical skills for an elite minority, most of whom were male.

FE college expansion continued and there was an emphasis on innovative learning programmes that aimed at reaching the more reluctant and disadvantaged learners, with the introduction of vocational qualifications such as City and Guilds and BTECs (formerly TEC/BEC). These qualifications were designed to provide individuals with practical skills that aligned with the needs of the changing economy, and they embedded 'the world of work' within broader educational programmes that included essential tools such as basic literacy, basic numeracy, the understanding of how to live and work together and respect for others and the individual (Kelly, 2001). However, the status of these programmes resulted in lower-skilled employment, and it was reported that only 40% of the workforce in the United Kingdom held qualifications relevant to their jobs compared with 85% in Germany (Thompson, 1995).

Conservative governments in the 1980s and 90s

Throughout the 1980s, the low status of FES in Britain continued and the sector shifted towards market-driven principles, reduced to 'narrow vocational training, where usefulness was gauged only in terms of the competence it produced in the workforce' (Kelly, 2001). Qualification reform was rife, with the establishment of a system of national vocational qualifications (NVQs) that were based on a statement of standards clearly aligned and relevant to work and assessment of skills to these specified standards. As manufacturing continued to decline and service-sector jobs grew, policy attention was also directed to supporting effective transitions from school to work via a pre-vocational education programme, with the creation of a new curriculum pathway for those between the ages of 14 and 18 for whom the traditional academic curriculum was unsuitable.

These programmes were centred on employability but became stigmatised as an option for failure or for learners who were not academically inclined. The 1990s also saw the introduction of the modern apprenticeships, which aimed to revitalise the system and make it more responsive to the needs of modern industries; however, concerns were quickly raised about the exploitation of cheap labour and they remained a second-choice option to academic programmes for learners (Keep and Mayhew, 1999).

Labour governments in the 1990s and 2000s

Continued technological advancements, globalisation and the rise of a knowledge-based economy required a workforce that could adapt to rapidly changing industries. The Labour government placed FES at the heart of their economic policy, with a significant focus on tackling skills shortages and making education more accessible, particularly for disadvantaged groups. Qualifications such as BTECs, NVQs and apprenticeships continued to play a key role, though there was a growing recognition of the need to integrate academic and vocational pathways to increase equity and create a more flexible and resilient workforce (Tomlinson, 2004). This led to the 14–19 education reforms that introduced diplomas in subjects such as engineering, health and IT that were designed to offer an alternative to traditional GCSEs and A-levels and aligned with the skills needs of the economy. However, these reforms were short-lived, and funding was withdrawn as soon as the Labour government lost power in 2010.

Coalition and Conservative governments in the 2010s and 2020s

Under Conservative leadership, the focus on FES shifted again, influenced by austerity policies, technological changes and global competition. Following the Wolf Report (Wolf, 2011), the government introduced reforms aimed at streamlining vocational qualifications and strengthening apprenticeships, with the creation of the apprenticeship levy in 2017, which required large employers to contribute to the cost of apprenticeships. Additionally, the Skills Plan (2016) and subsequent Skills and Post-16 Education Bill (2021) sought to provide more focused pathways for young people in an attempt to give technical education parity of esteem with academic routes, meet the needs of an evolving labour market and, crucially, to boost economic growth. This resulted in a new suite of qualification called T Levels and the proposal to defund any competing qualifications such as BTECs. With T Levels only offered at level 3, this created a division between the technical and vocational qualifications, resulting in what Esmond and Atkins (2022) refer to as a 'technical elite' whose higher-level technical skills were in high demand, with those unable to access T Levels destined for poor quality general vocational qualifications leading to low-skilled and low-paid employment.

Alongside these changes, the Covid-19 pandemic led to a shift in online learning and adoption of digital tools, and this not only highlighted the need for a flexible and resilient workforce but also the catastrophic inequalities in access to education. Post-pandemic policies were shaped by the need to address the disparities and focused on retraining opportunities but, significantly, there was a succession of government spending cuts and stagnation that ultimately marginalised a sector that, ironically, was highlighted as crucial to boosting economic growth.

Labour government in the 2020s

As we write this textbook, it is still unclear what the future of FES looks like under a Labour government, but their five missions suggest that FES will have a significant role to play in achieving them. The establishment of Skills England in place of IfATE, with the intention of supporting the workforce to remain competitive in the face of rapid technological and environmental changes, is a promising early step to place FES at the heart of Labour's policies.

As can be seen from this potted history of FES, there have been various attempts to reform the sector, largely through overhauling the curricula within it. But as we covered at the start of this chapter, over the course 30 years the sector has been influenced by 28 major pieces of legislation and more than 30 secretaries of state. This has meant that, unlike academic qualifications, which have remained largely unchanged with only small tweaks, the qualifications within FES have undergone huge transformations and, in some cases, these have only been short-lived with insufficient time given to see the impact.

An analogy for FES

David Russell (2017), former CEO of the ETF, once shared a simple analogy for the problem with FES, more specifically TVET qualifications, today. Let's look and then reflect on this characterisation:

Imagine you had a box full of Lego and that all the pieces in the box represented the education system and its qualifications. You can build whatever you want to but there are limited pieces.

You start by building a huge rocket ship that uses many of the bricks and looks like it was designed by a Lego expert – perfectly formed. This represents the prestigious A-level qualifications.

You look at the remaining pieces and manage to get enough for a satisfactory attempt at a car. There are some awkward looking parts but, on the whole, it looks like a Lego car and moves like one. This represents apprenticeships – a respected credential, but it isn't entirely clear where it belongs and how it fits into the system.

Finally, you are left with the remaining pieces and attempt to put something together that has meaning – something that looks a bit like a rocket ship but also a bit like a car, but there are not many pieces of Lego left to do this. This represents the rest of the TVET system.

In essence, the resources and commitment to maintaining the prestige of one qualification means that there are finite resources for everything else. There have been numerous attempts at creating technical and vocational qualifications, but nothing has stood the test of time.

> **REFLECT**
>
> Do you agree with this characterisation of the FE and skills sector? If you had the Lego box, would you dismantle and rebuild the education system, or would you keep parts of it?

At this point in the chapter we have a bit more information about the FES sector, how it has changed, the overarching causes that led to these changes and, importantly, the learners in FES and their backgrounds. To summarise the chapter so far:

- Government legislation, policies and regulations drive the focus in FES, and this is influenced by what is happening in society and the labour market.

- FES largely caters for learners who study TVET programmes rather than traditional academic programmes.

- Learners that study these programmes are often from poorer or minority backgrounds and often have little other option but to attend an FES institution.

- Some learners use FES as a second-choice option. As a result, FES in the UK has a low status compared to other sectors and comparable sectors in similar developed countries.

It is important for us to consider some of the implications of these bigger-picture challenges as teachers in the sector. In the next section, we shall explore what this means for teachers working in the FES sector and how this impacts us professionally.

1.4 Navigating professional duties and ethical and legal standards

In FES teaching specifically, the role requires us to make decisions that navigate complex issues around our professionalism and legal and ethical standards; in other words, what we must do legally and what we believe is morally the right or wrong thing to do. For example, in FES there is always a balance to strike between maintaining rigour with the academic standards while ensuring that our inclusive practice provides equitable opportunities for all to succeed. Alongside this, there is also the challenge of addressing the conflicts between aspirational targets that the institution sets in metrics such as attendance, retention, achievement of learners and the learners' individual needs. Striking the right balance can be a challenge.

> **REFLECT**
>
> Imagine a learner on your programme was struggling to attend because of a physical disability and this was impacting their learning and achievement on the programme. How would you navigate the situation while balancing the legal responsibilities you have in providing equal opportunity alongside institutional requirements for attendance and achievement rates?

Working within professional boundaries

Maintaining appropriate professional boundaries is essential for effective teaching and safeguarding learners. FES teachers work with diverse learner populations, including both young people and adults, which presents unique challenges in establishing consistent boundaries. The table below sets out some important professional boundaries in teacher-learner relationships.

Type of boundary	Defined
Emotional	Showing empathy and support while avoiding taking on the role of friend, therapist or parent.
Physical	Maintaining appropriate physical distance and avoiding unnecessary physical contact.
Social	Limiting social interactions outside the educational context, particularly on social media.
Temporal	Establishing clear parameters around availability and response times.
Knowledge	Recognising the limits of professional expertise and when to refer to specialists.

REFLECT

For the following examples, determine whether or not you think they cross the professional boundary of an FES teacher.

Example	Our take
A learner contacts you via email past 5pm asking for an urgent response about an assessment task. You respond later that evening.	This example relates to a temporal boundary, and while it does not necessarily cross a line, you would need to be careful to not set a precedent where the expectation becomes that your personal life and time are compromised by work.
In an engineering class, you are showing a learner how to perform a difficult technique and move their hand into a position without asking their permission.	This example relates to a physical boundary and requires a little more sensitivity. Ordinarily, physical touch should be avoided. However, sometimes manipulation into the correct position can be the only way to support your learners. In these instances, you must ask their permission prior to any form of physical contact, and it is always advisable to have others present observing. You must also be aware of things like religious convention, where it may not be appropriate to touch.
A learner approaches you asking for financial advice and you talk them through how to budget.	This example relates to a knowledge boundary, as financial advice is very much beyond most teachers' knowledge and skills. What you may think is sound financial advice may not be right for the learner, so always signpost them to colleagues within the institution. That said, if you are teaching accountancy or budget management, your subject expertise may position you to teach the broad fundamentals, but this does not constitute 'advice'.
You have a LinkedIn profile that is open access to anyone, and a learner chooses to follow you.	This relates to a social boundary, but in this case, it is a personal preference. You should be conscious of the messages you are putting into the social space, but this particular platform is a professional one and it could be argued that you are modelling professional practices for your learners. For personal social media spaces such as Instagram, the general advice from us is to keep it private.
A learner's relative has recently died, and you console them with a hug.	This relates to an emotional and physical boundary and is a really tricky one, because it can be natural to want to console your learners in instances like this. However, if you think about power dynamics, the learner is at their most vulnerable here, so physical contact should be avoided at all costs.
A learner declares that they are being emotionally abused by their parents, and you call them to check this is true.	This relates to an emotional and knowledge boundary and absolutely should not happen. Your role in any potential safeguarding issue must be to refer to the designated safeguarding lead (DSL). You should listen to all of the information presented to you, be sensitive to the information and accurately record it to enable you to pass it on to the DSL, but you should never check the legitimacy of a concern by contacting potential abusers.

> **Take it further...**
>
> Which type(s) of boundaries (i.e. emotional, physical, social, temporal, knowledge) do you think are relevant for each example in the previous activity?

For FES teachers, navigating these boundaries can be particularly challenging when working with adult learners who may be close in age or have significant life experience. In these contexts, it is important to maintain a professional demeanour while acknowledging the adult status of learners.

There are several guiding principles that can help FES teachers maintain appropriate boundaries. These include being consistent and ensuring that you apply the same standards and expectations to all learners to avoid favouritism or differential treatment. Furthermore, it is essential that you are transparent about your professional boundaries with learners from the outset and always aware of the teacher-learner power dynamics. Clear boundaries protect both learners and teachers, creating a safe and productive learning environment. When boundaries become blurred, both teaching effectiveness and learner wellbeing can be compromised.

Signposting and referral

An essential aspect of working within professional boundaries is recognising when learners' needs extend beyond your expertise or remit. Effective signposting and referral involve a series of steps, as we can see in figure 1.3.

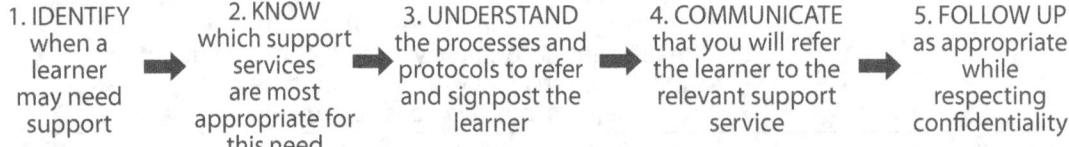

Figure 1.3 *Effective signposting and referral*

It is important that you develop a comprehensive understanding of the support network available to you and your learners within and beyond your institution, including:

- The DSL or safeguarding officer.
- Learning support services.
- Mental health and wellbeing support.
- Financial advice and hardship funds.
- Career guidance and progression support.
- Specialist external agencies (e.g. housing, addiction services).

By developing this understanding, you can ensure that learners receive appropriate support while maintaining clear professional boundaries.

Legislative and regulatory frameworks that impact professional boundaries

Earlier in this chapter, we identified a range of legislation that may impact the role (see page 11), and in the section above, we considered some of the types of boundaries we face in the role (see page 18). We now want to take this a step further and consider the implications of legislation in terms of our professional boundaries.

Legislation	Impact on professional boundaries	Case study
Equality Act 2010	Requires you to: • treat all learners fairly regardless of their protected characteristics • have an awareness of unconscious bias in your teaching, learning and assessment (see chapter 4, page 99) • ensure appropriate accommodations for learners without showing favouritism • create boundaries around personal views that may conflict with protected characteristics • carefully consider your teaching materials and examples.	A business studies lecturer regularly uses examples featuring only male entrepreneurs. When challenged by a female learner, he dismisses her concerns, suggesting, 'that's just how the business world is'. This represents a failure to maintain appropriate professional boundaries by allowing personal biases to influence teaching content, potentially violating the Act's provisions against discrimination. A more appropriate response would involve diversifying examples and acknowledging the learner's valid concerns.
SEND code of practice	Requires you to: • follow institutional expectations for reasonable adjustments without compromising learning standards • balance individual needs with group teaching responsibilities • maintain boundaries around self-disclosure of personal learning difficulties • adhere to the institution's guidance on the limits on the teacher's role versus specialist support professionals.	An English teacher becomes overly involved with a dyslexic learner, creating special materials and spending lunch breaks providing extra help. While well-intentioned, the teacher is crossing professional boundaries by assuming specialist responsibilities instead of working with learning support and external specialists as outlined in the SEND code of practice. This creates dependency and potentially unrealistic expectations for support that may not be sustainable or appropriate within their role.

Legislation	Impact on professional boundaries	Case study
Working together to safeguard children	Requires you to: • understand the reporting requirements over personal judgment • maintain boundaries around confidentiality and promise-keeping • maintain professional distances while building trusting relationships. • follow protocols for personal disclosures • be aware of power dynamics and vulnerability.	A performing arts teacher notices concerning bruises on a learner, who confides that they are being physically abused at home but begs the teacher not to tell anyone. The teacher, feeling the learner's trust is paramount, agrees to keep it secret but offers personal support outside college hours. This crosses professional boundaries by placing the teacher-learner relationship above safeguarding obligations, potentially endangering the learner further. Professional boundaries would require reporting to the designated safeguarding lead while maintaining appropriate support within the educational setting.
Prevent duty	Requires you to: • create boundaries around discussing controversial political topics • balance free speech with preventing radicalisation • follow protocols for addressing concerning viewpoints • distinguish between personal opinions and professional responsibilities • maintain neutrality while promoting critical thinking.	A sociology teacher passionate about social justice allows classroom discussions to become increasingly polarised when discussing terrorism. Instead of facilitating balanced debate, the teacher shares personal political views and fails to challenge extremist comments from learners. This crosses professional boundaries by neglecting the prevent duty requirement to maintain neutrality while promoting critical thinking. A more appropriate approach would involve facilitating balanced discussions, offering multiple perspectives and focusing on developing critical analysis skills.
Data Protection and GDPR	Requires you to: • adhere to clear boundaries around sharing learner information • follow institutional protocols for maintaining data security • consider the necessity before collecting personal data • limit use of personal devices for work purposes • maintain clear boundaries between personal and professional social media use.	A maths teacher takes home unmarked assessments containing personal data and leaves them in their car overnight. They later post anonymised but recognisable results on a personal social media account to celebrate high achievements. This crosses professional boundaries by failing to maintain data security and inappropriately sharing learner information. GDPR requires secure handling of personal data, clear consent for data sharing and maintaining appropriate boundaries between personal and professional digital spaces.

Digital boundaries and professionalism in online spaces

The increasing digitalisation of education has created new challenges for professional boundary management. FES teachers must navigate online spaces with the same professionalism they bring to physical classrooms while recognising the unique characteristics of digital interaction.

Key considerations for digital boundaries include:

- **Social media** – As teachers increasingly use online technology to fulfil their roles, it becomes harder to distinguish private from personal concerns. Maintaining separate personal and professional accounts, using privacy settings appropriately and considering the implications of connecting with learners on these platforms is paramount.

- **Communication channels** – It is important to establish clear guidelines for how and when learners can contact you digitally and ensure use of institutional systems rather than personal accounts.

- **Online teaching presence** – Maintaining a professional appearance and ensuring the environment (i.e. background), language and behaviour in virtual classrooms are appropriate.

- **Digital footprint** – As White (2016) notes, many young people believe they have the right to post anything they want on social media sites, but this could become a serious problem for their future careers as an electronic trail is created. Being conscious of the permanent nature of online content and how it could be perceived by learners, colleagues and employers is essential as a teacher.

Not only should you model the above to your learners to maintain professionalism in alignment with your duties, but you should also model this to support your learners' understanding and practices. Having conversations about what you are doing and why can go some way to supporting this.

Chapter summary

This chapter has explored the complex landscape of the FE and skills sector in the UK, from its historical development to its present form. We have examined how the sector caters to diverse learners over the age of 14, offering various pathways including technical education, vocational training and lifelong learning opportunities.

The FES sector operates within a dense network of legislative frameworks, policies and regulations that significantly influence teaching practices and professional responsibilities. The sector has undergone frequent transformations driven by political, economic and societal changes, contributing to its ongoing identity challenges and relatively low status compared to other educational sectors both domestically and internationally.

FES primarily serves learners from diverse backgrounds, including those pursuing second-chance education opportunities, vocational pathways and technical training, and as FES professionals we must navigate complex professional boundaries to create safe and effective learning environments while fulfilling our ethical and legal obligations.

The chapter has directly addressed Duty 7, providing a foundation for understanding professional boundaries and the legal and ethical standards that guide our work. As you develop your teaching practice, consider how the historical context, legislative framework and professional boundaries discussed here shape your specific teaching context and interactions with learners. Understanding these dimensions is essential for establishing clear expectations and fostering meaningful engagement among all learners in the FES sector.

References

Atkins, L. (2013). 'From Marginal Learning to Marginal Employment? The Real Impact of 'Learning' Employability Skills'. Power and Education, 5 (1), 28-37.

Crowther, G. (1959). The Crowther Report (1959): 15 to 18. Available at: http://www.educationengland.org.uk/documents/crowther/crowther1959-1.html (Accessed 12 July 2024).

Department for Education/ Department for Business, Energy and Industrial Strategy (DfE/DBEIS). (2016). The Post 16 Skills Plan. Available at: https://assets.publishing.service.gov.uk/government/uploads/system/uploads/attachment_data/file/536043/Post-16_Skills_Plan.pdf (Accessed 07 April 2025).

Education and Training Foundation (ETF). (2020). SO WHAT IS THE FE SECTOR? A GUIDE TO THE FURTHER EDUCATION SYSTEM IN ENGLAND. Available at: https://www.et-foundation.co.uk/wp-content/uploads/2020/08/200729-ETF-FE-Sector-Guide-RGB-v10.pdf (Accessed 20 June 2024)

Esmond, B. and Atkins, L. (2022). Education, Skills and Social Justice in a Polarising World. Between Technical Elites and Welfare Vocationalism. London: Routledge.

Hyland, T. (2014). 'Reconstructing Vocational Education and Training for the 21st Century: Mindfulness, Craft, and Values.' SAGE Open, 4(1), 1-15.

Keep, E. and Mayhew, K. (1999). 'The Assessment: Knowledge, Skills, and Competitiveness.' Oxford Review of Economic Policy, 15(1), 1-15.

Kelly, A. (2001). 'The Evolution of Key Skills: towards a Tawney paradigm.' Journal of Vocational Education and Training, 53 (1).

Simmons, R. (2016). Liberal studies and critical pedagogy in further education colleges: 'where their eyes would be opened' (sometimes), Oxford Review of Education, 42 (6), 692-706.

Thompson, P.J. (1995). 'Competence-based learning and qualifications in the UK.' Accounting Education, 4 (1), 5-15.

Thompson, R. (2009b). 'Social Class and Participation in Further Education: Evidence from the Youth Cohort Study of England and Wales.' British Journal of Sociology of Education, 30 (1), 29-42.

Tomlinson, M. (2004). 14-19 Curriculum and Qualifications Reform: Final Report of the Working Group on 14-19 Reform. Available at: https://education-uk.org/documents/pdfs/2004-tomlinson-report.pdf (Accessed 22 February 2024).

White, K (2016). Teacher Communication : A Guide to Relational, Organizational, and Classroom Communication, Rowman and Littlefield Publishers, Incorporated.

Wiliam, D. (2018). Embedded formative assessment. Second edition. Bloomington, Indiana: Solution Tree Press.

Williams, D. (2024). What's in a word? An Interdisciplinary Critical Discourse Analysis of 'Skill' in Technical and Vocational Education and Training in England. College of Arts, Humanities and Education, University of Derby.

Winch, C. (2018). 'Teachers' Know-How: A Philosophical Investigation.' Oxford: Wiley Blackwell.

Wolf, A. (2011). Review of Vocational Education – The Wolf Report. Available at: https://assets.publishing.service.gov.uk/government/uploads/system/uploads/attachment_data/file/180504/DFE-00031-2011.pdf (Accessed 17 July 2024).

Wolf, R. (2017). 'Inside views – perspectives on policy churn.' In, E. Norris and R. Adam's. All Change: Why Britain is so prone to policy reinvention, and what can be done about it, Institute for Government, 22-27.

Young, M. and Muller, J. (2013). 'On the powers of powerful knowledge.' Review of Education, 1(3), 229– 25.

Chapter 2 Professional duties and responsibilities of an FES teacher

Undertake relevant roles and duties and model sustainable practices, having regard to professional standards, demonstrating resilience and adaptability when dealing with challenge and change. (Duty 8)

Professionalism is not the job you do; it's how you do the job

Anonymous

2.1 Introduction

This chapter builds upon our previous exploration of the FE and skills sector, delving deeper into the wide range of professional duties and responsibilities that FES teachers must navigate daily. The role of an FES teacher extends far beyond classroom instruction, including administrative, pastoral and developmental duties that require a broad knowledge and skill set. As we established in chapter 2, there are numerous challenges presented by changes in policy and curriculum, the backgrounds of our learners and new technologies that require us to continuously develop our practice. This chapter will explore how FES teachers can not only meet these challenges but also model sustainable practices that benefit both their learners and their own professional wellbeing.

We will revisit some of the key legislative frameworks that inform FES teaching practice, examining how they shape day-to-day responsibilities and decision making. Additionally, we will consider the Education and Training Foundation's (ETF) professional standards and their importance in guiding professional conduct and development. By understanding these standards and integrating them into practice, FES teachers can ensure they are meeting the expectations of their role while also identifying opportunities for growth and improvement. We will explore strategies for balancing competing demands, working within professional boundaries and developing the resilience needed to thrive in this challenging – but rewarding – profession.

2.2 Responsibilities of an FES teacher

The role of an FES teacher is characterised by diversity and complexity. While teaching remains the core function, the boundaries of the role have expanded significantly in recent years to encompass a wide range of responsibilities. Understanding these responsibilities and the boundaries involved in the role is essential for effective practice and professional sustainability.

At its heart, the FES teacher role centres on several core responsibilities:

Core responsibility	Explained
Planning and delivering learning	This involves developing schemes of work, lesson plans and teaching resources that meet curriculum requirements and engage diverse learners. We explore this further in chapters 5 and 6.
Assessment and feedback	This involves designing and implementing assessment strategies, providing constructive feedback and tracking learners' progress. This is examined in detail in chapter 7.
Supporting learners' individual needs	This involves identifying individual learning needs and barriers and providing support to address them. It also includes providing tutorial support and fostering learner development that is explored in greater depth in chapter 4.
Quality assurance	This involves participating in moderation, verification and evaluation processes to maintain and improve teaching standards on the courses you teach. More information about this can be found in chapter 8.

As we can see, the responsibilities of an FES teacher require us to have knowledge and skills that extend beyond the classroom. In addition to the core responsibilities above, there are a range of other activities that we are responsible for, which include those in the table below.

Extended responsibility	Explained
Administrative duties	This involves maintaining accurate records, completing paperwork and using management information systems to monitor learners and their progression from the start to the end of their learning journey at your institution.
Pastoral care	This involves providing personal guidance, supporting learner wellbeing and addressing non-academic barriers to learning. Aside from formal tutorials, this may involve impromptu discussions with learners or liaising with other stakeholders (e.g. parents) to support the learners' progress.
Curriculum development	This involves drawing on evaluation data and stakeholder feedback to design and update course content to reflect industry needs and educational best practice.
Employer engagement	This involves building relationships with employers, facilitating work placements and ensuring curriculum relevance.
Marketing and recruitment	This involves contributing to promotional activities, open days and learner recruitment efforts.
Professional development	This involves you engaging in continuous learning, reflective practice and keeping up with subject developments.

The challenge for FES teachers lies in recognising which of these extended activities fall within their professional remit and which may require additional support or delegation. Effective teachers understand that while they may need to engage with all these areas, they cannot be specialists in everything and must therefore frequently work with others both within and beyond the organisation.

Balancing teaching with administrative, support and developmental duties

One of the most significant challenges facing FES teachers is the balancing act between teaching and any additional responsibilities. A typical teaching load may include 20–25 contact hours per week, but this represents only a portion of the overall workload. Research by the ETF (2023) indicates that on average, a full-time FES teacher spends around 22 hours per week on teaching (or providing cover), 5 hours per week planning and 5 hours per week assessing and marking. As we have seen in the tables above, these are just some of the core responsibilities that may be undertaken, so with additional responsibilities it is easy to see how challenging and demanding the role can be.

The need to balance can vary significantly depending on the institution, subject area and career stage. New teachers often find themselves spending disproportionate time on preparation while experienced teachers may take on additional curriculum development or quality assurance responsibilities.

Effective strategies for balancing these competing demands include:

- **Time blocking** – Allocating specific time slots for different aspects of the role, such as dedicated administration hours.

- **Prioritisation** – Distinguishing between urgent and important tasks using frameworks like the Eisenhower matrix.

- **Efficient planning** – Developing reusable resources and assessment materials that can be adapted rather than created from scratch.

- **Collaboration** – Working with colleagues to share resources, split administrative duties and provide mutual support.

- **Delegation** – Identifying tasks that can be appropriately delegated to support staff or learners (e.g. peer assessment activities).

> **REFLECT**
>
> What strategies do you currently use to balance your workload? Are there any responsibilities that you are finding difficult to manage?

Even with these strategies, the need to balance remains challenging. It is important for FES teachers to recognise that perfect balance is rarely achievable and that priorities will shift throughout the academic year. Accepting this reality is part of developing professional resilience, which we will explore later in this chapter.

The case study opposite illustrates the diverse nature of an FES teacher's working week, highlighting the integration of teaching, administrative, pastoral and developmental responsibilities. It demonstrates how FES teachers must be adept at switching between different roles throughout the day while maintaining their focus on supporting learners' learning and development.

Case study: A week in the life of Oliver, an FES eSports Teacher at a college in the Midlands

Day	Time	Activity
Monday	09:00–11:00	Teach Level 3 eSports (Year 1)
	11:00–12:00	Respond to learner emails and prepare for afternoon session
	12:00–13:00	Lunch and informal meeting with colleague about shared resources
	13:00–15:00	Teach Level 2 Introduction to eSports
	15:00–16:00	Individual tutorials with Level 2 learners (20 minutes each)
	16:00–17:00	Mark assignments and update tracking spreadsheet
Tuesday	09:00–11:00	Teach Level 3 eSports (Year 2)
	11:00–13:00	Curriculum development meeting for new T Level programme
	13:00–14:00	Lunch and catch up on emails
	14:00–16:00	Teach Level 2 Introduction to eSports
	16:00–17:00	Meeting with employer about work placement opportunities
Wednesday	09:00–11:00	Teach Level 3 eSports (Year 1)
	11:00–13:00	Standardisation meeting
	13:00–14:00	Lunch and preparation for afternoon session
	14:00–16:00	Teach Level 1 eSports administration
	16:00–17:30	Update schemes of work and lesson plans
Thursday	09:00–11:00	Teach Level 3 eSports (Year 2)
	11:00–12:00	Safeguarding training update
	12:00–13:00	Lunch and emails
	13:00–15:00	Teach Level 2 Introduction to eSports
	15:00–17:30	Department meeting
Friday	09:00–11:00	Teach Level 1 eSports
	11:00–12:00	Group tutorial with Level 3 eSports (Year 1)
	12:00–13:00	Lunch and informal professional development discussion with mentor
	13:00–14:00	Group tutorial with Level 3 eSports (Year 2)
	14:00–16:00	Preparation and planning for next week's lessons
	16:00–17:00	Make follow-up calls to learners with attendance concerns

> **Take it further...**
>
> Research the Eisenhower matrix and distinguish between the list of tasks you have this week. Did you find this helpful?

2.3 The dual professional

In FES, we also have a tension when it comes to our professional identity. In chapter 1, we spent some time considering what the FES sector is and who it serves. While there will always be anomalies, it is clear that a large number of our learners will come from backgrounds that are minority and marginalised, and that the sector has struggled to have a clear focus, finding itself inferior to other education sectors. Some of you may have once been an FES learner yourself and recognise some of the challenges raised in the chapter. Perhaps this is what has drawn you to teaching in FES. For others, you may not have experienced FES as a learner but recognise the value you can add to this sector based on your knowledge and experiences.

Many of you will be reading this as a 'trainee' FES teacher, but you will have come from entirely different backgrounds. Some will be graduates within the subject area you teach, perhaps straight out of university with little industry experience or perhaps joining teaching later in life having had working experience in the industry. Others may have taken an apprenticeship route and spent their working life mastering an occupation and be ready to share this experience with those wishing to follow a similar path. Whatever path you have chosen, you will likely have a level 3 or above qualification (A-level or equivalent) or significant industry experience in your subject specialism and therefore have subject expertise.

Subject expertise is important, particularly as the English FES system calls for its teachers to be 'dual professionals', whereby subject or occupational expertise is combined with excellent teaching and learning practices (CAVTL, 2014; ETF, 2022a), as illustrated in figure 2.1.

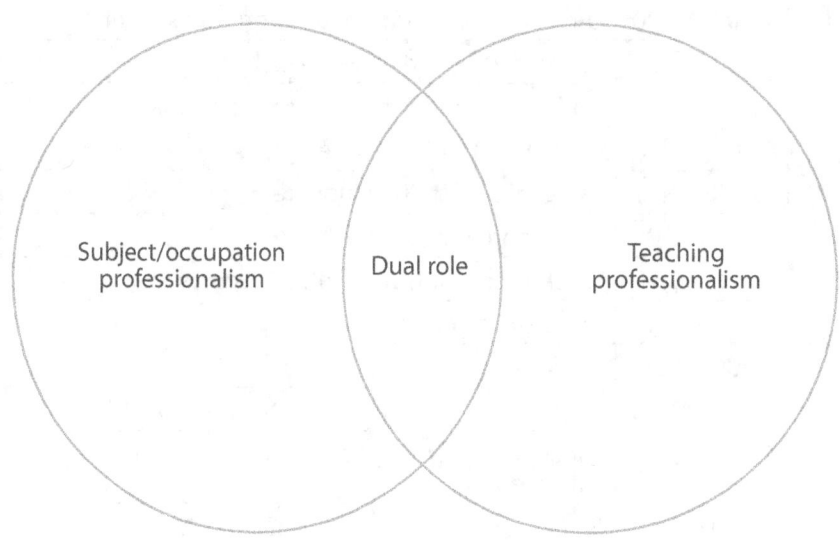

Figure 2.1 *Dual professionalism*

Though there are many ways of viewing professionalism, Millerson (1964) states that a profession must include the following:

- Intellectual training and education, i.e. a formal qualification to be studied.

- A skill based on theoretical knowledge, i.e. a recognised body of knowledge.
- The testing of competence, i.e. an exam or assessment to be passed.
- Closure of the profession by restrictive organisations, i.e. a professional membership body.
- A code of conduct, i.e. agreed behaviours for the role that all must comply with.
- An altruistic service in the affairs of others, i.e. a desire to help others.

> **Reflect**
>
> Think about the subject or occupational expertise that you are teaching. Are you a professional based on the above list? Do you agree with all of these aspects of a profession? What makes you a professional in your subject?

Teaching your subject is different to knowing it, and becoming a dual professional requires a deep understanding of the professional role you have in the education of others. Taking into account Millerson's list above, by undertaking your ITE and reading this textbook you are on your way to developing your teaching professionalism. But let us take a deeper look at each of these principles in turn and consider how you could meet all of these requirements.

Intellectual training and education

Despite the call for dual professionalism, the status of FES teachers has remained overshadowed by that of teachers in general education (Atkins and Tummons, 2017), and there has been a long-standing issue with respect to the mandating of ITE qualifications in the sector. In 2012, the Further Education Teachers' Qualifications (England) Regulations 2007 were revoked, meaning teaching qualifications were no longer mandated in the post-school sector (Lingfield, 2012). Consequently, FES institutions have been able to make their own decisions as to what qualifications their teaching staff should hold, allowing them to employ directly from industry.

This had many benefits, including meeting recruitment needs and being able to draw on current occupational expertise without the need for a teaching qualification. It also benefited the individual teacher; for example, a self-employed beautician could effectively become employed as a beauty teacher without loss of earnings. While some may question how this achieved dual professionalism (in respect of not having a teaching qualification prior to teaching), it is common practice for most institutions to support their teachers through a qualification to encourage quality teaching and learning and professionalism. Moreover, the majority of teachers entering the sector tend to have a desire to develop their practice for their own professional development and as part of their 'altruistic service in the affairs of others' (Millerson, 1964).

In the UK, there is a wide range of FES ITE qualifications between level 3 and level 7 under a range of titles and with varying requirements in terms of learning duration and assessment. Despite such variety, only those at level 5 or above are recognised as full teaching qualifications in the sector (DfE, 2024). Approximately 70% of those working in the FES sector have a level 5 or above teaching qualification (ETF, 2020), while over 10,000 individuals study one annually (ETF, 2016), with around a third of these within higher education institution (HEI) awarded provision. Typically, those studying ITE programmes as 'in-service' tend to be employed directly from the industry for their occupational expertise and, as a result, these individuals tend to be from craft- or skills-based subjects rather than general or 'academic' subjects (ETF, 2016). While in-service provision tends to be part-time training that trainee teachers undertake while employed in FES, pre-service provision is typically for trainee teachers before they enter employment and is often studied on a full-time basis.

The long-standing issues with the regulation of FES ITE have meant that curriculum guidance has been limited and, up until 2024, remained largely unchanged since 2007 (LLUK, 2008; ETF, 2016). From September 2024, as they seek to support sector-wide improvements, the DfE (2024) only recognise level 5 qualifications that are designed to support trainees to meet the level 5 learning and skills teacher occupational standards.

A skill based on theoretical knowledge

Unlike many secondary teacher education programmes, due to such a wide range of subject specialisms within the FE and skills sector (Crawley, 2005), ITE qualifications are largely generic in nature, meaning they tend not to focus on subject specialist teaching content (Loo, 2018) with much of the subject specialist support coming from a mentor in practice. Instead, the core 'taught' content is designed around generic knowledge, skill and behaviour standards (occupational standards) that have been created by a group of employers representing the wide-ranging FE and skills sector. These standards have been constructed from relations of similarity between elements of different subject specialist practices. While some would argue that this genericism weakens the profession (Williams, 2024), the attempt to create a standardised list of knowledge, skills and behaviours does provide a recognised body of knowledge that all trainee teachers can follow.

The testing of competence

As part of all formal qualifications, there are usually formal assessments of competence towards the respective learning outcomes or criteria. In the FES ITE programmes, which are mapped to occupational standards, they all have some form of portfolio development with a professional discussion alongside formal observations of teaching practice. Both of these assessment types should allow trainees to demonstrate that they can meet all of the occupational standards by the end of their programme of study. These formal assessments, therefore, allow for a test of competence in the profession, ensuring entry is restricted to only those who are able to meet these minimum standards

Closure of the profession by restrictive organisations

The professional membership body for the FES sector was first created in 2002 by the Institute for Learning (IfL); it was established to provide professional recognition, support and development for teachers, trainers and leaders within the FES sector. During its lifetime, professional membership was mandatory and free to all FES teachers, though as part of the coalition government's (2010–15) cuts to public spending, the IfL became voluntary and fee-paying, ultimately finding itself to be unsustainable. Power was then eventually transferred in 2013 to the Society for Education and Training (SET), an umbrella company of the ETF. Having spent ten years as SET, the professional membership body now resides solely with the ETF.

Trainee teachers currently benefit from free membership and can access a range of professional development opportunities and resources to support them. Not only does membership support these benefits, but you can also acquire several professional statuses from the organisation depending on your career status. For those who have recently completed a level 5 or above teaching qualification, you can undertake a period of professional formation leading to qualified teacher learning and skills (QTLS) status. This has legal parity with qualified teacher status (QTS), which primary and secondary teachers are awarded after the successful completion of their early career training period. Though it is not mandatory to have this status, it does provide recognition of your commitment to professional development (you can read more about this and other professional statuses in chapter 10).

A code of conduct

The institution you work or are doing a placement at will have a code of conduct for staff, but the ETF also supports your professionalism with a code of practice that all its members must comply with. This sets out the professional behaviours and conduct expected of its members and is underpinned by a set of professional standards, discussed in the next section. We will examine the code of practice further in chapter 8.

> **REFLECT**
>
> In terms of becoming a teaching professional, think back to Millerson's list of characteristics for a profession and identify which you meet and which you are not sure about. Set yourself a target for addressing any areas that you need to find out more about.

Considering Millerson's requirements, it is evident that becoming a teaching professional within FES is achievable and, coupled with your subject or occupational professionalism, becoming a dual professional is also within reach. This subject or occupational aspect to being a dual professional will come with various requirements, so ensure that you are clear about these and how you can adhere to them and maintain an up-to-date understanding of key subject knowledge and skills throughout your teaching career.

While 'dual professionalism' is an accepted term in the sector, Avis and Atkins (2017) highlight some issues with the notion of dual professionalism in FES. For instance, excelling as both a vocational and pedagogical expert simultaneously may create role conflict and risk diminishing the professional identify in one or the other; in other words, as you become increasingly 'professional' in teaching, it may be difficult to maintain currency and meet the demands of occupational professionalism. Avis and Atkins also argue that attempting to meet prescriptive standards may undermine autonomy, as teachers may feel constrained by the imposed standards. This becomes more of an issue of compliance, particularly where generic standards may not fully align with subject- or context-specific teaching practices.

> **REFLECT**
>
> Why is it important to maintain a focus on becoming a dual professional? How does this support your learners?

> **Take it further...**
> Read the critique of dual professionalism by Avis and Atkins (see the references section on page 41). Do you agree or disagree with this perspective? How will it inform your commitment to dual professionalism?

> **Tip for Teaching**
> Join your professional membership body for both your subject or occupation and as an FES teacher and benefit from the professional development, networking and support opportunities available to you.

2.4 Professional standards

While ITE programmes in FES are now designed to support trainees to meet the occupational standards, as part of their dual professional role, teachers within FES careers should aspire to meet the ETF's professional standards for teachers and trainers. These standards have been developed by a range of stakeholders in the sector to help teachers to excel in their teaching practice. As part of your professional responsibilities, it is important that you are able to consider your development in all aspects of the role, and the standards support this.

	Professional values and attributes	Learn more about this in chapter...
1	Critically reflect on and evaluate your practices, values, and beliefs to improve learner outcomes.	10
2	Promote and embed education for sustainable development (ESD) across learning and working practices.	2
3	Inspire, motivate and raise aspirations of learners by communicating high expectations and a passion for learning.	3
4	Support and develop learners' confidence, autonomy and thinking skills, taking account of their needs and starting points.	6, 7
5	Value and champion diversity, equality of opportunity, inclusion and social equity.	4
6	Develop collaborative and respectful relationships with learners, colleagues and external stakeholders.	8
7	Engage with and promote a culture of continuous learning and quality improvement.	8
Professional knowledge and understanding		
8	Develop and update knowledge of your subject specialism, taking account of new practices, research or industry requirements.	6
9	Critically review and apply your knowledge of educational research, pedagogy, and assessment to develop evidence-informed practice.	6

The ETF Professional Standards for Teachers and Trainers
© *Education and Training Foundation* www.et-foundation.co.uk

10	Share and update knowledge of effective practice with colleagues, networks or research communities to support improvement.	8
11	Develop and apply your knowledge of special educational needs and disabilities to create inclusive learning experiences.	4
12	Understand your teaching role and responsibilities and how these are influenced by legal, regulatory, institutional and ethical contexts.	1, 2
Professional skills		
13	Promote and support positive learner behaviour, attitudes and wellbeing.	3
14	Apply motivational, coaching and skill development strategies to help learners progress and achieve.	6
15	Plan and deliver learning programmes that are safe, inclusive, stretching and relevant to learners' needs.	5
16	Select and use digital technologies safely and effectively to promote learning.	5, 6
17	Develop learners' maths, English, digital and wider employability skills.	5, 9
18	Provide access to up-to-date information, advice and guidance so that learners can take ownership of their learning and make informed progression choices	9
19	Apply appropriate and fair methods of assessment and provide constructive and timely feedback to support learning and achievement.	7
20	Develop enrichment and progression opportunities for learners through collaboration with employers, higher education and/or community groups.	9

> **REFLECT**
>
> Complete a self-assessment against the professional standards above and identify those that are current strengths and those that may require development. You may wish to use the ETF's self-assessment tool which can be found on their website.

Professional standard 7 requires you to engage with continuous improvement of your practice and CPD can take many forms. Often your institution will require you to undertake mandatory training, such as safeguarding, as part of their compliance with the respective legislation. While this is essential to your development, top-down, one-sized-fits-all organisational approaches to CPD tend not to offer the professional growth expected by organisations or the individuals attending (Porter and Freeman, 2020). Darling-Hammond and colleagues (2017) define the key features of professional development based on an extensive review of effective teacher development, as we can see in the following table.

Features	Explained
Content focused	Content should be focused on the specific practices and ideally within the subject specialist area.
Incorporates active learning	Teachers should be able to actively engage in highly contextualised professional learning.
Supports collaboration	Teachers should be provided the space to share problems, practices and ideas.
Uses models of effective practice	In the same way we discuss success criteria in chapter 7 for effective assessment, teachers should have a clear understanding of expert practice or 'what good looks like' from observing colleagues or videos of the specific area of focus.
Provides coaching and expert support	Teachers can benefit from coaches and expert support informed by evidence and directly related to their specific needs.
Offers feedback and reflection	Time should be given for teachers to get input from others and to reflect on this and their own assessments to move towards what they perceive to be expert practice.
Is of sustained duration	For us, this is the crucial one. Teachers need time to learn, practise, reflect and refine their teaching practices.

REFLECT

Take a moment to record your professional development so far this year and create a log, outlining whether it was mandatory or self-directed and how many of the features above it met. You should also consider which of the professional standards it aligned to.

Take it further...

Identify those standards where you are developing well. Where do you need to focus more of your attention? Set an action plan for this.

In addition to a commitment to continuous improvement and given the nature of the FES sector – which caters for a diverse range of learners, often from marginalised communities – it is important that at the heart of your values, attitudes and beliefs is a commitment to inclusion. Though it may not be obvious, particularly if you are new to the term 'education for sustainable development' (ESD), Professional standard 2 encompasses this value and we believe it should be at the core of your practices.

2.5 Education for sustainable development

According to UNESCO (2020), education for sustainable development (ESD) equips learners with the knowledge, skills and values necessary to make informed decisions about their role in relation to the triple planetary crisis of climate change, pollution and loss of biodiversity. ESD is not just limited to environmental factors, it also extends to the promotion of individual and collective action to reduce inequalities in society, and the advancement of sustainable growth through industry innovation and responsible consumption and production. Some refer to these as the 3Ps of Planet, People, and Profit.

UNESCO sees education as the key to unlocking progress in all the global development goals. 17 sustainable development goals were adopted by all UN member states in 2015, providing a shared blueprint for peace and prosperity for people and the planet, now and into the future.

1. No poverty	2. Zero hunger	3. Good health and wellbeing	4. Quality education	5. Gender equality
6. Clean water and sanitation	7. Affordable and clean energy	8. Decent work and economic growth	9. Industry, innovation and infrastructure	10. Reduced inequalities
11. Sustainable cities and communities	12. Responsible consumption and production	13. Climate action	14. Life below water	15. Life on land
16. Peace, justice and strong institutions	17. Partnerships for the goals			

However, these goals are not without their critics; for example, Swain (2018) highlights the ambiguity and inconsistency of the goals and their application across developed and developing countries. Moreover, Haapanen et al (2016) highlight the huge tension between 'economic growth' and 'sustainability'. With finite resources on the planet, continuous growth will be difficult to achieve.

Despite this, research by the Learning and Work Institute (2021) found that 80% of UK jobs in 2030 will require green skills to some degree, and the European Centre for the Development of Vocational Training (CEDEFOP) (2023) have found that learners with sustainability competencies have improved employability, with employers increasingly valuing these skills across sectors. What is more, research by UNESCO (2020) shows that ESD in vocational education helps address inequalities, as climate change disproportionately affects disadvantaged communities, making sustainability literacy essential for social mobility. With this in mind, the UK government's sustainability and climate change strategy for education (DfE, 2022) explicitly called for embedding sustainability across all education levels, with FES increasingly playing a significant role in this.

But how does FES play this role? Research from the ETF (2022b) demonstrates that ESD approaches in FES improve learner engagement, retention and achievement through project-based and contextual learning. Their research also demonstrates that these approaches better prepare learners for complex workplace challenges. The evidence suggests that embedding ESD in FES is not just an ethical choice, but it genuinely offers tangible benefits to learners' outcomes, institutional performance and broader economic needs.

Case studies

Green construction skills

A provider in the north of England adopted an innovative approach to green construction skills where learners' programmes required them to conduct energy audits of college buildings and present retrofit recommendations, work on community projects and collaborate with learners from other subject areas to design and build a sustainable construction centre. To do this, teachers and managers:

- established partnerships with local eco-builders and sustainable materials suppliers
- embedded sustainable construction units in all construction courses from entry level to level 3
- introduced a level 4 qualification specifically in sustainable construction management.

Hospitality and catering curriculum transformation

A provider in the Midlands redesigned their curriculum around principles of circular economics in the food service industry. Learners managed a 'root-to-stem' cooking programme and seasonal menus that drew exclusively on locally sourced ingredients and helped to minimise food waste. This involved teachers and managers:

- establishing a college garden and small farm for food production
- creating partnerships with local organic producers and zero-waste shops
- developing specific assessment criteria related to sustainable practices.

Fashion and textiles revamp

A provider in the south of England revamped its fashion and textiles programmes to address the environmental impact of fast fashion and develop circular economy approaches. Learners were required to:

- run a clothing repair cafe for the local community
- create collections from reclaimed and recycled materials
- use food waste to develop natural dyeing processes
- create marketing campaigns for sustainable consumption
- deliver an end-of-year fashion show that featured exclusively sustainable collections.

This involved teachers and managers:

- introducing units and content on sustainable materials, ethical production and circular design
- establishing a textile recycling workshop and upcycling studio
- creating partnerships with ethical fashion brands and sustainable textile manufacturers
- developing specific assessment criteria related to sustainable practices.

> **REFLECT**
>
> It is evident that the institutions within each of these case studies worked closely in partnership with local industry to support their curriculum, while being innovative in developing project-based, real-world sustainability problems for learners. With this in mind, what could ESD look like in your subject?

> **Take it further...**
>
> If you would like to understand ESD further, visit the ETF website for resources and training for ESD: et-foundation.co.uk

2.6 Professional flexibility and resilience

As we have established throughout this chapter, the FES teacher's role is broad and encompasses many responsibilities, some of which you may not have been aware of. In addition to understanding these responsibilities and duties, we also need to be aware of the boundaries of our role and where another stakeholders' role begins. We explored earlier in the chapter how demanding the working week is when simply completing the core responsibilities of planning, teaching and assessment. Our practices as teachers need to be sustainable both for ourselves and the educational ecosystem in which we operate.

Sustainability is not just about environmental concerns but also creating teaching practices that can be maintained over time without depleting your personal resources. By modelling sustainable practices, FES teachers demonstrate to learners how to manage workloads, set priorities and maintain wellbeing in demanding professional environments. This may include creating efficient ways of working that reduce administrative burdens, establishing clear boundaries between work and life and collaborating with others. In chapter 8, we explore in detail how to work professionally and collaboratively, but as part of being resilient as an FES teacher it is important that you can recognise signs of stress and have some strategies to manage workload.

Identifying workplace stressors and coping strategies

Being able to recognise sources of work-related stress is the first step toward managing them effectively. Common stressors in FES teaching may include workload, particularly at key points in the year such as assessment and marking windows or when there are competing demands to manage. Another stressor may be challenging learner behaviour or managing conflict with a difficult team member, both of which require us to consider our communication skills and relationships (see chapters 3 and 8 respectively for more insight).

As we set out in chapter 1, the sector has been through a lot of change; as such, the precarious nature can provide a constant worry for us. Effective coping strategies will allow you to manage stress while maintaining your professional effectiveness. Different strategies work for different individuals, so reflective experimentation is key to developing a personalised approach to stress management. We have covered some of the ways that you can manage workload, but research in the field of positive psychology has shown further promising effects for teachers' wellbeing (Duckworth et al, 2009). Indeed, Avola and colleagues' (2025) review of interventions to prevent teacher burnout suggest the approaches in the table below may work for some individuals, depending on the context.

Intervention	Explanation
Physical activity	Incorporating regular physical exercise improves physical health and reduces stress.
Mindfulness and meditation	These practices aim to increase awareness and reduce stress.
Professional development	Opportunities for teachers to develop their skills and knowledge can enhance job satisfaction and reduce burnout.
Therapy-based techniques	Psychological therapies such as cognitive behavioural therapy (CBT) and counselling may help to support positive mental health and wellbeing.
Gratitude practices	Activities that encourage gratitude can improve mood and overall wellbeing.
Mixed activities	A combination of various activities including social and communal activities support holistic wellbeing.

> **REFLECT**
>
> What are your workplaces stressors and what coping strategies do you use to manage them? Are there things you would like to do more often?

> **Take it further...**
>
> Take a look at the Cooper-Gibson research (2018), which explores teacher workload, and see if you can identify with some of the strategies suggested for schoolteachers. You can read the research document here: rb.gy/gekehu

Support networks and resources

No teacher should face the challenges of the profession in isolation. Developing and utilising support networks is essential for sustainable practice, and this may involve mentoring relationships for guidance and perspective or joining peer support groups. In chapter 8, we explore the professional relationships with colleagues and other stakeholders in a little more detail and how to manage these through effective communication. In terms of accessing communities of practice, there are a host of networks that you can join for this with both online and in-person network events, for example the ETF's membership body or subject specialist groups such as the Learning and Skills Research Network (LSRN). These support systems not only provide practical assistance but also create a sense of collective resilience that helps individual teachers persevere through challenges.

Developing professional flexibility and resilience does not mean accepting unsustainable working conditions but rather developing the capacity to influence what can be changed while adapting effectively to what cannot. In doing so, you model the very resilience and adaptability that your learners will need in their future careers.

> **Tip for Teaching**
>
> If you are a trainee teacher, you can sign up as a free member of the ETF to access a range of webinars, resources and a community of over 23,000 members.

Chapter summary

In this chapter, we have explored the expansive role of the FES teacher, examining both core responsibilities and extended duties that define this challenging profession. We began by identifying the key responsibilities of planning, delivering learning, assessment, supporting individual needs and quality assurance before delving into the additional administrative, pastoral and developmental duties that often extend the teacher's role. We examined the challenge of balancing these competing demands, offering practical strategies for prioritisation, time management and collaboration.

The chapter then introduced the ETF professional standards as a framework for excellence, encouraging teachers to reflect on their practice against these benchmarks and identify areas for CPD. We examined ESD as a key aspect of Professional standard 2, exploring how sustainability can be embedded within teaching practice across different subject areas. The case studies demonstrated how innovative approaches to ESD can enhance learner engagement and outcomes while addressing critical global challenges. Finally, we focused on developing professional flexibility and resilience, recognising its importance for long-term success in the FES sector.

Throughout the chapter, we have emphasised that understanding professional duties and responsibilities involves more than simply knowing what tasks to perform. This requires developing a nuanced understanding of professional boundaries, legal and ethical frameworks and personal sustainability. By improving these aspects of professionalism, FES teachers can not only meet the diverse challenges of their role but also model the resilience, adaptability and sustainable practices that learners will need in their future careers.

References

Association of Colleges (2022) Green College Commitment: FE Climate Action Roadmap. London: Association of Colleges.

Avis, J., and Atkins, L. (2017). Youth Transitions, VET and the Making of Class: Changing Theorisations for Changing Times. Research in Post Compulsory Education, 22(2), 165-185.

Avola, P., Soini-Ikonen, T., Jyrkiäinen, A. et al. Interventions to Teacher Well-Being and Burnout A Scoping Review. Educ Psychol Rev 37, 11 (2025).

Atkins, L., and Tummons, J. (2017). Professionalism in vocational education: international perspectives. Research in Post-Compulsory Education, 22(3), 355–369.

CAVTL. (2014). Commission on Adult Vocational Teaching and Learning: one year on review. Learning and Skills Improvement Service, Coventry, England.

CEDEFOP (2023) Skills for the Green Transition: Vocational Education's Role in Sustainable Development. Luxembourg: Publications Office of the European Union.

CooperGibson Research. (2018). Exploring teacher workload: Qualitative research. Department for Education. Available at: https://assets.publishing.service.gov.uk/government/uploads/system/uploads/attachment_data/file/686734/Exploring_teacher_workload.pdf (Accessed 9 April 2025).

Crawley, J. (2005). In at the deep end. London: David Fulton.

Darling-Hammond, L., Hyler, M. E., Gardner, M. (2017). Effective Teacher Professional Development. Palo Alto, CA: Learning Policy Institute.

Department for Education (DfE). (2022). Sustainability and Climate Change Strategy for the Education and Children's Services Systems, London: HMSO.

Department for Education (DfE). (2024). Expectations for the delivery of initial teacher education for FE. Available at: https://www.gov.uk/government/publications/further-education-initial-teacher-education/expectations-for-the-delivery-of-initial-teacher-education-for-fe (Accessed 12 October 24).

Duckworth, A. L., Quinn, P. D., and Seligman, M. E. P. (2009). Positive predictors of teacher effectiveness. The Journal of Positive Psychology, 4(6), 540–547.

Education and Training Foundation (ETF). (2016). Qualifications in education and training Updated guidance on the teaching qualifications for the further education and skills sector. Available at: https://gatehouseawards.org/uploads/doc-library/guidance-for-qualifications-in-education-and-training-the-education-and-training-foundation-nov-2016.pdf (Accessed 19 July 2024).

Education and Training Foundation (ETF). (2020). Further Education Workforce Data for England: Analysis of the 2018-2019 Staff Individualised Record (SIR) data. Frontier Economics (March 2020). Available at: https://www.et-foundation.co.uk/wp-content/uploads/2020/06/SIR27-REPORT-FOR-PUBLICATION.pdf (Accessed 16 November 2024).

Education and Training Foundation (ETF). (2022a). Professional Standards for Teachers and Trainers. Available at: https://www.et-foundation.co.uk/professional-standards/teachers/ (Accessed 31 March 2025).

Education and Training Foundation (ETF). (2022b). Embedding Education for Sustainable Development in Further Education: Impact Assessment 2020-2022. London: ETF.

Education and Training Foundation (ETF). (2023). FE and WBL Education Workforce Survey report 2023. Available at: https://dera.ioe.ac.uk/id/eprint/41050/2/FE%20and%20WBL%20Education%20Workforce%20Survey%20report%202023_Redacted.pdf (Accessed 19 March 2025).

Haapanen, L. and Tapio, P. (2016). The Role of Economic Growth in Sustainable Development From The Perspective of 21st Century Growth Critique. Available at: https://sustainabledevelopment.un.org/content/documents/1007751_Haapanen%20et%20al._The%20role%20of%20economic%20growth%20in%20sustainable%20development%20from%20the%20perspective%20of%2021st%20century%20growth%20critique.pdf (Accessed 31 March 2025).

JISC and Education and Training Foundation (2023) Interdisciplinary Approaches to Sustainability Education in Further Education. Bristol: JISC.

Lifelong Learning UK (LLUK). (2007). Further Education Workforce Reforms, Explaining Initial Teacher Training, Continuing Professional Development and Principals' Qualifications in England. Available at: http://www.lifelonglearninguk.org/ittreforms/index.htm (Accessed 20 July 2024).

Learning and Work Institute (2021) Green Skills for the Future: Meeting Skills Needs for Net Zero. Leicester: LandW.

Lingfield, R. (2012). Professionalism in Further Education: Interim Report of the Independent Review Panel Established by the Minister of State for Further Education, Skills and Lifelong Learning. Available at: https://assets.publishing.service.gov.uk/government/uploads/system/uploads/attachment_data/file/623014/bis-12-670-professionalism-in-further-education-review-interim-report.pdf (Accessed 20 July 2024).

Loo, S. (2018). Multiple Dimensions of Teaching and Learning for Occupational Practice. London: Routledge.

Millerson, G. (1964). The Qualifying Associations. London: Routledge and Kegan Paul.

Porter, B.D., and Freeman, M.K. (2020). Experienced outcomes of a self-directed professional development program. Utah State University

Swain, R.B. (2018). 'A Critical Analysis of the Sustainable Development Goals'. In: Leal Filho, W. (eds) Handbook of Sustainability Science and Research. World Sustainability Series. Springer, Cham.

UNESCO. (2020). Education for Sustainable Development: A Roadmap. Paris: UNESCO.

UNESCO. (2022). Framework for the Implementation of Education for Sustainable Development (ESD) Beyond 2019. Paris: UNESCO.

Williams, D. (2024). What's in a word? An Interdisciplinary Critical Discourse Analysis of 'Skill' in Technical and Vocational Education and Training in England. College of Arts, Humanities and Education, University of Derby.

Chapter 3 The learning environment

Promote a passion for learning and set high expectations of all learners and support their personal and skills development. (Duty 1)

You establish what you establish.
Bill Rogers (1998)

3.1 Introduction

In this chapter we will explore how managing the learning environment promotes a passion for learning, and how setting high expectations for learners regarding personal and skill development enables them to practice behaviours conducive to learning, as well as preparing them for the workplace.

As FES teachers, one of the biggest concerns relates to our ability to 'manage' the behaviour of others. It is common to feel uncomfortable with being assertive, and dealing with confrontations, however, if our learners do not behave appropriately, there is little chance of any learning taking place. Therefore, teachers are right to think carefully about how they will navigate the behaviours of their learners from the outset, which requires a great deal more than asking someone to do something and them willingly adhering to those instructions, as you will find out in this chapter.

As FES teachers, we need to ensure that every choice we make in the classroom is purposeful and has a clear rationale and intended impact, which is ultimately to ensure that learners are given the greatest opportunities to progress and develop. So, although the guidance of this chapter will influence how you handle the behaviour in your classroom, we have chosen not to use the term 'behaviour management' in this context. This term, we feel, is far too narrow for an approach to enhancing behaviours conducive to learning and focusing on the ways we can manage our classrooms, engage learners and create opportunities for them to develop and progress effectively. Let us change our perception from one that is concerned with managing unwanted behaviours as they arise (in a reactive manner) to one that prevents those unwanted behaviours surfacing and promotes a passion for learning.

3.2 Setting the scene

When considering the learning environment in the FES skills sector, we first need to recognise that our learners are no longer at school and that the learning environment can vary significantly. In the main, learners will be studying qualifications that support progression towards the workplace, and therefore the educational establishment should reflect that. However, this does not come without challenge. According to Bennett (2018), due to the varied demographics of FES learners, who come from a wide range of backgrounds and in all ages and stages, the behaviours we face in the FES sector are complex, and trainee teachers need to be prepared for that. Here, the learners will not only develop personally but also professionally, and we therefore need to reflect on the kind of learning environment we want for them before we start considering how to create it.

Promoting a passion for learning within our own classrooms and learning spaces, considering the importance of building professional and effective relationships with learners and establishing routines and high expectations all begins with a joined-up approach across the institution, and more immediately, across the department you work in. To understand how this influences your own classroom, we will start with an awareness of institutional policy and procedure and how this can support you as an FES teacher to enhance the desired ethos and culture of the institution. We then outline proactive methods of creating behaviours conducive to learning through sections on how a teacher can develop 'teacher presence' and professional relationships with learners, before moving on to high expectations and creating positive learning spaces. Following this we then cover considerations for reactive approaches to challenging behaviours.

In summary, the content of this provides guidance on how to create a learning environment that feels safe, consistent, respectful and exciting, for both teachers and learners, and adequately prepares learners for the working environment.

3.3 Institutional culture and policy

As we explored in chapters 1 and 2, your institution will have a selection of policies in place to ensure that there are clear guidelines for both employees and learners within the institution. We will start the chapter here, as we consider the wider approaches to creating cultures that come from the initiatives set by the senior leadership team (SLT) who create all policies and procedures within the institution. These policies and procedures reflect a desired culture and always include a behaviour policy.

Depending on the institution's values and philosophy, the behaviour policy may reflect different approaches. On one end of the continuum, some may lean on behaviourist principles that mirror more traditional schools of thinking, assuming that behaviours are conditioned through reward and sanction. For example, when a learner demonstrates behaviours conducive to learning they gain rewards, whereas when a learner demonstrates behaviours not conducive to learning they lose their rewards or are sanctioned (Skinner, 1953). On the other hand, an institution's behaviour policy may focus on teaching positive behaviours by employing what is referred to as 'restorative practices'. These aim to restore relationships through discussion and reflection in order to develop an understanding of how our behaviour affects others (Dix, 2017).

In our experience, a good example of guidance is somewhere in between these two ends of the scale, such as the work of Bennett (2018), which focuses predominantly on how to address the behaviours of learners, as well as conduct yourself as a teacher, in order to avoid or respond to confrontational learner behaviours.

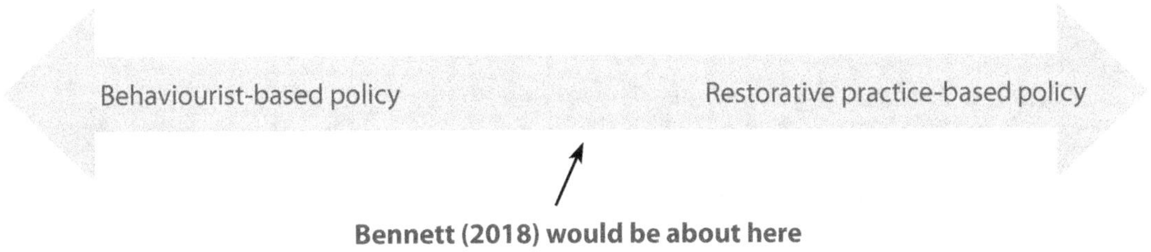

Figure 3.1 *Continuum of practice underpinning behaviour policy and procedure*

Procedures within the policy

The policy will include guidance on behaviour procedures, demonstrating the steps that are taken if a learner is deemed to have 'broken the rules'. This can be triggered by one incident, or several smaller incidents, that warrant 'cause for concern' slips (or something with a similar name) being filled out regarding the learner's behaviour. Clarity regarding these steps is extremely important as you need to be aware of what is deemed acceptable and unacceptable within the institution and what the process is should you need to use the procedure.

Underpinned by behaviourism

In figure 3.2 below, we can see an example of what the steps may be if the behaviour procedure is underpinned by a behaviourist approach focused on sanctions and the alteration of external behaviours.

Learner breaks the rules (or 3x cause for concern issued)
↓
Rule breaking is reported
↓
Senior staff Investigates Incident
Low level issue ➡ Verbal warning
Moderate level issue ➡ Written warning and meeting with senior staff
Serious level issue ➡ Disciplinary meeting with senior staff
↓
Disciplinary actions based on severity
First offense: Behaviour modification agreement signed
Repeat offense: Parental or guardian meeting (if appropriate)
Serious offense: Suspension or expulsion considered
↓
Support offered (e.g. behaviour contract, mentoring)
↓
Learner improves?
Yes ➡ Case closed
No ➡ Further disciplinary action

Figure 3.2 *Example flowchart from a behaviourist behaviour policy*

You can see here that the focus is on sanctions ('verbal warning', 'disciplinary meeting') in response to rule breaking, and if a learner repeatedly breaks the rules they are punished with suspension or expulsion. The challenge here is that, unlike general schools, in FES we cannot set detentions and isolation is not an available option. This is a good thing, as isolation and exclusion are highly problematic (Department for Education, 2019).

Behaviourist approaches can be deemed to be 'reductionist' (Bromfield, 2006), with claims that the approach ignores learners' emotions, context and cognition (Bromfield, 2006). Also, this approach relies heavily on extrinsic motivation (i.e. reward, punishment) rather than intrinsic motivations such as personal interests, goals and aspirations (Deci and Ryan, 2000).

Underpinned by restorative practice

Figure 3.3 below is an example of what the steps may be if the behaviour procedure is underpinned by a restorative approach that prioritises the understanding of our actions, practicing accountability and learning to repair broken-down relationships to change future behaviours (Dix, 2017).

Learner breaks the rules (or 3x cause for concern issued)
↓
Rule breaking is reported
Incident report logged for review by staff or peers involved
↓
Senior staff investigate the incident
Discussion takes place with those involved
Identify the nature and impact of the behaviour on others
Determine the appropriate restorative approach
↓
Restorative response based on severity
Low-level issue:
Restorative conversation with staff and learner
Learner reflects on their actions and impact
Moderate-level issue:
Mediation session with staff and affected parties
Opportunity for learner to take responsibility
Joint discussion on repairing relationships
Serious-level issue:
Restorative conference with all involved
Facilitated dialogue to address harm and solutions
↓
Restorative actions (as agreed in discussion)
Apology and reflection task (written or verbal apology, journalling)
Community repair (e.g. helping those affected, contributing positively to the community)
Behaviour support and mentoring (learner receives guidance and strategies for improvement)
↓
Follow-up and monitoring
Staff checks on learner's progress
Ensure restorative actions are completed
Provide additional support if needed
↓
Learner engagement in process?
Yes: Case closed and positive relationship built
No: Further restorative support needed (repeat mediation, mentoring or alternative approach)

Figure 3.3 *Example flowchart from a restorative practice behaviour policy*

As you can see, the example underpinned by restorative practice includes more of a focus on understanding our own actions and rebuilding relationships following that understanding. Restorative practice is deemed to be longer lasting as it challenges our perceptions of behaviours and changes our approach to similar situations in the future. A critique is that this method takes longer to implement, but the time spent should reduce reoccurrences of unwanted behaviours that are not conducive to learning (Dix, 2017).

> **REFLECT**
>
> Have a look at the policy at your workplace or placement and determine which theory it aligns to more. Consider how this aligns with your beliefs in relation to creating positive learning environments.

> **Take it further...**
>
> Think critically about whether a behaviourist or restorative practice can be used in FES, or if it needs to be somewhere in between.

Regardless of the underpinning theoretical approach, the policy will ensure a united approach within the institution when it comes to expectations regarding behaviours. This is delivered in two ways:

- If everyone adheres to the guidance in the policy, this strengthens your stance as you are in line with all other staff and learners are given clarity and consistency, which has many benefits for mental health and wellbeing.

- If you are clear on the policy and you enact it accordingly, you know that you are adhering to the 'rules' of your institution, which can give you confidence in your actions.

Policies are in place to protect and guide both staff and learners. Within Bennett's (2018) guide on managing difficult behaviours in colleges, he reminds us that we are not alone regarding challenging behaviours in the classroom and that we must work alongside our teams and managers to guide our learners to behave in ways that will enable them to engage in positive learning experiences. As such, it is more likely that the policy will focus on creating a positive learning environment and supporting learners to behave appropriately. After all, education is where we learn, and part of that learning includes managing yourself appropriately in society. In FES, this includes learning how to behave professionally in preparation for the workplace.

> **REFLECT**
>
> If you disagree with the policy, you still need to follow it; but if you really disagree with it, you need to decide if the culture of the provider is right for you. How do you feel about the guidance where you work now?

> **Take it further...**
>
> Motivation is commonly divided into two categories: intrinsic (or internal) and extrinsic (or external) motivation. The key difference between these is where the behaviour is thought by the actor to originate, known as the perceived locus of causality. When we are acting with our own volition, our motivation is said to be intrinsic, and when we are acting under duress or compulsion our motivation is extrinsic.
>
> So, intrinsically motivated activities are those that people do naturally and spontaneously when they feel they are able to follow their own interests.
>
> (Deci and Ryan, 2000)
>
> Of course, it is neither possible nor desirable to have learners solely follow their own interests during their studies, but we certainly want them to feel that they are in control of their behaviours and are empowered to act in a way that is not merely coerced or compelled. Do you think that the policy in your institution uses extrinsic or intrinsic motivation (or both) to guide learners in their behaviours? How effective do you think their chosen approach is?

Codes of conduct

It is very likely that an institution's behaviour policies will link to a learner code of conduct. This is a document that lists the expectations the institution has of learners in relation to dedication to their studies and appropriate conduct while on site or when representing the college. Learners generally sign this either before they enrol on the course or during the induction.

The code of conduct is the starting point for the learner, where expectations are clearly outlined and they confirm their agreement to these before enrolling onto their study programme. In an ideal world, the learners would read this code of conduct carefully, decide whether they are able to comply with the expectations and only sign it if they are completely sure that they are dedicated to demonstrating the behaviours identified.

A code of conduct is most effective when time has been dedicated to ensuring that learners understand the document, their responsibilities having agreed to it and what the implications are if they do not adhere to it.

> **REFLECT**
>
> Find out what the learner code of conduct covers in your place of work or placement setting. It should include things like expectations, academic integrity, respectful behaviour, attendance and punctuality, use of facilities and digital conduct.

> **Take it further...**
>
> When do learners sign the learner code of conduct at your institution? Take a moment to ask some of your learners when they signed it and what it said. Are your learners aware of what they agreed to?

It is important to make sure you are clear on the policies and processes within your institution as well as the culture regarding behaviour. If you do so, you will know how to escalate if you need to and be confident that your approach to creating positive learning environment is supported by your institution.

> **Tip for Teaching**
>
> If you are involved in administering a learner code of conduct, ensure that your learners spend time reading the expectations and generate some discussion regarding whether they feel they are able to adhere to them before they sign. This allows you to refer back to these discussions, if you need to, and ensures that learners are aware of the content of the document and the expectations while studying on the course.

It is possible, but unlikely, that your institutional policy and procedures will provide you with guidelines on the finer detail of managing your classroom and creating a positive learning environment. This is where you need to think about the kind of teacher you want to be, which will determine how you build relationships with learners that are carefully constructed through the application of a range of approaches, resulting in positive relationship development.

3.4 Teacher presence and your teaching space

You have a method of professional development in this area at your fingertips, and that is observing your colleagues (or at least having meaningful conversations with them about this where observing isn't an option) to see how they develop relationships with their learners that help create effective spaces to develop their professional and personal skills.

During these observations (or discussions if you do not manage to get into your colleagues' classrooms), you may notice that teachers will all have slightly different approaches to this. You may also notice that there are some key themes that will create positive learning environments where learners are passionate about their learning. In this section of the chapter, we will explore some of these themes in more detail.

To start with, people will tell you that your classroom or learning environment is your space, and this is absolutely right. Once you consider the learning environment to be your domain (whether online or face-to-face), your confidence will quickly grow.

Here are a few key actions you can take to communicate with learners that you are in charge of your space:

- Always welcome your learners into the learning space using their names. This demonstrates that you are in charge here, but you want them to come in and feel like they belong.

- Ensure that you have everything you need for the lesson, demonstrating that you are prepared. This will aid you to feel confident in your space and reassure learners that you care about their learning experience.

- Make sure you have a clear plan for what you intend to do with the time you are together in this space. This will enable you to give clear instructions, which again aids your confidence and demonstrates that you are the leader in this space.

Teacher positioning

Kounin (1970) referred to the ability to oversee all learners, both when working with individuals and being aware of what all others are doing at the same time, as 'withitness'. This allows you to not only assess all learners but also spot if there are behaviours not conducive to learning, such as phone use or low-level chatter, and also helps you to spot if a learner has their hand up or needs support.

As part of his ITE programme, Hitchcock (2022) completed action research which involved observing three teachers from different subjects, including geography computing and electronics. The teachers who were observed had the same classroom set-up, with all table rows facing the front of the classroom, and the same one learner in the class who was deemed to demonstrate challenging behaviours.

Hitchcock used heat maps to analyse how the position of the teacher impacted the behaviour of that one learner as well as the behaviour of the learners positioned around them.

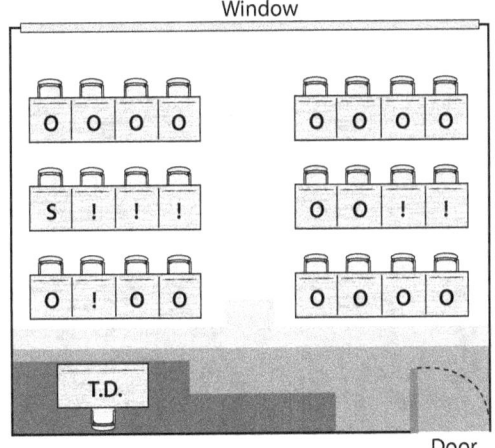

Key:
S – Student observed
T.D. – Teacher desk
! – Distracted/distractive student
O – Other student (not involved)
X – Empty space

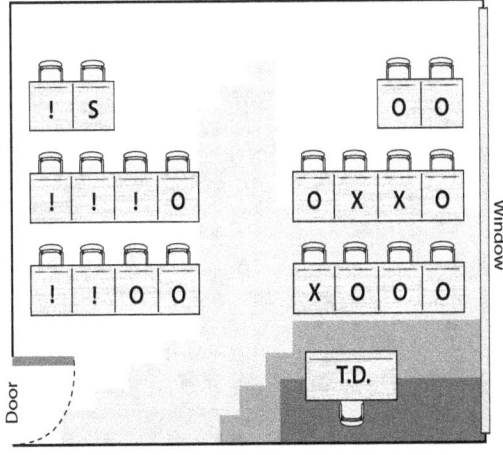

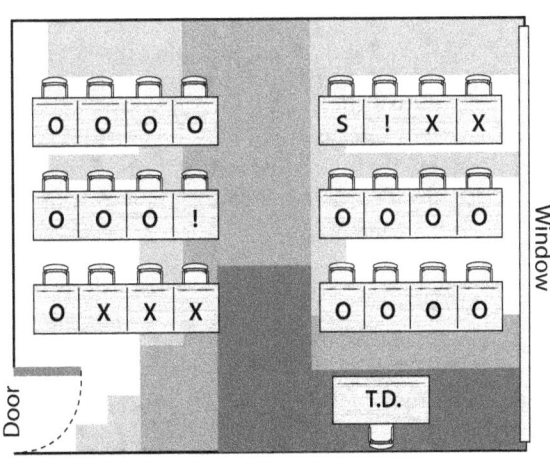

(Top) **Figure 3.4a** *Geography lesson seating plan*

(Bottom left) **Figure 3.4b** *Computing lesson seating plan*

(Bottom right) **Figure 3.4c** *Electronics lesson seating plan*

Findings

We can see from the images that Hitchcock has recorded the position of the teacher throughout the session (dark grey was the most time, medium grey the second most and light grey the least), and the impact this movement had on the behaviour of the learner (S) and those around them.

In figure 3.4a, we can see that the teacher spent the majority of the lesson at the front of the classroom only, leaving a total of six learners to behave in a way that demonstrated distraction due to the behaviour of S being observed.

In figure 3.4b, the teacher avoids S completely, resulting in another six learners being distracted by that learner.

Finally, in figure 3.4c we can see that the teacher covers the whole classroom and spends more time near S, resulting in just two learners being distracted during the session.

> **REFLECT**
>
> What can we learn from Hitchcock's findings? How do his findings reflect your own movement and positioning in the classroom? Think about where you position yourself and how this impacts the behaviour of your learners. Also, think about how your movement makes you more accessible for those who need support – does it make a difference to them?

Tip for Teaching

When teaching online, you have less ability to circulate, but you can ask for cameras to be turned on and make the session interactive in a way that allows you to assess whether or not learners are engaging and understanding the content, such as using the chat function or moving around breakout rooms.

It is clear that teacher positioning has an impact on learner behaviour, but now we need to consider how we can ensure that all learners get the support they need as well as keeping them on task. Figure 3.8 below demonstrates the actions we can take once we start a group of learners working on a task. These actions will help us understand how to promptly identify who needs help first (or who is not on task), who to progress to once those learners are on task and when to re-teach a class if required.

> **REFLECT**
>
> Is your classroom or learning environment a pleasant place to be? Are your chairs and tables (or stations) arranged in a way that encourage discussion, engagement with peers and teachers and an opportunity to feel comfortable as you learn. Can everyone see the board, you and your demonstrations? Are the resources they need readily available? Have you facilitated seating or station arrangements so that learners are sat near to the front but not too crowded together? Can you move around them freely to support those who need it most first, before checking in with other learners in the classroom?

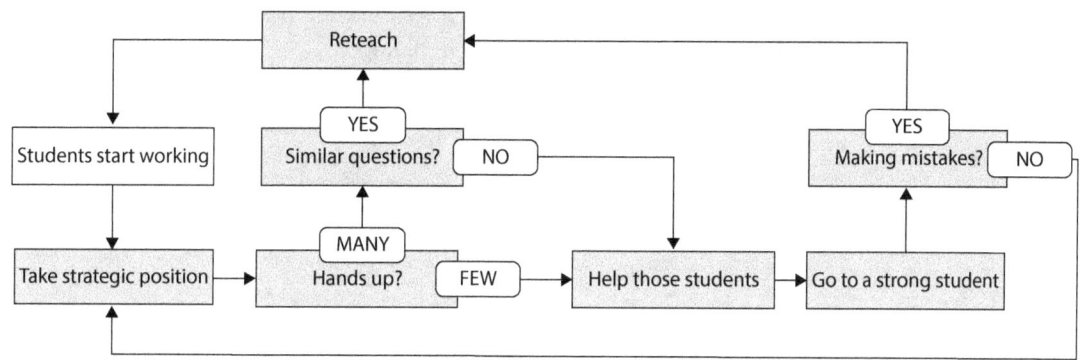

Figure 3.5 *'Running the room', adapted from Boxer (2021)*

This flowchart is helpful when observing learners with regards to unwanted behaviours, but it also allows the teacher to easily spot if any learner needs support before they get frustrated or distracted. Where learners sit not only dictates your movement around the learning environment but also guides you on your choices for approaching and questioning the learners.

3.5 Establishing professional relationships

Before you start establishing relationships with your learners, it is useful to consider what it is you are aiming for with regards to interactions with learners and what kind of teacher you want to be. This will shape your approach to building relationships and setting expectations.

Canter and Canter (1976) developed the distinction between assertive and non-assertive teachers:

- Assertive teachers communicate expectations clearly, are consistent with rule reinforcement and maintain a respectful and positive tone in communication.

- Non-assertive teachers do not communicate expectations clearly and avoid confronting unwanted behaviours, meaning boundaries in the classroom are unclear and inconsistent.

Of course, Canter and Canter concluded that the ideal approach for the teacher is the 'assertive' approach, and this can be executed in different ways. To delve slightly deeper, we will use the theory of Roberts (2023), who summarised four different types of teachers.

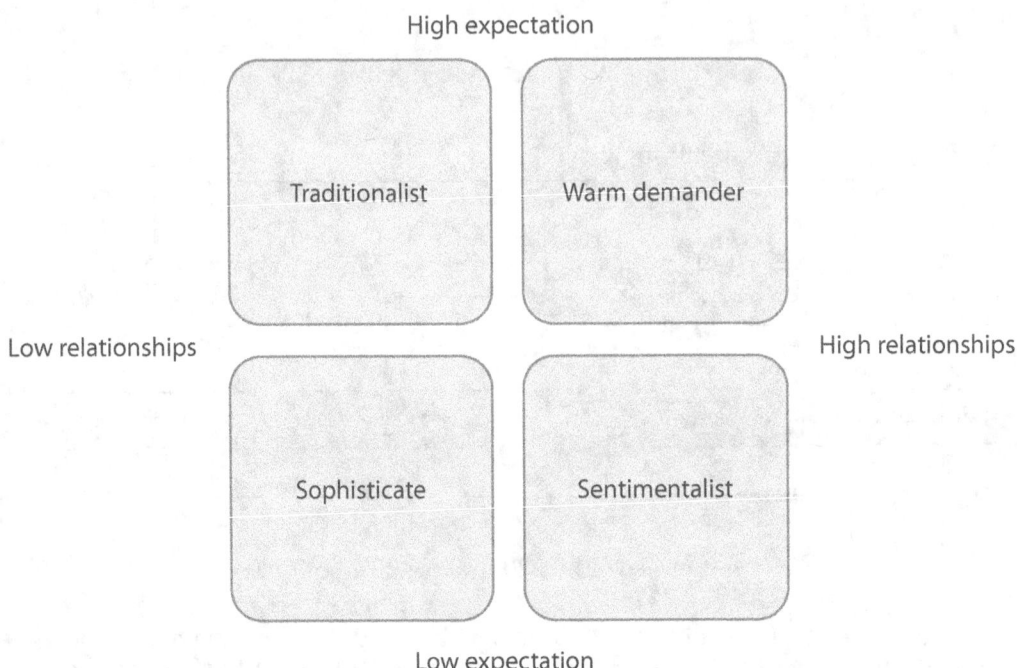

Figure 3.6 *The warm and cold teacher, adapted from Roberts (2023) and Kleinfield (1975)*

Type of teacher	What this looks like in action
Traditional – These teachers have high expectations of their learners but don't value their relationships with learners.	These are the teachers who tend to rely heavily on the sanctions to manage behaviours, rather than considering the impact of the learning environment and relationships (assertive).
Sophisticate – These teachers have low expectations of their learners so do not push them to be their best and also do not value relationships with learners.	These teachers do not care about learners making progress or about their personal development and are perhaps not suited to teaching (non-assertive).
Sentimentalist – These teachers are more concerned with the relationship with their learners without concerning themselves too much with the learners' progress.	These are the teachers who want to be known as 'cool teachers' or try to befriend learners rather than teach them effectively (non-assertive).
Warm demander – These teachers have, and uphold, high expectations of learners in regard to learning and behaviour. They also build strong, caring relationships, recognising the individual needs of learners and maintaining professional boundaries.	These teachers have high expectations of their learners but they will give them all the support they need to meet those expectations (assertive).

The importance of learning names

If you want to build relationships and demand high expectations of learners, you absolutely need to learn their names. Learning names helps you to achieve the following:

- **Demonstrate an appreciation of learners as individuals** – Being recognised by name, when for example when welcoming a learner into the learning environment, creates feelings of belonging in a group and recognition of the individuality of the learner.

- **Recognise contributions to the class** – Receiving feedback by name has more of an impact on the individual than if no name is used during feedback.

- **Enhance individual responsibility for the learners' own actions** – If a person is identified as an individual, they are more aware of their actions and less likely to engage in something 'because everyone else was doing it'.

- **Aim questions towards individuals** – This can be useful for cold calling (see chapter 7 for more detail on this) or inviting responses from individuals.

- **Gain learners' attention** – Being called out by name will receive a quicker response than 'you with the pink coat', for example, which will help with reinforcing expectations where necessary.

- **Keep the learners safe** – As above, calling someone by their name gets more immediate attention, which can be crucial in regard to health and safety.

> **Case study: What happens when we don't know our learners' names?**
>
> Mirabella goes to the head of sixth form (HoS) to complain about her chemistry teacher. She has been taught by them for six weeks so far and they still have not managed to learn her name. She also says that the teacher does not give her help when she asks for it.
>
> When the teacher was told that Mirabella had complained, they responded with, 'Who's Mirabella?'
>
> When the HoS then relayed the second part of Mirabella's complaint, the teacher said that the reason they had not helped the learner was because she had been caught playing dangerously with a Bunsen burner and was then told to work in silence.
>
> The HoS then asked if the learner who had to work in silence was definitely Mirabella, and the teacher replied, 'Yes, she definitely was.' The HoS replied, 'How would you know? You didn't know her name.'

REFLECT

What was the impact of not knowing Mirabella's name? Discuss with a peer or colleague the multiple challenges and issues that have arisen as a result of not knowing the learner's name.

It is not acceptable to create nicknames for names you find difficult to pronounce or to 'dead name' someone who has chosen to change their name themselves, so make sure you identify the best way for you to learn the preferred names of your learners.

Ways to learn people's names

If you have a good memory, or the group is small, play a name game. Ask learners to say their name and something they like, or an adjective that goes with their name (such as Dandy Dan or Marvellous Mike), or ask them to play a version of 'granny went to market' (a memory game where you add a new item to a shopping list and then list all the items identified by others in the game until someone cannot remember all the items) with the names until you have been round the whole class.

An example of this game is:

Learner 1: Hi, I'm Dandy Dan

Learner 2: Hi, this is Dandy Dan, and I'm Marvellous Mike.

Learner 3: Hi, this is Dandy Dan and Marvellous Mike, and I'm Tremendous Tyrone.

And so on, until you have a very long list that you have heard numerous times). This will help you to retain their names, and it is a bit of tension breaker when you are getting to know a new group.

Alternately, if your memory is not so good or you do not like the idea of a fun game (it is not for everyone), or you have so many learners it feels impossible to do it this way, you could:

- Use stickers for their names.
- Write their names on a piece of paper and fold it so it stands up in front of them.
- Use a seating plan.
- When teaching online, ask learners to have their name displayed on the call.

Tip for Teaching

Knowing people's names is key to developing positive relationships, so make sure you have a strategy planned for when you teach your learners.

Belonging

Belonging has two essential components: a sense of 'valued involvement' and a sense of 'fit'. The first of these describes the feeling of being accepted as a valued part of the system or environment, and the second is the feeling that a person has when their characteristics accord with or match those characteristics that are valued in the that environment (Asher and Weeks, 2014). A lack of a sense of belonging can be psychologically draining, and that sense of belonging is typically not something that can be created by the individual. Rather, belonging is created by a group or community (Nunn, 2021).

A learner feeling like they matter, through demonstrating genuine care, ensuring consistency with interactions and recognising them as an individual, adds a sense of agency to the feeling of belonging. Not only are learners welcome, but their presence makes a positive difference to the teacher, their peers and to their own learning. They have some control over how their learning progresses and are listened to by staff. In our teaching environments – and colleges more broadly – we should consider how we ensure our learners experience belonging. A lack of these can lead to marginalisation, which in turn impacts on our duty to be inclusive in our practice (see more on inclusivity in chapter 4).

> **REFLECT**
>
> How can you help your learners feel like they belong and matter in your classroom, department or college?

Relatedness

Relatedness describes the learner's sense of belonging in their environment and the extent to which they feel part of a group and share an identity with their peers. Importantly, this encompasses learner-teacher relatedness as well as learner-learner relatedness.

For sports teachers this will include learners wearing the college's sports kit. The kit became a source of pride, especially in fixtures against other colleges, and helped to establish a common identity among learners who would not have gelled in the normal course of their lives. Other uniforms such as coats and aprons (catering), overalls (motor vehicle) and scarves and cravats (travel and tourism) have similar group-cohering functions.

Clothing is by no means the only way to establish a shared identity or develop relatedness among group members. Escandell and Chu (2023) recommend that teachers show openness to prevent learners from self-silencing.

Learners are sometimes reticent to share their ideas when the environment does not feel supportive. The way a teacher responds to learner contributions sets the tone for future interactions. Humanising themselves through genuine interactions, active listening and responding positively to learners helps to establish a strong sense of relatedness and can lead to a learning environment characterised by mutual respect. Eye contact and open body language are important tools for a teacher to demonstrate openness. In these conditions, learners feel that they (and their views) are welcome, helping them feel more connected personally to one another and to the teacher.

> **REFLECT**
>
> How can you help your learners feel like they belong and matter in your classroom, department or college?

3.6 Creating a positive learning environment

Your learners need to know that their learning environment is a safe place, where mistakes can be made and confidence developed. Lemov (2015) refers to this as a 'culture of error', where an environment is purposefully built with the goal that learners feel psychologically safe enough to make mistakes and therefore develop an understanding that mistakes are part of learning.

To do this, teachers need to **'set the tone'** by normalising errors by addressing mistakes made by learners with curiosity (instead of correction) i.e. "How did you get that answer?" Or, "what made you think that?" Instead of: "No, that's wrong, how don't you know this?"

In accordance with the above, **errors should be used as a diagnostic tool**. If we can identify where the misunderstanding or misconception came from, we can address it and relearn the concept to enhance understanding.

As mentioned before, **psychological safety here is key**, so that learners feel safe enough to make the errors in the first place by attempting to respond to questions or tasks. You can imagine how much less progress is made in the classroom if learners aren't willing to try things out unless they are completely sure of the 'correct' outcome.

Consistency and routine

Routines create a calmer learning environment where learners can focus on the learning, which also contributes to creating the psychological safety mentioned above.

The table below highlights how impactful established routines are on learning and building relationships with your learners (see more on relationships in chapter 4).

Positive impact of routines	What this looks like	Impact on learner and teacher
Predictability	For a variety of reasons, some learners do not have stable lives outside of their education. If you can offer predictability for them within the classroom or the workplace, this reduces anxiety and provides the stability they need to be able to focus on learning. This means that when they enter your classroom, they find the same person with the same composure as always – calm, welcoming and ready to teach. They receive the same response regardless of their behaviours.	Solid relationships with teachers. When you are predictable and consistent, this strengthens the relationship between you and the learners as it reduces anxiety regarding your interactions regarding learning.
Consistency	Consistency is much like predictability, but consistency creates predictability for our learners. This can relate to the way you start each session, require the same resources stored in the same place or, most importantly, welcome learners into the learning environment.	If your mood is not consistent it makes you unpredictable, which can be a threat for those who do not experience consistency elsewhere. The way you interact with your learners needs to be consistent so the learners know where they stand with you.

Positive impact of routines	What this looks like	Impact on learner and teacher
Reduced anxiety	Knowing the routine is helpful for learners with a range of needs such as ADHD, autism and anxiety, but also for day-to-day anxieties such as: 'Who will I have to work with?' 'Where do I sit?' 'Have I got what I need for today's session?' 'Will my teacher be happy to see me or angry because the printer wasn't working before the lesson?'	To have a passion for learning, learners need to feel safe and have their anxieties reduced in any way that is feasible.
Effective use of learning time	Logistically, if there are routines in place, such as your learners knowing that as they enter the room, they need to ensure that their bags are safely put away and they have all the tools they need to start the session, this avoids wasting time settling, resettling and moving around to grab what they need.	There is more time for learning and less distractions for the learner.
Reduced requirements for revisits to 'the rules'	Keeping to a routine also contributes positively to reducing unwanted behaviours and certainly makes it easier to address those behaviours should they arise.	As above, there is more time for learning and less distractions for the learner.

There are many simple routines you can put in place to achieve the outcomes above. These include:

- Welcoming learners into the learning environment.
- Always starting your lesson on time.
- Having a seating plan.
- Taking a register.
- Revisiting expectations before you start the session (these could be expectations at the beginning of every session, including reference to policy or health and safety).
- Learners knowing where resources and tools are and that the expectation is to get what they need or wait for you to give out resources.

- Using starter activities such as retrieval tasks.

- Using an indicator that you want learners to listen to you (this needs to be something you are comfortable with; could be 'all eyes on me' or holding your hand in the air and saying 'hands up if you can hear me' or 'everyone look this way').

- Providing thinking time followed by cold calling (make it routine and the learners will be more likely to answer your questions, as they expect them).

- Dealing with behaviours that are not conducive to learning.

- Your classroom set-up.

- Always finishing your lesson on time – and not early, or this will become routine!

Resources

Even if you are not teaching in your regular learning environment, you can still bring the resources, lay them out neatly on a table and have an indicator on the board for what learners each need before the lesson or activity begins. Making sure that you are well prepared for the lesson will inevitably make the session run more smoothly, but it will also demonstrate your dedication to the learners as you have considered the content of the session carefully and provided what they need in order for them to learn and progress. Make sure you consider who your learners are and what their needs are so that they feel safe and seen (see chapter 4 on learner needs).

Grouping learners

A seating plan is where you set out where you want your learners to sit and is a very useful tool when it comes to encouraging behaviour conducive to learning. You can organise them based on the following goals:

- Avoiding unwanted challenging behaviour, such as by separating chatty friends or people who you know can't get along, or pairing people who you know will work well together (such as when a learner is reluctant to talk in pairs if they are not sat with someone they are comfortable with).

- Enhancing learning opportunities by pairing learners who are working on similar projects, to enhance the knowledge in a group of learners or for group work.

- Helping you to remember the names of the learners in your class. You can use the seating plan to pose questions using names as well.

You may find the idea of a seating plan a bit overwhelming, but if you are working with a mentor, you can ask them to support you with this. If you are not teaching with a mentor by your side, then make sure to give a clear rationale for using a seating plan (not just that you are separating learners to avoid unwanted behaviours!) as learners are less likely to argue against it if they understand the reason. Equally, this is your classroom or learning environment, so make it routine that you move them around for learning purposes and they will become accustomed to it.

Of course, there are more subtle ways of grouping learners than a seating plan, such as:

- Assigning learners numbers and asking that all the '1s' sit together, all the '2s' etc.

- Giving out cards with pairs or sets (could be a jigsaw), and the learners have to find their partner or group.

- Using QR codes the learners have to scan, which provide guidance on a topic they are working on (four learners could have the same topic, for example).

- Assigning learners to four corners of the room, seemingly at random, even though you have planned out who you want to work together.

Learner positioning in the learning space

There are a variety of ways you can set up classroom seating in a traditional classroom setting or learner positioning during practical sessions and activities. Three common examples are U-shaped tables, rows and small, grouped tables.

For theory classes, U-shaped tables are a useful way to facilitate inclusive discussions; for practical classes, they are an effective way to invite learners to stand around a demonstration so they can all see. In either scenario, this set-up allows the teacher to carry out effective question and answer sessions with all learners in the group.

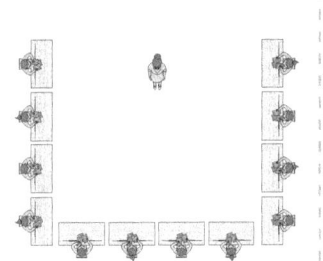

Figure 3.7 *U-shape tables or learner positioning with teacher in the middle of the 'U'*

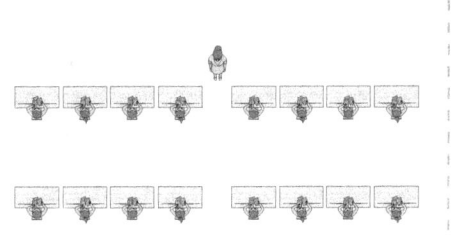

Figure 3.8 *Tables set up in rows*

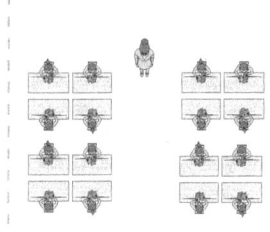

Figure 3.9 *Tables and learning set-up for groups*

Arranging seating in rows is good for reducing unwanted chatter in the classroom and ensuring all eyes are facing forward. This may also be necessary in practical classrooms such as science labs, beauty salons or kitchens so teachers can move around the room easily, see the practices taking place and ask questions during practical sessions.

Small, grouped tables will work best for group work in a theory class, as they allow the teacher to circulate freely to support learners. This set-up can also be replicated within a practical setting such a gym or workshop, where learners are at various stations around the room and the teacher needs to circulate.

Tip for Teaching

Whatever the set-up in your room, always try to make sure the learners are facing you and can look at the board easily. This makes it more comfortable for them and easier for you to notice if they turn their heads when they shouldn't or if they need support, as well as giving them the opportunity to access information you are sharing as the teacher.

3.7 Establishing and maintaining high expectations

Establishing clear expectations with your learners is at the very core of positive behaviours in the learning environment. Below is a short case study that demonstrates why expectations are so important.

> **Case study**
>
> Think about an occasion where you have been somewhere new. Let's choose a restaurant as an example. You enter the restaurant for the first time and the questions between you and your companion go a bit like this:
>
> 'Do we just choose our own table?' 'Do we order at the bar, or do they come to us?' 'Where are the toilets?' 'Should I take my cap off, or do you think it's okay to keep it on in here?'
>
> Sound familiar? Unless we are given instructions in a new setting, we can feel slightly on edge until someone tells us what to do.
>
> Think about the scenario again – you arrive at the restaurant, but this time you are met by a friendly but assertive member of staff.
>
> Staff member: 'Hello, table for two? I will take you over when you are ready. The toilets are just over there. I will come and take your order in a moment. Would you like me to take your hat?'
>
> You: 'Phew! We know exactly what to expect, so we can settle in and enjoy our delicious meal. We will absolutely come here again.'

It is a similar situation in the learning environment. If your learners know exactly what is expected of them, not only can they adhere to those expectations but they are also able to relax into the session, enjoy the learning experience and focus their attention on the content being taught.

Always be clear when providing guidance to learners in an institution. This may be represented in college expectation posters in classroom settings, or you may need to gather these from your colleagues if you are teaching in a workplace setting where you may not find these kinds of posters displayed. Use these posters as a starting point, making sure that any rules decided are in line with the guidelines created by the institution.

The time to outline expectations is when you first start teaching the learners. There are several ways of doing this, such as the below examples of ways to approach this task that adhere to Roberts' (2023) teacher types outlined on page 54.

- The 'traditional teacher' approach – Tell the learners your expectations without discussion. This will make things clear, but it won't contribute positively to relationship building.

- The 'warm demander' approach – Develop mutually agreeable expectations. One way you could do this is to generate discussion about what learners want for themselves in the classroom and should therefore give to others.

This process enables the learners to recognise the rationale for each of the expectations or rules, thus creating a reference point for the teacher if these expectations are not met. Do make sure that you start with the institution's expectations here though and ensure that the rules identified are in line with them.

Tip for Teaching

Rights and responsibilities in the classroom

1. Instruct learners to make a list of what their rights are in the classroom. Examples are to feel safe, be allowed to learn, be respected and work in a clean environment.

2. Then, instruct the learners to identify what their responsibilities are in order for their peers to receive the same rights. They could create a table such as the example below.

It is my right to...	Therefore, it is my responsibility to...
Feel safe in the classroom	Contribute to a safe environment for others where no one is subjected to bullying.
Be allowed to learn	Allow others to learn by not being disruptive or talking over others.
Be respected	Be respectful to others (refer to Equality Act here).
Work in a clean environment	Keep the environment clean by tidying up, eating outside the classroom and only allowing water in the classroom.

3. Now, create your rules for the classroom out of the responsibilities. Avoid terms like 'no being disrespectful' or 'no food' and opt for more positive rules such as 'respect one another by listening and using respectful language' or 'eat outside the classroom and only drink water while in class'.

Once the rules are created, you have a final discussion with learners inviting them to either agree or disagree to the classroom rules. You now have a common understanding and agreement on the rules of the classroom.

REFLECT

What expectations and information can you relate to your learners to ease them into your learning environment?

---

① **Respect.** Listen actively and respect different opinions.

② **Responsibility.** Be punctual, be prepared.

③ **Engagement.** Participate positively in lessons and activities.

④ **Professionalism.** Use appropriate language.

⑤ **Wellbeing.** Maintain a safe, inclusive space for all.

⑥ **Be part of a positive learning community!**

Figure 3.10 *Example expectations poster*

Once you have outlined and agreed expectations, if learners break them then you need to call them up on it. Remind them that they agreed to be respectful and that they need to demonstrate the responsibilities they have in relation to other peoples' rights. Again, consistency is key. You have a reference point in the form of your agreed rules to remind the learners what they agreed to and why they agreed to it.

Some teachers have a reminder of the rules on the first slide of every session, much like the poster on page 63. This is a great way to pick up on any rules that were not adhered to the last time the group was together. If you always do this, it will start to feel natural (and consistent) and learners will know that their behaviours will be addressed where necessary.

Stick to the rules!

If you have said that learners should eat outside the classroom, then that is where they eat. The trick is to never enter any grey areas with your expectations. For example: 'Is soup okay?' 'If soup is okay, can I bring a stew in?' 'If stew is okay, can I just have this steak in the back here?'

If there is no food on the classroom, then there is no food in the classroom. Never bend the rule for one learner. This only slips into inconsistency, which means your classroom is no longer a predictable, consistent and safe place for your learners – or for you.

> **REFLECT**
>
> How do your colleagues on a placement or in the workplace outline expectations? Do they do this as an activity at the start of the year, where they created expectations as a group? Do they refer to institution posters displayed on the walls? Do they use a slide at the beginning of every session that is personal to them, or agreed with the department? Or do they not have any expectations to draw on at all?
>
> Once you have identified what your colleagues use, think about how they use it as a tool, or consider the impact it has if teachers do not establish and refer to agreed expectations.

> **Tip for Teaching**
>
> Make sure that you are able to adhere to the same rules. This will give the rules (and you) more credibility and make them universal for all learners, regardless of age.

3.8 Maintaining high expectations

Of course, there will always be occasions where the proactive methods of developing high expectations and the application of teacher presence will not be enough to maintain constant behaviours conducive to learning. Below, you will find advice and guidance regarding reactive responses to behaviours in your positive learning environments.

Difficult conversations

Not only do you need to establish routines, but you also need to promptly address any unwanted behaviours in your learning environment. Let us discuss some reactive approaches to managing your learning environment while remembering that our learners are no longer in the school environment and that we are preparing them for the workplace.

Challenging inappropriate behaviour is a vital part of maintaining a safe and respectful learning environment (for more information on this, see chapter 2). We have a duty to address issues promptly and consistently while remaining calm and objective; this is easier said than done but following a simple process of clearly communicating expectations and the consequences of not meeting these helps learners to understand the impact of their actions.

Handling difficult conversations is an essential skill for teachers as you often need to address sensitive topics. Whether discussing a learner's performance, addressing concerns with a parent or managing a conflict with a colleague, the key is to approach the conversation with empathy, clarity and professionalism. Active listening plays a crucial role in ensuring that the other person feels heard, and this can help de-escalate tension and foster a productive dialogue. Active listening involves demonstrating you have heard what has been said to you by rephrasing to demonstrate your understanding.

Teachers should focus on facts rather than emotions, use neutral language and provide constructive solutions. Preparing for these conversations by anticipating potential reactions and planning responses can also improve outcomes and maintain positive relationships.

Use of 'we' language

> 'We've got a really interesting topic to learn about today!'
>
> 'We've had some great results in our recent assignment!'
>
> 'Are we ready to begin?'
>
> 'We're cooking with gas now!'

Each of these phrasings is intended to convey the idea that learning is a shared journey and that you, the teacher, are as invested in it as you hope your learners are. 'We' language allows you to let a group down gently if they are underperforming or need a reprimand but also helps to share praise when a lesson or assessment has gone well or if general levels of effort and application have increased. In many ways you represent the organisation to the learners, and their feeling of belonging and being welcome in the organisation can be shaped by the language you use to relate to them.

Separating the behaviour from the individual

When challenging behaviour, it is necessary to separate the behaviour from the individual. By using 'I' statements such as 'I noticed that X', rather than accusatory language such as 'you did X', you can reduce the likelihood of defensive reactions.

Even referring to the impact of the behaviour of the individual rather than the individual themselves can be effective; for example, 'talking over others is making it hard to hear what they have to say' rather than 'you are being too loud.'

Consider your tone and volume

Considering your own volume and the tone of your voice, as well as the words that you use, will have an impact on how learners respond to your reminders of expectations.

For example, instead of shouting 'Meg, you know you aren't supposed to drink fizzy drinks in class, get rid of it now', try a softer tone, such as 'Meg, pop that fizzy drink away for me, you know we don't allow them, thanks.'

Another approach to challenging unwanted behaviours is to give the learner the impression that they are doing you a favour if they comply. For example, say 'do me a favour and pop that can away, thanks', followed by a smile.

Both of these approaches are more likely to get a positive response to a request from a young person or adult as they are less confrontational than a demand for compliance.

Direct with respect

It is also good practice to say 'thank you' to learners while giving clear and direct instructions, rather than 'please', when requesting actions or modifying behaviours so that they are conducive to learning. For example, instead of 'Please Adam, listen to others while they are talking' you say, 'Listen to others while they are speaking, Adam. Thank you.' (Cowley, 2010). This means that you are being direct but you are also maintaining respectful relationships while communicating your requests. It also avoids you sounding timid, when you might feel that way!

One-on-one discussions

In some cases, private conversations may be more effective than public reprimands. Restorative approaches such as encouraging learners to reflect on their behaviour and its impact on others can promote accountability and positive change.

Attendance and punctuality

This chapter holds a great deal of information regarding how we can support behaviours conducive to learning, but there is one very simple rule we can follow as a starting point: be curious about your learners, find out about their lives and their needs and then keep them in mind.

In the case study opposite you will find a common occurrence in the classroom which can lead to disruption, or behaviour conducive to learning, depending on whether we consider the needs of our learners, or not.

3.9 Returning to the policy

If you apply the techniques outlined in this chapter you should be able to create a positive learning environment, but there will always be occasions where you will need to react in the moment to unwanted behaviours when a learner is not complying with all the above.

When working with people, there is always the chance that emotions run high. There are some learners who provoke during an altercation with a teacher, and in this scenario you need to take a breath and remember that this behaviour is unlikely to be about you. It is more likely to do with something that has happened outside the classroom, or in education prior to this interaction with you. So, promptly focus on reminding yourself of this before you say anything that may escalate your emotion or the emotion of the learner.

Case study

There will be rules regarding expectations of attendance and punctuality, but there is less likely to be guidelines on how you respond to lateness. Make sure to always start your lesson on time, even if some learners are late. This shows that you respect the efforts of those who are on time have made, reinforcing their values and beliefs that you should be on time to class.

For those learners who are late: think about if they have been caught in the rain, if their bike tyre had burst or if they missed the bus because they were feeding their siblings. They arrive at college late and their teacher immediately responds by shouting at them to get outside and wait there until invited in.

What impact would that have on the individual who has had a bad day but made it in anyway? What impact does that have on learning? Is it disruptive?

Of course it is disruptive. You have interrupted the flow of the class, left to reprimand the learner and hindered any chance of them coming into the room ready to learn.

What impact does that have on you, the teacher, who should be focusing on the class?

You lose track of what you were talking about, have to take the chance of leaving the room and therefore creating opportunities for learners to go off task, and you could feel flustered due to confrontation.

There are different schools of thought on this topic, but if you are seeking to provide your learners with consistency and a safe place to learn and respect, the above reaction is likely to hinder the creation of the positive learning environment.

The purpose of attendance to class is to learn, so it makes sense that lateness should cause the least amount of disruption possible.

A welcome, point to a seat and carry on teaching, allowing the learner to settle in before being asked about their lateness and promptly included in the lesson is much more conducive to learning.

If all else fails and you are unable to address the behaviours of an individual on a one-on-one basis, refer back to the policies and procedures outlined at the beginning of this chapter.

> **REFLECT**
>
> According to your policy, what should you do if a learner refuses to engage with the tasks set in your classroom?

Take it further...

For further reading Sherrington and Caviglioli's (2020) Walkthru books each include a section on Behaviour and Relationships.

Identify what you want to improve in regards to behaviour and relationships, choose a method from the books and apply it using the step-by-step instructions they offer, which includes application and reflection on impact.

Chapter summary

This chapter has explored how you can develop your knowledge of practice and theory in relation to Duty 1: 'Promote a passion for learning and set high expectations of all learners and support their personal and skills development.'

To do this, we have looked at:

- Behaviour policy and procedure
- Creating a positive learning environment
- Establishing expectations
- Upholding your positive learning environment

In the next chapter, we will build on these concepts, developing your knowledge of how to work with individual learners in FES and enhancing a culture of belonging that contributes to the learning environment, but from an individual learner perspective.

References

Asher, S. R., and Weeks, M. S. (2014) Loneliness and belongingness in the college years. In R. J. Coplan and J. C. Bowker (Eds)., The handbook of solitude: Psychological perspectives on social isolations, social withdrawal, and being alone (pp. 283-301). Wiley Blackwell,

Bennett, T. (2018) Managing difficult behaviour in colleges. London: UNISON.

Boxer, A. (2021) Teaching Secondary Science: A Complete Guide. John Catt. Melton, Woodbridge.

Bromfield, C., 2006. PGCE secondary trainee teachers & effective behaviour management: An evaluation and commentary. Support for learning, 21(4), pp.188-193

Canter, L. and Canter, M. (1976) Assertive Discipline: A Take-Charge Approach for Today's Educator. Los Angeles: Canter and Associates.

Cents-Boonstra, M., Lichtwarck-Aschoff, A., Denessen, E., Aelterman, N., and Haerens, L. (2020) 'Fostering learner engagement with motivating teaching: an observation study of teacher and learner behaviours', Research Papers in Education, 36(6), pp. 754–779. doi: 10.1080/02671522.2020.1767184.

Cowley, S. (2010) Getting Your Class to Behave. 2nd edn. London: Continuum International Publishing Group.

Deci, E.L. and Ryan, R.M., (2000). The "What" and "Why" of Goal Pursuits: Human Needs and the Self-Determination of Behavior. Psychological Inquiry, 11(4), pp.227-268. Available at: https://doi.org/10.1207/S15327965PLI1104_01

Department for Education (2019) Timpson review of school exclusion. London: Department for Education.

Dix, P (2017) When the Adults Change, Everything Changes. Wales: Independent Thinking Press.

Dubeau, A., Plante, I. and Frenay, M. (2017) Achievement Profiles of Learners in High School Vocational Training Programs. Vocations and Learning 10, 101–120. https://doi.org/10.1007/s12186-016-9163-6

Escandell, S., and Chu, T. L. (Alan). (2023). Implementing Relatedness-Supportive Teaching Strategies to Promote Learning in the College Classroom. Teaching of Psychology, 50(4), 441-447. https://doi.org/10.1177/00986283211046873

Hitchcock (2022) Case Study: Write a critical evaluation of the learner behaviour. Unpublished Assignment. University of Derby.

Kounin, J. (1970). Discipline and group management in classrooms. New York: Rinehart and Winston.

Lemov, D. (2015) Teach like a champion 2.0: 62 techniques that put students on the path to college. 2nd edn. San Francisco: Jossey-Bass.

Niemiec, C.P. and Ryan, R.M., (2009). Autonomy, competence, and relatedness in the classroom: Applying self-determination theory to educational practice. Theory and Research in Education, 7(2), pp.133-144. Available at: https://doi.org/10.1177/1477878509104318.

Nunn, L.M., 2021. College belonging: How first-year and first-generation students navigate campus life. Rutgers University Press.

Pelletier, L.G., Séguin-Lévesque, C. and Legault, L. (2002) 'Pressure from above and pressure from below as determinants of teachers' motivation and teaching behaviors', Journal of Educational Psychology 94: 186–196

Roberts, H. (2023) Bothered. London: Crown House Publishing.

Rogers, C. R. (1969) Freedom to Learn. Columbus, OH: Charles E. Merrill Publishing Company.

Roth, G., Assor, A., Kanat-Maymon, Y. and Kaplan, H. (2007) 'Autonomous motivation for teaching: How self-determined teaching may lead to self-determined learning', Journal of Educational Psychology 99: 761–74

Sherrington, T. and Caviglioli, O. (2020) Teaching WalkThrus: Five-Step Guides to Instructional Coaching. [Place of publication]: John Catt Educational.

Skinner, B.F. (1953) Science and Human Behaviour. New York: Macmillan.

Chapter 4 Meeting learner needs

Work in a manner that values diversity and actively promotes equality of opportunity and inclusion by responding to the needs of all students. (Duty 5)

Every person in [an educational] community should be free to be themselves, to feel seen, to feel safe, to feel supported and to feel like they belong.
Brassington and Brett (2023)

4.1 Introduction

This chapter aims to outline what it means to value diversity, to demonstrate how we can actively promote equality of opportunity and inclusion and to ensure you provide all learners with appropriate support and teaching to succeed, regardless of background, ability or individual characteristics.

The learner cohort in FES is arguably more diverse than any other education sector due to such a diverse range of education opportunities. As discussed in chapter 1, qualifications offered across the sector range from entry level to higher education, across different domains, such as academic and vocational, and different contexts, such as colleges and community learning. With around 3,112,870 students, including 16-18 and 19+ (DfE, 2025a) and 284,190 apprenticeships who started in August 2024 to April 2025 (DfE, 2025b), it is unsurprising that the sector needs to cater for a wide range of ages, levels of experience and abilities. Such diversity and complexity attract learners from different backgrounds with a range of needs and motivations for learning. This presents challenges when attempting to meet the needs of every learner progressing through the sector; but not only do we have a legal duty to support these learners, we also have a moral duty as teachers to enable every learner to make progress.

Throughout this chapter, we endeavour to support you to understand the diversity of your cohort and provide a range of strategies that will help you to meet their needs, promote equality of opportunity and an inclusive learning environment where all, regardless of background, can thrive. In doing so, we will summarise key legislation that informs and shapes inclusive practice as well as covering some of the key terms we need to understand as FES teachers in regard to Duty 5. We will then provide examples of how the legislation works in practice and how to identify and meet learner needs, first by expanding your understanding of each protected characteristic and then moving on to other elements of learners' background which may contribute to their needs as FES learners. Finally, we will move on to methods of ensuring equality of opportunity for learners, finishing with how to address discrimination in the FES sector.

Please note, the terminology regarding both protected characteristics and marginalised groups changes over time. At the time this book was written, we have endeavoured to use the most inclusive language in all cases.

4.2 Valuing diversity

What do we mean when we say that FES teachers should value diversity? To value something is to see its worth or importance in our lives and communities. In respect to diversity, it can be interpreted in one of two ways:

- To value diversity, we appreciate (and respect) difference and variety.
- Where we are inclusive of all individuals; for example, in regard to cultural, social, ability and disability, gender, age, race and religion.

Therefore, to value diversity is to see it, adapt your approaches to communication and learning accordingly and appreciate how difference enriches our lives and society.

4.3 Legal and ethical considerations

The starting point for this chapter must be our legal duty as FES teachers. We need to understand these legal duties before starting to consider how we can adhere to them. As we discussed in chapters 1 and 2, legislation, regulations and policies have a significant impact on our role, and this is no more evident than when we are thinking about our learners and ensuring equitable access to education.

In this chapter, we want to consider three main pieces of legislation and guidance that can help us understand our role in meeting learners' needs and that will inform policy within your institution. While the Equality Act 2010 and SEND Code of Practice (2014) have already been introduced in chapter 1, here we look at them specifically through the lens of inclusion and meeting learner needs. We also include the Joint Council for Qualifications (JCQ) guidelines in the table below to enhance your understanding of access arrangements for examinations.

Legislation	Relevance to inclusion	Relevant terminology and practice
Equality Act (2010)	This policy protects individuals against discrimination, victimisation and harassment in relation to the nine 'protected characteristics', which are: age, disability, gender reassignment, marriage and civil partnership, pregnancy and maternity, race, religion or belief and sex and sexual orientation.	The act refers to 'reasonable adjustments' for those with disabilities. The adjustments made can vary enormously and should always be individualised to the learner. These can include large font, providing lecture notes in advance, recording sessions, coloured overlays, quiet rooms, adjusted lighting, ramps, lifts and accessible toilets, gender neutral toilets, remote or hybrid learning options, flexible timetabling, support workers, note takers, wellbeing support and visual timetables, as some examples.
SEND Code of Practice (2014)	This policy outlines the legal requirements for teachers working with young people who have diagnosed and undiagnosed disabilities. (Chapter 7 covers legal requirements for FES, specifically.)	The policy uses the term 'best endeavours' in relation to the support provided to those protected by this legislation. This means we are legally required to do everything that can reasonably be expected to support FES learners who have, or are suspected to have, SEND needs. This can include making reasonable adjustments (as above), monitoring progress, training staff, providing targeted interventions and wellbeing support. It is expected that this is all put in place without waiting for an educational health care plan (EHCP) to be in place before acting (see the assessments table on page 73 for more detail on EHCPs).

Legislation	Relevance to inclusion	Relevant terminology and practice
JCQ Guidelines for Access Arrangements and Reasonable Adjustments (2024)	This document provides guidance on what we refer to as 'access arrangements', which are put in place to make access to summative assessments or examinations fair and equitable for all taking part.	Access arrangements are put in place for learners to provide them with equal opportunity for achievement in exams. These can include 25% extra time, a reader or a scribe, the use of a laptop or other assistive technology tools like screen readers or voice to text software, coloured screens or paper, rest breaks and a reflection of 'normal ways of working' (which can include any of the above).

4.4 Identifying learner needs

Now that we understand our legal responsibilities with regards to meeting learner needs, we can begin to consider what information we need to gather to meet these obligations.

Assessments of individual needs

There are several ways we gather information about the needs of individual learners through different types of assessment. We will cover the various principles of assessment that centre primarily on learning and progress in chapter 7, but in the context of assessing learners' individual needs, we will think about the principles in another way to enable us to identify potential barriers to learning. These barriers can begin to form even before learners join us at our institution and can remain in place until the end of the programme (or the time they leave).

Type of assessment	What it tells us
Initial assessment	
Assessment at application regarding learning needs and support plans	As learners apply for their programme, there is usually a question on the application form that asks them to identify whether they have any learning needs or disabilities or if they have had support in previous education. Note that many learners will not report their learning needs at this stage, sometimes due to previous negative experiences and a fear of stigma attached to disability.
Prior attainment	You will be able to build an idea of your learners' interests and strengths from their prior attainment, i.e. grades.
English and maths	Your institution may require your learners to complete English and maths initial assessments that provide you with knowledge of what level they are working at (on that day, but this is not necessarily a true reflection of their ability). These range from Entry 1 (below GCSE level) to Level 2 (GCSE level).
Protected characteristics	Those which have been gathered throughout the application and interview process will be available to you if your institution provides this information (Equality Act, 2010).

Type of assessment	What it tells us
Diagnostic assessment	
Learner support	If the learner has identified that they have a need on the enrolment form, this will trigger an interview with learner support, who will assess prior support given.
EHCP	This is put in place if a young person or adult has special educational needs. This can be created during childhood and be amended by the relevant stakeholders (teachers and education psychologists, SENDCos etc.) until the learner is 25 years old.
Getting to know your learners	During any induction period (yours or the learners'), take time to get to know your learners, find out what they did before they signed up to the course (were they in industry or education, or elsewhere?) and about their interests and aspirations.

As we will discuss in chapter 8, close collaborative working with other stakeholders will help you to effectively support your learners. It requires a great team effort to gather this initial data, with some of it coming through applications, and the learners themselves, others from the learning support team or previous providers and, on occasion, from previous teachers. Your English and maths team may also be involved in assessing these skills through coordinating the English and maths initial assessments. Once all the data has been gathered from multiple sources, it is often placed on a digital platform that can be accessed and added to during the learners' journey. Where institutions do not have software, they may require you to create a manual group profile that contains much of the detail outlined in the table above.

> **Take it further**: There is a debate regarding initial assessments in English and maths regarding moving away from deficit approaches (Dampier et al, 2019) to initial assessment, i.e. pointing out what learners don't know and filling those gaps, and moving towards a skills based approach where we find out what skills learners do have and how we can build on those in regards to literacy and numeracy (Zychowicz, 2022). Consider which approach you think is more beneficial for your learners, and why.

Group profile or individualised learning plan

The data gathered regarding your learners will inform what is referred to as a 'group (or class) profile'. Sometimes this may be referred to as an individualised learning plan (ILP) if the data is stored separately for each learner, rather than as a collective. This will help you to pre-empt some of the needs your learners may have. You will need to update these plans as you learn more and, if they are your personal tutor group, you will need to share this profile with other teachers who are teaching them other units or modules. In all cases when accessing or collecting learner data, you must adhere to GDPR guidelines (see chapter 2 for more detail on this).

As an FES teacher, you are likely to see a range of ages among your learners and so a range of retained information or ability in English and maths (indicated by your initial assessment outcomes). You will need to take this in to account when planning and facilitating learning, as well as any learner needs (both identified and unidentified).

A simplified example of a group profile may look like the following table.

Learner number	Age	English assessment	Maths assessment	Learning need	Additional information
100456	16–18	Level 2	Level 1	ADHD	Requires fidget toys to aid concentration and reduce anxiety
100378	16–18	Entry 3	Level 1	None	Grade 4 in English GCSE
100283	19+	Level 2	Level 2	None	O-levels only
100293	19+	Level 2	Level 1	Visually impaired	Size 18 font required
100789	16–18	Level 1	Entry 3	Dyslexia	Extra time for reading

The assessments in the table on page 72-73 will not always capture the detail we need to know about our learners. For this reason, you must have conversations with learners about their needs, as well as creating ILPs, if your aim is to truly understand them. This forms part of our continual assessment, where we establish what works for our learners through discussion and experimentation in the learning environment, which enables us to adapt our teaching to meet learner needs.

Planning for learners' needs

As we have established, the diversity of our learners will bring a variety of needs that we need to consider. We will now outline some of these needs using the nine protected characteristics in the Equality Act 2010 as a framework. We will provide suggested actions, pedagogical approaches and considerations which could support learners with these characteristics. Some of these are grouped together to demonstrate how they are interlinked. This ensures that the needs are considered in relation to key legislation that impacts the role.

Age

In an FES class, you could have learners whose ages range from 14 to any age above. This will have an impact on learner needs. Consider how a learners' previous education (whether that was the previous year or decades ago) will create discrepancies in the classroom, including a range of abilities in industry, digital or study skills. Consider the generalised responsibilities of different age groups with regards to caring for others, work or the pressures of running a home.

An area of consideration that is often neglected regarding age is the impact that menopause has on retention of information, brain fog, anxiety and physical symptoms such as hot flushes, muscle and joint pains and difficulty sleeping (NHS, 2022).

> **REFLECT**
>
> Think about the different ages of the learners you have in your classroom and how you could utilise the knowledge of older learners (such as previous experience or industry knowledge) and of those younger learners (such as more recent knowledge from education) in a task you have planned for this week.

Disability

According to the Equality Act (2010), disabilities that are protected includes learning, physical and prolonged (such as mental health). There are two models we intend to consider when discussing disability, introduced by disability activist Mike Oliver in the 1980s (Oliver, 2013).

Oliver labels these models as:

- **Medical model of disability**. This is where a disability is due to physical or cognitive impairments, suggesting that these impairments need to be 'fixed'. This view is perhaps more related to medical interventions such as medication or occupational therapies.

- **Social model of disability**. This is where the individual is disabled by the barriers and attitudes in society that stop them from thriving and living happily, meaning it is society that needs to be 'fixed' to address the disability. This includes inaccessible buildings and transport as well as the need to challenge stereotypes, negative attitudes and prejudices.

We will refer throughout to the social model of disability, as this is suitable for teachers who can make reasonable adjustments to their environment and the methods of communication to combat prejudice and reduce barriers to learning.

Neurodiversity

Neurodiversity is a term coined by Singer (1999) that describes the natural differences in the ways the brain works, also referred to as 'cognition'. This can be divided further into specific learning disabilities and difficulties, such as autism, ADHD and dyslexia, but as a group it brings those together who are not deemed to be 'neurotypical', a word which means that the brain processes information in the way that most individuals in society do.

The table below includes examples of the more specific disabilities alongside a brief summary of more generic challenges and some ideas (in addition to any reasonable adjustments identified by learner support). These are starting points for ways you can support your learners before you get to know their individual needs more specifically.

The descriptions in the table below and on the next few pages are brief, therefore you will need to research the needs of your learners in detail and try different approaches to provide them with support. This is not an exhaustive list of the disabilities you may encounter in your group and remember, all learners experience needs differently, even if they have the same label as another learner in the group.

Condition	Description and symptoms	Ideas for adjustments
Obsessive compulsive disorder (OCD)	According to the NHS, a person with OCD will usually experience frequent obsessive thoughts and compulsive behaviours. An obsession is an unwanted and unpleasant thought, image or urge that repeatedly enters your mind, causing feelings of anxiety, disgust or unease. A compulsion is a repetitive behaviour or mental act that someone feels they need to do to temporarily relieve the unpleasant feelings brought on by the obsessive thought. For example, someone with an obsessive fear of being burgled may feel they need to check all the windows and doors are locked several times before they can leave their house.	As OCD can manifest in a wide variety of ways, you need to signpost learners to learner support and follow the guidance given by those professionals in order to support your learners effectively.

Condition	Description and symptoms	Ideas for adjustments
Dyslexia	According to the NHS, a person with dyslexia may: - read and write very slowly - confuse the order of letters in words - be confused by letters that look similar and write letters the wrong way round (such as 'b' and 'd') - have poor or inconsistent spelling - understand information when told verbally but have difficulty with information that is written down - find it hard to carry out a sequence of directions - struggle with planning and organisation. Bear in mind that people with dyslexia often have good skills in other areas, such as creative thinking and problem solving.	Chunk, dual coding and scaffolding information and the use of memory aids will help avoid cognitive overload. Some learners will benefit from the use of reading rulers, different coloured paper (if they have scotopic sensitivity) or the use of sans serif fonts (but not Comic Sans, as it is not age appropriate for FES).
Dyscalculia	Individuals with dyscalculia have a severe and persistent difficulty with understanding numbers which affects their daily life and education. A current working definition is provided by the British Dyslexia Association: Dyscalculia is a specific and persistent difficulty in understanding numbers, which can lead to a diverse range of difficulties with maths. It will be unexpected in relation to age, level of education and experience and occurs across all ages and abilities. Maths difficulties are best thought of as a continuum, not a distinct category, and they have many causal factors. Dyscalculia falls at one end of the spectrum and will be distinguishable from other maths issues due to the severity of difficulties with number sense, including subitising, symbolic and non-symbolic magnitude comparison and ordering. It can occur singly but often co-occurs with other specific learning difficulties, maths anxiety and medical conditions.	Chunk, dual coding and scaffolding information will help avoid cognitive overload. Some learners will benefit from the use calculators and different coloured paper and memory aids.

Condition	Description and symptoms	Ideas for adjustments
Attention deficit hyperactivity disorder (ADHD)	According to the NHS, symptoms of ADHD involve the inability to pay attention to things (being inattentive), having high energy levels (being hyperactive) and the inability to control impulses (being impulsive). People may show signs of being inattentive, such as: - being easily distracted or forgetful - finding it hard to organise your time - finding it hard to follow instructions or finish tasks - losing things often, like your wallet, mobile or keys. People may show signs of being hyperactive and impulsive, including: - having a lot of energy or feeling restless - being very talkative or interrupting conversations - making quick decisions without thinking about what could happen as a result. Most people with ADHD will have symptoms of both the inattentive and hyperactive-impulsive type, though some only show signs of one type.	Chunking is key here, as small, achievable tasks will help keep the learner engaged. Reduce teacher talk, tasks and scaffolding information. Ensure that you are aware of the routines that need to remain and those that can change without causing dysregulation. Offer options to learners who get distressed when they are given instructions that they don't want to follow. Give count downs to changes in activity (perhaps 10 minutes, 5 minutes, 1 minute, then change). Use memory aids to support with occasions when learners experience short-term memory.
Dyspraxia	According to the NHS, if a person has dyspraxia it may affect: - their co-ordination, balance and movement - how they learn new skills, think and remember information at work and home - their daily living skills, such as dressing or preparing meals - their ability to write, type, draw and grasp small objects - how they function in social situations - how they deal with your emotions - time management, planning and personal organisation skills.	Adhere to health and safety requirements, consider how the room is laid out (whether it is easy to walk across the room) provide maps where necessary and a laptop or device if required.

Condition	Description and symptoms	Ideas for adjustments
Autism	According to the NHS, autistic people may: <ul><li>find it hard to communicate and interact with other people</li><li>find it hard to understand how other people think or feel</li><li>find things like bright lights or loud noises overwhelming, stressful or uncomfortable</li><li>get anxious or upset about unfamiliar situations and social events</li><li>take longer to understand information</li><li>do or think the same things over and over.</li></ul>	Provide clear instructions that do not need interpretation. Know which routines need to remain and which can be altered. Consider the sensory elements within the room and allow recommended protection against these, such as headphones for loud noises or dimmed lighting.

You will notice that there are certain activities or suggestions that are relevant to more than one impairment within the table – at this point we want to remind you that not all suggestions will work for all learners. You need to communicate with learners about what works best for them, try different things and then seek their evaluation of whatever you have tried.

Emotional and social needs

The learners in your care will have a variety of social and emotional needs, but we must acknowledge boundaries when it comes to supporting our learners with needs that we are not trained to deal with.

In relation to challenges such as anxiety and depression, there are a wide range of forms and reasons for these to emerge for a learner, so we must be careful to signpost our learners to the correct support for their emotions and mental health. Our role is to support the learners with making progress in their learning.

Recognising the symptoms of anxiety and depression allows us to signpost our learners promptly should we see them manifest. Trying to support learners with anxiety or depression ourselves can make the symptoms worse and have disastrous consequences, so just stick to supporting their learning in any way you can and making reasonable adjustments which will help them to achieve and progress.

Condition	Description and symptoms	Ideas for adjustments
Anxiety	According to the NHS, anxiety is a feeling of unease, such as worry or fear, that can be mild or severe. Anxiety is a feeling of stress, panic or fear that can affect someone's everyday life physically and psychologically. Generalised anxiety disorder (GAD) is a long-term condition where a person feels anxious about a wide range of issues.	Listen carefully to learners' fears and worries and make reasonable adjustments to support their engagement in the learning. For example, both anxiety and depression can make learners reluctant to answer questions in front of their peers, so consider ways you can hear their voice but perhaps on a 1:1 or in smaller groups, which is less intimidating. Learners may also experience brain fog, so providing the opportunity to think about questions before you require an answer will also be helpful, as well as scaffolding and chunking learning.
Depression	Some of the psychological symptoms of depression include continuous low mood or sadness, feeling hopeless and helpless, having low self-esteem, feeling tearful, feeling guilt-ridden, feeling irritable and intolerant of others, having no motivation or interest in things, finding it difficult to make decisions, not getting any enjoyment out of life, feeling anxious or worried or having suicidal thoughts or thoughts of harming oneself. Some of the physical symptoms of depression include moving or speaking more slowly than usual, changes in appetite or weight (usually decreased, but sometimes increased), unexplained aches and pains, lack of energy or disturbed sleep (for example, finding it difficult to fall asleep at night or waking up very early in the morning). Some of the social symptoms of depression include avoiding contact with friends and taking part in fewer social activities and neglecting hobbies and interests.	

Physical disability

A learner with a physical disability will have an idea of what may meet their needs in learning, but just like those who are neurodivergent, the learners may not be aware of the support that is available to them in their institution.

With physical disabilities, take guidance from risk-assessments and support plans, as well as discussing reasonable adjustments and amendments to practice that learners feel support their learning. Ensure that you keep the dialogue open by asking for evaluations on approaches to learning this way, you continue to build a picture of what does and does not work when supporting your learners as individuals.

Condition	Ideas for adjustments
Visual impairment	Consider the room layout, where the learner sits and if they need resources before or during the session (such as large print text or worksheets). Some learners may benefit from a magnifying glass for reading. Consider your learner's need if a task requires them to move around a classroom. Seek out what you have available in regard to Braille, audio books and captioning using assistive technology.
Hearing impairment	Consider the layout of the room with regards to the ability to lip read. Also, consider how an echoey room could impact hearing. You can use a technique that is referred to as 'looping in', where a hearing aid can be linked to audio.
Arthritis or other physical disability, chronic fatigue syndrome, fibromyalgia	For these ailments, pain, brain fog (sometimes due to medication) and exhaustion are key symptoms which may impact learning. Consider your learner's need if a task requires them to move around a classroom, how you can make it accessible to them and ensure they are not excluded from the task. Provide thinking time and the same approach to others who may have occasions where they have limited short term memory, methods such as chunking, use of memory aids and scaffolding.
Epilepsy, diabetes, narcolepsy	For these three ailments symptoms can escalate quickly and learners may need medication, and or interventions, to address those symptoms, preventatively and reactively. Know the signs and what to do if your learner needs help. Be aware of potential triggers and manage your classroom to avoid these.
Dysgraphia	The learner may have challenges in holding pens and writing. Provide use of a laptop or device where possible.

The physical impairments listed in this table can vary enormously. For any of these impairments, refer to support plans and speak to the learner to find out what they have put in place in the past to help them.

Keep in mind that if a learner has not been in education for some time, they may not know what is available to them.

Remember that not all learners will have a diagnosis, but if they have symptoms of any disabilities, difficulties or impairments they will still need the right support, and it is your legal duty to provide that according to the SEND Code of Practice.

REFLECT

DfE data from 2024–25 (2025c) found that 19.5% of FES learners self-declared a learning disability or difficulty. It is likely that your institutions' information is more accurate than this, as many learners will not disclose their learning need unless it is necessary due to a fear of the stigma they feel may be attached to the need they have. What percentage of the learners in your taught groups have a diagnosed or self-declared learning disability or difficulty? Does the data correlate with the findings of the DfE?

> **Take it further...**
>
> For one or more of your learners with a disability, research the different ways you can meet their needs within your next taught session. Choose a method of support that you have found in the literature and trial it with your learner. Reflect afterwards on how impactful the method was. (See chapter 10 for more on methods of reflection.)

For up-to-date terminology in relation to disability, consult the following guidance on the GOV.UK website: 'Inclusive language: words to use and avoid when writing about disability'.

Gender reassignment, marriage and civil partnership and sex and sexual orientation

It's important to acknowledge that elements of these protected characteristics are potentially contentious topics at present which could influence significant change in relation to policy and legislation. We have statutory and non-statutory guidance which is likely to change in the foreseeable future, so please do ensure that you are following statutory guidance, and policy within your institution, in relation to inclusivity regarding gender reassignment, marriage and civil partnership and sex and sexual orientation.

Lesbian, Gay, Bisexual, Transgender, Queer/Questioning (LGBTQ+) is a broad umbrella term. Below is some general good practice on being inclusive when it comes to the LGBTQ+ community. We can do this in several ways, but we will start with the language we use in the learning environment (and beyond) which demonstrates inclusivity and allyship to the LGBTQ+ community members.

What heteronormativity or cisnormativity looks like	What you should do instead
You make assumptions that the learner has a mum and dad (this is also inappropriate due to the diversity of family set-ups).	Refer to parents and caregivers as just that – parents and caregivers. This way, you aren't assuming their sexual orientations or whether they are married, in a civil partnership, or indeed, two people.
You assume that people are in heterosexual relationships.	Use the term 'partner' if you must (talking about relationships with learners at all can be problematic; see chapter 2 for more information).
You only discuss heterosexual relationships when facilitating sex education.	This is dismissive of the range of relationships learners may have
You set up your example scenarios who are in heterosexual relationships. For example: 'Mr. Ahmed decided to buy his girlfriend three presents, but he only has £10. How much should he spend on each present?'	Use a variety of non-heterosexual relationships in your worked examples. For example: 'Ahmed decided to buy his partner three presents, but he only has £10. How much should he spend on each present?'
You forget to use a person's preferred name.	Ensure you know peoples' preferred names (see chapter 3 for further information on the importance of learner names).
You misgender a person.	If you do this, you should discreetly apologise and correct yourself.

What heteronormativity or cisnormativity looks like	What you should do instead
You get the attention of the class by calling out 'right then girls and boys' or 'lads and ladies'.	Use the term 'folks', which is inclusive of all, or you could refer to them as subject specialists e.g. mathematicians, scientists or mechanics (Brassington and Brett, 2023).
Only using the terms Miss, Mrs or Mr.	Use the term 'Mx' for those who are nonbinary (if those individuals would like you to do so).

These are just a few examples we have provided to encourage you to pre-empt and recognise opportunities for inclusivity. This is something that takes conscious practice to address, so do not worry if you make a mistake as you are learning to be more inclusive.

> **REFLECT**
>
> Consider how you can make your classroom a more LGBTQ+ safe place. To read in more detail about LGBTQ+ and education, read Brett and Brassington (2023) Pride and Progress: Making Schools LGBT+ Inclusive Spaces.

> **Take it further...**
>
> For up-to-date terminology in regard to LGBTQ+, refer to the UCU's 'LGBT+: A Guide to Language in Use' document.

Logistical considerations

Although gender is not currently identified in the protected characteristics, we need to be aware that FES is widely understood to be 'gendered' (Marope, Chakroun and Holmes, 2015; Hegna, 2017) in the sense that most young people engaging with technical, vocational education and training (TVET) do so with programmes related to gendered occupations, such as hair and beauty (typically females) and construction (typically males). As a result, there will be individuals who can feel 'othered' due to their gender, such as a female learner studying construction, or a male learner studying hair and beauty.

When this happens, there are a few considerations we could explore to meet our learners' needs, for example:

- Am I actively aware that those of all genders are catered for regarding toilets and changing areas?

- Is there provision in place for gendered role models or support networks within the department?

- Am I tuned in to current gender issues such as the 'manosphere' and incels (part of 'prevent' training)?

- Am I aware of current issues in LGBTQ+ communities?

> **REFLECT**
>
> How could issues such as the 'manosphere' impact your context? What guidance is there from institutional policy on how to address issues of this nature?

Pregnancy and maternity

As educators we need to know the challenges that learners who are pregnant, breastfeeding or returning from maternity leave may face in relation to their education, particularly regarding the emotional, mental and physical effects of pregnancy. Pregnancy can cause symptoms such as feeling faint, physical pain like cramps or pelvic girdle pain, headaches, nose bleeds, tiredness and vomiting (NHS, 2024). Return from maternity leave can be challenging for a mother due to the emotional bonds they have with their babies and the hormones they have surging through their body during this time, especially when breast feeding.

Pregnant learners should have risk assessments that you can refer to, which are conducted by those with overall responsibility for health and safety at the institution (though remember that we are all responsible for health and safety). These assessments highlight any risk related to pregnancy including illness and challenges that may arise in a practical environment. Make sure you are aware of the requirements of that risk assessment, and be sure to query if the learner doesn't have one in place.

> **REFLECT**
>
> Imagine a learner has just disclosed a pregnancy to you. While waiting for a risk assessment to be undertaken, what immediate changes to your learning environment and expectations can you make in order to meet their immediate needs? What pedagogical approaches can you use which have been identified throughout this chapter?

Race and religion, culture or belief

Let us begin with an understanding of the difference between race and ethnicity. According to Smedley and Smedley (2005), 'race has no genetic or scientific basis.' It is a social construction to group people by skin colour and appearance. Ethnicity, Bilge et al (2021) argue, 'is a communicative process that establishes a distinct identity for its members through cultural commonalities such as race, language, religion or national heritage,' which is why we have grouped race, religion, culture or belief together here, as they all contribute to a person's ethnicity. (Note they are not grouped this way in the Equality Act (2010)).

Based on these definitions, ethnicity is a more complex identity that is built on similarities that transcend skin colour and appearance. We will explore learner needs in regard to race specifically before moving on to religion, culture and belief.

Race

According to data from the Office for Learners (2020), the awarding gap between white and black learners in higher education achieving first-class or upper second-class degrees was around 13.5%, highlighting that black learners were less likely to achieve higher level degree classifications than their white counterparts. The data also shows that Gypsy, Traveller and Roma learners suffered from even wider attainment gaps. Although there is little to no research relating to attainment gaps in FES, it is useful to be aware of the research here to avoid the same gaps in achievement within the FES sector.

Gutman and Younas (2024) identified three main reasons for the awarding gap in higher education:

- Participants reported lower expectations and prejudices, which resulted in a perceived need to apply extra effort to achieve.

- This is the case among both teaching staff and the curriculum, making learners feel isolated and negatively impacting their sense of belonging.

- A lack of integration with other minority ethnic peers leads to a sense of disconnection.

The participants of the Gutman and Younas (2024) study recommended an increased awareness of the attainment gap, so that teachers are conscious of ways to address and reduce these gaps in the curriculum. They suggested that creating opportunities for peer groups for those individuals from an ethnic global majority (a term used to move away from white-centric terms like 'ethic minority' when referring to non-white individuals) we can achieve a more inclusive educational environment where teachers identify ways to enhance opportunities for all. Also, by enhancing the diversity of the curriculum, we can create learning spaces where our diverse learners feel seen and celebrated, rather than othered and ignored. (You may be familiar with the term 'decolonising the curriculum', which gained prominence through the learner-led campaign, 'Why is my curriculum white?', at the University of College London in 2015.)

> **REFLECT**
>
> Think about the learners you teach. Are you able to understand and address the reasons for the attainment gaps identified by Gutman and Younas? Can you create opportunities for your learners to engage with peers from global majority groups?

Religion, culture or belief

The religions, cultures and beliefs of learners are less likely to be collected as part of an initial assessment; instead, they are something you will learn through discussions and getting to know your learners as individuals. For this protected characteristic, it is helpful if we know a little about religion, particularly if religious beliefs have an impact on day-to-day work in the learning environment and on learner experience.

Of course, every individual will follow their religion in their own manner, so never assume that a person will interpret the same religion or beliefs in the same way (including atheist and agnostic beliefs).

Tradition	It is helpful to learn about religious traditions your learners may engage in. For instance, during Ramadan our Muslim learners won't eat or drink during daylight hours. This can impact energy levels and therefore ability to engage with certain activities, or for some, this could have medical implications. Muslim learners will also need to pray more often during this period, so we should be helpful with regards to enabling this to happen throughout the day.
Holiday	Most religious groups (and different countries) have holiday or celebration periods. This includes Ramadan and Eid in Islam, Chinese New Year, Hanukkah in Judaism, Easter in Christianity and Winter and Summer Solstice for Wiccans. It is helpful to download an Equality and Diversity calendar (there are many online to choose from) which includes these and other important dates for your learners.
Dress	There are some religions which have restrictions on diets. Some examples include Halal meat, or restrictions on eating certain animals. This could be impactful particularly in teaching catering, or hospitality, but also if you engage in celebratory treats with your learners in class, i.e. providing sweets etc., so do ensure you are aware of dietary restrictions so that your learners can be included.
Diet	Some learners who practice certain religions will wear headdresses or hijabs, or full outfits which form part of their religion. Other religions will require that women do not undress in front of others or show their hair in public. This needs to be considered in vocational education in a few different ways, with regards to how uniform can be adapted to meet religious requirements as well as the professional requirements, and can need to be considered when learners are studying subjects such as hairdressing and beauty therapy, or sports massage, for instance, both for the learners themselves and for their clients.

Figure 4.1 *Religious considerations in the classroom*

> **Take it further...**
> For up-to-date terminology in relation to ethnicity, consult 'Writing about ethnicity' on the GOV.UK website.

Learner backgrounds

We believe there is a need to consider both socioeconomic status and ESOL (English speakers of other languages) learners or learners using EAL (English as an additional language).

> **REFLECT**
> What do you think is missing from the nine protected characteristics? What other elements of a learner's identity creates learning needs or barriers to learning?

Learner background	Expert definition/ description	Starting points and tips to support (these will grow as you get to know the individual learner)
Socioeconomic status	Atkins (2013) identified that the majority of young people undertaking vocational education programmes are drawn from lower socioeconomic groups, often with a history of low achievement in school alongside additional characteristics associated with social exclusion such as learning difficulties and disabilities.	We must consider how we can motivate young people who may not value education or have had a previous negative experience in secondary education. Learning resources (such as study space at home and digital devices) available to young people from working class backgrounds also must be considered in order to promote equality of opportunity.
ESOL or EAL	In England, these learners are identified as those who are 'exposed to a language at home that is known or believed to be other than English' (The Bell Foundation (n.d.)). Teaching strategies for ESOL or EAL learners or learners from diverse cultural backgrounds vary in relation to their proficiency in English, of which there are five stages between fluent and new to English. (The Bell Foundation)	For those who are fluent or competent, they need little to no additional support as a learner using ESL, but for those who are New to English, Early Acquisition or Developing Competence there are several methods of support that you can put in place as a starting point. These include the use of images used to support with communication and provide context (dual coding), a reduction in colloquialisms and unnecessary dialogue from the teacher, an inclusion of reference to a variety of cultures, scaffolded support, rephrasing your instructions when needed, and chunking information. For more guidance on how to support ESOL/EAL learners, see recommendations below from The Bell Foundation website.

The Bell Foundation offers guidance and resources for teaching and supporting learners who use EAL. EAL is predominantly a primary and secondary term for ESOL learners (the term we use in FES). The resources and recommendations provided by The Bell Foundation are mainly specific to the primary and secondary sectors, but when examined hold a wealth of knowledge that can be applied in the FES sector. Below, we can see the Five Principles to Guide EAL pedagogy, identified for teaching learners using EAL.

> **Take it further...**
>
> For further reading on how to support ESOL learners or learners who use EAL, visit The Bell Foundation's website for free training and resources.

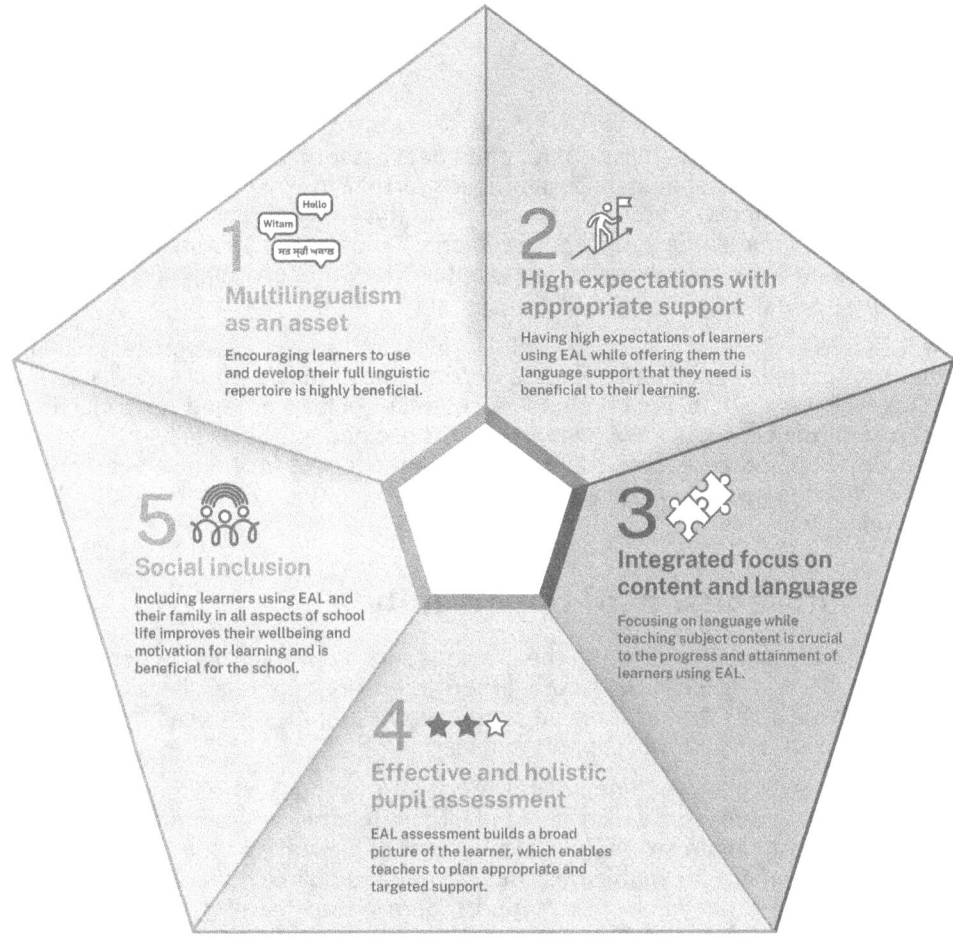

Figure 4.2 *Five principles to guide EAL pedagogy. Copyright © The Bell Educational Trust Limited (operating as The Bell Foundation). www.bell-foundation.org.uk*

Intersectionality

Learners can be affected by multiple protected characteristics, as well as more elements of their identity. This is understood as 'intersectionality', a term coined by Crenshaw (1989), whose research recognised that everyone has a selection of identified characteristics that complement one another, making every individual unique.

It is helpful for FES teachers to recognise the uniqueness of every individual, emphasising the need for conversations and observations that enable us as teachers to recognise and address our learners' diverse needs. (Barriers to progression due to various elements of protected characteristics and learner backgrounds are covered in more detail in chapter 9.)

> **Take it further...**
>
> Just like learners, we teachers also have intersectional identities which bring us both privilege (where we are the majority) and marginalisation (where we are the minority). There has more recently been an uplift in literature celebrating the diverse identities of educators, such as the work of Wilson (2023) in Diverse Educators: a Manifesto.
>
> Consider your own intersectional identity and how you can use your privilege, and your lived experience of being within minority groups, to reduce barriers to learning and meet learner needs.

Ongoing assessment

Following the collection of initial assessment and data gathering, you have the responsibility of developing your understanding of learner needs further so you can provide them with the same access to education as all other learners. To do this, you need to have open and honest conversations with your learners, but these can only happen after you have established relationships based on trust with them (see chapter 3 for more on building relationships with learners).

As we will discuss in chapter 7, it is also useful to include learners in the process of self-assessment, which helps to enhance their understanding of their own progress and enables them to take ownership of it. The continued assessment of learner needs not only provides the teacher with the knowledge we need to meet those needs, but equally the continued discussion with the learner teaches them how to identify needs for themselves. This provides the learners with the necessary skills they need to continue to do this throughout their lives, not just during our lessons.

4.5 Promoting equality of opportunity

This section of the chapter builds upon the previous section by focusing on how we can use the knowledge we have gained about our learners to ensure that, regardless of background or ability, they have access to the same educational opportunities. This can be achieved by providing fair access to resources, support and learning.

While some learners will tell you immediately what interventions or reasonable adjustments they had in previous education, which can feed into your initial assessment, for others who may feel vulnerable in relation to their learning needs, it may take a little longer to find out how best to support them. To enable this, you will need to build a relationship with them through demonstrating that you want to support them in their learning, as well as observing their responses to activities rather than asking them directly.

The behaviour iceberg

Your learners will not always communicate verbally to share how they feel or identify what they need to be able to succeed, sometimes this communication will be via their body language or behaviour.

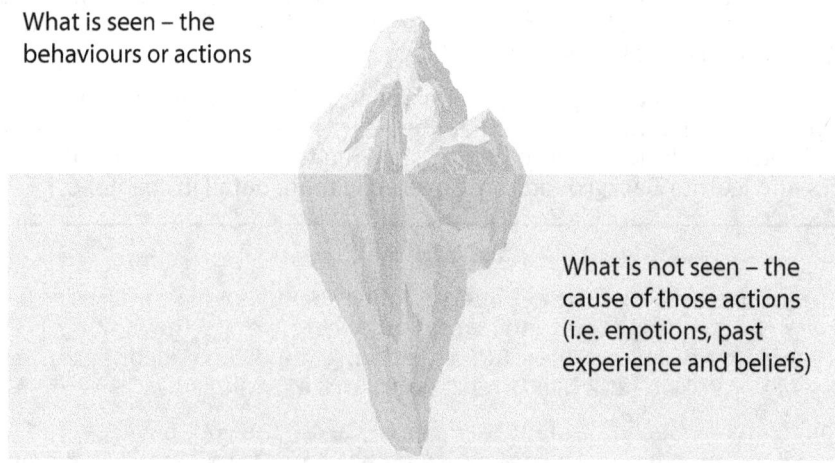

Figure 4.3 *The behaviour iceberg*

Although the 'behaviour iceberg' was originally designed in research regarding autism, the same concept can be applied to any behaviours we see in the learning environment, enabling us to consider the reason for these behaviours and how they can manifest. Understanding this helps us to consider what can be put in place to reduce frustrations and barriers through the application of reasonable adjustments or adapting how you teach a certain topic to provide access to learning for all.

> **Tip for Teaching**
>
> To start to generate these discussions, seek feedback from all learners on their learning experiences. You can do this through conversation either as a class discussion or on a one-to-one basis.
>
> Just like with creating a safe learning environment (as discussed in chapter 3), the key is to be consistent with your message that you have high expectations of your learners but that you will provide the support they need to meet those expectations.

Understanding learners' needs is imperative if we hope to respond to them in a way that provides equality of opportunity. We will explore how we can use pedagogical approaches to address the needs of all learners and aid their progress.

Adaptive teaching and responding to learner needs

In previous years we would have been advising trainee teachers to differentiate for learners in order to consider what learners can achieve and amend our expectations for each learner accordingly. Differentiation takes various forms, such as task-variation (different tasks printed on a variety of different coloured sheets, all with different levels of activities on each colour). Another popular approach was the 'all, most, some' objectives to differentiate by ability, as shown in the following figure.

Catering Session 5: Learning Objectives

- **All learners will be able to**: Identify basic kitchen utensils and their uses.

- **Most learners will be able to**: Use a variety of cutting techniques with the correct kitchen knives (e.g. dice, batonnet, julienne).

- **Some learners will be able to**: Adjust techniques for different food types and preparation requirements.

Figure 4.4 *Example of 'all, most, some' objectives*

> **REFLECT**
>
> Do you think that this approach allows for appropriate stretch and challenge activities for some learners? How would you ensure that the learners in the 'all' group progress to the same level as those in the 'some' group? What impact could 'all, most, some' have on learner motivation?

There are two negatives to the differentiation approach. Firstly, differentiation was distorted to become a process of creating several different plans for each lesson to account for different learners' needs, which was both time consuming and unsustainable (Eaton, 2022). However, since the introduction of generative AI as a teacher's tool to create resources (which significantly reduces the time a teacher may spend on creating meaningful resources), there may be room to create multiple resources to support the different needs of learners. For example, AI can be used to create a worksheet with different levels of scaffolding to ensure that all learners are challenged appropriately (see chapter 6 for more on scaffolding).

The second major criticism of previous versions of differentiation is the way that the approach was misused in classrooms, resulting in different expectations for learners that did not aid progression fairly or provide equal opportunities for all to access the knowledge and skills they needed. For example, teachers were inhibiting learners by identifying lower-level expectations or learning outcomes for them when they could have achieved more (Raso, 2023). Learners were also given the option to choose their own outcomes, with some taking easier options that led to them doing less than they were capable of.

In recent times, a wider-used approach to differentiation and meeting learner needs is adaptive teaching, which prioritises the view that any learner may surprise us at any moment. Adaptive teaching is referred to in chapter 6, where we explore the use of formative feedback to understand a learner's progress, which then informs the level of scaffolding that we should put in place so that all learners are enabled to meet the same outcomes.

Figure 4.5 is an example of how we can prepare to adapt our approaches to teaching in order to enable our learners to meet high expectations within the classroom, consider their starting points and put scaffolding in place to support them to succeed.

4.5 Promoting equality of opportunity

Before teaching

Anticipate barriers

For example:
- Different levels of prior knowledge
- SEND
- ESOL

Plan to address them

For example:
- Supply background knowledge
- Plan to scaffold
- Teach vocabulary

Assessments inform planning and in-the-moment adaptations

Use assessments to elicit evidence of learning

For example:
- Questioning
- Talk
- Learning activities
- Answers on sticky notes or mini whiteboards

During teaching

Examples of in-the-moment adaptations

- Adjust the level of challenge
- Change language
- Clarify what 'good' looks like
- Use an analogy
- Use peer tutoring
- Highlight essential content

Figure 4.5 *Understanding effective teaching, adapted from Eaton (2022)*

Adapting teaching resources

This is where differentiation in the form of different resources and the adaptation of resources is important for learners when providing access to course materials. As we have established in this section, we have a duty to ask learners what they think they need in regard to alternative resources; but you may also need to do further research to determine ways to better meet their needs.

If we are armed with knowledge of learners and their needs, we should be able to adapt teaching effectively to meet these needs as they relate to learning. Now we will explore how we can use our subject specialist knowledge to meet our learners' needs and support their progress.

Case study: Adaptive teaching in a GCSE English resit class

Luna, a trainee teacher, asks her learners to read a story to themselves that fills one side of A4. The story is set in a pile dwelling.

The learners resist completing the task and make comments like:

> 'This is way too much reading for me.'
>
> 'I don't even know what a pile dwelling is.'
>
> 'I can't concentrate with everyone talking!'

If Luna responds to these comments by demanding compliance, seeing the behaviour as the issue, not listening to the comments made by the learners and assuming they have a deeper meaning, this will likely end with the learners refusing to read, and everyone is left feeling annoyed with their comments dismissed.

Alternatively, if Luna adapts her approach in response to the learners finding reading long texts difficult, she could respond like this:

1. 'Let me show you a little trick.' Luna proceeds to fold the paper in half or provides a second piece of paper to cover the paragraphs so the learner can just see one paragraph at a time. This reduces cognitive overload and allows the learners to tackle one section of the text at a time.

2. Before the lesson, Luna reads the text, identifies what parts her learners are unlikely to be familiar with and provides a simple image on the board so they know what they are reading about and can visualise what they are reading with ease, thus reducing cognitive overload.

Figure 4.6 *Pile dwellings*

3. Before asking the learners to read the text, Luna asks everyone to read in silence, as some cannot concentrate when they are trying to read. The quiet in the room also reduces cognitive overload.

The second approach shows that Luna is still trying to get the learners to read by adapting her pedagogical approaches, such as adding in chunking and scaffolding. This way, the learners are able to read the text and progress to the next activity.

> **REFLECT**
>
> Can you think of a lesson where something similar has happened when you were teaching? Think about what the learners were saying as they rejected the activity. What deeper reason could there be for this behaviour? What could you do about it?

Tip for Teaching

This case study highlights the importance of listening to learner voice to help identify methods of meeting learner needs. Next time your learners identify a barrier with an activity, ask them what they think they or you could do to remove or reduce the barrier.

Pedagogical content knowledge

Becoming a specialist subject teacher enables us to pre-empt challenges like those outlined in the case study above. In this section, we will consider what it means to be a subject specialist teacher and how we can communicate the knowledge and skills of our subjects successfully to learners in the FES sector using our pedagogical content knowledge (PCK).

Research by Coe et al (2014) showed that PCK had the strongest evidence of impact on learner outcomes, followed by quality of instruction, classroom climate and classroom management.

Shulman (1986) argued that to become a subject specialist teacher, you must be a specialist not only in the subject itself, but in the pedagogies that enable you to plan methods of teaching and learning that communicate your subject knowledge most effectively. (See chapter 6 for more on pedagogy.)

According to Shulman:

> [Subject specialist teachers should know] the most regularly taught topics in one's subject area, the most useful forms of representation of those ideas, the most powerful analogies, illustrations, examples, explanations, and demonstrations – in a word, the ways of representing and formulating the subject that make it comprehensible to others.

By this, Shulman means that we need to know the best teaching methods (or pedagogical approaches) to help learners to understand the content of the course.

Shulman also talked about a subject specialist teacher's ability to pre-empt challenging topics within the subject specialism, as well as the needs of the learners with regard to their 'different ages and backgrounds' so that, as teachers, we can apply different pedagogical approaches to the same concepts, in order to communicate them effectively to learners.

> [It] also includes an understanding of what makes the learning of specific concepts easy or difficult – the conceptions and preconceptions that learners of different ages and backgrounds bring with them to the learning.

To summarise, Shulman argued that to teach our subjects effectively, we need knowledge of the subject (what) plus knowledge of the pedagogical approaches available to us (how) in order to be able to communicate our subject effectively through the application of PCK.

This is where we know how best to sequence knowledge and skills, make complex concepts understandable and pre-empt misconceptions in our subject as well as support needs.

Shulman argued that we develop PCK through the acquisition of three different types of knowledge which:

- is evidence-informed
- comes from knowledge and experience of ourselves and others
- is the ability to make choices on how to approach the teaching of a subject, using all the knowledge gained as above.

Case study

Milo is planning for a media lesson for which one of the objectives is to analyse a movie clip and explain how mise-en-scène conveys character, narrative and meaning.

Milo knows from the last lesson that the group struggle with interpreting how mise-en-scène creates meaning in media. He has one autistic learner who finds this particularly challenging. So, before the lesson he does the following:

- Develops his propositional knowledge by researching methods of teaching this topic.
- Develops his case knowledge by seeking the experiences of others teaching this subject, from colleagues in the staffroom, colleagues on online networks and by speaking to one of the SEND specialists who works at the college.
- Uses this selection of methods to develop his strategic knowledge.

REFLECT

Consider a topic you have taught recently that your learners found tricky to learn and is therefore tricky to teach (also known as a problematic concept). Now follow the same steps as Milo and apply the knowledge you gain to addressing the concept.

Take it further...

Return to the tables in Section 4.4 of this chapter. Look at the right-hand columns and, using your pedagogical content knowledge, make a list of recommendations for adapting teaching resources.

You could list the following three categories for reference:

- Tailoring learning materials, activities and teaching approaches to meet individual learner requirements.
- Using assistive technology.
- Accessible formats for learners with sensory impairments.

PCK is discussed in more detail, and in relation to curriculum planning, in chapter 5.

Trauma informed practice

Now that we have considered pedagogical, subject and assessment focused methods of adaption to teaching to enable learning, we will outline trauma-informed practices in education. Trauma informed approaches to education have more recently been adapted from psychology and counselling to teaching, and are now beginning to be included within teacher training (Boylan et al, 2023). The premise of this is that we recognise that within each cohort we teach, there will be learners who have had traumatic experiences, and it removes barriers for them if we consciously approach teaching with this information in mind.

According to the Substance Abuse and Mental Health Services Administration (SAMHSA) (2023) trauma can arise from short-term and chronic long-term events.

Examples of traumatic events include, but are not limited to:

- Physical, sexual, and emotional abuse
- Living with a family member with physical or mental health conditions or substance use disorders
- Domestic violence or sexual assault
- Chronic poverty, racism, discrimination, or oppression
- Violence in the community, war, or terrorism
- Living through a natural disaster or other period of distress.

Of course, trauma varies due to lived experience and personal interpretation and response, but we are aware of some common indicators and causes of trauma in our learners lives at the present time, indicating a need for FES teachers to be aware of this approach to learner support. These include (but are not limited to) mental health statistics climbing, with 20.3% of eight to 16-year-olds, 23.3% of 17 to 19-year-olds, and 21.7% of 0 to 25-year-olds reported to have probable mental disorders (NHS, 2023). Another example is the dramatic increase in online grooming crimes in children (NSPCC, 2024) with a rise of 89% from 2018 to 2024, as just two examples. We also know that learners in FES recently experienced the trauma of a world-wide pandemic, which impacted them as individuals, as well as people's experience of education worldwide, which has led to challenges in returning to and progressing through education in recent years (Ofsted, 2022).

The National Education Union (2024) published helpful guidance informed by SAMHSA's (2014) six key principles fundamental to a trauma informed approach, for use in education.

Principle from NEU (2024)	What this could look like in education
Safety	We should ensure we understand what safety means to individuals, families, and communities. Without this understanding, we cannot create a sense of safety for all. We should recognise and respond to different experiences, across ages, cultures, races, and demographics—including staff and co-workers. Safety includes physical, emotional, and interpersonal safety.

Principle from NEU (2024)	What this could look like in education
Trust	Services, operations, and decisions must be transparent to build and maintain trust.
	Transparency includes openness in difficult decision-making and collaborative engagement.
	Trust begins with a culture of connection in relationships.
	Many people with trauma histories have experienced unsafe or disrespectful interactions, and rebuilding trust is key to supporting resilience.
Peer support	This principle emphasises embedding peer support throughout services.
	Peer support should include opportunities for self-help and mutual aid among service users and staff.
	The focus is on mutuality and possibility.
	Deep, mutual connections between staff, leaders, and service recipients are crucial.
Collaboration	A trauma-informed approach requires collaborative, shoulder-to-shoulder work.
	It breaks down hierarchies and power imbalances.
	Mutuality and standing together must be embedded in organisational culture.
Empowerment, voice and choice	Organisations must believe in and support the possibility of recovery.
	They must highlight the strengths and abilities within people and communities.
	Because many trauma survivors have experienced coercion, offering choice is vital.
	A person must have choice.
Cultural, historical and gender issues	Trauma-informed services must move beyond cultural stereotypes and biases.
	They should be gender-responsive, promote the value and worth of cultural connections and address historical trauma.

Of course, we are not able to support our learners to overcome this trauma from a counselling or psychological perspective, this is beyond our remit and our professional boundaries as teachers, but we can support learners who have experienced trauma and who carry post-traumatic stress with them into our institutions and learning environments if we are able to follow the guidance outlined in this section of the chapter.

Take it further...

For further reading on trauma informed practice in education, visit the links in the reference list from NEU (2024) and SAMHAS (2014: 2023) in this section to learn more.

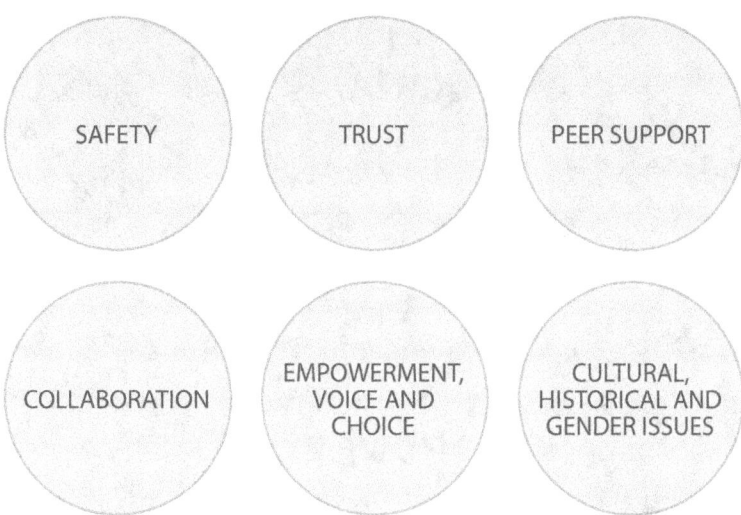

Figure 4.7 Six principles of the trauma-informed approach and practice. © The Lancashire Violence Reduction Network www.traumainformedlancashire.co.uk

4.6 Promoting inclusion

The author and critic bell hooks, whose work focused on intersections of race, gender and class, wrote that 'encountering difference… will afford [people] the opportunity to nurture spiritual and intellectual growth in new and varied ways' (1994:113).

Diversifying the curriculum

In the spirit of the work of hooks, we encourage you to represent different groups of individuals throughout your taught programmes by diversifying the content of the curriculum. By doing this, we can promote representation of marginal groups wherever possible while remembering that relatable resources and examples have their merits (for more on this, see chapter 5). Research into GCSE English resit learners and their reading preferences (Kemp, 2024) identified that learners who read in their own time felt that the curriculum did not offer a wide range of diverse texts and those who did not read outside of school did not notice the lack of diversity. This demonstrated that learners who were only exposed to literature at school were unaware of the diversity of literature available, highlighting the importance of educators sharing wider resources from marginalised groups. Our learners may not know that these groups exist, which is problematic for those who do not feel represented in the specialists, literature and examples we give in our classrooms. If they do not see this diversity in the learning environment, they are unlikely to see it at all.

There are multiple ways that we diversify the curriculum, from making reference to art from other cultures to studying the work of individuals from marginalised groups. See the Wheel of Power/Privilege overleaf for the diversity of identified marginalised groups. The table that follows includes some subject-specific examples.

Figure 4.8 *The wheel of power and privilege*

Subject	Example of diversifying
Art	Artwork from a range of cultures and countries.
Photography	Researching using diverse photographers' work as primary research.
Science, technology, engineering and maths (STEM)	Focusing on female specialist contributors to the field.
Sport	Learning about athletes with disabilities and from a range of cultures.
English	Studying literature representing a range of marginalised groups.

> **REFLECT**
>
> Think about how you could represent experts, writers, artists or specialists in your area who are from marginalised groups.

4.7 Challenging discrimination and prejudice

Unconscious bias

Unconscious bias can form in relation to any protected characteristic, so as teachers we need to be aware of this so we can address our own unconscious biases before they impact on our learners negatively.

> **REFLECT**
>
> A father and his son are involved in a horrific car crash, and the father died at the scene. The child was taken to hospital and rushed into the operating theatre. The surgeon immediately pulled away and said, 'I can't operate on this boy; he's my son.' How can this be?

Some people struggle to work out a solution to this problem. One solution is that the surgeon is the boy's mother, but some may not have considered this as they assumed the surgeon was male, which is an example of unconscious bias where a role has been gendered.

However, this solution is heteronormative (assuming that relationships are all heterosexual) because the surgeon may be male and be the boy's other father. Indeed, assigning a gender at all to the surgeon is problematic, but our experiences often lead to such assumptions. Regardless of your immediate response, the purpose of this exercise is to show that our understanding is influenced by our experiences and attitudes.

Stereotyping, discrimination, victimisation and harassment

Some people are confident in challenging others, but even the most confident teacher can feel unnerved about addressing discrimination and harassment. However, it is our duty to model inclusive attitudes and behaviours, both morally and legally (see the Equality Act 2010 in chapter 2).

It is imperative that we show allyship to our learners and act as role models for any of them who may be exposed to discriminatory language and actions elsewhere in their lives. Below is the IDEA framework (Reid, 2022), which you may find useful for doing this.

I	Interrupt the discrimination, harassment or victimisation that is taking place.
D	Describe what you heard them saying or saw them doing, e.g. 'I just heard you using discriminatory language in regard to XYZ'.
E	Explaining the significance of what they have said. This can be specific or as simple as 'what you are doing or saying is against the law in accordance with the Equality Act.'
A	Action or apology. At this point, you invite the learner to apologise or assign an action. An action could be that you would like the learner to attend a talk on Equality Act 2010 with their head of department, for example.

Having a framework like this can remove the anxiety around confrontation. Also, taking action against discrimination, harassment and victimisation empowers learners to challenge stereotypes and prejudices themselves.

Using the IDEA framework can also develop a higher awareness of discrimination, including the (usually unintentional) use of microaggressions, a term originally coined by Pierce (1970) that refers to everyday comments or actions that may seem small or harmless but are actually insulting in relation to elements of their identity. These comments or insults are less easy to spot but can be very damaging over time.

Examples of microaggressions include:

- Being surprised a female learner is good at mechanics. 'You're actually really good at this!' may feel like a compliment but is gender bias.

- Repeatedly using the name a learner was given at birth when they have expressed a wish to go by another name, or mispronouncing a learner's name even after being corrected is disrespectful regarding their identity.

- After someone says where they live, asking them 'where are you really from?' can imply that they do not really belong.

- Repeatedly misgendering someone when they have expressed their preferred pronouns is also disrespectful of their wishes and identity.

- Suggesting that people from different cultures are fast runners, good at maths or careful with their money are all types of stereotyping.

By bringing attention to microaggressions and discrimination, we are actively demonstrating our allyship to learners and colleagues, and by encouraging open discussions about cultural awareness, social justice and inclusivity, we are educating our learners to become allies themselves.

> **REFLECT**
>
> Look at the wheel of power and privilege on page 98. Where are you powerful or privileged, and where are you marginalised? Discuss with a peer how you can use your privilege to help others who are marginalised.

> **Take it further...**
>
> For more information on what can be referred to as 'anti-oppressive' education, read Freire, P. (2000) Pedagogy of the Oppressed. 30th anniversary edn. translated by M.B. Ramos, London: Bloomsbury Academic.

Chapter summary

In this chapter, we have outlined how to 'work in a manner that values diversity and actively promote equality of opportunity and inclusion by responding to the needs of all learners' (Duty 5). To do this, we have firstly demonstrated how meeting the diverse needs of learners requires an understanding of the legal frameworks that govern education. Here we focused on the Equality Act (2010), the SEND Code of Practice (2014) and the JCQ Guidelines for Access Arrangements (2024). These not only protect the rights of individuals but also set clear expectations for the FES teacher.

The section that followed emphasised how insight into learner backgrounds and individual needs is crucial for identifying and removing barriers to learning. We then outlined the continuous process of gathering key data — academic, social, educational, and cultural — which aids inclusion, diversity and belonging, from enrolment and throughout the learning journey, in order to be able to teach learners inclusively. Understanding learners' backgrounds, identities, and experiences allows educators to tailor their approach to teaching, learning and assessment and foster meaningful connections with the learners. Inclusive methods of teaching, learning and assessment which enable flexible and responsive teaching were discussed, including adapting content, delivery methods, and assessment strategies to meet varied needs. Finally, the chapter provided readers with methods for diversifying the curriculum to reflect a broader spectrum of voices, histories, and perspectives, aiding learners' understanding of the world, and enabling them to feel seen and valued.

This chapter supports readers to work in a manner that values diversity and actively promotes equality of opportunity and inclusion in FES, empowering learners to not only make great progress but also become thoughtful and inclusive citizens.

References

Atkins, L. (2013). 'From Marginal Learning to Marginal Employment? The Real Impact of 'Learning' Employability Skills'. Power and Education, 5 (1): 28-37.

Bilge, N., Marino, M. I. and Webb, L. M. (2021) 'Definitions of Ethnicity in Communication Scholarship: A New Perspective', Howard Journal of Communications, 32(3), pp. 213–234. doi: 10.1080/10646175.2021.1871869.

Boylan, M., Truelove, L., Pearse, S., O'Brien, S., Sheehan, H., Cowell, T. and Long, E. (2023) 'Developing trauma-informed teacher education in England', London Review of Education, 21(1), pp. 29. Available at: https://doi.org/10.14324/LRE.21.1.29 (Accessed 11 June 2025).

Brett, A. and Brassington, J. (2023) Pride and Progress: Making Schools LGBT+ Inclusive Spaces. London: SAGE Publishing.

British Dyslexia Association (no date) British Dyslexia Association. Available at: https://www.bdadyslexia.org.uk/ (Accessed 8 April 2025).

Colley, H., (2006). Learning to labour with feeling: Class, gender and emotion in childcare education and training. Contemporary Issues in Early Childhood, 7(1), pp.15-29.

Coe, R., Aloisi, C., Higgins, S., and Major, L. E. (2014) What makes great teaching? Review of the underpinning research.

Crenshaw, K., 1989. Demarginalizing the intersection of race and sex: A Black feminist critique of antidiscrimination doctrine, feminist theory and antiracist politics. University of Chicago Legal Forum, 1989(1), pp.139–167.

Dampier, G., Baker, L.A., Spencely, C., Edwards, N.J., White, E. and Taylor, A.M., 2019. Avoiding the deficit model and defining student success: Perspectives from a new foundation year context. Journal of the Foundation Year Network, 2, pp.41-52.

Department for Education (2025a) Further education and skills, Academic year 2024/25. [online] Explore Education Statistics. Available at: https://explore-education-statistics.service.gov.uk/find-statistics/further-education-and-skills/2024-25 [Accessed 2 September 2025].

Department for Education (2025b) Apprenticeships, Academic year 2024/25. [online] Explore Education Statistics.

Available at: https://explore-education-statistics.service.gov.uk/find-statistics/apprenticeships/2024-25 [Accessed 2 September 2025].

Department for Education (2025c) Further education and skills, Academic year 2024/25. Explore Education Statistics. Published 17 July 2025. Available at: https://explore-education-statistics.service.gov.uk/find-statistics/further-education-and-skills/2024-25 (Accessed 2 September 2025).

Department for Education and Department of Health. (2015) Special educational needs and disability code of practice: 0 to 25 years. London: Department for Education. Available at: https://www.gov.uk/government/publications/send-code-of-practice-0-to-25 (Accessed 8 April 2025).

Duckworth, S. (2020) The Wheel of Power and Privilege.

Eaton, (2022) EEF blog: Moving from 'differentiation' to 'adaptive teaching': What does adaptive teaching mean for Education South West? Available at: EEF blog: Moving from 'differentiation' to 'adaptive teaching' | EEF. [Accessed 08 April 25].

Freire, P. (2000) Pedagogy of the Oppressed. 30th anniversary edn. Translated by M.B. Ramos. London: Bloomsbury Academic.

Gov.uk (2010) Equality Act 2010: Chapter 15. London: The Stationery Office. Available at: https://www.legislation.gov.uk/ukpga/2010/15/contents (Accessed 8 April 2025). SEND Code of Conduct.

Gutman, L.M. and Younas, F. (2024) 'Understanding the awarding gap through the lived experiences of minority ethnic students: An intersectional approach', British Educational Research Journal [Online]. Available at: https://doi.org/10.1002/berj.4108 (Accessed 9 April 2025).

Hegna, K. (2017). 'Conflicts, competition and social support in female-dominated vocational education-breaking or reaffirming stereotypical femininity?' Journal of Vocational Education and Training, 69 (2): 196-213.

hooks, b. (1994) Teaching to Transgress: Education as the Practice of Freedom. New York: Routledge.

JCQ (2024) Access Arrangements and Reasonable Adjustments: 1st September 2024 to 1st August 2025. London. JCQ.

Kemp, B. (2024) 'The Books they Show People', The Use of English, (1), pp. 96–100. English Association. Available at: https://englishassociation.ac.uk/wp-content/uploads/2025/02/The-Use-of-English-76.1-Autumn-2024.pdf (Accessed 10 April 2025).

Marope, P.T.M., Chakroun, B., Holmes, K.P. (2015). Unleashing the Potential: Transforming Technical and Vocational Education and Training. UNESCO.

National Education Union (NEU) (2024) Six Principles of the Trauma-Informed Approach. London: National Education Union.

NHS, 2022. Menopause - Symptoms. [online] Available at: https://www.nhs.uk/conditions/menopause/symptoms/ [Accessed 10 June 2025].

NHS, 2024. Common health problems in pregnancy. [online] Available at: https://www.nhs.uk/conditions/pregnancy-and-baby/common-health-problems-pregnancy/ [Accessed 10 June 2025].

NHS England, 2023. One in five children and young people had a probable mental disorder in 2023. [online] Available at: https://www.england.nhs.uk/2023/11/one-in-five-children-and-young-people-had-a-probable-mental-disorder-in-2023/ [Accessed 10 June 2025].

NSPCC (2024) 'Online grooming crimes against children increase by 89% in six years', NSPCC News & Opinion, 14 October. Available at: https://www.nspcc.org.uk/about-us/news-opinion/2024/online-grooming-crimes-increase/ (Accessed 2 September 2025).

Office for Standards in Education, Children's Services and Skills (Ofsted) (2022) Education recovery in further education and skills providers: spring 2022. Research and analysis. [Online] Available at: https://www.gov.uk/government/publications/education-recovery-in-further-education-and-skills-providers-spring-2022/education-recovery-in-further-education-and-skills-providers-spring-2022 (Accessed 11 June 2025).

Oliver, M., 2013. The social model of disability: Thirty years on. Disability & society, 28(7), pp.1024-1026.

Pierce, C.M. (1970) 'Offensive mechanisms', in Barbour, F.B. (ed.) The Black Seventies. Boston, MA: Porter Sargent, pp. 265–282.

Raso, G. (2023) 'From differentiation to adaptive teaching: what does this really mean?', NACE, 13 March. Available at: https://www.nace.co.uk/blog/from-differentiation-to-adaptive-teaching-what-does-this-really-mean/ (Accessed 8 April 2025).

Reid, S. (2022) 'IDEA: A Framework For Challenging Discrimination in the Moment', LinkedIn, 9 December. Available at: https://www.linkedin.com/posts/shonaghreid_idea-a-framework-for-challenging-discrimination-activity-7015738647853289472-GB7B (Accessed 8 April 2025).

Substance Abuse and Mental Health Services Administration (SAMHSA) (2014) SAMHSA's Concept of Trauma and Guidance for a Trauma-Informed Approach. HHS Publication No. (SMA) 14-4884. Rockville, MD: Substance Abuse and Mental Health Services Administration.

Substance Abuse and Mental Health Services Administration (SAMHSA) (2023) Practical Guide for Implementing a Trauma-Informed Approach. HHS Publication No. PEP23-06-05-005. Rockville, MD: Substance Abuse and Mental Health Services Administration.

Schopler, E. (1995) 'Behavioural and educational approaches to autism', Journal of Autism and Developmental Disorders, 25(2), pp. 239–246.

Singer, J., (1999). Why can't you be normal for once in your life? From a "problem with no name" to the emergence of a new category of difference. In: M. Corker and S. French, eds. 1999. Disability Discourse. Buckingham: Open University Press, pp.59–67.

Shulman, L.S. (1986) Those who understand: knowledge growth in teaching, Educational Researcher, 15 (2), pp. 4–14. https://doi.org/10.3102/0013189X015002004

Smedley, A. and Smedley, B.D. (2005) 'Race as biology is fiction, racism as a social problem is real', American Psychologist, 60(1), pp. 16–26.

The Bell Foundation (n.d.) What is EAL in education? Available at: https://www.bell-foundation.org.uk/resources/guidance/classroom-guidance/what-is-eal-in-education/ (Accessed 8 April 2025).

Thompson, R. (2009) Social class and participation in further education: Evidence from the Youth Cohort Study of England and Wales. Journal of Further and Higher Education, 33(3), pp. 243–253. doi:10.1080/03098770903026131.

UCL (2015) 'Why is My Curriculum White?', UCL News, 9 March. Available at: https://www.ucl.ac.uk/news/2015/mar/why-my-curriculum-white (Accessed 8 April 2025).

Wilson, H. (ed.) (2023) Diverse educators: A manifesto. London: Sage.

Zychowicz, P., 2022. Adult education: A critical analysis of initial assessment procedures in community learning in the United Kingdom. Kultura-Społeczeństwo-Edukacja, (2), pp.55-71.

Chapter 5 Curriculum

Demonstrate, maintain and evidence excellent pedagogy, subject, curriculum and industry knowledge and practice. (Duty 3)

Educational programs will be more effective in the long run if they produce a more focused, but truly mastered, repertoire rather than a broad but fragile repertoire.

Binder (1996)

5.1 Introduction to chapters 5, 6 and 7

In the next three chapters we will look at curriculum, pedagogy and assessment. Bernstein (1973) defines these terms as follows (emphasis ours):

Curriculum defines what counts as valid knowledge, pedagogy defines what counts as a valid transmission of knowledge and evaluation (i.e. assessment) defines what counts as a valid realisation of this knowledge on the part of the taught.

The interplay between curriculum, pedagogy and assessment is so significant that this chapter and the two that follow will tread unavoidably on each other's conceptual toes. Decisions made in one of these areas have substantial implications in the other two; for example, as soon as we begin talking about assessment, we must talk about lesson objectives, which brings pedagogy into view. As soon as we begin talking about curriculum, we must talk about retrieval practice, which brings assessment into view. There is no escape from thinking about these levels of practice in mutually reinforcing terms, so while we have addressed each individually in the following chapters for clarity's sake, these conceptual crosslinks will repeatedly emerge.

5.2 What is a curriculum?

As with so many things in education, there is scant agreement on a definition of 'curriculum'. Here is one from Stenhouse (1975):

A curriculum is an attempt to communicate the essential principles and features of an educational proposal in such a form that it is open to critical scrutiny and capable of effective translation into practice.

So, is the curriculum the structure of the plan or the content of the plan? Or is it the document that contains the plan? Perhaps it is some combination of these. We can at least begin by saying this: curriculum is the 'what' and 'when' of teaching.

In this chapter, we take the view that a curriculum is not just the content that is taught but also the organisation of that content or domain, which requires us to consider links between concepts and must also include a temporal dimension. In fact, the idea that a curriculum has a temporal dimension is inherent in the word itself, which comes from the Latin currere, meaning 'to run'. As we delve into curriculum considerations, we will bear in mind that a curriculum – just like those to whom it is delivered – is 'going somewhere'.

How should we assess the quality of a curriculum? Stenhouse would lead us to conclude that there are two features of a curriculum: is it open to critical scrutiny and can it be translated into practice? If the proof of the pudding is in the eating, the proof of the curriculum is in the teaching.

> **REFLECT**
>
> Your teaching setting may have medium- and long-term plans, lesson plans or schemes of work. How well integrated are assessment and pedagogy into these plans?

What should be in the curriculum?

Where is your curriculum going? Throughout this chapter, we argue that the curriculum is akin to following a map to go on a journey – and we will make extensive use of this metaphor throughout. The curriculum is the journey through an existing domain of knowledge, skills and behaviours; each domain has its own landscape and routes. You can explore on your own or go with a tour guide; you can linger in some places and skip past others; you can visit some landmarks in groups or head out alone.

Most novice teachers have little input into the design of a curriculum, and many FES courses are so tightly structured around a specification and its related assessment outcomes that curriculum planning and design may not seem like a pressing concern. However, we will see in this chapter that, given the interconnections between curriculum, pedagogy and assessment, a strong grasp of key curriculum ideas is very helpful for teachers at the chalkface.

Following a brief introduction to some of the cultural considerations that underpin curriculum design, we will go on to discuss types of curricula, curriculum models and intentions, curriculum content and further considerations for those tasked with putting this all into practice.

Key term	Definition
Syllabus	A document or set of documents that outline how a course will be administered.
Specification	A document outlining the expected content coverage as well as assessment outcomes for that content
Scheme of work/ learning	A document that schematises and operationalises the curriculum. Typically divided into chunks of lessons, and often referencing the content from the specification, assessment outcomes, and teaching and learning activities.

Let us begin by asking the question, what should be included in the curriculum? Or perhaps, a more telling question: what should be left out? These are value judgments and are unavoidable. Value judgments have always underpinned curriculum decisions and will continue to underpin those decisions that shape the curricula that you teach.

In recent decades, secondary schools in England have increasingly emphasised the need for a 'knowledge-rich curriculum'. But what does this mean, and is it relevant for us in FES? Does 'rich' mean abundant, in the sense that a millionaire is rich, or concentrated, in the sense that millionaire shortbread is rich? How do we decide what knowledge is included or excluded? Should the curriculum introduce learners to the 'best that has been thought and said', or should it seek for contemporary relevance? To revive an old debate, is studying the works of Shakespeare a 'richer' experience than studying the works of Stormzy? Perhaps this is a false dichotomy. Before answering, you are going to have to consult your own values and philosophy.

> **REFLECT**
>
> Is studying the works of Shakespeare a 'richer' experience than studying the works of Stormzy?
>
> Why or why not? What does your answer reveal about your perspective on education? Can you identify the personal and professional values (or even biases) you are using to make this judgment? Even better, have these discussions with your peers and colleagues.

Should we look at this in another way altogether? Could we swap the word *knowledge* for something else? What about a subject-specific skills-rich curriculum, a professional behaviour-rich curriculum, an experience-rich curriculum or even a values-rich curriculum?

Knowledge, skills and behaviours

A good curriculum ought to provide learners with the opportunity to develop knowledge, skills and behaviours in their area of study, as well as the values and attitudes that will help them succeed. Alongside these elements, learners should have access to the artefacts – vocational, technical, and intellectual – of their subject of study and be taught to use them proficiently and independently.

What do we mean when we say 'knowledge, skills and behaviours'? First, let's distinguish between these terms, which are sometimes used interchangeably.

Term	Defined	Example
Knowledge	The information, facts, concepts and understanding a learner must possess. It encompasses both theoretical and practical understanding relevant to a subject or field.	The Level 3 Diploma in Health and Social Care covers knowledge about care standards, health and safety procedures and legislation relevant to care work. BTEC Level 3 National Diploma in Business includes theoretical knowledge such as business management theories and economic concepts.

Term	Defined	Example
Skills	The ability to perform tasks and apply knowledge in practical situations. They can be cognitive (thinking skills), technical (manual skills) or interpersonal (communication and teamwork).	Apprenticeships in Plumbing involve developing technical skills in pipefitting, installation and maintenance. A-level Physics emphasises cognitive and problem-solving skills.
Behaviours	The attitudes and personal qualities that influence how learners interact with others and approach their work. This includes professional conduct, ethics and interpersonal skills.	An NVQ in Leadership and Management develops leadership behaviours such as decision making, problem solving and ethical leadership. The T Level in Health develops behaviours like empathy, responsibility and professional ethics.

> **REFLECT**
>
> List some of the knowledge, skills and behaviours within the curriculum or learning content that you have taught.

For general academic programmes aligned with progression to higher-level study, much of the content has been well-established over many years, primarily driven by universities and awarding organisation requirements.

In the context of a rapidly evolving labour market, the current government focus on meeting employers' needs means that they have adopted a central role in the development of occupational standards for technical and vocational education and training programmes within FES. Skills England (formerly the Institute for Apprenticeships and Technical Education [IfATE]) are responsible for organising and approving these standards and programmes, and they apply to apprenticeships and recently developed technical qualifications (such as T Levels). Each occupational standard contains a series of knowledge, skills and behaviour expectations, and by the end of the programme of study learners should be able to provide evidence that they meet all of these.

It was once suggested that there were over 200 subjects in FES (Crawley, 2005), so selecting and ordering knowledge, skills and behaviours poses a significant challenge. Some subjects have a strong and clear understanding of the knowledge and skills within it, which means that the language and practices (discourses) are clearer; these tend to be traditional and 'higher status' subjects. For example, in maths the rules and boundaries of the subject are well-established, and it is distinctly different from other subject areas. As a result of this, what may and may not be taught is largely agreed upon, with the teacher having very little control over the selection, organisation and pacing. This tends to result in more teacher-directed practices.

A subject like travel and tourism, on the other hand is made up of multiple, interrelated subjects – a bit of business, a bit of geography, a bit of performing arts – so it does not have its own distinct specialised language and practices. This is the case with many TVET disciplines that bring together different knowledge and skills alongside workplace practices.

Power, knowledge and 'powerful knowledge'

Drawing on the theoretical work of Bernstein (2000), it could be argued that the knowledge, skills and behaviours selected for each qualification or subject will privilege some social groups over others.

Bernstein argues that there are two distinct forms of knowledge: vertical discourse and horizontal discourse. A vertical discourse consists of knowledge that it is 'context-independent knowledge conserved through intricate social formations' (Hordern, 2017). This refers to types of knowledge that have a strong structure and rules for the way it is shared; there are certain things that individuals should know, and there are certain ways of teaching this knowledge (as in the maths example above). This knowledge tends to sit within the intellectualised 'academic' subjects such as English, chemistry, history or economics. Bernstein suggests that because this knowledge structured in a vertical discourse, the power and status it affords is accessible only to some, which in turn reinforces divisions in education and society more broadly. Widening access to this form of knowledge, according to Young and Muller (2013), Wheelahan (2007, 2010, 2015) and others, has the potential to reorganise social distributions of power.

On the other hand, knowledge structured in horizontal discourse is always context-specific and circulated through 'unsystematic social processes' (Bernstein, 2000). This means that the knowledge is likely to be specific to a particular job and tacit; in other words, it cannot be directly taught and as a result is segmented and has weak rules. Where vertical discourse is ordered and explicit, horizontal discourse is perhaps best described as messy and situated in practice.

The TVET sector has many subjects that draw upon the single disciplines to align it to employment; for example, engineering merges the more structured disciplines of physics with more contemporary fields such as management to represent a new area of practice (Beck and Young, 2005). Most TVET subjects have weaker classifications as they are formed from multiple applied subjects. According to Bernstein, this has the effect of marginalising groups and individuals, which is significant for the way social relations play out within TVET.

Many researchers in the TVET sector argue that all TVET programmes should not just consist of the knowledge associated with the discipline but also on 'powerful knowledge' that enables learners to critique and challenge that knowledge and the social consequences of the discourses it upholds.

> **REFLECT**
>
> Is the knowledge taught in your subject structured horizontally, or vertically? Are there established methods for teaching certain things, or have you got more freedom to teach the knowledge and skills in your curriculum?
>
> Do your learners have the opportunity to learn powerful knowledge? What could be the impact of this on their progression?

What is a skill?

Winch (2010) asserts that typical understandings of skills involve 'activities that involve dexterity and sensorimotor co-ordination', such as sawing a piece of wood or kneading bread. These understandings are 'an ability, usually learned, to act in certain ways in relation to tasks'. Winch goes on to explain that the possession of a skill is subject to normative appraisal, in that the skill can be appraised based on how skilfully it was performed rather than whether or not it was done; for example, the wood was sawn with precision, or the bread was kneaded with efficiency. Winch also suggests that a skill is usually performed with intention; for example, individuals must purposefully carry out the task and exercise an appropriate skill.

We think this is a clear definition of 'skill', but the term is so common in FES that it has become detached from its intended meaning. Winch's work highlights some of the ways in which it has become inflated beyond its original meaning and the consequences of this.

One such issue is referred to as moderate, benign inflation. Mental arithmetic, for example, doesn't quite fit Winch's definition; it fails to involve dexterity and sensorimotor co-ordination, but it is learned in relation to the task, you can be more or less good at it and it is performed with intention. Therefore, it could be argued to be a skill. There will be many more mental skills that could be associated with the characteristics outlined here, though some take it a little too far and immoderately inflate the term.

The desire to isolate and teach generic, transferable skills has become more prevalent since technological advancements, and the rapid growth of service industries have led to a change in the labour market (Keep, 2014). The development of flexible skills has been deemed more necessary for a world in which futures are increasingly unpredictable. However, as Winch (2010) suggests, the concept of generic, transferable skills immoderately inflates the definition of 'skill'; for example, for generic, transferable skills such as problem solving to really be considered a skill, they would need to be immediately applicable to a range of tasks and be applied to new tasks without significant knowledge or additional skills. Without being immediately applicable to a task, they cannot be characterised as general or generic.

Having a general skill of 'problem solving' would mean that the mechanic who can diagnose and fix an issue with a car's gearbox would be able to transfer this skill to diagnose and repair a fault on a personal computer. The skill of problem solving is therefore not a clearly structured process, as the two very different problems require different processes of problem solving. While the discrete skills of replacing a part may be quite similar (using a hand tool, for example), arguably the skill is then a physical skill rather than the generic mental skill of problem solving. The mechanic also requires a different body of knowledge to be able to solve problems involving a computer.

Wheelahan et al (2022) argue that the pervasive notion of generic skills is empty in two forms. First, they are conceptually empty – they are taught without content. And second, they are socially empty in that they are removed from the context in which they are used, which cuts the holder off from communities of practice.

There is also the issue that if one were to be labelled as a 'good problem solver', for example, one may wrongly believe oneself to have the skill of problem solving in all cases. This is where the idea of reification applies to general thinking skills; for example, if X can do Y skilfully, it is assumed that there must be a skill of Y-ing and that X has it (Johnson and Siegal, 2010). We are tempted to believe that there is a 'skill' to be identified, isolated and trained for. Thus, there is, in effect, a jump from talk of performing an action well or successfully to the existence of some specific, discrete skill (or skills) that is possessed and exercised by the performer (Johnson and Siegal, 2010).

> **REFLECT**
>
> Think back to the background of your learners and reflect on what this could mean for the knowledge and skills they enter your programme with. What do they not know or be able to do? What learning habits do we need to be mindful of?

Are social skills really skills?

Immoderate inflation of skill also arises when it is aligned to personal attributes, often called social, soft or interpersonal skills. According to Winch (2010), it is not appropriate to apply the concept of skill to dealing with others as it removes agency from individuals. For example, communication is and should be unscripted; it should give both speaker and responder choice in how they react.

Barrow's (1987) perspective on these 'skills' is that learners have not been trained to perform particular behaviours, but they have a certain character that is steeped in various areas of understanding. For example, being sociable or pleasant is arguably a matter of being a certain kind of person and having an understanding of particular people and situations. Individuals therefore demonstrate soft skills in the sense that they listen well, show concern and greet or shake hands with others, but these are more social conventions than skills. The skill is actually the ability to exercise these conventions at appropriate times and in the right way for the present context.

There may be occasions where this is a legitimate application of the concept of the skill – knowing when to listen and to explain in different ways to aid the completion of a task. However, characterising communications with people as a 'skill' not only distorts the moral orientation towards other people, but rather than respecting agency they are seen as objects to be overcome (Winch, 2010). This also suggests that there is a 'generalisability' of the skill, which is doubtful given the concerns already addressed.

> **REFLECT**
>
> What skills are prioritised in your curriculum or by your institution? What is the reason for this? How impactful is this on supporting learners' progression?

It is undeniable that a very important part of our sector's remit is preparing learners for the world of work, and this must inform our curriculum choices. But what if this is too narrowly utilitarian a view of what the curriculum ought to include? Some have argued for a 'character curriculum' in which learners are taught intellectual, moral, civic and performance virtues in pursuit of the Aristotelian ideal of phronesis, meaning practical wisdom (Jubilee Centre, 2022). We are cautioned by Winch not to see these things as skills to be deployed but as characteristics to be embodied. Since we send learners out to work in a divided and divisive public square, is this something we can afford to overlook as teachers in FES? Or is the moral formation of our learners someone else's job?

> **REFLECT**
>
> Have you ever considered your role as an educator to include teaching learners how to be wise or virtuous? We tend not to speak in these terms in our professional lives – perhaps we should!

Who should construct the curriculum?

Plainly, since we're using terms like values, virtues, power and privilege, we can recognise that a curriculum is an unavoidably cultural artefact. Since curricula do not emerge fully formed out of the ether, each one is a culturally conditioned product constructed out of thousands of little (and not so little) decisions, with each decision made by a teacher or leader whose own educational perspectives directed their decision making.

Perhaps they were right, perhaps they were wrong; but before we begin tearing down the curriculum and redesigning it, we should take note of G.K. Chesterton's parable of the fence. Imagine you come across a fence and you think the best thing is for the fence to be removed. Chesterton would recommend a pause before action to think through the reasons for the fence being there – perhaps the fence is there for a reason you haven't yet considered. As Chesterton wrote:

If you don't see the use of it, I certainly won't let you clear it away. Go away and think. Then, when you can come back and tell me that you do see the use of it, I may allow you to destroy it.

You should always begin by asking, why is this curriculum structured in this way? Why have these modules been chosen? Why this knowledge, these skills, these behaviours? What are the messages inherent in this curriculum? Once we have a grasp of these things, we can start making changes for the better without reintroducing the problems or dilemmas that the existing curriculum was designed to solve. Chesterton would also warn to us to be mindful that unintended consequences will undoubtedly appear because of our curricular choices, and we should be prepared to acknowledge this and course correct where needed.

Diversifying the curriculum is a key tenet of contemporary education in FES. Widening the experience of learners so that they encounter a range of ideas and perspectives is incredibly valuable. Marginal voices, peripheral viewpoints and less-well known perspectives can and should be offered and evaluated alongside more well-established voices, ideas and approaches. Learner voice can be a particularly helpful way of assessing the broadness of an educational offer. We should take the opportunity to listen to the perspectives of those who are living and breathing the curricula we are delivering – insight is invaluable (we will explore learner voice in more depth in chapter 8).

Most teachers and educators are idealists of one sort or another, and so we tend to fall into self-perpetuating groups and tribes. One group may believe that education should prioritise preparing learners for the workplace and another may argue that education is a sufficient end-in-itself. One group may consider themselves progressive and another may prefer the traditionalist approach.

Our caution is to beware of grand statements about curricula – whether you intuitively agree with them or not – and be prepared to change your mind when the evidence changes. Be prepared to make trade-offs, too; you will not get your way with every curriculum decision, but nor will any of your colleagues. It is unlikely you will get to set your own assessment outcomes, for example – these are usually set by an awarding body or exam board – so you will have to accept that the outcomes influence the structure and content of your curriculum. The aim of this chapter is not to persuade you of one tribe's view (though that may end up happening), but to help you make better, more informed decisions about curriculum for the sake of your leaners.

> **REFLECT**
>
> What would you do if you disagree with your mentor or colleagues about what should be taught?

Explicit versus implicit curricula

It is useful to consider a taxonomy of curriculum that makes a distinction between explicit and implicit curricula. An explicit curriculum is the sum of all that is intended to be taught and is normally represented by official documentation, such as specifications, schemes of work and lesson plans. The explicit curriculum is that which is consciously planned, delivered, assessed and reported on; in other words, it is overt.

An implicit curriculum, by contrast, consists of all that is taught in an educational setting that does not appear in formal documentation. The content of this curriculum may be taught by the teacher through his or her attitudes, behaviours or even unplanned, in-class digressions, or it may be those lessons are picked up by learners from the culture of the institution. This type of curriculum is also known as a 'hidden' or 'covert' curriculum.

Explicit curriculum	Implicit curriculum
Enacted	Hidden
Overt	Covert
Planned	Unplanned

Formal, non-formal and informal learning

Given the extent of the implicit elements of any curriculum, perhaps a more realistic approach to curriculum language would be to talk about learning rather than teaching. Not only do learners sometimes not learn what you teach them, they also sometimes learn what you did not teach them. The diagram overleaf outlines one way of understanding the relationship between education, curriculum and learning. In this model there are three types of learning:

- **Formal learning** – the learning that is planned and intended by the curriculum. In practice, some aspects of the taught curriculum are not learned.

- **Non-formal learning** – the learning that is outside of the curriculum but within the confines of the learner's educational experience (i.e. extracurricular activities, school values and social skills).

- **Informal learning** – the learning that takes place outside of the educational experience, such as through self-teaching, social clubs and activities and friendship groups.

For the remainder of this chapter, we will narrow our focus to the design features of formal learning in an explicit, planned and guided curriculum. We will look at different curriculum models, think about the selection of appropriate content and outline some important considerations for putting it all together ready for teaching.

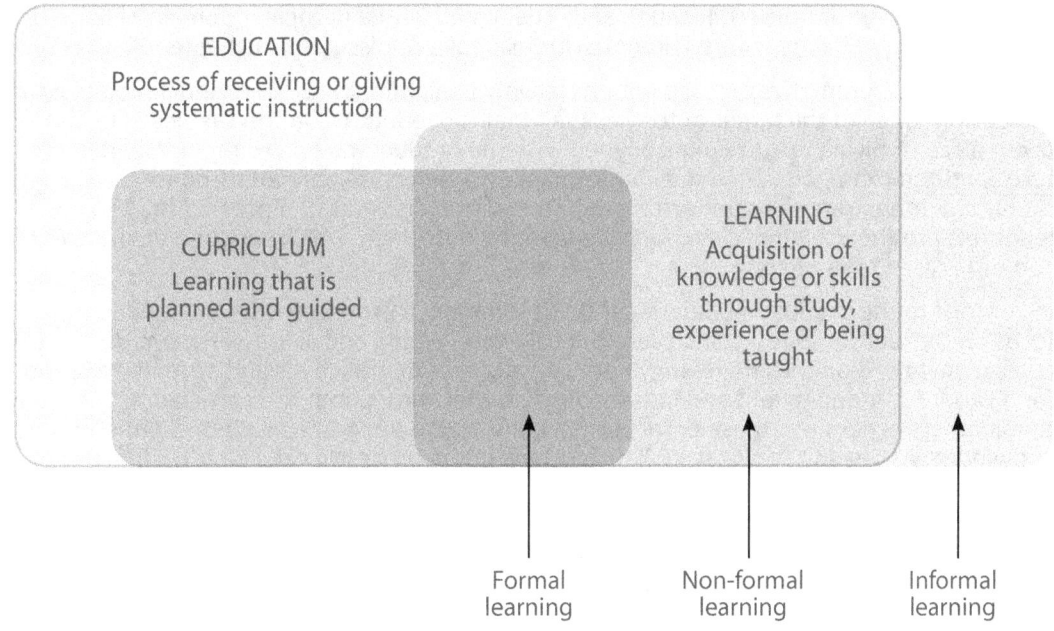

Figure 5.1 *Three types of learning. Adapted from Johnson, M., and Majewska, D. (2022)*

5.3 Designing a curriculum – models and intentions

If an educational program is to be planned and if efforts for continued improvement are to be made, it is very necessary to have some conception of the goals that are being aimed at. These educational objectives become the criteria by which materials are selected, content is outlined, instructional procedures are developed and tests and examinations are prepared.

In this quotation, Tyler (1949) – in his seminal text on curriculum – is proposing that outcomes (objectives, goals and aims) are to be identified prior to the planning of a curriculum. This is eminently sensible, and although we can enjoy and make space for serendipitous learning along the way, it means that we have a way of assessing both the quality of the curriculum itself and the learners' progress through it.

Once the intentions of a curriculum have been specified, we can begin to think about how to structure the curriculum. Now we turn to the various models that may be of use.

Process versus product

When thinking about curriculum models, perhaps the most important initial consideration is whether we are hoping to design a curriculum according to a process model, a product model or some combination of both (Abie, 2014).

A product model of the curriculum focuses on learner outcomes. In this model, learners are being directed to a destination that is typically the demonstration of some form of competency, perhaps an academic or vocational skill. In this model, the teacher's role is central – they instruct, direct and tell. A curriculum based on the product model tends to be delivered in clearly defined and delineated chunks of learning, which have been pre-planned by the teacher (or another colleague), and is delivered with a particular domain of learning in focus (cognitive, affective or psychomotor for example, as discussed in chapter 6).

Formative and summative assessment is relatively straightforward in a product model, as the performance of the target outcomes is all that is needed to confirm that learning has taken place. Typically, a curriculum aligned with the product model will require learners to take a written exam, present a final performance or undertake a timed response to a task in order to demonstrate their understanding. One of the strengths of a product model is that it lends itself to the design of clear, tangible learning outcomes, which can then be more easily communicated to learners.

In contrast to the product model's focus on destination, a process model is intended to focus on the learner journey and therefore values reflection and self-assessment. As such, a curriculum based on this model may not use outcomes or objectives and instead make room for a variety of independent and individualised routes throughout the curriculum. It is hoped that learners experience these curricula in a holistic way, integrating values, experience and knowledge. As a result of this flexibility, teaching in the process model typically looks more like guidance, facilitation or enabling of discovery or inquiry.

Standardised assessment is trickier in the process model, so review and reflection come to the fore as tools for assessing whether learning intentions have been met. Ongoing assessment is more common, such as the building of a portfolio (like the portfolios common in teacher training courses) or the collection of a set of artefacts.

> **REFLECT**
>
> Curriculum design choices do not happen in a vacuum. How could some of the factors below influence the model of curriculum you, your department or institution choose to follow?
>
> - Learner demographics, experience, and attainment.
> - Reporting of learner progress data (and other accountability measures).
> - The financial needs and capabilities of your institution.
> - Local skills needs.
> - Ofsted's inspection framework.

It is true that the product and process model approaches have some relationship to the (rather tiresome) progressive education versus traditional education debate that has raged on social media for the best part of the last decade. Traditionalists are derided for their joyless focus on standardised testing and learner outcomes (product model), while progressives are lambasted for their fluffy, guide-on-the-side approach that centres on learner experience (process model).

However, these arguments are not fair or correct, because neither model entirely jettisons the strengths of the other. Process models are not a free-for-all where learners do what they please, nor are product models rigid and unforgiving where learners are pressed into a metaphorical cookie cutter. Instead, these are conceptual poles that help to keep you oriented as you plan your curriculum. Your curriculum needs both a journey and a destination.

Product models	Process models
Destination	Journey
Outcomes focused	Process focused
Learning objectives	Learning Intentions
Outcomes in cognitive, affective and psychomotor domains	Holistic outcomes linking domains
Teacher centred	Learner-centred (independent and individualised)
Teacher as instructor	Teacher as facilitator or enabler
Externally assessed	Self-assessment and review or reflection

From Abie (2014)

Tip for Teaching

Do not let learners take shortcuts during the process and jump straight to the end point. Beware of setting learning outcomes that can be achieved without the need for your learner to think, engage or reflect.

Linear, spiral, network and web models

Ashbee (2021) introduces the concept of 'manthanology', a term that describes to what extent the structure of a subject domain demands that it be taught in a particular chronological order. To understand the 'internal temporal logic' of a domain we can pose the question, does your subject have elements that must be taught prior to other elements and cannot be taught in a different order? If so, how many and what are they? When designing a curriculum, this is an important consideration. We should know how the subject domain is structured according to its own inner logic, conceptual links and pathways and use this knowledge to guide what we teach and when, as well as what we assess and when.

The shape of a curriculum can therefore be conceptualised in several helpful ways, each of which implies a particular set of considerations for its design derived from the manthanology of the respective subject domains. Ireland and Mouthaan (2020) identify four curriculum models: linear, spiral, network and web.

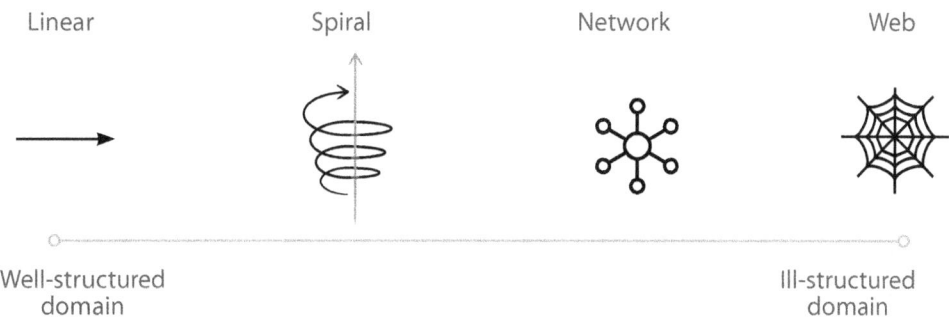

Figure 5.2 *Four curriculum models*

Linear and spiral models can be valuable for curricula that provide a 'well-structured knowledge domain' (Ireland and Mouthaan 2020, 7). Well-structured subjects are 'highly directional' in the sense that their internal structures demand that topics are learned in a specific order, one step at a time. They are also structured around 'vertical discourse' (Bernstein 1999), where the subject tends toward increasingly abstract concepts. We could consider maths to be one such subject; there is often a direct link between previously learned concepts in the domain and their follow-on concepts. Without a secure grasp of the prior concept, the later concept cannot be learned. This type of highly directional subject has what Ashbee (2021) defines as a 'manthanology of necessity'.

Linear and spiral models can be easy to follow for both teacher and learner, and as they tend to be based around uncomplicated learning outcomes or checkpoints they provide a simple structure for lesson planning. Spiral models originate with Bruner (1960), who suggested that a linear curriculum model fails to account for the need to revisit previously learned concepts in increasingly complex contexts. In the spiral curriculum model, previously learned concepts provide the core principles for the next layer of learning.

While a spiral curriculum model is an adaptation of the linear model, both network and web models can be classed as non-linear models. Network and web models are most applicable in knowledge domains that are 'ill-structured' (Feltovich et al, 1993) or 'adirectional', where the order in which topics are taught is much less critical. Bernstein (2000) designates this form of knowledge as 'horizontal discourse'; learners can be led through the domain via several different routes, each of which is equally valid. We may consider fine art or dance to be such a subject. If enough prior learning exists, later learning can be successful. These subjects have a manthanology of sufficiency (Ashbee, 2021).

All subject domains exist on this spectrum, and there are no subjects that exhibit no internal temporal logic, but for some subjects this logic dictates the structure of the curriculum while for others it is much less critical.

Take it further...

The extent to which this is a relevant consideration in practice depends on the specification of the qualification you are teaching, and in FES an individual teacher's power over this is perhaps even more limited than in earlier phases of education. It is likely that some parts of the curriculum need to be sequenced in a particular order and others can be experienced by learners in a less essential order.

- What kind of subject are you teaching?
- Does your subject have a manthanology of necessity, or of sufficiency?
- Is your subject highly directional, or is it 'adirectional'?
- What about different topics within the boundaries of your subject?

Take it further...

There is a whole host of other curriculum models and intentions that have been left out of this textbook. You may want to consider researching the examples in the following table and identifying the strengths and weaknesses of each along with their possible uses in your classroom.

Curriculum model/Intention	Description
Universal design for learning	A curriculum design approach that provides all learners with multiple means of engagement, representation, action and expression.
Emergent curriculum	A curriculum centring the interests of the learners, in which the teacher responds to their curiosity and largely facilitates. Outcomes are open ended.
Null curriculum	The knowledge, skills and behaviours that may legitimately be included in a curriculum offer but are deliberately and consciously excluded.
Authentic curriculum	A curriculum that provides learners with meaningful tasks with real-world relevance.
Personalised curriculum	A curriculum that provides learners with a range of choices about their learning, based around the provision of individualised (or very small group) instruction.

5.4 Designing a curriculum – content

In this section, we think about the decisions we need to make when selecting and organising curriculum content, with a focus on establishing curriculum-level objectives and outcomes.

Pedagogical content knowledge, subject specialism and dual professionalism

Imagine you wanted to learn all about Rome, and so you plan a visit. You call up your friend who is a tour guide and ask him, 'Where should I go to learn all about Rome?' You tell him you want to know about the most important buildings, the most significant monuments and the best place to get a gelato. 'How should I know?' he replies. 'I'm a tour guide in London'.

Talking about curriculum in the abstract – even with teachers – is a bit like asking a London tour guide to plan a tour around Rome. We may share an understanding that our learners want to see the metaphorical buildings and monuments of their chosen discipline, but without domain specific knowledge, all we have is abstracts. Which buildings? Which monuments? What route?

We can talk to a motor vehicle or fine art lecturer about threshold concepts, sequencing and spaced practice, but we cannot tell them what these may look like in their curriculum because we do not have the necessary domain expertise. We do not have the domain knowledge to identify how to chunk an ESOL (English for speakers of other languages) course, no matter how well we understand the concept of chunking. When it comes to designing an effective curriculum, domain knowledge is indispensable (Hanley and Thompson, 2021), so while it is of value to have a shared language and a set of key curriculum tools and concepts to guide us, the construction of a curriculum requires subject specialist thinking that cannot be bypassed.

Pedagogical content knowledge (PCK) is a requirement for good curriculum design. Shulman (1986) defines PCK as 'the ways of representing and formulating the subject that makes it comprehensible to others.' PCK is a concept that describes the way in which a teacher's pedagogical skills interact and overlap with their subject content knowledge to enable them to be an effective teacher.

An example of a pedagogical skill is using analogies to show how a novel concept mirrors something learners already know and understand, while an example of content knowledge is the way in which vasoconstriction and vasodilation work to change the pressure in a blood vessel during exercise. Bringing this pedagogical skill and specific content knowledge together could involve using an analogy of spraying a younger sibling with water from a tap or a garden hose by partially covering the outlet with a thumb. The teacher could use this analogy to explain why pressure changes in a blood vessel in relation to its diameter.

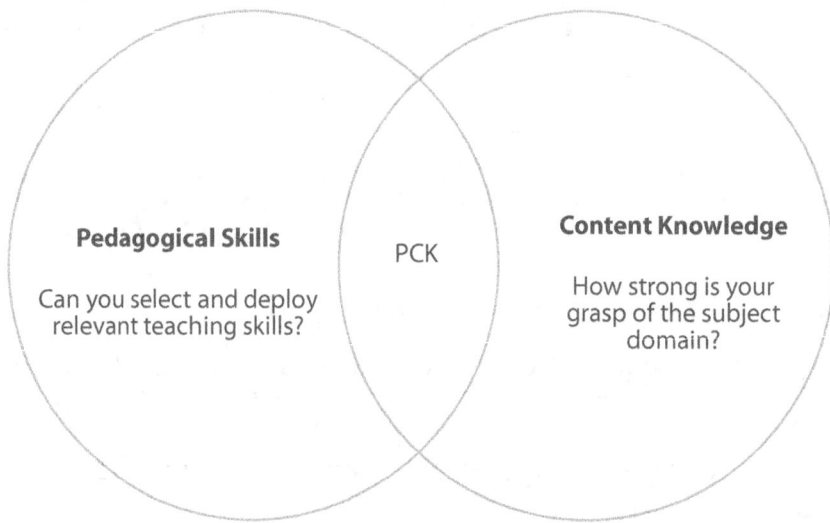

Figure 5.3 *Bringing pedagogical skills and content knowledge together*

Coe et al (2014) argue that PCK has a strong influence on learner outcomes, more so than a teacher's professional behaviours, beliefs or even their classroom management.

PCK can be especially helpful for spotting where in the domain troublesome knowledge resides (Meyer and Land, 2003). These are the points in the curriculum journey at which learners are most likely to develop misconceptions because the new learning is either counterintuitive or clashes with simplified versions of that knowledge already committed to memory. Often, the difficulty experienced in mastering troublesome knowledge means that once a learner has 'crossed the threshold' there is now a range of possible further understanding that they could not have previously envisioned. For this reason, Meyer and Land define such concepts as threshold concepts.

> **REFLECT**
>
> What troublesome knowledge and threshold concepts are found in your subject? Perhaps you have noticed learners consistently getting the same thing wrong. Why is this, and how can you help them? What new knowledge awaits them on the other side of the threshold?

The concept of PCK gives the lie to two false views of teaching. The first false view is that if you just have great subject knowledge, you can be an effective teacher. The second false view – and one that is more commonly heard in education – is that a good teacher can teach any subject. Neither view is correct. As discussed in chapter 2, when considering the dual professional in FES, both pedagogical skills and strong subject knowledge are needed to be an effective teacher and be well placed to optimise PCK.

Tip for Teaching

Evens et al (2015) analysed research on PCK development for teachers across educational levels to discover which of the following sources of PCK were most profitable.

- Teaching experience
- PCK courses
- Disciplinary knowledge
- Observation
- Cooperation with colleagues
- Reflection

All six activities were shown to have their role to play in developing PCK, but the findings were particularly positive about the value of reflection for PCK development, especially where that reflection becomes a habitual feature of a teacher's practice. If there's a reason for you not to skip the reflection sections of this textbook, this is it! Consider how, in the busyness of the FES environment, you could build in time for quality reflection on your practice.

Thankfully, Evens and colleagues also note that merely introducing teachers to the concept of PCK was shown to be a helpful step towards improving PCK.

If you are teaching vocational or technical qualifications it is important to stay on top of the developments in your sector. If you have left an industry to teach in FES, it becomes very important to consider how you can maintain industry expertise. You should be careful that you are not teaching leaners outmoded or outdated practices. Are you up to date with the tools of the trade and the changing approaches in your industry? Dual professionals have an advantage here.

REFLECT

How can you stay up to date with the industry you are training learners for?

Take it further...

Can you think of any examples of content knowledge in your subject that has become outdated?

Establishing curriculum objectives

The stage at which you decide on your curriculum objectives will already be contingent on the type of curriculum you propose to construct. A process curriculum may take a more relaxed approach to defining curriculum objectives, while a product curriculum will necessitate attending to these first.

Biggs (2003) proposes the concept of constructive alignment to guide the process of curriculum design. Biggs argues that in order to best construct their knowledge of a subject, learners should follow a course in which there is an alignment between curriculum, pedagogy and assessment such that each element is mutually reinforcing and coheres with the other two. The first step to this alignment, in Biggs's view, is to establish 'intended learning outcomes (ILOs)'. (Note that ILOs is Biggs' term, which I will therefore use here. Chapter 7 deals with assessment terminology in more detail.)

There are various versions of Biggs' approach, but here is a simple one from the organisation Advance Higher Education:

- **Define** ILOs.

- **Choose** teaching and learning activities likely to lead to the ILOs.

- **Assess** learners' actual learning outcomes against the ILOs.

- **Arrive** at a final grade.

ILOs should be focused on the learner rather than the teacher because they 'define what learners are supposed to be able to do with the content they have learned' (Biggs, 2014). Biggs (2003) therefore recommends that ILOs incorporate verbs that can serve as 'markers throughout the system' reappearing in the activities and assessments that learners undertake as they move towards the respective ILOs. It is the verb that establishes the alignment between these elements.

In selecting verbs for our ILOs, we could borrow from Biggs' own SOLO model (Biggs and Tang, 2011) or use verbs taken from Blooms' revised taxonomy (Anderson and Krathwohl, 2001). Figure 5.4 below shows some of these verbs laid side by side. Note in the table that verbs are linked to different orders of skills, with Bloom arranging his verbs on a scale from lower to higher order skills and Biggs using a continuum from surface to deep learning. (You can read more about higher and lower order skills in chapter 7.)

Bloom's revised taxonomy	Sample verbs		Biggs' SOLO taxonomy
Create	Adapt, build, compose, construct, create, design, develop, estimate, imagine, improve, invent, modify, originate, predict, propose, solve	Create, formulate, generate, hypothesise, reflect, theorise	Extended abstract
Evaluate	Agree, assess, conclude, criteria, criticise, decide, defend, disprove, evaluate, interpret, judge, justify, prioritise, prove, rate, recommend		
Analyse	Analyse, categorise, classify, compare, conclusion, contrast, discover, examine, inspect, simplify, take part in	Analyse, apply, argue, compare, contrast, criticise, explain causes, relate, justify	Relational
Apply	Apply, choose, construct, develop, experiment with, identify, interview, model, organise, plan, select, solve, utilise		
Understand	Classify, compare, contrast, demonstrate, explain, extend, illustrate, infer, interpret, relate, rephrase, show, summarise	Combine, describe, enumerate, perform serial skills, list	Multi-structural
Remember	Choose, define, find, label, list, match, name, omit, recall, relate, select, show, spell, tell	Identify, name, follow simple procedure	Uni-structural

(Left axis: Higher order → Lower order. Right axis: Deep learning → Surface learning.)

Figure 5.4 *Bloom's and Biggs' taxonomies*

> **Take it further...**
> Choose a topic from your subject and try to write an ILO for each step of either Bloom's or Biggs's taxonomy. For each ILO you write, borrow verbs from the figure above. Do you already have a sense of what different activities may be needed to help learners get to each of the ILOs?

Once ILOs have been devised, the teacher should carefully design the teaching and learning activities that are most likely to lead learners to meeting the ILOs. At this point, Biggs notes that although the assessment tasks may be the final consideration for the teacher, they will be the first thing learners will consider. When learners receive an assessment brief, for example, they will typically use it to help them focus their efforts on meeting that brief and jettison any activities they deem superfluous. Biggs (2003) calls this assessment 'backwash'. They will judge the quality and worth of the teaching and learning activities according to how well they feel they prepare them for that assessment. Thus, if the assessment is clearly communicated, understood by the learner and well-linked to the ILOs, the probability of learner engagement is increased as is the likelihood of achieving the ILOs. Also, there will hopefully be no surprises for the learners when they get their feedback! (You can find out more about the principles of assessment in chapter 7.)

> **REFLECT**
> Many colleges select their awarding bodies based on assessment type and rely on backwash from there. Is this the right approach? How does your college or department select which awarding body qualifications you will teach?

Wiggins and McTighe's (2005) 'backwards design' model agrees with Biggs that 'desired results' (ILOs for Biggs) should be designed first, but it is more explicit in recommending that assessments are planned before learning activities. This is done because 'assessments operationalise constructs' (Wiliam 2010), which means that until you design the assessment your intentions remain intangible and uninterpreted.

Wiggins and McTighe propose three stages for those following their model:

- **Set learning goals** – identify the desired results or objectives of the curriculum.
- **Design assessments** – determine what counts as evidence of achievement.
- **Activities and materials** – plan the learning tasks and produce resources.

In summary, Biggs' key assertion is the need to first define outcomes to align all other aspects of curriculum, while Wiggins and McTighe emphasise the need to design assessments before learning activities. (Designing activities and materials will be covered in chapter 6 and designing assessments will be discussed in chapter 7.)

> **Take it further...**
> Both Bloom's and Biggs's taxonomies have come in for criticism in recent years. Take some time to critically investigate what the problems associated with each may be.

5.5 Designing a curriculum – considerations

In this section, we will look at some practical considerations for designing a curriculum. Schema theory provides us with a basis on which to build our understanding and then we investigate a series of related ideas including cumulative dysfluency, the relationship between learning and performance and the crucial but often overlooked importance of forgetting. Throughout the section, we will explore what these ideas tell us about effective curriculum sequencing and pose practice-focused questions for you to consider.

Schema theory

Melton's (1963) early work on memory suggested that there are three stages of learning and memory, which he identified as encoding, storage and retrieval. Encoding and retrieval are dealt with in chapter 6, but here we need to identify why an understanding of how we store our learning can help us make good decisions about how we plan our curriculum.

Storage refers to the way in which what is being processed in the working memory is secured in long-term memory (which we will explore in more detail in chapter 6). Being able to store learning in long-term memory is of no real use unless it can be retrieved, in which case the nature of the storage system becomes very important. So how is the storage system of the long-term memory structured for facilitating retrieval? It is schema theory that answers this question and helps us make sense of the dynamic relationship between encoding and retrieval.

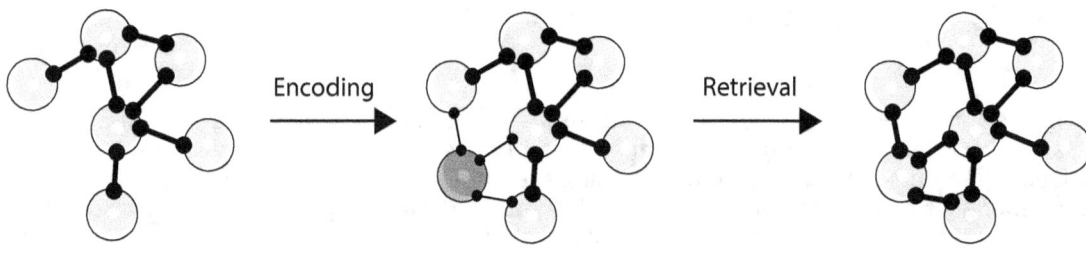

Figure 5.5 *Schema development*

What are schemas?

Schemas (or schemata) are theorised as networks of memories held in long-term storage that are both categorised and linked. All your memories are stored in schemas; you may have many well-connected memories or few disparate ones. The purpose of learning is not only to add memories to these schemas, but to create more and more links.

Think of the London Underground map. The map is made up of nodes (stations) and links between them (lines). The links and nodes on the map refer to real places and routes and help you plot out your route to a destination.

To go from Earl's Court to Covent Garden, you could take the District Line to Embankment, then the Northern Line to Leicester Square, and then the Piccadilly Line for a short hop to your destination. You would get there in the end, but it would be far easier just to take the Piccadilly Line the whole way. But what if you did not know that the Piccadilly Line goes directly from Earl's Court to Covent Garden? You would be restricted to the route you know despite it being less efficient.

A learner's sketchy schema for a procedure does not necessarily mean they will not be able to find their way to the destination by completing a task, getting the correct answer or demonstrating a skill, but it probably means they are metaphorically going the long way around. The more nodes and the more links between those nodes, the more knowledgeable and skilful our learners become – and their knowledge becomes more easily usable. Part of the teacher's responsibility is to help learners build schemas by making explicit for them how new ideas link and mesh with their existing understanding.

So schemas are like living maps, always under construction and always being refined to better represent the real world and function more efficiently. The more nodes and links we have constructed the more routes we can find to a solution, and the more likely we are to find the best shortcut to a destination. Our thinking becomes ever more efficient the more we build our schemas.

We build schemas through encoding and we consolidate them through retrieval. But what do we know about how we use our schemas in further learning?

Using schemas

In a seminal study in 1973, Simon and Chase asked chess players to study the board positions of several chess pieces for a few seconds and then, without referring to the board, try to recall the positions. Participants were either grandmasters, intermediate players or novices. When shown board layouts from real games that had taken place, the grandmaster did best in recalling the positions; however, when shown random board layouts with the same number of pieces, there was no difference in how well the participants did in recalling the positions of the pieces.

What this revealed is important. In the board layouts from real games, the position of the pieces was meaningful to the grandmaster in ways they were not to the other two less advanced players. While looking at the same set of environmental cues and stimuli, the chess master sees more than the other players because he is looking from the vantage point of his own more advanced schemas. Schemas help guide selective attention and productive noticing when faced with novel situations, but for meaningless layouts where the information in long-term memory is of no use, the working memory capacity of a grandmaster and a novice exhibit essentially the same limitations in both capacity and duration.

Evidently, working memory capacity is augmented by long-term memory. The more that is stored in long-term memory, the more the working memory can do. When a schema is larger, more linked and more secure, it can then function as a scaffold for the acquisition of new knowledge. Consequently, novice learning is slow and expert learning is fast, and we should plan our curricula with this in mind. We should also plan for novel concepts and skills to be introduced slowly and deliberately, with plenty of practice through which learners can make links with their existing schemas. But what happens if we go too fast?

> **REFLECT**
>
> How do schema theory and the findings of Simon and Chase help establish the importance of checking for prior knowledge?

Cumulative dysfluency

The word fluency (and its antonym, dysfluency) describes the quality of skilled performance; we readily use the term in relation to musical performance or foreign language acquisition. Fluency is more than mastery, as it adds a temporal component to the quality of a skill or behaviour. Take bricklaying as an example of the difference between mastery and fluency. Let's say two bricklayers build a wall and the quality of the build is equal in every regard, but one finishes in four hours and the other takes four days. Both have mastered the skill as far as the outcome is concerned, but the first has achieved fluency. Binder (1996) argues that it is not enough to learn to mastery – fluency is all important.

In figure 5.6 below, each block represents a concept, idea or skill. At each level, component skills combine to enable the learning of compound skills at the next level. Where a component skill has not yet been developed to fluency, the compound skill will necessarily be dysfluent. Thus, fluency (not merely mastery) is the sought-after quality of performance before a teacher moves on to the next 'layer' of learning. Over time, as the teacher presses on with their teaching, the dysfluency inherent in component tasks accumulates until it becomes prohibitive to learner progress. The learner's learning then stalls.

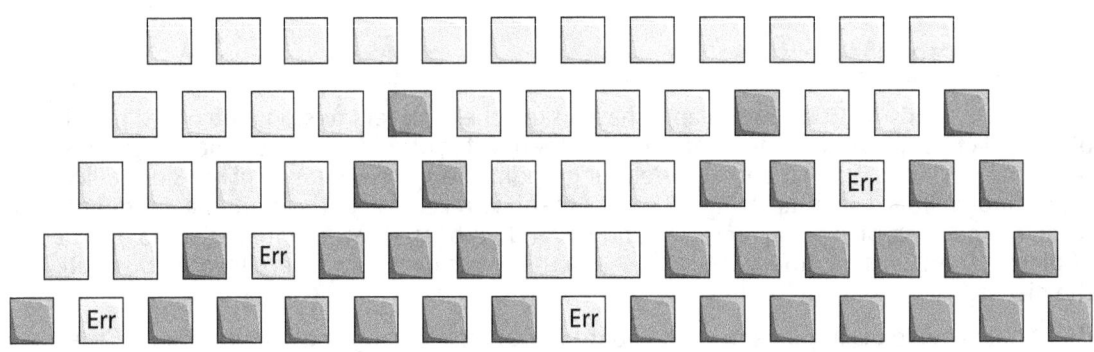

Figure 5.6 *Cumulative dysfluency model*

If you have ever played Jenga, you will be aware that the more gaps there are in the lower levels, the less stable the whole tower is. Teaching can be like Jenga in reverse – if you can find the gaps and fill them, you can stabilise the whole tower ready to be built on further. Dysfluency in any of the component skills will always lead to dysfluency in the compound skill, though it may not affect mastery. This is where careful assessment of learner progress is critical; moving on to the next thing when the component skill is not yet secure and fluent is storing up trouble ahead.

Binder (1996) suggests that cumulative dysfluency may be 'the most important factor in long-term learner failure', and Gallagher et al (2006) propose that cumulative dysfluency 'may be the antecedent of academic underachievement'. On top of all this, there are a range of consequences of dysfluency in the literature (see figure 5.7 below). Coping strategies in the classroom would include asking to go to the toilet, copying from a friend, making jokes or giving silly answers to questions to deflect attention away from themselves. Clearly, designing the curriculum to be carefully and thoughtfully sequenced to maximise fluency is critical.

McDowell, Keenan and Kerr (2002) identify a twin-horned dilemma that arises when fluency is not prioritised across the timeframe of the curriculum and teachers move on prematurely.

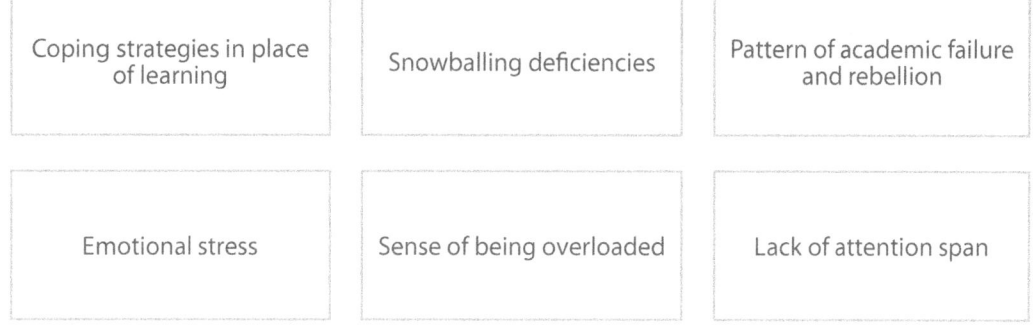

Figure 5.7 *Consequences of dysfluency*

These tasks were no longer under instruction [...] which indicates that their teachers may have been unaware of the extent to which the participants were still experiencing difficulty performing these basic skills. More worrying still is that even if they were aware of these difficulties, teachers may have felt unable to do anything to remediate these problems.

What can be done? We will discuss the available strategies for in-lesson adaptation in chapter 6, but it is even more critical that your curriculum has responsiveness built into it. It may not be appropriate or possible to alter the intended outcomes or the assessments, but all tasks and activities should be adjustable.

Tip for Teaching

Set up your scheme of work so it is a 'live' document. Alter and amend as you go based on formative assessment feedback.

Imagine your printer adds a letter 'e' to the end of every line of text in your handouts. What would you do? Say that you have a whiteout solution ready to amend each rogue letter before giving the resource to your learners; you have solved the problem but have not really solved the problem. You need to go back to the root cause of the error and fix it. This is what Binder (1996) is imploring us to understand. Pedagogical practice (such as scaffolding and worked examples) can sometimes be used to mask a problem that is created at the level of curriculum. It would be better in the long run to fix the root error than to paste pedagogical paper over curriculum cracks.

Learning versus performance

Considering the dangers of cumulative dysfluency, understanding the distinction between performance and learning is key to effective curriculum sequencing, especially if we are looking to establish fluency in our leaners.

Soderstrom and Bjork (2015) define learning as the 'relatively permanent changes in comprehension, understanding and skills of the types that will support long-term retention and transfer.' Problematically, learning is invisible and can only be inferred from behaviour.

However, if we ask learners to demonstrate their learning during acquisition of that learning, what we are seeing is performance, which Soderstrom and Bjork argue is 'often an unreliable index'. This is made even more critical when we grapple with the counterintuitive fact that their research suggests that success during learning seems not to be a guarantee of successful long-term retention and doing poorly in the moment may even equate to better retention in the long term.

This means that our choice of when (at what point in the curriculum) to ask learners to exhibit the target behaviour (whether writing an essay, making a pastry or handling a chihuahua) will impact the validity of the inferences about their learning that we can make from the behaviour. We need to ensure that we locate the assessment of learner learning at a point in time away from the learning event, so that we can be surer that what we are seeing is evidence of learning rather than evidence of mere performance.

Incidentally, it is important for application across varied FES subjects to recognise that Soderstrom and Bjork's findings are applicable to both verbal and motor learning.

Case study

A teacher teaches a group of learners a new set of concepts in the first lesson of the day. The learners then take a five-minute break before their next lesson with the same teacher in a computer room. On their return the teacher tells them, 'Please go to your online assignment portfolio and write up the learning from this morning's lesson.' The learners write up the learning and, with some help and prompting, they each produce a couple of good summary paragraphs of the morning's content. The teacher does this all year long. When it is time to submit and grade the portfolios, the learners all achieve excellent results.

Quite apart from the questionable ethics of the practice, how much actual learning have these learners accomplished? How much of what they have written would they be able to remember in six weeks' time? Should this type of practice be prevented, or is it part and parcel of the system?

In designing a curriculum, we want to ensure that we provide maximum opportunity for learners to develop fluency in the relevant knowledge, skills and behaviours without them or us getting caught in the trap of confusing performance with learning. How can we keep from falling into this trap? We must understand the essential ingredient for effective curriculum structure: forgetting.

The forgetting curve

Ebbinghaus' 'forgetting curve' was first devised in a context far removed from teaching in the FES sector in the 21st century (Ebbinghaus 1985). Having said this, the central findings have been convincingly replicated in more recent times (Murre and Dros, 2015), and so the key concepts remain very helpful to us when designing a curriculum.

For our purposes, we can identify three important ideas from Ebbinghaus' work as shown in this curve:

- As soon as we learn something, we begin to forget it.

- Each time we review that learning, the rate of forgetting slows.

- Later reviews of learning can occur with longer time gaps without loss of impact.

What do these ideas mean for our curriculum planning? First, we should interrupt our learners' forgetting by providing them with retrieval tasks, and second, we should optimally space those tasks chronologically.

Practically, it makes sense that a retrieval opportunity is baked into the start of a lesson, as these will typically be after a break in learning or after a lesson earlier in the day on a different topic. The first of Rosenshine's (2012) principles of instruction is daily review, which tells us we should 'begin each lesson with a short review of previous learning'. In some instances, retrieval practice may even happen mid-lesson because whenever new content is to be taught, it is good practice to get your learners to retrieve relevant prior learning, which will help them contextualise and make sense of that new content.

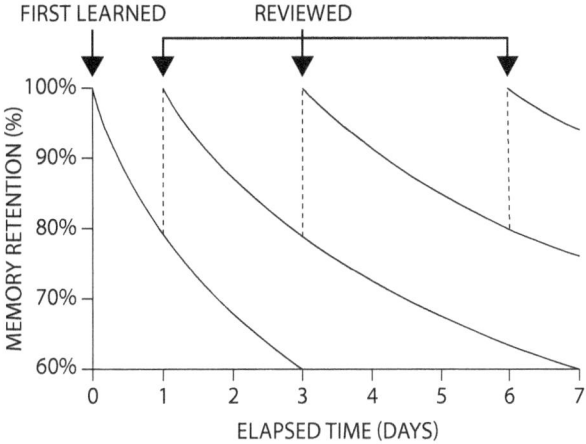

Figure 5.8 *Ebbinghaus' 'forgetting curve'*

REFLECT

How many strategies, techniques or activities can you think of to get your learners to retrieve their prior learning?

Tip for Teaching

These retrieval opportunities should be a key part of your planning, not only at lesson-level but in the longer term as well. If you are using schemes of work (as most FES establishments do), your retrieval practice should be included in them.

Rosenshine suggests that if learners achieve 80% in a retrieval test, the teacher should conclude that they have sufficient mastery of that material to be ready to move on. This is where our first difficulty arises. Quite apart from what we've already established about fluency, there is variation in the research evidence as to how many times a learner should visit a concept before they achieve 80% accuracy in their retrieval. Nuthall (2007) famously coined the 'three times rule', suggesting that revisiting an idea three times means learners are likely to recall the content with about 80% accuracy. More recently, Koedinger et al (2023) have asserted that a 'learner needs about seven learning opportunities to master a typical knowledge component', although there is 'substantial variation' between learners in this regard. It worth mentioning that Nuthall was referring to visiting and revisiting concepts in their compound state (he used the term 'complete set of information'), while Koedinger et al studied discrete 'knowledge components'. In any case, all are agreed – us included – that repetition is fundamental to the establishment of durable learning and should therefore be planned into a curriculum.

> **Take it further...**
>
> Have a discussion with your subject mentor and colleagues about which ideas and activities need to be revisited most often, and why. In your teaching context, have you noticed how many times your learners need to experience an idea before they 'get it'? Is it different for knowledge, skills and behaviours?

The second practical approach that we can derive from Ebbinghaus's forgetting curve is that we should space the practice across learning events, rather than blocking or using a massed practice approach.

Blocked or massed practice is the repetitive focus on a single skill with no variation until that skill is demonstrated to a level of proficiency. You could spend several hours honing a single skill, such as repeatedly practicing star piping as part of a patisserie module. The problem with overuse of blocked practice is that it does not tell us much about whether that skill is going to be retained in the long term and so can give the impression that learners are 'making progress' when in fact they are not. If your learner is producing excellent star piping after four lessons of blocked practice, you may conclude that you never have to return to that technique and move on to the next skill, such as round piping (see figure 5.9 below). On top of that, you may report to your line manager that your learners are ready for their final exam, only to discover their performance has deteriorated.

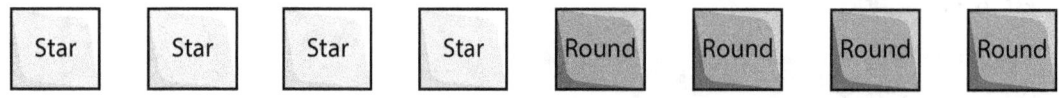

Figure 5.9 *Blocked or massed practice*

Spaced practice is preferable to blocked practice as it allows for retrieval. What factors should we consider when locating these retrieval events in our curriculum? Retrieval events should be positioned in the curriculum to account for two interacting factors: some time must pass prior to retrieval, but not too much time should pass prior to retrieval.

Why is this? It is important that the retrieval is from long-term memory rather than working memory. A very small space of time between the first and second learning events may not show learning, only performance (Soderstrom and Bjork, 2015), as the material is still held in short-term memory; this tells us little about the quality or durability of the encoding (see chapter 6 for more on this distinction).

The time gaps between practice events allow for forgetting to occur, such that when retrieval takes place it is more effortful for the learner and more likely to be from long term memory, thereby consolidating that memory. Bjork and Bjork (2011) use the term 'desirable difficulties' to describe the level of challenge needed in a learning event to provoke long term retention. Importantly for FES, this holds for both cognitive and motor skills. In our catering example

> ### Tip for Teaching
>
> If you assess your learners on what you just taught them, this can be helpful for checking their understanding but unhelpful as an indicator of who will best retain that learning over time. Sometimes poor performance in a test during acquisition is the sign of productive struggle that in time will mean that the learner remembers more than their peers who sail through the lesson and give you all the right answers out of their working memory.

(see figure 5.10 below), the curriculum structure allows learners to have three retrieval practice events after first learning to produce star piping, which means their practice is likely to be more of a struggle but also more durable.

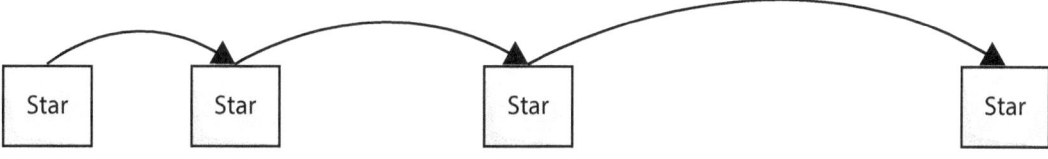

Figure 5.10 *Spaced practice*

> **REFLECT**
>
> Bjork and Bjork's data show that learners believe that blocked practice helps them learn better even after experiencing the benefits of spaced practice. Why do you think this is?

The quality and extent of retrieval should determine the spacing of the next retrieval practice event. Performance on a formative assessment (having accounted for the distinction between performance and learning) enables you to decide whether their understanding is secure, partial or absent. You are making inferences about their learning from the performance in tests, but the more secure their learning appears to be the longer you can leave it until the next retrieval event of the concept or skill being assessed. Sadly, this is not an exact science; you will still have to make some inferences and assumptions, but the quality of your assessment design will help you ensure those assumptions and inferences are reasonably valid. (See chapter 7 for more on assessment validity and reliability).

Interleaving is an approach to spaced practice that mixes up the practice of separate (though related) skills while still incorporating spacing between practice events.

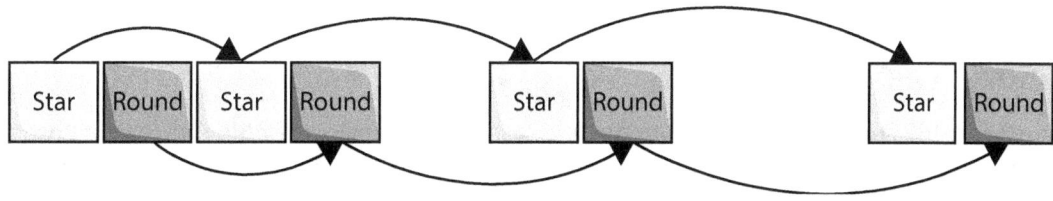

Figure 5.11 *Interleaving*

Interleaving optimises curriculum time by filling the gaps that are demanded by spacing, but it provides some other interesting benefits as well. To return one last time to our catering example in figure 5.11, the interleaving of star piping with round piping means that not only are the benefits of retrieval practice experienced for both skills, but learners are also more likely to have learned subtle differences between the techniques, which may improve both retention and transfer to new contexts.

> **Take it further...**
>
> What tensions can you see between some of the concepts in this chapter? And what pressures could there be to revert to less well evidenced methods in our day-to-day practice?

> **REFLECT**
>
> Are we nearly there yet?
>
> Repeatedly in this chapter we have relied on an extended metaphor: the curriculum as map and itinerary. You may think we have stretched this metaphor to breaking point!
>
> As we conclude, consider whether you think this metaphor is an apt one. What ideas may have been overemphasised by thinking in this way, and what concepts may have been overlooked or concealed?

Summary

In this chapter we have considered what a curriculum is and the models and intentions, content and considerations that make up the designing of a curriculum. We began by thinking about the sociocultural factors that influence curriculum content and what constitutes 'powerful knowledge', before pressing on to think about different models of curriculum. Process and product models are often pitted against each other, but we tried to strike a balance in seeing the benefits each provides. We established a key recurring idea that the internal structure of the subject domain should be the thing that guides our decisions about curriculum models and intentions, and we thought about how to integrate new and existing knowledge together over time into learner schemas.

We clarified the key difference between learning and performance and, drawing on Ebbinghaus's seminal work on forgetting (Ebbinghaus, 1885), we established some important considerations for the spacing of teaching and assessment through time.

Hopefully these insights will help you as you consider the 'what' and the 'when' of your teaching.

References

Abie, S. (2014) Curriculum Models: Product versus Process. Journal of Education and Practice 5:35, 152-154.

Anderson, L.W. and Krathwohl, D.R. (2001) A taxonomy for teaching, learning, and assessing: A revision of Bloom's taxonomy of educational objectives. New York: Longman

Ashbee, R. (2021). Curriculum: Theory, Culture and the Subject Specialisms

References

(1st ed.). Routledge. https://doi.org/10.4324/9781003039594

Barrow, R (1987). "Skill Talk," Journal of Philosophy of Education, 21 (2), 187-195.

Beck, J. and Young, M.F.D. (2005). 'The assault on the professions and the restructuring of academic and professional identities: a Bernsteinian analysis'. British Journal of Sociology of Education, 26: 183-197.

Bernstein, B. (1973). Class, Codes and Control (Vol. 2). London: Routledge & Kegan Paul.

Bernstein, B. (1999). Vertical and Horizontal Discourse: An Essay. British Journal of Sociology of Education, 20(2), 157–173

Bernstein, B. (2000). Pedagogy, Symbolic Control and Identity: Theory, Research, Critique (revised edition). Oxford: Rowman and Littlefield.

Biggs, J. (2003). Aligning teaching for constructing learning (online). The Higher Education Academy. Available https://www.advance-he.ac.uk/knowledge-hub/aligning-teaching-constructing-learning [Accessed 08 April 25]

Biggs, J. (2014). Constructive alignment in university teaching. Higher Education Research and Development Society of Australasia (HERDSA). HERDSA Review of Higher Education v.1 p.5-22.

Biggs and Tang (2011) Teaching for Quality Learning at University: What the Student Does (4th ed.). Maidenhead: McGraw-Hill

Binder, C. (1996) Behavioral fluency: evolution of a new paradigm. The Behavior Analyst, 19, 163-167 Available http://binde1.verio.com/wb_fluency.org/Publications/Binder1996.pdf. [Accessed 08 April 25]

Bjork, E. L., & Bjork, R. A. (2014). Making things hard on yourself, but in a good way: Creating desirable difficulties to enhance learning. In M. A. Gernsbacher and J. Pomerantz (Eds.), Psychology and the real world: Essays illustrating fundamental contributions to society (2nd edition). (pp. 59-68). New York: Worth

Bruner, J. S. (1960). The process of education. Harvard University Press.

Coe, R., Aloisi, C., Higgins, S. and Elliot Major, L. (2014) What makes great teaching? Review of the underpinning research. Sutton Trust. pp. 18-22

Crawley, J. (2005). In at the deep end. London: David Fulton.

Ebbinghaus H (1885) Memory: A contribution to experimental psychology. Ruger HA, Bussenius CE, translators (1913). New York: Teachers College, Columbia University.

Evens, M., Elen, J., and Depaepe, F. (2015) Developing Pedagogical Content Knowledge: Lessons Learned from Intervention Studies, Education Research International. http://dx.doi.org/10.1155/2015/790417

Feltovich, P. J., Spiro, R. J., & Coulson, R. L. (1993). Learning, teaching, and testing for complex conceptual understanding. In Test theory for a new generation of tests. (pp.181–217). Lawrence Erlbaum Associates, Inc.

Gallagher, E., Bones, R., & Lombe, J. (2006) Precision teaching and education: Is fluency the missing link between success and failure? Irish Educational Studies, 25 (01), 93-105, DOI: 10.1080/03323310600597642.

Hanley, P. and Thompson, R. (2021). ''Generic pedagogy is not enough': Teacher educators and subject-specialist pedagogy in the Further Education and Skills sector in England.' Teaching and Teacher Education, 98: 1-14.

Hordern, J. (2017) 'Bernstein's sociology of knowledge and education(al) studies'. In, Whitty, G. and Furlong, J., eds. Knowledge and the study of education: an international exploration. Didcot: Symposium: 191-210

Ireland, J. and Mouthaan, M. (2020) 'Perspectives on curriculum design: comparing the spiral and the network models', Research Matters, Issue 30, Autumn 2020, pp. 7-12.

Johnson, S. and Siegal, H. (2010). Teaching Thinking Skills. London: Continuum International Publishing Group.

Jubilee Cente (2022) The Jubilee Centre Framework for Character Education in Schools. 3rd edn. Birmingham: University of Birmingham, Jubilee Centre for Character and Virtues. ISBN: 9780704429789.

Keep, E. (2014). What Does Skills Policy Look Like Now the Money Has Run Out? Available at: https://www.aoc.co.uk/sites/default/files/What_Does_Skills_Policy_Look_Like_Now_the_Money_Has_Run_Out__0.pdf (Accessed 09 May 2021).

Koedinger, K.R., Carvalho, P.F., Liu, R. and McLaughlin, E.A. (2023) An astonishing regularity in student learning rate. Proceedings of the National Academy of Sciences, 120(5)

McDowell, C., Keenan, M., & Kerr, K.P. (2002) Comparing levels of dysfluency among students with mild learning difficulties and typical students. Journal of Precision Teaching and Celeration. 18 (2), 37-48. Available https://celeration.org/wp-content/uploads/2017/02/JPTC_V18.02_06.pdf [Accessed 12 April 19]

Melton, A. W. (1963). Implications of short-term memory for a general theory of memory. Journal of Verbal Learning and Verbal Behavior, 2, 1–21.

Meyer JHF & Land R (2003) 'Threshold Concepts and Troublesome Knowledge (1) – Linkages to Ways of Thinking and Practising' in Improving Student Learning – Ten Years On. Rust, C (ed), OCSLD, Oxford

Murre J.M.J. & Dros J. (2015) Replication and Analysis of Ebbinghaus' Forgetting Curve. PLOS ONE 10(7): e0120644. https://doi.org/10.1371/journal.pone.0120644

Nuthall, G. (2007). The Hidden Lives of Learners. Wellington, NZ: NZCER Press.

Rosenshine, B. (2012) Principles of Instruction: Research-Based Strategies That All Teachers Should Know. American Educator, 36 (1), 12-19, 39.

Shulman, L.S. (1986) Those who understand: knowledge growth in teaching, Educational Researcher, 15 (2), pp. 4–14. https://doi.org/10.3102/0013189X015002004

Simon, H.A. & Chase, W. (1973). Skill in chess. American Scientist, 61, 394-403.

Soderstrom, N. C., & Bjork, R. A. (2015). Learning versus performance: An integrative review. Perspectives on Psychological Science, 10(2), 176-199.

Stenhouse, L. (1975). An introduction to curriculum research and development. London: Heinemann.

Tyler, R. W. (1949). Basic principles of curriculum and instruction. Chicago: University of Chicago Press.

Wheelahan, L. (2010). Why knowledge matters: a social realist argument. Abingdon, Oxon: Routledge.

Wheelahan, L. (2007). 'How competency-based training locks the working class out of powerful knowledge: a modified Bernsteinian analysis.' British Journal of Sociology of Education, 28 (5): 637-651.

Wheelahan, L. (2015). 'Not just skills: what a focus on knowledge means for vocational education.' Journal of Curriculum Studies, 47: 750 - 762.

Wheelahan, L., Moodie, G., Doughney, J. (2022). 'Challenging the skills fetish.' British Journal of Sociology of Education ,43 (3): 475-494.

Wiggins, G., & McTighe, J. (2005). Understanding by design (2nd ed.). Upper Saddle River, NJ: Prentice Hall

Wiliam, D. (2010). What Counts as Evidence of Educational Achievement? The Role of Constructs in the Pursuit of Equity in Assessment. Review of Research in Education, 34(1), 254-284. https://doi.org/10.3102/0091732X09351544

Winch, C. (2010). Dimensions of Expertise: A Conceptual Exploration of Vocational Knowledge. Vancouver, CA: Continuum.

Young, M. and Muller, J. (2013). 'On the powers of powerful knowledge.' Review of Education, 1(3): 229– 25

Chapter 6 Pedagogy

Plan, deliver and evaluate effective evidence-informed teaching using assessment, relevant systems and safe use of technology to support learning (Duty 4)

Serious consideration of pedagogy is largely missing in vocational education and ... vocational learners are the losers as a result of this omission

Lucas et al (2012)

6.1 Introduction

The aim of this chapter is to respond to Lucas's concern in the quotation above by taking serious consideration of pedagogy in the context of FES for the sake of our learners. Most of the chapter is structured around three key domains of learning: affective, cognitive and psychomotor. It should be remembered that our learners are whole people with bodies, brains and beliefs, and they deserve the effort of their teachers and lecturers to consider them as whole people when they arrive in the classroom.

In chapter 5, we considered some key ideas around curriculum structure and how instruction, practice and assessment should be spaced over time. This chapter will focus more closely on your 'in-the-moment' practice as you teach.

If curriculum is the 'what' and 'when' of teaching, then pedagogy is the 'how'. In this chapter, we consider further what we mean by pedagogy, what good pedagogy looks like in the FES context and some of the ways in which teachers can become evidence-informed in their pedagogical practice.

6.2 Pedagogy

Given the amount of writing already on the subject, it is perhaps worth admitting here that a universally satisfactory definition of pedagogy will probably continue to elude us. Even so, some common features can be unearthed from previous attempts. Here are two such attempts.

Alexander (2004) argues that:

Pedagogy is the act of teaching together with its attendant discourse. It is what one needs to know and the skills one needs to command in order to make and justify the many different kinds of decisions of which teaching is constituted.

And Bernstein (2000) asserts that:

Pedagogy is a sustained process whereby somebody acquires new forms or develops existing forms of conduct, knowledge, practice and criteria from somebody or something deemed to be an appropriate provider and evaluator.

Drawing from these and other definitions, Hanley et al (2018) have suggested that pedagogy should be thought of as having four dimensions, as we can see in figure 6.1.

FOUR DIMENSIONS OF PEDAGOGY

Content

The knowledge, skills and attributes that students are given the opportunity to learn

Process

What happens (or potentially can happen) in educational environments

Knowledge

The knowledge that teachers have about pedagogical content, processes and their possible outcomes, including knowledge about their students and the context in which they are learning

Decision making

The processes and actions through which teachers come to decisions about what will happen in their classrooms and to what purpose

Figure 6.1 *Four dimensions of pedagogy*

All four of these dimensions are developed in this chapter but also spill out beyond its confines. For example, you will find some aspects of 'pedagogy as decision making' explored further in chapter 7 and 'pedagogy as knowledge about learners' in chapter 3.

Towards the end of the chapter, we will address the question of subject-specificity, a discussion we began in chapter 5: to what extent do different subjects require uniquely tailored pedagogies rather than a generic pedagogy? By providing a general overview of pedagogy before addressing the question, you may already have an intimation of the nature of my answer!

I want to note that though pedagogy is the more commonly used term in education, some FES practitioners prefer the term 'andragogy' to describe their theoretical approach to teaching. Pedagogy is derived from the classical Greek word for 'child', while andragogy is derived from the classical Greek word for 'man', denoting an adult. FES is of course not confined to the teaching of adults but does typically involve learners over the age of 16, so clearly there is an argument that can be made for using the term andragogy. However, in my view, the precision introduced is probably not worth the confusion potentially caused by a change in terminology; therefore, for the remainder of the chapter I will continue to use the word pedagogy.

6.3 Pedagogical philosophies

At this point of a teaching textbook, you may expect to find discussion of philosophical approaches to education such as behaviourism, constructivism (cognitive and social), enactivism or critical pedagogies – these are absent in this textbook. Despite such discussions being a staple part of the teacher training industry for decades, we are sceptical about the value to practitioners of such philosophising. For this reason, we include a table here that signposts you to some philosophical approaches that you may wish to investigate.

Philosophy	Key idea	Proponent(s)	Text(s)
Behaviourism	Learning is shaped by reinforcement and punishment. Observable behaviours are the focus.	B.F. Skinner, John Watson	Science and Human Behavior (Skinner); Psychology as the Behaviorist Views It (Watson)
Cognitive constructivism	Learning is an active process of building on prior knowledge. Focuses on mental processes.	Jean Piaget, Jerome Bruner, Daniel Willingham	The Psychology of Intelligence (Piaget); The Process of Education (Bruner); Why Don't Students Like School? (Willingham)
Social constructivism	Knowledge is constructed collaboratively through social interaction.	Lev Vygotsky	Mind in Society (Vygotsky)
Enactivism	Learning is rooted in action, experience and embodied cognition.	Francisco Varela, Eleanor Rosch, Evan Thompson	The Embodied Mind (Varela, Rosch and Thompson)
Critical pedagogies	Education challenges power structures, encourages critical thinking and promotes social justice.	Paulo Freire, bell hooks	Pedagogy of the Oppressed (Freire); Teaching to Transgress (hooks)

These philosophies also apply to digital pedagogy, with more traditional approaches viewing digital tools as supplements to conventional teaching methods while maintaining the core educational principles. On the other hand, more critical approaches emphasise digital citizenship, ethics and social justice through advocating for open-source tools and open educational resources. However, pedagogical philosophies are not all directly comparable because not all of them seek to ask or answer the same kinds of questions about the nature of learning. In reading about them, you may notice both sharp disagreements as well as areas of commonality, which will hopefully prompt you to think carefully about your own pedagogical philosophy.

Take it further...

Research the above and write your own philosophical position statement for your professional development portfolio.

From here on, in a knowingly pragmatic fashion, we will focus on theories of learning and their application in different FES contexts. As we have already established, if curriculum is the 'what' and 'when' of teaching, then pedagogy is the 'how'. There are multiple pedagogical approaches available to you as a teacher, some of which are competing and others that are complementary. Part of becoming an expert teacher is understanding the pedagogies available to you, when they are best deployed and to what extent they are evidence informed.

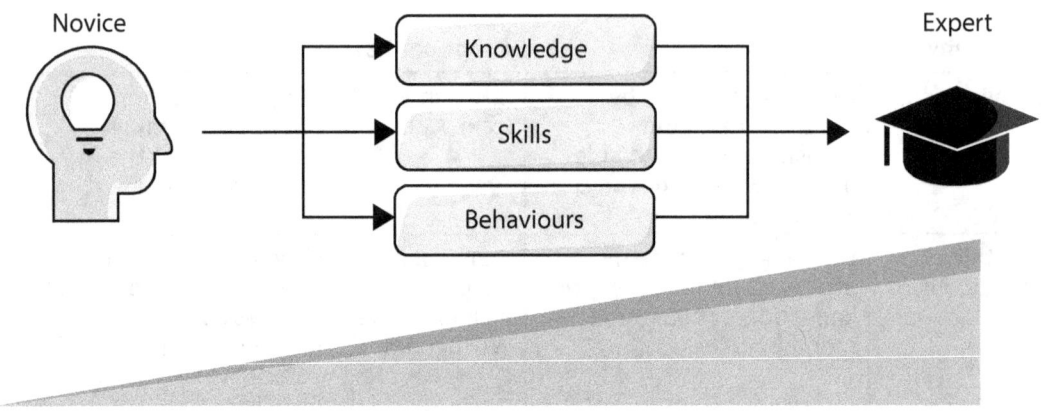

Figure 6.2 *Transition to independence*

Chapter 5 introduced the idea that a curriculum has a temporal feature; in other words, that our purpose in teaching is to assist learners to move over time from being a novice to being an expert, transitioning them to independence as they go. 'Novice' and 'expert' are relative terms of course, so we can validly speak of moving from knowing less to knowing more. How can we help our learners navigate their way to expertise?

6.4 Theories of learning and their application

A theory of learning or model of the learning process underpins a practitioner's pedagogical decision making. In this section, we outline a range of theoretical and conceptual models for how learning happens. For each, there will be a description of the theory along with exemplars, case studies and questions to help you consider how you could incorporate the theory or concept into your mental model of how learning happens. Having done this, you will be well placed to synthesise the best research evidence with your own expertise and judgment and be equipped to make evidence-informed choices for your own teaching context.

All theories are approximations. They rely on metaphor and abstractions. But that does not mean they are not valid or helpful. For example, just because the brain is not a computer, this does not mean that using a metaphor of a computer is necessarily without validity. Part of the skill of incorporating a theory into your mental model for teaching and learning is to identify the utility of the concept rather than getting hung up on philosophical questions that lurk beneath the surface. Our advice is to keep your learners at the forefront of your thinking as you read through the following sections.

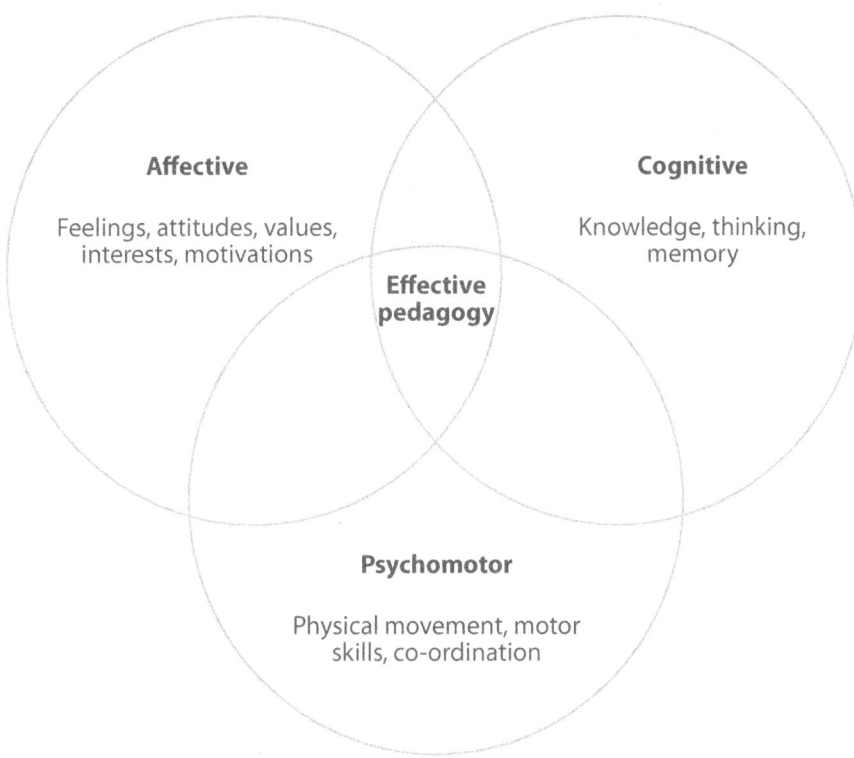

Figure 6.3 *Bloom's pedagogy domains*

The theories included here do not represent an exhaustive survey but are those that we believe to have the greatest utility for the FES teacher. The theories have been categorised according to their focus – some focus on cognitive aspects of learning, (such as cognitive load theory), some on the affective (such as SDT), some on the psychomotor domain (such as embodied cognition) and others combine these domains in unique ways (such as MARGE). There are, of course, some theories, concepts and practices that have been omitted from this textbook (such as learning styles, 'brain gym' and Maslow's hierarchy of needs) due to them being unsupported by evidence.

These three domains have been taken from the seminal work of Bloom (1956). While careless use of Bloom's taxonomy of learning outcomes has come in for criticism in the wake of findings from cognitive science and associated disciplines (Agarwal 2019), these top-level categories are certainly helpful in ensuring that the whole learner is factored into our discussion of pedagogy. In the next section, we consider each of the domains separately for simplicity, but we should recognise that the domains are mutually reinforcing and interact with each other, because our knowing, doing and feeling are all fundamentally interconnected (Neary 2002). These three domains have been memorably labelled 'head, heart and hands' (Orr 1992, Sipos et al. 2008).

6.5 Heart – affective and social theories of learning

The first of Bloom's three domains that we will consider is the affective domain, which despite being deemed the 'gateway to learning' has also been described as the 'most overlooked of the three domains' (Pierre and Oughton, 2007). Among educators, 'affect' is often used as a synonym for 'emotion', but this is imprecise and narrows its meaning too much. 'Affect' is a broad term that encompasses emotion-driven and emotion-laden states such as motivation, engagement and attention but also includes beliefs, values and attitudes. In addition, 'affect' also includes the intensity of these states and their durability and trajectory. Clearly, these things are of importance to our learners and their experiences in our classrooms, and so it would be wise for us to understand the nature of their influence and impact. We begin with a detailed discussion of motivation and engagement before moving on to broader affective theories.

In the FES classroom, the factors that affect motivation and engagement are numerous, and studies in similar contexts have shown that learners often enter vocational training having experienced motivational challenges in their learning journey (Dubeau, Plante and Frenay 2017; Cents-Boonstra et al, 2018). It is fair to say that this is a feature of the FES sector in the UK but is one that affords us the privilege of making a tangible difference to our learners' lives and career prospects.

It would be wrong and unfair to us as teachers to suggest that we ought to be motivational gurus, and that the levels of engagement and inspiration felt by our learners are entirely within our power to create. We should remember that not every learner success (or failure) is down to the teacher's actions in the classroom. This would be too great a burden to bear and would probably end up narrowing the profession to extraverts with extraordinary personalities, abounding with indefatigable enthusiasm – introverts can be great teachers too! As we discuss motivation, we must remember the myriad complex social and interpersonal factors that shape the teaching environment and our learners' experiences within it.

But we are not off the hook completely – clearly there is a very important role to be played by teachers in the motivation of their learners. But we can set and uphold high expectations and provide the support needed to get there by applying both motivational theory and individual support.

Shimamura's MARGE

MARGE stands for motivate, attend, relate, generate and evaluate (Shimamura, 2018). We will consider only the first two: motivation and attention, as the other three concepts relate more closely to the cognitive domain and will therefore be addressed in the next section.

Shimamura argues that motivation is intrinsically linked to the brain's reward circuitry and the release of the pleasure hormone dopamine, and so the teacher's role is to work out how to 'engage the reward circuit in the service of learning'. Key to this is instilling curiosity in our learners.

How can we encourage our learners to be curious? Here are some of Shimamura's suggestions:

- Big questions
- Overarching frameworks
- Storytelling
- Aesthetic questions

'Big questions' are questions that invite learners to consider a consequential issue of subject relevance but to do so from within their own value system. Shimamura advises starting a lesson with a big question that can guide the learners as they try to answer it by making sense of the lesson content.

'Overarching frameworks' are mental structures into which learners can place their new and developing understanding. This can be as simple as providing an acronym as a structure to be infilled (such as MARGE), as you are hopefully doing as you read this. Any structure that

> **REFLECT**
>
> One of the things that makes these kinds of questions motivating and engaging is that the discussion often has a low bar to entry. Learners can share their initial thoughts, starting points and presuppositions without fear of getting the wrong answer. (Do be careful about the phrasing of your questions if you are going to be asking about divisive or emotionally charged topics.)
>
> Here are some big questions that have been posed to sport learners:
>
> - Should fighting in ice hockey be banned?
> - Should performance enhancing drugs (PEDs) be made completely legal in sport?
> - Should clubs be prohibited from advertising gambling apps and websites?
> - Should team initiation ceremonies be stopped?
> - Is it okay to win a penalty by diving?
> - What are the big questions of your subject?

is shared with a learner prior to the learning event is known as an advance organiser – these include graphic organisers, grids to fill out, analogies or stories.

'Storytelling' can be a powerful tool for engagement, especially when the characters in the story are relatable or known by the learners themselves. A story has an inbuilt structure or framework that learners can follow and use in the organisation of their own understanding. Carefully selected documentaries, talking heads and personal anecdotes can all be of use in this regard. Here is a simple example of a storyline that provides a structure for the learning of the stages of the bone remodelling process in level 3 sport.

Storyline	My old fireplace was dated, and there were cracks in the stone surround. My wife said we should get it sorted before it falls apart.	I knocked out the stone surround with a hammer and chisel, making a bit of a mess (it was quite a lot of fun, though)!	I cleaned the area by bagging up all the old stone surround and taking it off to the tip for disposal.	I used new bricks to create the new fireplace, securing them in place with mortar and checking it was solid.	You can't see all the brickwork, but the facing bricks give the fireplace a rustic look, which my wife likes!
Application	Osteoclasts respond to a signal from the bone. (e.g. mechanical stress or damage)	Osteoclasts dig a cavity (in spongy bone) or a tunnel (in compact bone).	Pre-osteoblasts arrive and become osteoblasts. Debris is dissolved and osteoclasts 'die'.	Osteoblasts line the cavity and produce a matrix which is hardened by calcium and phosphorous.	Some osteoblasts become lining cells, and some remain in the new bone.
Key term	Activation	Resorption	Reversal	Formation	Quiescence

Finally, Shimamura recommends asking 'aesthetic questions' such as 'what do you like about this?' or 'what is good about this?' The idea here is to deliberately engage the learners' emotions in thinking about a topic to foster motivation.

A warning! Coe et al (2014) remind us that while motivation is essential for learning, it is not sufficient for learning. Your learners are not wind-up toys; a teacher's job is much more than turning the key and letting them go. In fact, motivation has been shown to be a poor proxy for learning; teachers can be tempted to believe that because their learners are motivated (or 'engaged') they must be learning. This misunderstanding can be exacerbated by confusing episodic memory with semantic memory; your learners may remember that three weeks ago you had a heated discussion about the merits and demerits of fighting in ice hockey, but that does not mean they can recall any of the key arguments.

For Shimamura, attention follows on from motivation. Once learners are motivated to learn, they must direct their attention to the taught content, making use of their capacity for selective attention. It is important we help them with this because, as Shimamura (2018) reminds us, 'attention takes effort.'

Selective attention is our ability to focus on the things we choose to focus on while simultaneously dampening down potentially distracting inputs from our environment. This cognitive ability, paired with top-down processing in which we use our existing knowledge to guide our focus, enables us to pay attention in lessons and make sense of the content. The teacher can help learners by making explicit those things they should be focusing on.

Shimamura suggests that the first few minutes of a lesson are of vital importance, as this is the time when mind-wandering is most likely to occur. He recommends starting lessons by grabbing learner attention (some of the strategies suggested by Shimamura to motivate learners are pertinent). Shimamura further advises establishing learning goals at the outset, reviewing the links between already learned and new material and using real world examples.

> **REFLECT**
>
> Consider the following questions:
> - What is motivation?
> - What motivates you to learn something new?
> - Is short-term motivation cultivated differently compared to long-term motivation?
> - What is the relationship between motivation, support and success?

Self-determination theory

In contrast to MARGE, self-determination theory (SDT) is a systemic theory that places much greater emphasis on how the structure of the environment influences motivation rather than on the cognition of the individual. The structure of the environment includes (for our purposes) the teacher's behaviour and their level of competence, or, more accurately, the learner's perception of the teacher's competence. These can have a significant impact on motivation (Cents-Boonstra et al, 2020) and disaffection (Wilding, 2015) among learners.

The theory has implications for many facets of our practice, but here our focus is narrow. We will be asking the question, 'how can SDT inform our pedagogy?' Each of Deci and Ryan's three strands (autonomy, relatedness and competence) have implications for the way that we teach our learners. Ahmadi et al (2022) summarised their extensive research with a table of teacher motivational behaviours (TMBs) that either support or thwart learners' development of autonomy, relatedness and competence. In the next section, we have included a selection of the most potent TMBs from Ahmadi's table in a slimmed-down and adapted format.

Autonomy

Research shows that self-directed learning interventions among adolescents positively impacted both enjoyment and effort (Schweder and Raufelder, 2022). As a result, a synthesis of self-directed and teacher-directed approaches appear to help maintain optimal learner motivation (Schweder and Raufelder, 2024).

Sherrington's (2018) 'mode A/mode B' distinction is a helpful approach here. He suggests an 80/20 split between what he calls 'mode A' teaching (teacher-directed: modelling, practice, questioning, testing) and 'mode B' teaching (learner-directed: exploration, discovery learning, hands-on experience). The balance between these is yours to consider.

> **REFLECT**
>
> In your subject, what knowledge, skills and behaviours may lend themselves to being taught via mode A teaching, and which may be better taught via mode B teaching?

	Behaviour	**Description**	**Function**
Supportive	Allow for learner input or choice.	Create opportunities for learners to meaningfully direct the activities they do in class.	Allows learners to choose tasks that align with their priorities and capabilities; supports the ownership of the behaviour.
	Teach in learners' preferred ways.	Use knowledge gleaned about the learner values and preferences to design class activities customized to them.	Aligns lesson activities to learner's intrinsic reasons for learning rather than imposing extrinsic reasons.
	Provide rationales.	Explain the reason to perform the behaviour.	Learners understand why they are doing an activity and ideally aligns the task to a learner's values.
Thwarting	Use of pressuring language.	Using pressuring or controlling language when explaining tasks, providing feedback and so forth.	Increases perceived external pressure to complete the task for imposed reasons.
	Set up activities that exclude some learners.	Set up activities so there are times where some learners are not doing anything.	Learners do not have opportunities to engage even if they want to.
	Set pressuring deadlines.	Allow a capped amount of time for a task or remind learners they are running out of time.	Adds pressure on learners to work faster and finish tasks when teacher says to.

Autonomy *(Ahmadi et al, 2022)*

Relatedness

To be 'relatedness-supportive', Escandell and Chu (2023) suggest that a teacher should seek to help learners make connections between their learning and real life by using relatable graphics, diagrams, vocabulary and descriptions. This does not mean simply using clips from loved TV shows (although it could!) but rather working out how learning materials and real life can be connected in meaningful ways. Perhaps the best way to achieve this is to help learners apply their learning in real-life scenarios.

> **Tip for Teaching**
>
> While using relatable examples to aid learning can be a helpful tool, be careful you are not limiting learners to the circumference of their existing experience and understanding. Mix up your examples and give them new things to think about as well as drawing on the familiar.

Relatedness is supported by developing a learner-centred environment, which for Escandell and Chu (2023) is one contrasted with authoritarianism and control. Paired work, small group work and real-life applications are all promoted as means to achieve a learner-centred classroom, but we would caution against a priori commitment to types of delivery without reference to the learners' levels of mastery in the process or concepts under instruction.

I remind you of Coe's (et al, 2014) injunction not to conflate or confuse engagement with learning. In short, when attempting to achieve relatedness, you should not always be led by learner preferences. Learners do not always know how they learn best, and ultimately it is your role and responsibility as an educator to determine the nature of the teaching that goes on in your classroom. You must balance these things with insights into effective pedagogy from other approaches, which we will cover later in this chapter as we turn to pedagogies of the cognitive and psychomotor domains.

Ahmadi's (et al, 2022) relatedness-supportive strategies are summarised in the table opposite.

Competence

Competence refers to each learner's sense that success is within their grasp. It is extremely difficult to motivate yourself, or anyone else, to attempt a task that you don't believe is possible to accomplish. Imagine you are asked to perform a forward dive with four and a half somersaults from a 10-metre platform – how likely are you to give it a go?

Vygotsky (1978) proposed that learners should be provided work that is sufficiently challenging but within reach of their present competency level – he called this the zone of proximal development (ZPD). Setting work beyond that level and out of the reach of the learner would lead to demotivation and failure, as would setting work that was already mastered. It should be noted that competence is highly domain-specific; you can have mastered high-level concepts in engineering and also be a terrible baker!

Additionally, motivation is dependent not on the actual levels of learner competence, nor on the teacher's assessment of learner competence, but on each learner's own perception of their competence. This is closely related to another important component of competence called academic self-concept. Academic self-concept is also correlated with performance (Chen et al, 2013).

	Behaviour	**Description**	**Function**
Supportive	Show unconditional positive regard.	Act warmly toward learners, especially ones who are challenging or who find the course challenging.	Ensures performance mistakes or behavioural misconduct are not met with ego-threatening behaviour.
	Ask about learners' progress, welfare and feelings.	Show interest in how learners are doing, both emotionally and in their mastery of content.	Shows care and encourages learners to express themselves openly, so they connect with their teacher.
	Expressing affection.	Be warm and kind to learners.	Learners feel they are cared for.
Thwarting	Ignoring learners.	During times when attending to learners would be appropriate the teacher maintains distance or does not direct attention to the learner.	Makes learners feel they are not valued or cared for and that their efforts are not noticed.
	Using abusive language.	Calling learners by hurtful names when they misbehave.	Performance mistakes and behavioural misconduct are met with competence-threatening punishment.
	Provide punishments unfairly.	Provide punishments unfairly so learners who misbehave are treated unequally.	Means structures are perceived as unreliable and learners feel incompetent in terms of their ability to behave.

Relatedness (Ahmadi et al, 2022)

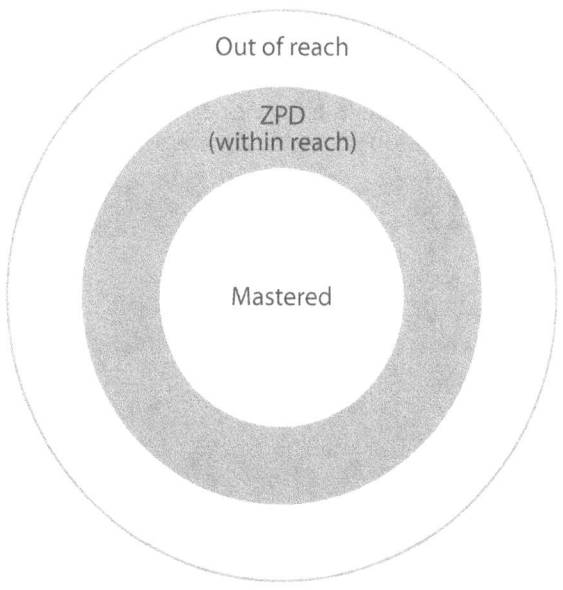

Figure 6.4 *Vygotsky's zone of proximal development (ZPD)*

There is yet another layer of complexity here because research has repeatedly shown that self-perceptions of competence are not always accurate. In fact, boys generally assume themselves to be more competent than more objective measures of learning could indicate, while girls assume themselves to be less competent than those more objective measures (Herbet and Stipek, 2005). This is one of my favourite findings to reveal to trainees, as it usually receives smiles and self-deprecating nods of acceptance right across the room.

In a fascinating interplay of these two qualifiers (self-perception and domain specificity) it is interesting that while a learner's sense of competence also appears to be domain specific, this is most especially true for girls (Frome and Eccles, 1998). This suggests perhaps that boys' sense of competence is more transferable or durable than girls', who tend to underestimate their abilities in fields not stereotypically associated with female excellence.

There are two interrelated pedagogical strategies that emerge from this way of conceptualising learner competence: scaffolding and formative feedback. Bruner (1978) introduced the concept of scaffolding to explain how instruction in the ZPD should occur. Scaffolding refers to any activity whereby a learner who has not yet mastered a concept or skill is supported to complete it. This could be achieved through guidance from a teacher or co-operation with a more competent peer. In either case, the presence of a 'more knowledgeable other' (MKO) is vital.

Optimal levels of challenge are difficult to precisely design, and a teacher needs to avail themself of formative feedback about their learners' progress that can inform the next steps for both teacher and learner (we will explore this further in chapter 7). This is known as responsive or adaptive teaching. Being informed by regular in-the-moment feedback on learner understanding and their developing competence means we teachers can set work for them that genuinely does fall into the ZPD.

We want our learners to experience what Bjork and Bjork (2011) have termed 'desirable difficulties', and regular formative feedback enables us to tweak the level of scaffolding being used. Given that learners often have faulty perceptions of their own capabilities, we teachers should use formative feedback to make competence visible to learners so that they too are better informed about their own progress.

How do we (and our learners) know if we have hit the ZPD sweet spot? Rosenshine (2012) suggests the use of 80% correct answers as a rule of thumb. Where learners are achieving 80%, this indicates that they are having substantial success but are still being challenged. Anything higher suggests that the content is too easy, which may negatively affect motivation. Of course, there remains the problem of establishing what 80% looks like in any given formative assessment in FES; it may be a helpful indicator in a GCSE maths resit lesson, but it is less clear cut when it comes to hairdressing or dog grooming!

Tip for Teaching

Teach to the top through high-level examples

Mansworth (2021) is critical of Vygotsky's ZPD, arguing that pitching the level of a lesson or task 'just above' the current level of the learner is often insufficiently challenging or aspirational. Instead, she argues that alongside examples that are 'just above', teachers should make use of high-level examples. A high-level example is one that is well above the learners' current level of mastery.

Think about using examples from those who are considered experts in the domain. Who are the great practitioners of your subject or vocation? Can learners be encouraged to strive for high levels of mastery exemplified by the accomplishments of these greats? Of course! Just make sure that the scaffolding is well planned.

	Behaviour	Description	Function
Supportive	Provide optional challenge.	Offer learners more challenging tasks if they find it too easy, or easier tasks if they find it too difficult.	Learners get the right amount of challenge for them.
	Provide specific feedback.	Provide feedback that targets a specific strategy for improvement.	Clarifies path toward goal achievement.
	Praise improvement or effort.	Provide praise that targets the improvement or effort from the learner.	Affirms learners' progress and improvement.
Thwarting	Publicly present critical feedback.	Provide critical feedback in public so other learners can hear.	Increases risk of feedback being ego-threatening.
	Criticise a fixed quality.	Provides critical feedback that targets a fixed quality.	Emphasises the importance of inherent abilities for achieving success and insinuates that a learner cannot grow in their learning.
	Criticise losing via peer comparison.	Tell learners when they are not doing as well as others.	Emphasises peer comparison for establishing a sense of competence, meaning few learners experience success by being the best.

Competence (Ahmadi et al 2022)

> **REFLECT**
>
> Are your needs as a teacher being supported? How could this affect your sense of self-determination as well as your motivation to teach and psychological wellbeing?

Social theories of learning

Having dealt in some detail with motivation as a component of 'affect', we now zoom out conceptually to take a wider look at where motivation and affect fit within broader social theories of learning. We are encouraged in this by Pierre and Oughton (2007):

Instructional designers should not use the affective domain only for a learner's motivation to learn, but consider how to engage learners in deeper learning through the use of this domain with appropriate pedagogy and evaluation methods.

Even after a cursory glance at the table above on competence, you may be able to see why the theories and concepts so far discussed – which focus on motivation, self-determination and affect – are grouped under the heading of affective and social theories. Some of the themes here (such as belonging) have already been discussed, but widening the scope beyond motivation can help us benefit from thinking about how our pedagogic practice can incorporate further social aspects of learning.

A social theory of learning, according to Wenger (1998), integrates four interconnected components: community, practice, identity and meaning.

Figure 6.5 *Features of social theories of learning*

Wenger's central assertion is that learning proceeds from interactions within the learning community of which the learner is a member. For Wenger therefore, the key influence in social learning is the nature, structure and practice of the community or learning group. As the group interacts to work on a project or carry out a practice, as they share their developing understanding, and co-construct meaning for that community, each member comes to adopt an identity tied to their membership of that group. From this perspective a teacher's role (if a teacher is needed at all) is to set up or facilitate learner engagement within a 'community of practice' that is conducive to learning the desired knowledge, skills and behaviours. Wenger's provocative exclamation that 'learning cannot be designed' (1998) highlights his emphasis on the organic, social determinants of learning versus a more formalised, planned curriculum approach. Instead, the community of practice is 'a living curriculum' (Wenger-Traynor, 2015).

> **REFLECT**
>
> To what extent are your learners – as they develop skills for a future career – being embedded in a community of practice? How could you foster this? What opportunities do they have for cultivating a professional identity that is tied to their developing practice? How much contact to they have with 'the real thing'?

Bandura's social learning theory

Perhaps the best-known social learning theory is that of Bandura. Bandura's (1977) theory propounds the idea that we learn our behaviours, moods, actions, feelings and sense of confidence from interacting with others and interpret our experiences by thinking about those interactions. Bandura thus modified behaviourism with key ideas from cognitivism, and to account for this much of the research that has stemmed from Bandura's earlier work is conducted under the rubric of social cognitive theory (Bandura, 1986).

Self-efficacy is a critical construct within Bandura's theory; the term describes a person's perceived capacity to succeed at a given task. In this sense it is a very similar concept to the academic self-concept already discussed, so we will avoid repetition of strategies under the competence subheading above. However, according to Bandura, self-efficacy is bolstered by four factors, which are shown in figure 6.6 below along with a quotation from Bandura's seminal 1977 paper.

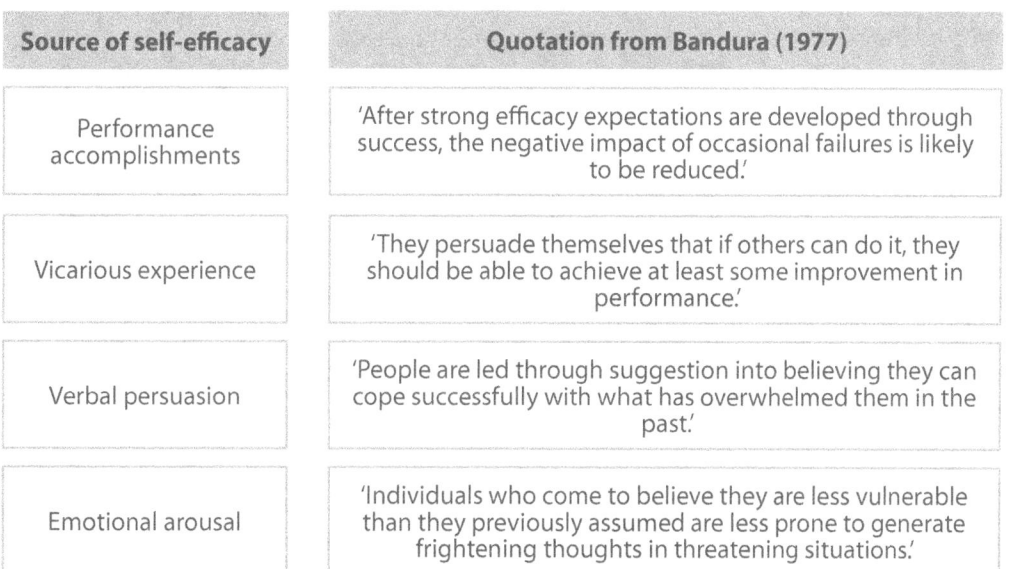

Figure 6.6 *Sources of self-efficacy in Bandura's social learning theory (SLT)*

Performance accomplishments are the strongest source of self-efficacy. Our learners' sense of their own capability is very closely tied to their previous achievements, both in negative and positive directions – a 'winning streak' is a real thing! It makes sense to help learners achieve some early 'wins' in their studies, whether early during a course or at the outset of each lesson. This can set the conditions for a virtuous circle of self-efficacy.

Vicarious experience and verbal persuasion are less potent as sources of self-efficacy than performance accomplishments but do still have a role to play. When learners can observe others performing skills and activities successfully, this can lead to an increase in their own sense of what is achievable. This is especially true when the person they are observing is felt to be like them in meaningful ways, such as gender, age or class. The words that you use as a teacher to praise, encourage or reprimand are also a source of self-efficacy in your learners. Take care to praise your learners.

Emotional arousal is the most volatile source of self-efficacy, as emotional states fluctuate along with the cognitive appraisal of these states. When learners interpret the features of their physiological state as nervousness, they are more likely to experience a lack of self-efficacy. If you as a teacher can either reduce your learners' exposure to stressful situations or model coping strategies for situations that are unavoidable (such as an examination or observed final assessment), then learner self-efficacy can be better safeguarded.

Each of these sources of self-efficacy can be positively influenced by teacher behaviour. Ultimately, you want your learners to have a high assurance in their capabilities; as Dubeau, Plante and Frenay (2017) state:

> *Learners with a high assurance in their capabilities approach tasks as challenges to be overcome. In contrast, people who doubt their capabilities [withdraw from or avoid] difficult tasks and give up readily in face of difficulties.*

Niemiec and Ryan (2009) prefer self-determination theory and are critical of Bandura's self-efficacy theory, believing that it 'denies functional significance to autonomy.' If learners feel they can complete a task, will that really be sufficient motivation for them to exhibit motivated behaviour towards task completion, regardless of whether they have a sense of willingness towards it? Pitching material to our learners at the right level of difficulty is essential but not enough, as we ought also to think of ways to help them establish a rationale for task completion. What reasons for working hard and persisting through challenge do you give to your learners? What reasons do you give to yourself?

Tip for Teaching

Tip for teaching: Develop your self-efficacy as a teacher

The research is not univocal about the impact of teacher self-efficacy (TSE) on learner attainment (Jerrim, Sims and Oliver, 2023), but there do appear to be correlations between TSE and a range of positive outcomes.

Teacher self-efficacy has been found to be linked to 'a range of instructional outcomes, teacher instructional behaviour, and teacher well-being, including learner motivation, learner engagement, learner achievement, learner self-efficacy, teacher work satisfaction, work commitment, teacher effectiveness and instructional behaviour' (Mok and Moore, 2019).

How can you develop your self-efficacy as a teacher?

- **Performance accomplishments** – Think about how far you've come already. Remind yourself of specific, identifiable successful moments in your teaching experience so far. Remember how it felt for your learners to finally grasp something that you taught them.

- **Vicarious experience** – Visit other teachers and watch them teach. From a self-efficacy point of view, it may be particularly helpful to go and watch teachers who are newly qualified, rather than those that have been doing it for years. You may be able to see yourself in them and be encouraged.

- **Verbal persuasion** – Ask a mentor for some positive feedback and get someone in your corner who is going to tell you 'well done'. You could even write yourself some encouraging notes!

- **Emotional arousal** – Sports competitors are masters at reframing their emotional states so that their self-efficacy is not degraded and reinterpreting their performance flaws through attribution retraining. When they are nervous, they say 'pressure is a privilege', and reinterpret the butterflies as meaning their body is preparing them for the performance. As a teacher, you can do this too.

6.6 Head – cognitive theories of learning

In the UK over the past two decades, there has been an explosion in interest in the application of cognitive science principles relating to teaching and learning. While this has been a welcome corrective to some of the less well-evidenced practices of years gone by, the quality of implementation of cognitive approaches across FES remains sketchy.

Part of the reason for this is that much of the teacher-facing literature that has been produced under this banner has been aimed at secondary schools. The transfer of secondary-shaped pedagogy into FES – where there is less uniformity of context – is not straightforward and poses a significant challenge to practice in our sector. This section explores the value of grappling with cognitive theories of learning for teachers in the FES sector but – in response to the challenge of application – will continually press you to think carefully about how this could look in your context.

Given the utility, wide applicability and robust evidence base of cognitive theories of learning, this section will be the longest in this chapter.

Working memory models

An understanding of human cognitive architecture underpins all the cognitive theories in this section. But before we get into these models and theories we should establish the boundaries of what we are talking about. Knowledge can be categorised according to the way it is learned; Geary (2005) suggests that some knowledge is 'biologically primary' and some is 'biologically secondary'. Our biology as humans structures us to learn some things from the environment around us with little or no effort and without instruction. This includes native language acquisition and facial recognition.

Sadly, experience confirms that we cannot learn everything the same way that we learned to walk, recognise our family members or speak our native language. Most of the learning that takes place in schools and colleges is 'biologically secondary' and, as such, takes considerable mental effort. But why is this? Willingham's simple memory model (2009) is a good place to start.

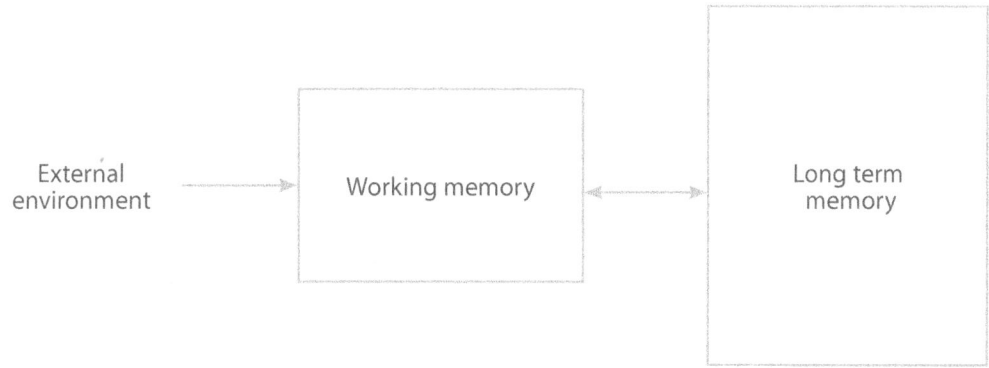

Figure 6.7 *Willingham's simple memory model*

We perceive our external environment with our senses and attend to the features of this environment, which are passed to the working memory. Working memory is synonymous with consciousness; that is, if you are conscious of it, you are processing it in your working memory. A prerequisite for learning is focusing your attention on the selected features of the external environment that you wish to learn. A teacher's job is, in the first instance, to ensure their learners are consciously attending to the to-be-learned material that is under instruction. You can't learn something subconsciously; you must think. As Willingham (2009) says, 'memory is the residue of thought'.

The long-term Memory is the second feature of the human mind in this model, and it is here where the 'residue of thought' is found and where we 'store' our learning. The theories addressed below outline how all this works.

Having laid the foundation with Willingham's simple working memory model, the remainder of this section has been divided into two. The first set of theories and concepts relate to how our learners encode novel learning from working memory into their long-term memory, and the second set relate to how our learners retrieve prior learning from long-term memory into working memory. Crudely, we begin with how stuff goes in and then look at how stuff comes back out again. We begin with cognitive load theory (CLT) and multimedia theories. Then, we will outline and apply theories of retrieval practice and generative learning before concluding this section by addressing several metacognitive approaches to learning.

Cognitive load theory

Sweller's CLT is arguably the most influential educational psychology theory of the past 20 years in the UK and is, in educationalist Dylan Wiliam's estimation, 'the single most important thing for teachers to know' (Wiliam, 2017).

CLT builds on the work of Baddeley and Hitch (1974), with acknowledgement that the working memory – when learning biologically secondary information – is limited in both capacity and duration. Working memory capacity is limited to processing around three or four novel elements at a time (Cowan, 2005), and working memory duration is also severely limited (Barrouillet and Camos, 2012). As soon as attention is moved away from whatever you are thinking about, that 'memory trace' begins to decay, and this decay takes 'a few seconds' (Atkinson, Allen and Waterman, 2021). In addition to this, the already limited working memory suffers from depletion when cognitive effort is expended on similar concepts or ideas for a prolonged period (Chen et al, 2018).

While the exact limits of capacity and duration are disputed there is unanimity that the limitations are substantial and educationally significant. These constraints are a fundamental reason why we find it hard to learn new things. Importantly for teachers and lecturers in FES, research shows that while our working memory does develop continuously during childhood, it typically reaches adult levels between the ages of 14 and 15 (Gathercole et al, 2004).

CLT's name comes from the idea that whatever we are thinking about exerts a 'load' on our mental resources. Put simply, there are some ideas, concepts and skills that are 'weightier' than others – they take more effort to process and can be said to induce greater cognitive load (Reif, 2010).

As far as teaching and learning is concerned, there are two components to cognitive load for you to be aware of. Intrinsic load is the term given to the processing effort required to make sense of the taught content – the target knowledge, skill or behaviour. This is the stuff you want your learners to learn. The second component is called extraneous load and is the cognitive effort required to carry out the learning task. The task itself may be a worksheet, a demonstration, a peer discussion or any number of activities, each of which induces a load. The intrinsic and extraneous loads together make up the overall cognitive load.

Think of cognitive load as if it were a parcel. The weight of the parcel is the sum of the weight of the packaging and the weight of its contents. The purpose of the packaging is merely to deliver the contents; it needs to be robust enough to carry the contents to the recipient, but if it is unduly heavy or unnecessarily large it will cost more to send, making the process inefficient. Intrinsic load is like the contents of the parcel, representing the learning that you are trying to deliver to the long-term memory of your learner. Extraneous load is represented by the packaging; it is necessary, but it is important not to allow it to become unduly cumbersome or inefficient.

There are several ways to fall foul of the working memory's finite capacity. In figure 6.8 below, the first two tasks are both overloading the working memory of the learner. In task 1, the content is simply too complex for the learner at this point of their learning journey. Even though the task itself is simple, the difficulty inherent in the content means that the learner is overloaded. Task 2 is more careless on the teacher's behalf; the content is pitched at a level that the learner could understand but the task is too complex. Perhaps the task contained too many steps, or perhaps when the teacher explained it they used vocabulary that the learner did not understand; whatever the reason, the learner's processing capacity is exceeded. Wong et al. (2020) remind us that 'a situation where a learner is faced with high extraneous and intrinsic load simultaneously must be avoided at all costs.'

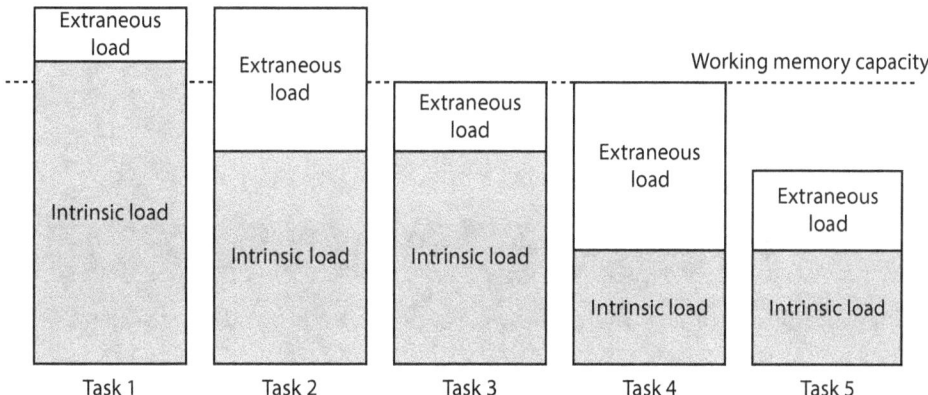

Figure 6.8 *Intrinsic and extraneous load*

Tasks 3 and 4 both make use of the full capacity of working memory without exceeding it, and for this learner the experience will be one of working hard but with a good chance of success. Task 3 is preferable to task 4 because the balance between intrinsic and extraneous load means more of the target learning is taking place.

Task 5 is extremely inefficient. To have so much working memory capacity available but unused is a risk – the task is likely to be so easy for the learner that they may well lose interest. Plus, when you have a packed curriculum to get through, there is little time to waste with such inefficient teaching.

Determining the likely cognitive load of a task is not easy. While the number of elements of information to be processed is worth considering, Sweller et al (2011) argue that for teachers the exact limit of novel elements is 'probably irrelevant' and that a more essential contributing factor to the load induced is the element interactivity of the novel ideas being processed in the working memory (Chen, Paas and Sweller, 2023). Element interactivity describes the extent to which to-be-learned elements depend on each other for processing; the greater the element interactivity, the more load is induced. For example, learning a range of isolated facts (such as the names of car engine parts) induces a lower cognitive load than learning about how those same parts of a car engine work together.

Tip for Teaching

Manage the cognitive load of tasks by reducing extraneous load and optimising intrinsic load.

If you are teaching something that you suspect your learners will find complex or difficult, consider first how you could present the content in smaller chunks. After this, think about how you could 'package' the task in as straightforward a structure as possible and pay close attention to the clarity of your instruction. Simple tasks with few steps are best.

If you want to introduce more complex, multi-step tasks, consider reusing a bank of task strategies and increase the complexity of the content slowly. This way, as learners become familiar with the task strategy, it will induce less of a load. For example, if you are using a carousel activity for the first time, it makes sense to use a simple version first until learners get used to what is happening. Then next time you can provide them with more complex content

Tip for Teaching

Reduce the complexity of new material by carefully chunking and sequencing tasks

Hopefully it is obvious that presenting too much information in one go makes learning difficult for your learners and you should avoid doing so. But element interactivity is a more fundamental concern when it comes to teaching knowledge, skills or behaviours that are new to your learners. Consider chunking your lessons not solely based on the volume of material you are teaching but on its complexity.

Discerning the complexity of material that you, as a subject expert, have already mastered is itself difficult, but this is where discussions with other teachers of your subject are crucial. Talk to expert colleagues about their experiences of teaching your subject. Exam boards and awarding organisations routinely publish examiners' reports (sometimes called external verifier or standards verifier reports) and reading back through previous versions of these may also help build a picture of where your subject's complexities lie. If you can identify common misconceptions or concepts and ideas that are critical for later learning, you can focus your attention on how you will teach that material.

This all seems rather inefficient. If working memory is so limited, it creates something of a bottleneck between the environment and the long-term memory. Given these constraints, how do we as humans ever go beyond simple factual recall and on to comparison, analysis and even creativity? CLT has an answer, and it involves the function of the long-term memory.

The long-term memory store is, in theory, infinite. While we have some good ideas about the limitations of working memory, we are not yet certain of the limits of long-term memory. For a teacher, it makes sense to conceive of the long-term memory as being functionally unlimited. This is great news for teachers and learners because of how items retrieved from the long-term memory interact with novel information in the working memory.

The simplest way to explain this distinction is that when information is new to us it exerts a load on our working memory, but when it is familiar and well-learned it does not. Sweller, van Merrienboer and Paas (2019) argue that:

> *Working memory was limited in capacity and duration when dealing with novel information but these limitations effectively disappeared when working memory dealt with information transferred from long-term memory.*

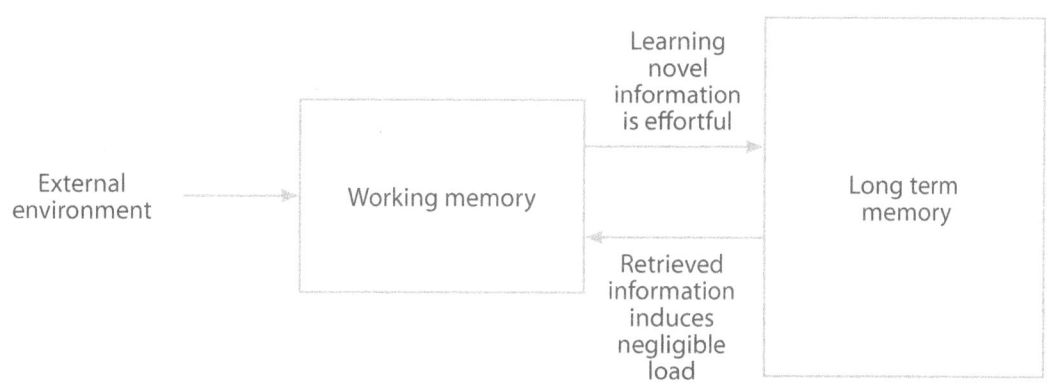

Figure 6.9 *The role of long-term memory in CLT*

Given this fact, it becomes clear that what a learner has already learned becomes a critical factor in that learners' ability to learn something new. It is axiomatic in education that, as Ausubel (1968) famously wrote: 'The most important single factor influencing learning is what the learner already knows. Ascertain this and teach him accordingly.'

The reason it is so important is that the relevant knowledge stored in long-term memory is drawn into working memory during processing of new information and acts as a kind of internal scaffold. If the learner has a wealth of existing relevant knowledge, they can use this to help them organise the novel information, meaning less cognitive load is induced. The more you know, therefore, the faster you learn; or, put another way, novice learning is slow and expert learning is fast.

> **REFLECT**
>
> Look at this list of letters. Can you make sense of them?
>
> TN TD AVEI TVBB CSK Y
>
> Now look again, but this time keep in mind that the letters relate to British television channels.
>
> Did the 'scaffold' of television channels, which was (hopefully!) drawn from your long-term memory, help you make sense of the list of letters? This is dependent on your prior knowledge of television channels, of course, but you can probably see how what you already know can help you process new material. Here are those letters again.
>
> TNT DAVE ITV BBC SKY

Crucially, since expertise is domain-specific, this effect is also domain-specific. I can be an expert in one domain (say, plumbing) and a novice in another (catering). The available prior knowledge that your learners can call upon to help them process new information is going to differ from topic to topic, not to mention learner by learner.

Tip for Teaching

When planning and delivering your lessons, keep in mind that the working memory of a novice is different to that of an expert and that within a class of learners there may be a range of prior knowledge and attainment in the topic under instruction. Be aware that what you can do with minimal cognitive effort is a result of your own learning, not necessarily because the content itself is 'easy'. Do not assume too much about your learners' levels of knowledge or understanding – I once discovered a learner of mine thought that humans had eight lungs!

Because of this 'curse of knowledge', effective initial assessment of learner starting points and existing misconceptions becomes extremely important. There are some clues that will help you predict likely starting points; for example, FES learners are typically enrolled at a particular level of course, which gives some early indication to the teacher as to their experience and knowledge in that subject. Even so, it is advisable to undertake some form of prior knowledge check with your learners before moving on to delivering new material.

If we are to accept the utility of the account of human cognition set out by CLT – and it seems sensible to do so given the extent and quality of supporting research – what other pedagogical approaches does CLT imply or predict? These predictions are known as 'effects' and can be independently tested. Some of the most well-attested effects of CLT are found in the table below, which has been adapted from Sweller, van Merriënboer and Paas (2019). You can find further effects in their article.

Effect	Description
Goal-free effect	Replace conventional tasks with goal-free tasks that provide learners with a non-specific goal.
Worked example effect	Replace conventional tasks with worked examples that provide learners with a solution that they must study carefully.
Split-attention effect	Replace multiple sources of information, distributed either in space or time, with one integrated source of information.
Redundancy effect	Replace multiple sources of information that are self-contained (i.e. they can be understood on their own) with one source of information.
Modality effect	Replace a written explanatory text and another source of visual information (unimodal) with a spoken explanatory text and the visual source of information (multimodal)
Self-explanation effect	Replace separate worked examples or completion tasks with enriched ones containing prompts, asking learners to self-explain the given information.
Expertise reversal effect	Cognitive load effects that are found for low-expertise learners (e.g. worked example effect, goal-free effect) are typically not found or even reversed for high-expertise learners.
Transient information effect	Cognitive load effects that are found for transient information are typically not found for non-transient or less transient information.

> **REFLECT**
>
> What impact could these effects have on our classroom practice? Given what you have now learned about CLT, can you propose how practices that account for these effects may be helpful?

The 'worked example effect' is one of the best-supported effects that is predicted by CLT. Using worked examples in instruction has been shown to provide an 'efficiency advantage' (Renkl, 2013) to teachers and learners, which means the same outcomes being achieved in a shorter timeframe. In one study investigating the impact of teaching using worked examples, a three-year maths curriculum was taught in two years, with the learners even producing slightly better results than learners on the standard timetable (Zhu and Simon, 1987).

When a problem that requires a specific solution is presented to learners, they must draw upon their mental resources to solve the problem while holding the solution in mind. If learners are not aware of the steps required to get them from problem to solution (because they are novices), they will tend to adopt a trial-and-error approach. Unfortunately, this is an extremely cognitively demanding and time-consuming approach to problem solving and can lead quickly to frustration and demotivation.

A worked example, by contrast, provides the solution as part of the instruction and invites learners to interrogate the steps that will help them build towards the solution. In this case, the learner's working memory resources can be wholly directed to the stages or the principles that underpin the skilled performance of the target learning without being concerned initially with the final output. As Sweller (2006) puts it: 'The probability of successful learning following a worked example is dramatically increased compared to learning following problem solving.'

There are myriad ways of using worked examples; here is a step-by-step guide along with a couple of different possible applications for FES.

Steps	Scaffold	Patisserie (catering)	Past paper question (GCSE English)
Provide or demonstrate a completed version of the task or problem.	I do…	Demonstrate how to make a chocolate éclair or show a video of the process. Show completed versions.	On the visualiser, teacher annotates a previously written paragraph in answer to a past paper question while learners take notes.
Direct learner attention to small chunks of that task or problem.		Pause during demonstration to verbalise what is being done (e.g. baking or piping). Teacher asks the learners questions to check their understanding at each step.	Teacher live writes second paragraph and narrates the process, referring to established paragraph structures and key subject terminology that learners already know.
Guide practice of small chunks prior to whole task completion.	We do…	Learners roll pastry or fill éclairs with guidance and feedback from teacher. Teacher asks, 'What is the next step?'	Teacher provides keywords and sentence starters, and learner use their notes from the model to write a paragraph in pairs.
Learners complete the task or problem independently after the worked example.	You do…	Learners produce chocolate éclairs independently using correct techniques without reminders.	Learner writes independently.

> **REFLECT**
>
> How can you make use of the worked example effect in your context? Think of a lesson you are soon to be teaching and consider whether you have already provided a worked example or can implement one to better support your learners.

A word of caution: selecting worked examples for use in your teaching requires some careful consideration. Poorly chosen examples can easily confuse learners if the features to be learned are not easily recognised in the worked example (Wesenberg et al, 2024). Ambiguity in the chosen example can increase the likelihood of learners developing misconceptions, even when teacher verbalisations try to diminish that ambiguity.

Using non-examples and incorrect solutions as worked examples – where the teacher presents and deconstructs a poor or inaccurate version of the solution – is a very effective strategy but suffers from the same issues as selecting a good example. If there is any ambiguity as to why the example is a poor example or why it is wrong, this may introduce errors into learner understanding that become difficult to remediate. For this reason, using non-examples and incorrect examples is more likely to benefit learners who are further along in their learning (Grosse and Renkl, 2006).

Tip for Teaching

Use FAME as a guide for getting the most out of your worked examples

The Education Endowment Foundation (2022) has developed the FAME approach:

- **Fading** – Remove solution steps, ideally in reverse order, when you judge that the learner is ready.
- **Alternating** – Switch between worked examples, instruction and learner practice.
- **Mistakes** – As your learners grow in competence, add mistakes into the worked examples for them to spot and solve.
- **Explanation** – Verbalise your thought processes during the worked example and then get learners to do the same when working on their own.

The 'expertise reversal effect' describes the situation by which the instructional strategies that are successful for novices become ineffective and ultimately counterproductive for learners who have developed expertise in the domain of study. You do not want learners to become reliant on the support of a scaffold – this is akin to learned helplessness. Novices will usually benefit from diagrams carefully paired with text, but once a degree of expertise is reached the text becomes redundant and using diagrams without text has been shown to be a more effective strategy (Kalyuga, Chandler and Sweller, 1998). The teacher should use sufficient scaffolding to ensure learners' working memory is not overloaded, but no more than is necessary. All scaffolding, including worked examples, can induce the expertise reversal effect.

Tip for Teaching

Fading scaffolding as learners move towards expertise

Once a learner has achieved a level of proficiency or mastery in a topic and no longer needs any external scaffolding, consider how you can fade this scaffolding and allow them to rely on their prior knowledge to manage their cognitive load.

The goal is not simply to make it harder for them, because you could do this by adding ambiguity to the task with unclear instructions. Instead, you are trying to create 'desirable difficulties' (Bjork and Bjork, 2011) for your learners by providing just the right amount of

> **Tip for Teaching (...continued)**
>
> challenge. Here are some examples:
>
> - If you have previously provided learners with sentence starters or a writing frame, remove these (or cover them up if they are on the wall).
>
> - If you have previously allowed learners to have their books in front of them during quizzes and tests, ask them to put these away.
>
> - If you have previously provided learners with worked examples, ask them to complete the task without assistance.
>
> - If you have previously allowed learners to work in pairs on a task, ask them to work individually.
>
> - If you have previously provided verbal reminders during a task that you have asked your learners to practise, refrain from giving these.

Multimedia theories

Multimedia theories take us one step further, as they describe how the learner's working memory processes information presented in differing modalities such as visual, auditory or kinaesthetic. We will look in depth at Paivio's dual coding theory (DCT) and Mayer's cognitive theory of multimedia learning (CTML).

Before moving on, it is important at this point to emphasise that it would be inaccurate to suppose that since multimedia theories use terms such as visual, auditory and kinaesthetic, they provide any support whatever for the notion of learning styles. The myth of learning styles – that each learner has an innate style of learning and a teacher will be more successful if they present all material to that learner in the specific modality of their learning style – has been repeatedly and soundly discredited (Willingham, 2018). Aside from instances where a leaner's perceptual apparatus is impaired (such as by visual or auditory impairments or processing disorders), the evidence is clear that all learners benefit from being taught using a range of modalities chosen to best convey the subject matter or skill to be learned. (The important issue of individual difference among learners is relevant to all that follows but has been discussed in greater depth in chapter 4.)

Dual coding theory (DCT)

DCT is conceptually congruent with the working memory model of Baddeley and Hitch (1974). Strictly speaking, 'dual coding' is a description of how memory traces are stored in the long-term memory when congruent information is presented to visual and verbal channels of the working memory simultaneously. In educational practice, it has come to denote a particular way of presenting information during instruction that takes account of the dual-channel structure of working memory.

Allan Paivio (1971) theorised that the working memory has two distinct but interacting channels via which information is processed in the working memory before transfer to the long-term memory. The first channel includes the visuospatial sketchpad that processes visual information and helps us makes sense of what we see (examples include charts, diagrams and colours). The visuospatial sketchpad enables us to see relationships between items literally 'at a glance'. For a teacher, the layout of slides, worksheets or posters is not inconsequential; we can help or hinder our learners' processing of visual information through careful design of resources.

The second channel includes the phonological loop, which processes sound and differs from the visuospatial sketchpad in that its processing is sequential. Your phonological loop allows subvocal rehearsal (or internal re-hearing) of sounds that you have just heard. When a teacher is speaking, a normally functioning phonological loop allows a learner to replay the teacher's words in their head.

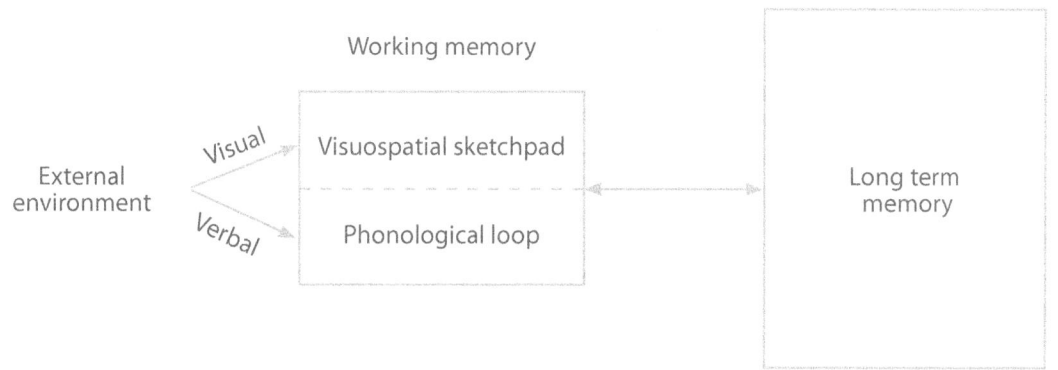

Figure 6.10 *Dual coding theory*

DCT tells us that, when the two systems are used in tandem (congruently and simultaneously) they will interact to enable more secure learning to take place. More precisely, when learning novel material via two modalities, the memory trace that is encoded into long-term memory retains a referential linkage between what was presented to the visual channel and what was presented to the verbal channel.

This referential linkage appears to provide a surprising benefit. Research by Mayer and Anderson (1992) indicates that learning via dual coded instruction not only enhances retrieval strength but also enhances the learners' ability to come up with creative solutions to unseen problems. Mayer and Anderson's research shows that of several groups taught under a range of conditions, one group outperformed all the others when asked to suggest possible creative solutions to a problem they had not previously encountered: 'on tests of creative problem solving, only the group receiving concurrent presentation of words and pictures performed better than the group receiving no instruction.' Incredibly, their findings showed that groups who had been taught the content via a single modality were unable to provide more creative solutions than the control group who had received no instruction at all!

REFLECT

Imagine another educator says to you that teaching using multiple modalities is just the same as teaching according to learning styles. How would you counter that argument?

Take it further...

Ask a colleague to read the next paragraph, and - at the same time - read it aloud to them. Then ask them the questions that follow.

The water cycle describes how water moves through the Earth and atmosphere. It includes four main stages: evaporation, where the sun heats water in rivers, lakes, or oceans and turns it into vapour; condensation, where the vapour cools and forms clouds; precipitation, where water falls as rain, snow, or hail; and collection, where water gathers back in bodies of water and the cycle starts again

- *What is the process called when water turns into vapour?*
- *During which stage does water fall as rain or snow?*

Your colleague may have struggled to answer the questions, as attempting to read and listen to you read to them utilises the same verbal channels to their working memory: you speaking to them and their inner voice as they read.

Now try again where you read the above passage to them, but they are only to look at the visual below.

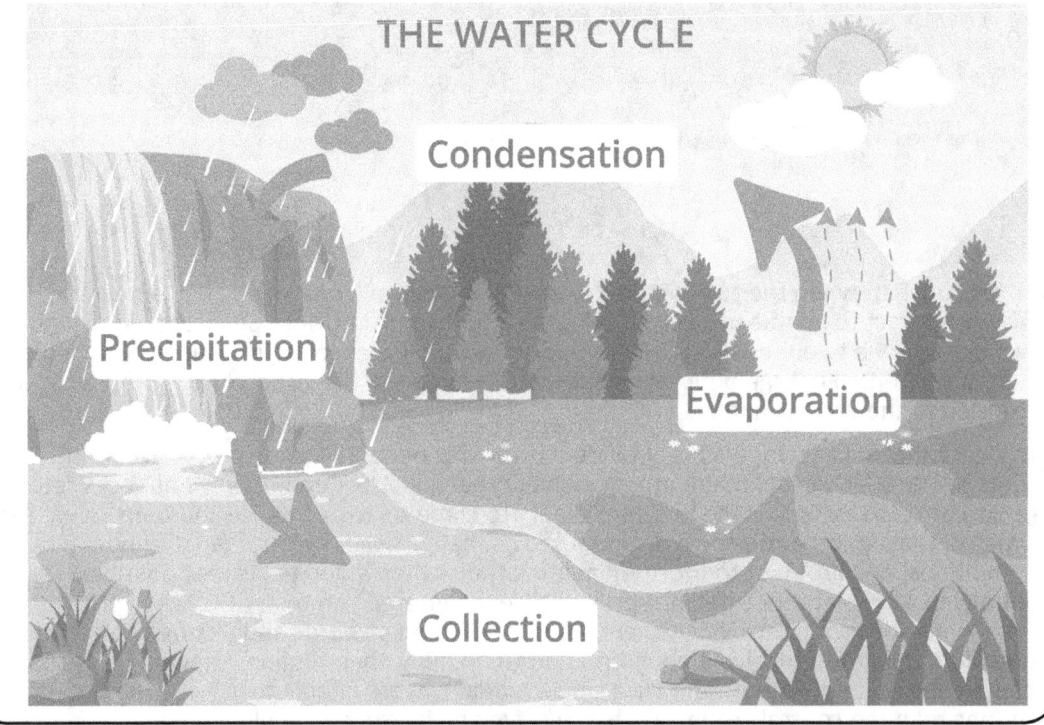

DCT suggests that it is the thoughtful pairing of verbal and visual instruction that enables learners to excel in problem solving and creativity. But beware: a poorly constructed visual or a lack of congruence between text and visual can increase cognitive load and cause learners to miss out on the benefits inherent in 'dual coded' instruction.

> **Tip for Teaching**
>
> **Avoid the selective interference effect**
>
> One effect that is supported by DCT is the selective interference effect. Simply, your learners cannot complete two simultaneous tasks if they are in just one 'code' or channel (visual or verbal). As soon as learners are asked to perform simultaneous tasks in the same 'code' their performance decreases due to overloading of that channel. For example, if you place text on the whiteboard or screen at the front of the room, learners will typically begin to read it, creating subvocal rehearsal (reading it in their heads). If you then begin giving verbal instructions, which also utilise the verbal channel, the learners are unable to process those simultaneously and will have to select one or the other of those inputs for their attention.
>
> You could solve this problem when presenting new information to a class by minimising the number of words on your teaching slides and using a hide and reveal function to bring up only those words you want learners to read at any point in the lesson. Another way of solving the problem of overloading a single channel is to replace words with diagrams so that your speech can be processed by the learner's verbal channel while the learner processes the diagram via their visual channel.
>
> A step-by-step teacher demonstration where you verbalise your thought processes makes effective use of the dual channel structure of working memory. This kind of demonstration is the bread and butter of teaching for technical and vocational subjects, and its efficacy is backed by solid research evidence.

Cognitive theory of multimedia learning

A second relevant multimedia theory is Richard Mayer's CTML (2005). CTML rests on three assumptions. The first two – that working memory is limited in capacity and working memory is divided into visual and verbal channels – have already been described. Mayer's third assumption is that learners actively try to make sense of the taught material by processing, organising and finally integrating it with their existing understanding. He called this the 'active processing assumption'.

Mayer proposed a three-step process by which learners actively process the contents of their working memory – learners must select, organise, and integrate (SOI). In this SOI framework, learners would need to select from among the many sensory inputs that are being drawn continuously into their consciousness. Having done so, they must focus on the selected information – hopefully these are relevant to the learning aims of the session! Then, with those elements in working memory, a learner will actively attempt to organise, categorise and order them, linking them to one another and to relevant prior learning. After integrating old and new learning, the learner passes these newly augmented mental representations and knowledge structures into long-term memory for storage.

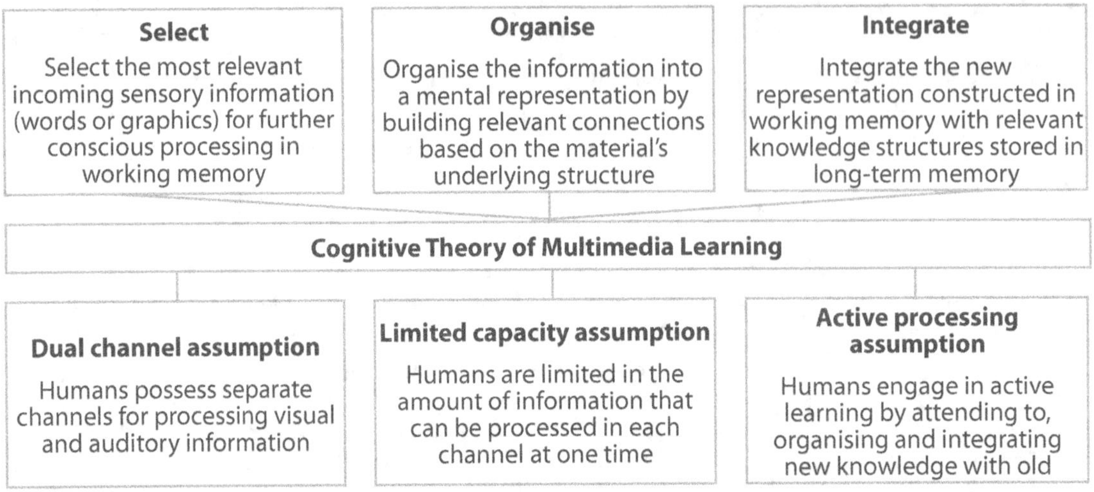

Cognitive Theory of Multimedia Learning

Select
Select the most relevant incoming sensory information (words or graphics) for further conscious processing in working memory

Organise
Organise the information into a mental representation by building relevant connections based on the material's underlying structure

Integrate
Integrate the new representation constructed in working memory with relevant knowledge structures stored in long-term memory

Dual channel assumption
Humans possess separate channels for processing visual and auditory information

Limited capacity assumption
Humans are limited in the amount of information that can be processed in each channel at one time

Active processing assumption
Humans engage in active learning by attending to, organising and integrating new knowledge with old

Figure 6.11 *Mayer's cognitive theory of multimedia learning*

Tip for Teaching

Help your learners to select, organise and integrate information into long-term memory

Hopefully they will get better at it, but initially guiding learner attention helps them to select the relevant information that you want them to learn. You can guide their attention in many ways, but perhaps the most helpful tip is to strip away all extraneous features of your teaching environment and process so that distractions are kept to a minimum. Clear away any clutter in the learning environment and streamline your slides, resources and explanations. We discuss more about how to do this with Mayer's 12 instructional principles below.

Organising information happens in the learner's working memory. Providing scaffolds for learners that reveal the underlying structure of the material you want them to learn. This may include using drawing diagrams to show relationships, tables to reveal comparisons, teaching mnemonics, acronyms and acrostics to outline multi-step processes. Diagrams are particularly helpful as they can not only be used to reveal relationships between concepts, but – as we have learned in the previous section – benefit from the advantages of dual coding. In our own teaching, we have used a single diagram as the basis for an entire lesson. The shell of the diagram can be shared with learners initially, and they can fill the blanks, add their own notes and be invited to verbalise their developing understanding as the lesson progresses.

Mayer has developed 12 principles that are of relevance to teachers, which are summarised in figure 6.12.

Some of Mayer's principles relate specifically to on-screen teaching, and these will be of use to teachers who teach via online learning platforms. The principles can be grouped according to their intention. The first five principles focus on reducing inefficiency in the presentation of information to a learner, reducing the need for processing of extraneous information. The next three principles focus on helping learners organise and integrate their new learning.

1. Coherence principle	2. Signalling principle	3. Redundancy principle
Exclude extraneous material	Highlight the organisation of the essential material	Use graphics and narration, not graphics, narration and printed text
4. Spatial contiguity principle	5. Temporal contiguity principle	6. Segmenting principle
Place words and pictures near each other on the page or screen	Present corresponding words and pictures at the same time	Present learning in user-paced segments not as a continuous unit
7. Pre-training principle	8. Modality principle	9. Multimedia principle
Give pre-training in the names and characteristics of key components	Use graphics and narration, not graphics and printed text	Use words and pictures, not just words
10. Personalisation principle	11. Voice principle	12. Image principle
Use a conversational rather than a formal style	Speak in a friendly human voice and avoid using a machine voice	Your image does not need to be on screen

Figure 6.12 *Mayer's 12 multimedia instructional principles*

The final four principles relate predominantly to online teaching and are relatively self-explanatory. Here, we pick out a few that are most relevant for the widest range of teaching environments. Let us look at the coherence, signalling and contiguity principles.

The coherence principle ('exclude extraneous material') is, in our view, the most neglected of the group. Given the fragility of the human attention span and the myriads of distractions that bombard our learners even in their classrooms, the importance of removing unnecessary content from slides, handouts, workbooks, explanations and classrooms is difficult to overstate. We have already discussed the need for learners to select relevant information to pass into their limited working memory. Teachers can help their learners out by not making this step harder than it needs to be – if it is not essential, cut it out!

The signalling principle ('highlight the organisation of the essential material') is the second of the 12 principles that we think is of particular importance. As Fiorella and Mayer (2015a) have shown, the more effectively learners can actively generate links and connections between the material in their working memory, the more efficiently and meaningfully they will be able to integrate their new learning with their existing knowledge framework. Signalling does include pointing at things that learners should be attending to while you speak, such as a component of a car engine or a part of a reptile, but it is a wider principle. Signalling also means showing learners – whether verbally or visually – how the ideas they are contemplating relate to each other and to their prior knowledge. Diagrams are extremely useful for this but must be carefully constructed to avoid introducing misconceptions about how ideas, processes and actions are internally structured or relate to each other.

A grasp of the two contiguity principles will help a teacher bring together some of the key aspects of dual coding and the CTML. The spatial contiguity principle recommends presenting corresponding words and pictures near each other in space, such as on screen or on handouts. For example, if you are teaching with a labelled diagram, try to place the labels close to the thing they label rather than expecting a reader to move their eyes from label to diagram and back again (this switching induces unnecessary cognitive load).

Also, when the teacher is speaking, they should be speaking about whatever the learners are being directed to look at. The temporal contiguity principle suggests avoiding placing a picture or diagram on the board and then speaking about something else. Your learners' working memories are trying to make connections – help them out!

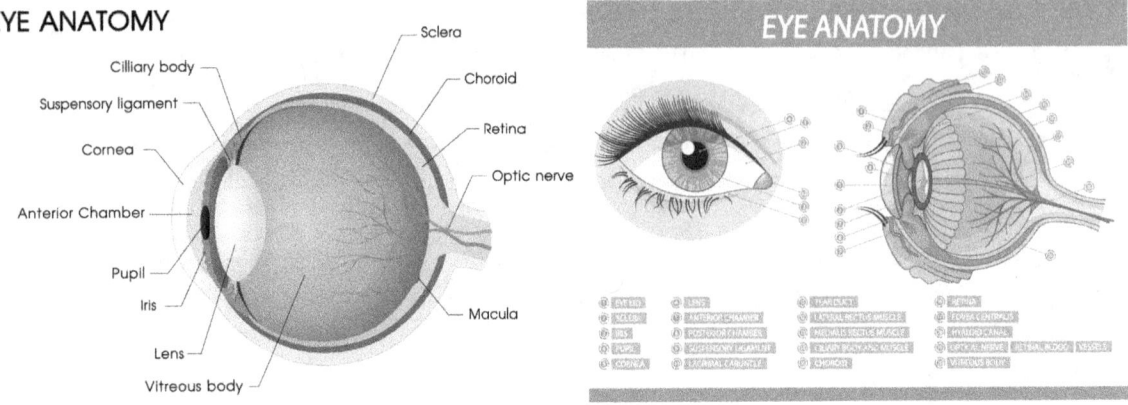

Figure 6.13 *Examples of good (left) and poor (right) spatial contiguity*

Tip for Teaching

Use Oliver Caviglioli's design guide

Caviglioli (2019) has provided a helpful practical synthesis of these concepts for teachers. He suggests that there are four simple things to bear in mind when designing resources, whether they are slides, handouts, booklets or anything else you plan to give to your learners as a learning stimulus. These key principles are cut, chunk, align and restrain.

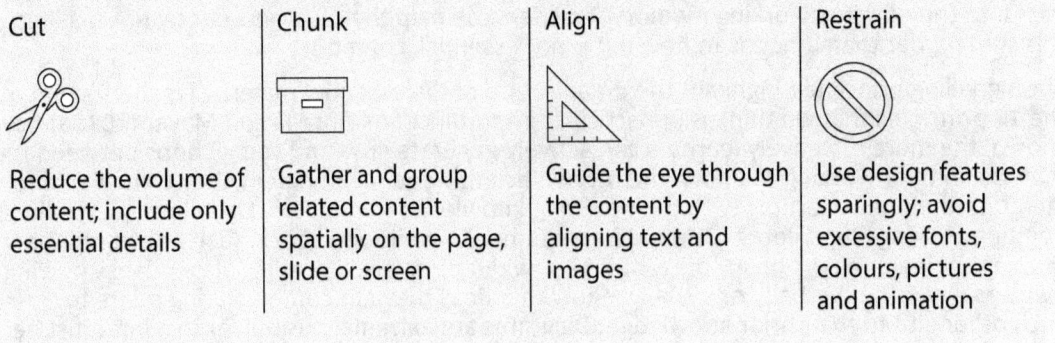

Cut	Chunk	Align	Restrain
Reduce the volume of content; include only essential details	Gather and group related content spatially on the page, slide or screen	Guide the eye through the content by aligning text and images	Use design features sparingly; avoid excessive fonts, colours, pictures and animation

REFLECT

Look at the slide at the top of the next page. Using what you have understood from the sections above, try to explain what design changes you could make to the slide for use in a teaching environment.

Design Principles

CUT
Reduce how much content there is on the slide by only including all the essential details and leaving out anything that is not necessary or does not help make the point you are trying to make.

Chunk
Gather and group related content spatially on the page, slide or screen

Align
Guide the eye through content by aligning text and images

Restrain
Use design features sparingly; avoid excessive fonts, colours, pictures and animations

> **Take it further...**
> The reflect task has been presented with the assumption that the learners are neurotypical and have no impairments to their visual or auditory processes. How would you consider the above research to support neurodiverse learners? How would you consider the above in supporting learners with visual or hearing impairments?

Retrieval practice

So far in this cognitive theories of learning section, we have focused on how an understanding of human cognitive architecture helps us to get novel information 'in' to our learners (encoding), but learning is as much about retrieval as it is encoding. In fact, as alluded to in the schemas section in chapter 5 (see page 122), retrieval is the whole point of encoding. There is little reason to learn something if you cannot remember it when it is needed.

We want our learners to be more proficient at recalling what they have previously learned, so it should encourage us that practicing retrieval improves retrieval. In chapter 5, we discussed planning for retrieval opportunities in the curriculum, so here we will focus on 'why' and 'how' retrieval practice should be built into your learners' lessons.

Why is retrieval practice so important? Retrieval practice is not primarily a formative assessment tool (Agarwal et al, 2020), although there may be some formative inferences that can be made from your learners' retrieval practice outputs. Instead, retrieval practice should be thought of as a learning event that takes advantage of the testing effect (Roediger and Karpicke, 2006) as well as a means by which we can activate the prior knowledge of a learner.

The testing effect is a simple but important benefit of retrieval practice. When we ask our learners to retrieve prior learning from their long-term memory, this search of long-term memory for responses has the effect of strengthening the neural connections that were laid down in the encoding process during acquisition. In fact, Roediger and Karpicke (2006) showed that testing improves long-term retention more effectively than re-studying.

Regular opportunities to retrieve previously learned ideas, skills and behaviours secure these in long-term memory by increasing both the retrieval strength (how easily something is recalled) and the storage strength (how durable or secure that memory is). What is more, the testing effect has been shown to be independent of cognitive ability – all learners at all levels benefit from the testing effect (Jonsson et al, 2020), and so all learners at all levels should be practicing retrieval.

A second important benefit of retrieval practice is its value in activating prior learning. When our learners are asked to recall something that will be of use to them in the lesson, they are activating their prior learning. Bringing previously learned skills and knowledge back into working memory prior to the presentation of new material helps learners make connections and strengthen the related schema. A simple way to conceive of this is that retrieval practice makes the relevant schemas 'sticky', and so new knowledge is more readily incorporated into existing knowledge.

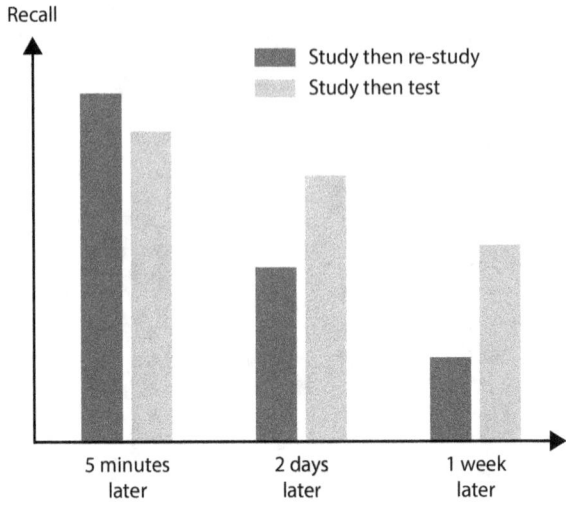

Figure 6.14 *Effects of testing and re-studying on long-term memory*

Tip for Teaching

Rather than randomly selecting previous taught content for your learners to review, think carefully about what prior learning could reinforce the new learning and ask learners to complete retrieval practice of those ideas.

For example, in an art class, if you are going to be teaching about complementary colour theory for the first time, you will want to activate your learners' prior understanding of colour fundamentals (primary colours, colour wheel relationships) and perhaps some of the colour terminology (hue, saturation, value) and visual principles (contrast, harmony) that will help them access the examples of complementary colour applications that you will be using later in the lesson.

When selecting or designing retrieval practice activities for your learners, consider whether you want to use free recall or cued recall. Free recall is where you give learners a topic and ask them to recall (usually by writing down) everything they can about that topic (this is sometimes called a brain dump). Free recall allows learners to review previously learned content but also forces them to engage with the organisation of that knowledge in their schemas (Zaromb and Roediger, 2010). This approach can have motivational benefits as it does not exclude those who have minimal prior learning to draw on. It may also be a helpful strategy to develop some curiosity in a new topic, although this is not a benefit derived specifically from the testing effect.

Cued recall is another useful way of doing retrieval practice. A 'cue' is anything that assists a learner in retrieving information that due to low retrieval strength could not otherwise be retrieved. An example of this may be using meaningful icons next to empty text boxes that learners are required to fill out. Including the first letter of an answer or supplying some other contextual information may also serve as a cue. Typically, the cue should have been present in the initial learning event, so that it was stored alongside – or in the same schema as – the knowledge you are trying to retrieve. This is called the encoding specificity principle (Tulving and Thompson, 1973).

If you have produced resources using the dual coding principles above, you will probably have lots of ready-made cued recall activities. You could use a knowledge organiser during instruction in a lesson, and then for the following lesson starter simply delete the words, provide learners with the images and see how much they can recall using those images as cues. A presentation slide can be cleared of text, printed out and used in the same way, or it could be as simple as the three tables below, which fade the scaffolding and can be used in subsequent lessons as distributed practice. The intention ultimately is to strengthen retrieval to the extent that the cues are no longer required.

Retrieval 1

Type of bone	Function	Example
L	Leverage and red blood cell production	
S	Weight bearing	
F	Protection	
S	Reducing friction across a joint, embedded in a tendon	
I	Individualised functions	

Retrieval 2

Type of bone	Function	Example
L		
S		
F		
S		
I		

Retrieval 3

Type of bone	Function	Example

Other examples of tasks that could incorporate retrieval practice include quizzes, self-explanations, elaborative interrogation, summarising, flashcards, mapping and matching tasks. (You will find guidelines for effective design of multiple-choice questions (MCQs) in chapter 7.)

Whatever method you choose, the key is to set up the task in such a way that a learner's working memory is being supplied with items from their own long-term memory and not some other source. Normally this is best achieved when retrieval practice is done individually and without notes. While there are many benefits of paired and group work, there is a greater risk that learners can 'get the right answer' without having to go through processes that will strengthen their ability to remember the 'right answer'.

> **REFLECT**
>
> How could you set up and manage a paired retrieval practice activity without losing the key element of retrieval from long-term memory?

We have already established that retrieval practice should be considered as a learning event rather than as a formative assessment opportunity, but it is well worth your time to check learners' answers so that you can identify any misconceptions that learners have about their learning (Kang et al, 2007). It may be that you spot some inaccuracies in their recall that mean re-teaching is warranted.

Generative learning

Generative learning describes the way in which learners make sense of what they are learning by incorporating it into their existing understanding. This process does not happen by default (Fiorella, 2023) and the learner must be prompted (usually by the teacher) to engage in some of organisation and integration of the topic at hand. Fiorella has categorised generative learning activities (GLAs) into three sense-making modes: explaining, visualising and enacting.

'Explaining' relates to generating coherent verbal statements about what is being learned. These statements can be written or spoken and may or may not be shared with another learner or with the teacher. Learning by teaching a topic to a real or imagined other is a good example of an explaining GLA. The intention of this type of GLA is for the learner to create generalisations about the topic that can be transferred into new situations and contexts.

'Visualising' relates to generating coherent images and diagrams that display how an idea is structured, such as how the parts of an idea relate to its whole or how concepts can be placed in hierarchy or sequence. A visualising GLA could be some form of drawing, mapping or imagining. This type of GLA supports the learner to categorise their knowledge by considering its internal links and relationships.

'Enacting' describes an activity that requires the learner to generate coherent movement to represent relationships in the to be learned materials, whether physical or conceptual. Interestingly, enacting can include imagined movement, where learners visualise moving objects or their own bodies to represent key ideas. Learners could also be asked to use manipulatives (physical objects that can be moved around) to demonstrate their thinking.

Tip for Teaching

Fiorella and Mayer (2015b) have suggested eight strategies for generative learning. Whichever strategies you choose, your learners will need to be taught how to do each one and then supported as they have a go. Some are harder to master than others, so teacher modelling will be very helpful.

- **Summarising** – Create a written or oral summary of the material. This is best used for learning from short text passages with relatively simple concepts or concepts that are not highly spatial. Highly spatial concepts would be better taught using visualising or enacting strategies.
- **Mapping** – Create a concept map, knowledge map or graphic organiser. It may take learners some time to learn how to do this well, but it is very effective in learning from explanatory text passages.
- **Drawing** – Create a drawing that depicts the text. Instruction should be very specific about what to draw and the elements to be drawn should be simple enough (perhaps even copied from the board or the margin of the worksheet).
- **Imagining** – Imagine a drawing that depicts the text. Currently less well evidenced but shows promise as an effective strategy when implemented carefully. As with drawing there should be clear prompting for learners as to what they should be imagining.
- **Self-testing** – Give yourself a practice test of the material. Useful for both simple factual recall and more complex conceptual recall. Self-testing is one of the GLAs that has strong support for its utility right across the age range (Brod, 2020), probably because it takes very little training for learners to learn how to use this strategy.
- **Self-explaining** – Create a written or oral explanation of the material. This is a well-supported strategy that is particularly helpful for making sense of conceptually difficult material.
- **Teaching** – Explain the material to others. Much of the benefit of this strategy comes from the expectation that you will later have to explain your learning to someone else rather than the actual act of teaching someone else (which also has some benefit, of course). Tell your learners in advance that this is what they will be doing.
- **Enacting** – Move objects to act out the material. This unique strategy has a growing support, but learners will need help to identify gestures, movements and manipulation of objects that represent underlying concepts.

Here is the good news for FES: generative learning strategies appear to be increasingly effective as learners get closer to university age (Brod, 2020). It seems likely that this is due to the increased prior knowledge held in dense, interconnected schemas, but this is not something to be taken for granted. It remains important to assess the prior knowledge of learners before we begin to teach them and to check for understanding regularly.

When should GLAs be deployed? Given the value of generative learning, these strategies can and should be deployed often. Fiorella provides us with a summary table on the next page.

Timing	Purpose	Function	Example
Before instruction	Preparatory activity	Knowledge activation	Generating predictions prior to a demonstration
During instruction	Sense-making activity	Knowledge construction	Creating drawing from a provided science text
After instruction	Retrieval activity	Knowledge consolidation	Writing an explanation after each part of a video lesson

> **REFLECT**
>
> How could you use digital tools to set and manage both GLAs and retrieval practice activities for your learners? What tools are available? If you are not sure, ask your mentor and teaching peers.

Shimamura's MARGE revisited

We return briefly to the last three letters of Shimamura's MARGE acronym – relate, generate and evaluate – to consolidate what we now know about both retrieval practice and generative learning and to introduce the importance of learner self-evaluation.

In MARGE, R stands for 'relate'. To build schemas – interconnected and organised webs of knowledge – in long-term memory, learners must integrate new and existing knowledge by linking them together. This linking, or 'relational binding', taking place is, according to Shimamura (2018), 'as important as the new information itself.' Organising our knowledge during learning helps encode it into more easily retrievable schemas.

This clustering or chunking reminds us of the organising step of Mayer's SOI model. Shimamura suggests that to provoke this process we should consider how we can get our learners to do three things: categorise, compare and contrast – the three Cs. There are lots of ways of achieving this, but here are some that Shimamura recommends:

- **Devise acronyms** – Use a word (e.g. MARGE) as cued recall for related ideas (useful for lists).
- **Develop visual images** – Link concepts by imaging a picture containing both.
- **Elaborative interrogation** – Generate questions about your learning by asking why or how.
- **Mental imagery (still or moving)** – You could imagine your own documentary on the topic.
- **Metaphors and analogies** – Identify things you already know that are like the new learning.

- **Draw schematic representations** – Produce hierarchical outlines or concept maps to show how new ideas relate to one another and to others you already know.

A note: Shimamura recognises the first two can be helpful for recall of facts where there are 'arbitrary associations' between the elements being learned – like the low-element interactivity concept of CLT – but that most learning aims for much more than factual recall. Shimamura goes on to offer recommendations 3–6 more useful for the integration required to ensure lasting and productive learning.

Tip for Teaching

Consider when you could use these different types of schematic representations to assist your learners in categorising, comparing and contrasting their understanding of a concept.

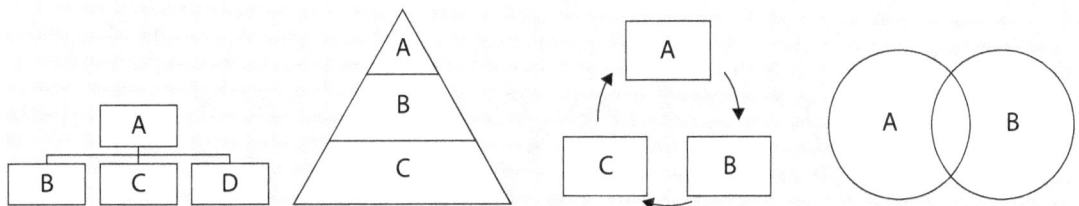

For example, in business studies you could ask your learners to use their prior knowledge to generate comparisons and contrasts between two businesses using a Venn diagram.

- Which concepts from your subject lend themselves to being organised in each of these ways?
- Which of these could you use to help your learners generate one or more of the three Cs?

For other types of schematics and how to use them, see Caviglioli and Goodwin (2021).

G stands for 'generate'. Shimamura agrees with Fiorella and Mayer (2015) that memory consolidation is best achieved when our learners are asked to do something with what they have learned. Shimamura (2018) says that the 'key to long-lasting memories is the reactivation and elaboration of pertinent information after initial learning.' In using our knowledge and repeatedly pressing it into service, we become proficient in its use, just as we do when using a tool such as a mortar board, keyboard or skateboard. This proficiency then enables us to repurpose our knowledge in different scenarios or contexts. This is known as 'transfer' and is the essential ingredient of creative thinking required for problem solving.

'Evaluate' is the final concept in Shimamura's MARGE acronym. Shimamura suggests that to get beyond the 'illusion of knowing' – where we think we have learned something but in fact we have not – learners should use a range of strategies to evaluate both the accuracy and durability of their own learning; this way, they will know whether their assumptions about what they know match up with the reality! It is easier to build up a personal picture of what you do and don't know if you are regularly engaged in self-testing.

Shimamura recommends delaying a test for a period after the initial learning event, using generative activities to check what you have forgotten, interleaving retrieval by mixing up topics being tested and repeating the tests several times.

> **REFLECT**
>
> Reflect: Evaluate your learning so far through using elaborative interrogation.
>
> For each of the methods Shimamura recommends above, use theories and concepts already covered in this textbook to explain why he recommends them. What gaps in your understanding have you just uncovered? What do you need to go back and revisit? Perhaps you could use some of Shimamura's strategies yourself!

Metacognitive approaches

Metacognition is typically described as 'thinking about thinking' (Mahdavi 2014), and there is a growing literature focusing on the value of engaging learners in metacognitive activities as part of their learning. Perry et al (2018) report that there is 'strong evidence' of metacognition's 'very positive effect on pupil outcomes' and Veenman et al (2004) showed that metacognitive ability is a strong predictor of learning. The Education Endowment Foundation (2021) report that across secondary and primary schools explicit teaching of metacognitive strategies is 'worth the equivalent of an additional seven months' progress when used well.'

Nelson and Narens's (1990) model of metacognition proposes a relationship between cognition – the thinking our learners do about a topic – and metacognition – our learners'

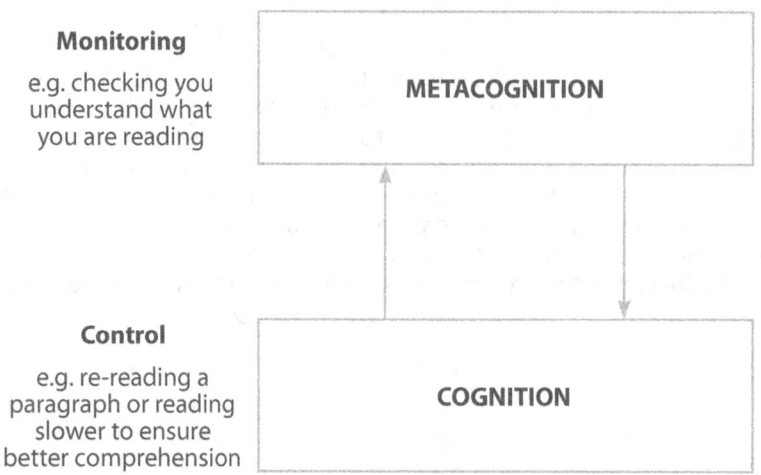

Figure 6.15 *Nelson and Narens' model of metacognition*

thinking about effective cognitive strategies and how to implement them. During a learning task we may find ourselves monitoring our own developing understanding, asking interrogative questions such as 'what have I understood?' or 'do I need to re-read that paragraph?' The answers to these self-posed metacognitive questions may then inform the next steps in our cognition. We may select a new cognitive strategy such as re-reading, drawing a diagram or verbalising our understanding to a peer; when we then deploy that strategy, we are taking control of our cognition.

> **Tip for Teaching**
>
> After you have set a task or activity, pair up your learners and ask them to discuss, 'How am I going to tackle this task', or 'What strategies could I use to do this well?' This will require them to think metacognitively.

Let us take this a step deeper. There are two aspects of metacognition that help us to monitor and control our cognition: metacognitive knowledge and metacognitive regulation (Flavell, 1976; Jacobs and Paris, 1987). Metacognitive knowledge refers to what a learner knows about different types of learning task, available cognitive strategies and themselves as learners. This metacognitive knowledge exists in the long-term memory and provides a store of strategies and approaches from which the learner can select.

Once a learner has been presented with a learning task, metacognitive regulation begins. This can be seen as the application of metacognitive knowledge. Based on their understanding of the learning task, a learner plans, monitors and evaluates their use of cognitive tools as they try to arrive at an understanding of the material. Planning includes selecting from among the cognitive strategies they have in their metacognitive knowledge, and monitoring happens during the learning task where the learners assess their use of the cognitive tool (they may change their chosen tool or technique according to their level of success in the task). Finally, once the learning task is complete, the learner will evaluate their use of the tool and update their metacognitive knowledge.

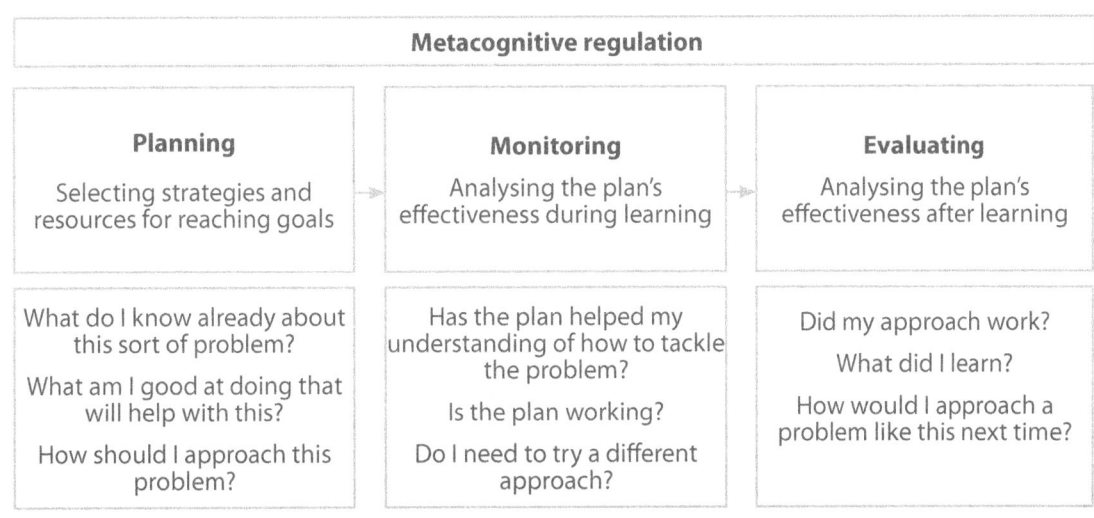

Figure 6.16 *Metacognitive regulation*

> **REFLECT**
>
> Metacognitive strategies are the tools in the toolshed, while metacognitive regulation is how you use the tool. Just as with a saw, hammer or sander, the tools themselves can be put to multiple uses but are designed to assist with specific types of tasks. You could try to use a hammer to cut wood, but this would be inefficient to say the least. The ability to select the right cognitive tool for the job is part of metacognitive regulation.
>
> What metacognitive tools do you possess? Let us investigate your own metacognitive regulation by trying a calculation. Try to work out 53 x 145, and think about these questions as you do so:
>
> - Plan
>   * Which cognitive strategies for calculations are you good at using?
>   * Which strategies could be helpful here?
>   * Which strategy will you try first?
>   * Will you need any physical resources?
> - Monitor
>   * Are you aware of how you are getting on?
>   * Are you finding it easy or hard, and can you say why?
>   * Have you had to change strategy?
>   * What new strategy did you try?
> - Evaluate
>   * Will you use the same strategy next time?
>   * What were the difficulties in using the strategy you chose?

To some extent, metacognitive regulation happens automatically in all our learners. But there is evidence to suggest that teaching learners a range of subject-appropriate metacognitive strategies can move them from using their metacognition tacitly through awareness towards being strategic and reflective users of these techniques (Perkins 1992). In fact, becoming a strategic or reflective user of metacognitive skills may contribute to learner performance that otherwise may be hindered by the learner's cognitive skills (Veenman et al, 2004).

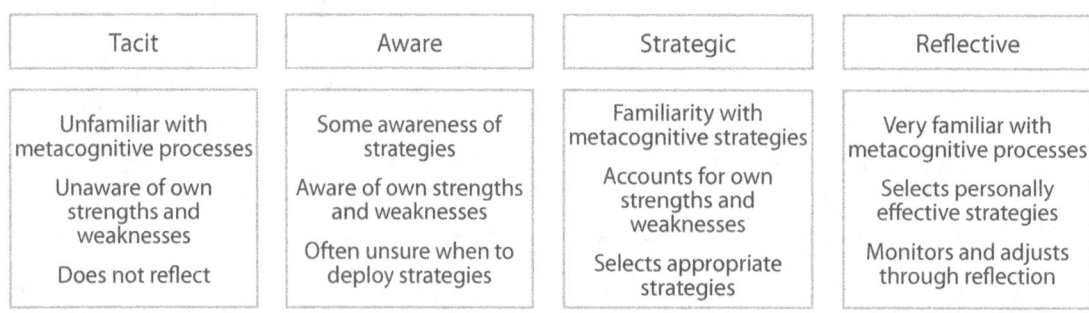

Figure 6.17 *Perkins' four levels of metacognitive awareness*

There is some debate in the literature about whether metacognitive skills are transferable or domain-dependent, and this will influence whether we teach metacognition discretely through 'learning to learn' sessions or whether it is best taught while being embedded in the subject. Veenman et al (2004) suggest that 'metacognitive skilfulness is a general, person-related characteristic [...] rather than being domain-specific.' In contrast, Perry et al (2018) have suggested that metacognitive strategies should be taught in conjunction with subject content because learners find it hard to select and apply generic skills to specific tasks. Additionally, some research has suggested that metacognition moves towards becoming domain-general with maturation (Geurten et al, 2018).

On balance, it is probably prudent to teach learners metacognitive strategies in the context of the subject domain. This way, the central pedagogic intention – developing the quality of subject-specific cognition – remains central. To do this, teachers should help learners understand how and when to apply relevant strategies and provide opportunities for metacognitive practice that is embedded in the subject. It is therefore a key part of your pedagogical content knowledge (PCK) as a teacher to understand which metacognitive strategies are best deployed for the various components of your subject.

> **Take it further...**
>
> Use the Education Endowment Foundation's (2021) seven-step model below to explicitly teach metacognitive strategies to your learners, which are increasingly learner-centred as you go down the list. Choosing which step to begin with will depend on the learners' prior metacognitive knowledge.

Let's apply the seven steps to teaching a topic using mind-mapping (Buzan and Buzan, 1993) as a metacognitive tool. You could provide an example from your own subject at each step.

Step	Strategy	Application
Activating prior knowledge	The teacher asks the learners what they can remember about how to construct a mind map, and when they have used one before.	If learners have previously used a mind map, the teacher encourages them to look back at their previous mind map in their notes.
Explicit strategy instruction	The teacher reminds the learners of the key features and purpose of a mind map.	Learners are instructed to use different colours for each concept branch. Lines split and branch out from a central concept and words and pictures are added along the lines.
Modelling of learned strategy	The teacher models completion of one branch of the mind map, verbalising their thought processes as she does so.	On the whiteboard, the teacher draws a main branch from the centre, adding the key word. The branch splits in two, which the teacher labels before reminding learners of their meaning. The teacher continues to add to the mind map while verbalising her metacognitive regulation.

Step	Strategy	Application
Memorisation of learned strategy	The teacher checks that learners have understood and remember how to implement the strategy by asking questions or quizzing.	The teacher asks learners to turn and talk to their partner and explain the process and key features of mind mapping, as well as what resources will be needed. She then checks for understanding with a cold-call Q and A.
Guided practice	Learners complete one more branch and the teacher circulates to check the quality of work, asking learners to explain their thinking.	Learners add the remaining branches. The teacher asks questions about both learner cognition and metacognition. Questions may include: 'How has this activity helped you makes sense of the topic?'
Independent practice	Learners complete the rest of the mind map on their own.	Learners complete the mind map. The teacher continues to circulate.
Structured reflection	Learners reflect on how useful the mind map tool has been, and what they could do differently next time.	Learners are asked to write down on their mind maps three things that the mind map helped them with, two things they would do different next time, and one other concept or idea they think it may be useful for.

6.7 Hands – psychomotor theories of learning

The third of Bloom's categories is the psychomotor domain, by which he means physical movement and motor skills as coordinated by the brain.

In our experience – and despite their at-first-glance usefulness for our sector – psychomotor theories are perhaps the least consciously incorporated into FES teaching practice. There has been a great deal of ink spilled on social and affective learning theories, and – in more recent decades – on cognitive theories, but the psychomotor domain remains the poor cousin despite the practical nature of much learning within FES. It is rather telling that when Bloom and colleagues set out to write a handbook for each of the three domains, a handbook for the psychomotor domain was never completed or published.

This relegation of the psychomotor domain is longstanding and has endured despite some educationalists having raised the alarm at various points since the establishment of education as a social science. Dewey (Thorburn, 2020), Montessori (Rathunde, 2009) and Piaget (Marshall, 2016) all incorporated the body in their frameworks, and yet the 'cultural othering of the body in academia' (Clughen, 2023) has persisted. Over three decades ago, hooks (1994) argued provocatively that 'individuals enter the classroom to teach as though only the mind is present and not the body.' More recently, in a scathing review of the educational landscape, Claxton argued that most learners in the UK are being taught in 'somatically impoverished classrooms' (Claxton, 2015). This impoverishment perpetuates the 'knowing-doing gap'.

How many learners know that a sentence or a proper noun should begin with a capital letter? And how many of them then go on to use capital letters properly in their assignments? This is the knowing-doing gap. This gap describes the disconnect between theoretical and practical knowledge; between declarative and procedural knowledge; between the abstract and the concrete; between 'knowing that' and 'knowing how' (Winch, 2010). In FES, where skilled practice in a vocational field is the end goal of many FES curricula, we should immediately recognise the value of teaching that incorporates the psychomotor domain.

Our assertion is that the knowing-doing gap is best bridged with careful application of pedagogies that account for the psychomotor domain, placed alongside the cognitive and affective domains. In making this claim, we readily acknowledge that this has often been done poorly and to the detriment of learner learning. One such poor application of psychomotor pedagogies is the 'brain gym', whose advocates have made unevidenced claims for its impact and effectiveness (Hyatt, 2007; Spaulding et al, 2010; Watson and Kelso, 2014). But while 'brain gym' is the wrong answer, the question remains: how should we help our learners cultivate embodied 'know how' and not merely a disembodied 'know that'?

To answer this question, this section will begin with a consideration of the benefits and pitfalls of Kolb's somewhat contested experiential learning theory (ELT). Then we will investigate the comparatively recent concept of embodied cognition along with the related extended mind thesis. We will then consider three categories of human movement that may assist in teaching and learning: gestures, whole-body movements and physical activity (Mavilidi et al, 2022). Finally, taking a parting shot at disembodied pedagogies, we will consider the concept of tacit knowledge and whether the nature of learning in a vocational field may best be thought of as becoming a connoisseur.

Experiential learning theory

At the outset of this chapter, we noted that experience alone without reflection means it is possible to be experienced in a field without being an expert. This is as true for our learners in their learning as it is for us as teachers. It is inadequate to simply assume that learners will achieve the required learning outcome by giving them unmediated, unscaffolded or unguided experiences of the thing they should be learning. As Kolb (2014) reminds us:

> *Truth is not manifest in experience; it must be inferred by a process of learning that questions preconceptions of direct experience, tempers the vividness and emotion of experience with critical reflection and extracts the correct lessons from the consequences of action.*

What Kolb is saying is that we cannot expect expertise to emerge from experience as a matter of course. The teacher's job is more than providing

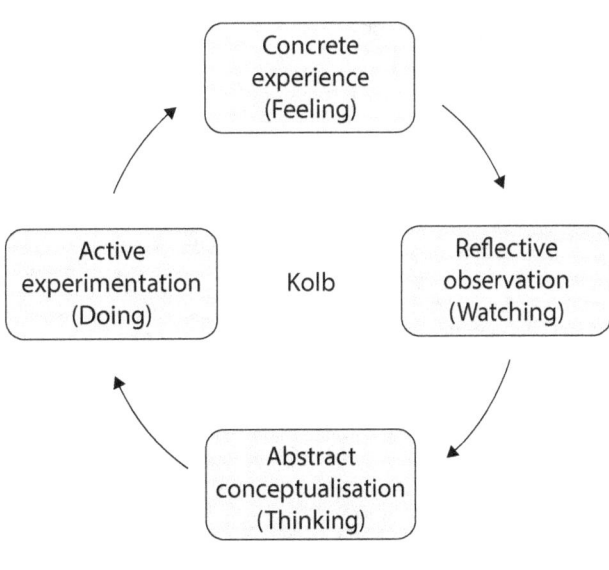

Figure 6.18 *Kolb's learning cycle*

experiences for her learners and hoping they will extract the key points for themselves. Any pedagogical approach that centres learner experience as the primary stimulus for learning must account for this. We will discuss the risks inherent in this approach shortly, but first we will consider how Kolb's theory can be implemented if done so carefully.

There are other versions of ELT, but Kolb's is the best known. Kolb has suggested that there are four stages of learning that form a 'learning cycle'. Notice how Kolb has attempted to include both the concrete and abstract and relate them to one another through metacognitive processes.

First, a learner begins with a concrete experience where they engage with a concept or idea in its compound or final state. In practice this is often done through problem-based or project-based approaches where learners 'have a go' or participate in an industry-standard event. Learners are then asked to reflect upon their experience, making sense of it from their own perspective. Kolb's approach has been criticised for failing to specify that reflection should be critical reflection (Morris, 2020). This critical reflection can be guided by the teacher using a reflective model such as Gibbs (1988), Schon (1983) or Borton (1970).

Through reflection, learners are encouraged to abstract the key concepts and features from their experience to produce a tentative working hypothesis (Miettinen, 2000) which can then be repurposed or practiced in a new situation. The value of an abstract conceptualisation is tied closely to the quality of the reflection that came before it. Active experimentation then provides further concrete experience for the learner to draw from and refine their understanding or performance.

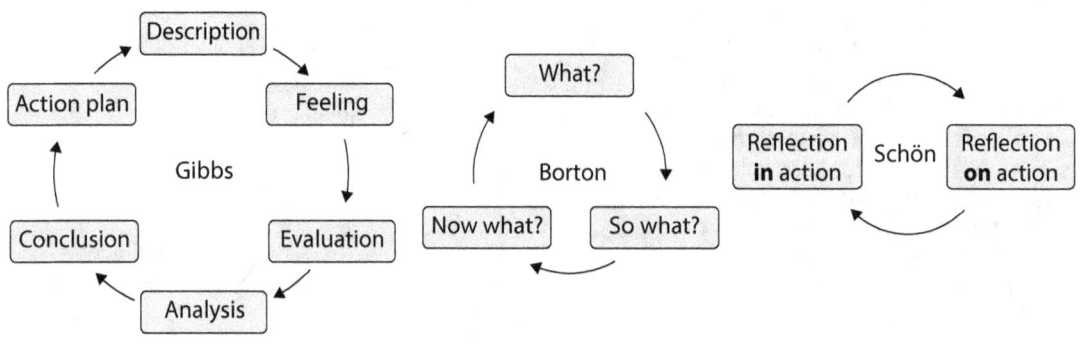

Figure 6.19 *Reflective models*

Proponents of ELT argue that situated experiences provide opportunities for both authentic and situated learning, that is often said to be missing from other approaches. ELT argues that it is precisely the embeddedness of the experience which gives the approach its pedagogic value. Retaining this means that learners directly experience the many relationships between the to-be-learned material and the context of its application, which is thought to be lost or diluted in more deconstructed approaches.

What could experiential learning look like in FES? A sports teacher may ask her learners to participate in an authentic training session delivered by an experienced coach. During the session they are told to pay attention to their thoughts, feelings and perceptions, which they will have chance to discuss in more depth later. At the end of the session, learners may be asked to review video footage of their participation and discuss in small groups why the coach made the decisions they did, and how those decisions influenced their learning in the session. After this, they may be asked to work in pairs or alone to construct a general model for a good coaching session which is then turned into a session plan. Finally, using their session plan, they may be given the opportunity to lead their own coaching session for their peers.

> **REFLECT**
>
> How could you use each of Kolb's learning cycle stages to provide an experiential learning opportunity for your learners? Consider:
> - What experiences would be suitable?
> - What activities would you use to ensure this was adequately scaffolded?
> - Would the approach be better suited to novices or near-experts?

In a synthesis of 88 peer-reviewed research studies, Ranken et al (2023) discovered a wide range of benefits of using experiential learning strategies with children aged 4–14. Benefits related to motivation and engagement, agency and wellbeing, while mixed results were reported for academic achievement. The extent to which these are still applicable in FES is a question to be pondered.

Critics of ELT point to the clear evidence that unguided or minimally guided instruction is a very inefficient mode of teaching (Kirschner, Sweller and Clark, 2006). The rejoinder may be that, when done well, experiential learning (whether problem-based or inquiry based) is neither unguided nor minimally guided, but highly scaffolded (Hmelo-Silver, Duncan and Chinn, 2007). Additionally, there is support for the idea that problem-solving prior to explicit instruction has beneficial outcomes for learning of cognitive skills and early-stage learning of motor skills (Loibl and Leukel, 2023). Since motor skills (movements) are a critical part of many FES subjects (sport, dance, performing arts, hairdressing, catering and patisserie) we should take these claims seriously.

> **REFLECT**
>
> What movements are integral to your subject? What actions should learners learn? What does fluency look like in these movements? How are these refined?

Loibl, Roll and Rummel (2017) argue that when learners are asked to acquire new motor skills through problem solving there are three key mechanisms at work that contribute to the success of the approach. These mechanisms bolster the claims of ELT.

- **Activation of prior knowledge** – In the search for solutions, learners naturally engage their (often intuitive) prior knowledge as a guide, strengthening that prior knowledge and providing a lens through which to attend to the new learning.

- **Awareness of knowledge gaps** – Through 'productive failure' learners recognise those areas of their skill that is causing their performance to be unsuccessful or impeded. This then primes them to attend to the features of subsequent instruction that will help them fill these gaps.

- **Recognition of deep features of the target concept** – With teacher assistance and through comparisons of different learner solutions, learners come to identify the underlying structures of the target concept or skill and can use this to guide the repair of their flawed or incomplete mental models.

So, having presented the theory and some evidence for its effective application, we can now identify some risks of adopting an ELT approach and possible solutions for the FES teacher.

Risks of adopting an ELT approach

Risk	Explanation	Possible solutions
Learners remember the wrong things	Our cognitive architecture prioritises episodic memory over semantic memory. Learners may remember details irrelevant to the target learning, such as who was in their group.	Point out key events during the experience. Use reflective models immediately after the experience. Film the experience and allow the learners to re-watch.
Risk of cognitive overload	Learners with limited prior knowledge may struggle to attend to all the necessary features of the experience. They may also feel the experience to be overwhelming or stressful.	Encourage learners to look for certain features by giving out a prompt sheet or asking scaffolding questions.
Risk of misconceptions	With so many elements that a learner could focus on, it would be easy for a learner to develop a flawed understanding of the target concept, which may not be realised until problems occur in later learning.	Provide opportunities for a prompt debrief. Respond to misconceptions immediately.
Entrenching learning gaps	If existing schemas help learners make sense of new experiences, learners with more prior knowledge will be advantaged over learners with less prior knowledge.	Locate the experience at a point in the curriculum where learners have a strong grasp of key prior knowledge.
Entrenching social disparities	Socioeconomic background correlates to a range of life experiences, so learning gaps entrenched by experiential approaches may reinforce socioeconomic disparities.	Be aware of the demographic of the learner group. Select the types of experiences with a focus on inclusivity.
Teacher workload	Depending on the experience, setting up a 'real-life' experience is potentially time consuming.	Share experience planning with colleagues. Invite a guest to run a 'real-life' session.

Not all of Kolb's work can be supported by empirical evidence, most notably his use of ELT to propose a learning style inventory (Coffield et al, 2004). To be fair, Kolb envisioned learning styles as semi-permanent orientations or preferences rather than fixed personality traits, but for us, this is not enough to rescue his learning styles inventory from its flawed premise.

These qualms with ELT are not to be taken to mean that experiential learning approaches should be dismissed and certainly not that the psychomotor domain is of no importance for shaping your classroom practice. We turn now to other approaches within the psychomotor domain that have utility in the FES classroom.

Embodied cognition and the extended mind

This section will deal with the concepts of embodied, situated and distributed cognition, focusing mainly on embodied cognition. Before outlining the pedagogical ramifications of these fascinating concepts, it is worth noting the parent theory from which these are derived: the extended mind thesis (EMT). The EMT is a provocative idea proposed by cognitive scientist David Chalmers and philosopher Andy Clark (1998) that seeks to answer the prickly question, 'Where does the mind stop and the rest of the world begin?'

According to EMT, our cognition reaches beyond our brain through perception-action loops at a range of scales and modes. Cognition happens in the mind but also runs to and from the body, to and from the environment and to and from other minds.

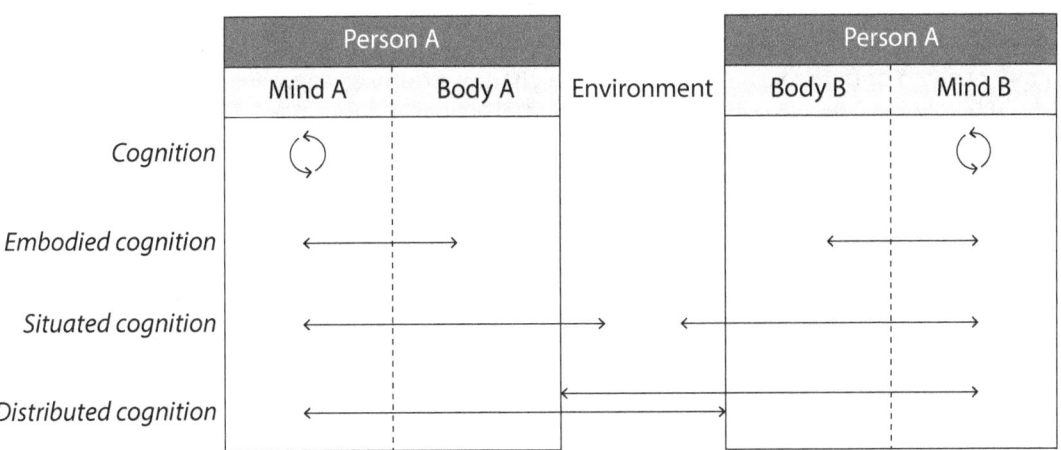

Figure 6.20 *Movement of cognition*

These modes of cognition have also been categorised as the 4Es – embodied, embedded, enactive and extended cognition – which relate in turn to how the body, the environment, movement and tools assist in our making sense of the world around us (Stanciu, 2023).

If the EMT is to inform our pedagogy, we must widen our view of what cognition is and what counts as a tool of cognition, and we must widen our view of the channels along which that cognition flows. If we really do think with (in, or through?) our bodies, what does that mean for our learners? If we think with the environment, with tools and with the minds of others, how does this all play out in our teaching practice? For many of us, this will require a paradigm shift. We will begin with embodied cognition.

Embodied cognition and the haptic modality

We educators are being challenged by hooks, Claxton, and others to work out how we could bring bodies into our classrooms. Schilhab and Groth (2024) argue that:

All learning is through and through embodied, perceptual, biased, and sensorially rich, involving and evolving the learner and the world to an extent that transgresses traditionally conjectured boundaries.

Macrine and Fugate (2022) implore teachers to consider the extent of learners' 'sensorimotor engagement' with their own learning. If we accept the claims of embodied cognition as a way of responding to this challenge, what implications come to the fore for our teaching practice? Hrach (2021) suggests that 'an embodied teaching practice requires recasting cognition as a whole-body enterprise.'

In getting started with this enterprise, we should lay some of the theoretical groundwork for embodied cognition. In doing so, we find some help from perhaps an unlikely quarter: CLT. From within the conceptual framework of CLT, Sweller et al (2019) argues that involving the motor system not only 'seems to reduce load on working memory during instruction' but it also results in a 'richer encoding and therefore richer cognitive representations.' Put in the simplest terms, involving our body's movement in our learning helps us remember more. As well as the benefit of improved retention, Sullivan (2018) adds that 'higher levels of embodiment in learning tasks appear to increase levels of learner engagement and effort.' The promise of embodied cognition is significant but, as we have already noted with reference to 'brain gym', there are strategies that are supported by research and others that are not.

DCT (Paivio, 1971) shows us that presenting coherently integrated instructional materials simultaneously to both the visual and the verbal channels reduces cognitive load on the learner and may even increase the transferability of the learned materials. One suggestion of embodied cognition theory is that visual and verbal modalities can be augmented by the body and its movements, which can be considered as a third modality: the haptic modality (Webb et al (2022)). Since movement can be used to dynamically simulate knowledge (Barsalou, (2008)), delivering learning to learners in visual, verbal and haptic modes will help our learners learn more effectively.

If this is the case, now we can conceive of movement as instructional tool, and this opens a range of possibilities. How can we go about 'engaging learners in physical activities that are aligned with target concepts' (Lindgren et al, 2022)? Mavilidi et al (2022) propose three main ways in which movement can be used to support instruction: teaching with gesture, teaching with whole-body movements and teaching with physical activity.

Teaching with gesture

When we speak, we gesture; it is almost impossible to stop yourself from doing it. In fact, congenitally blind people who have never seen another person gesture will make gestures as they speak (Iverson et al., 2000). This indicates that there is something fundamental about our use of gesture and it is no mere addendum to the spoken word (Goldin-Meadow, 2004). Some studies show that gesture even precedes speech and helps us to think of what we want to say (ter Bekke, Drijvers and Holler, 2024). Humans are particularly adept at processing objects that are within reach, specifically in the 'perihand space' where gesture occurs (Cosman and Vecera, 2010).

Not only does making gestures help with our cognition, but watching other people's gestures does too. Gestures support the listener to make inferences about the meaning of the speaker because 'the human brain understands actions by motor simulation' (Calvo-Merino et al, 2005). The mechanism for this is the mirror neuron system.

Imagine your football team has scored a goal, a towering header from a fizzing cross. After the replay, the camera shows you the reaction of the bench. As the player leaps to head the ball into the goal, the manager, absorbed by the game, jerks his head forward as if he is the one heading the ball. Why does he do this? When absorbed by what is happening in the environment, mirror neurons fire to replicate the movement we are watching, as if we were the ones making that movement.

This was discovered by noticing that the same neural reward circuitry of monkeys that lit up when they were given a banana would also light up when they saw another monkey given a banana (Rizollatti et al, 1996). In some sense their mirror neurons helped them indwell the experience of the other monkey and adopt it as their own experience. This is significant because it suggests that the motor replication of another's movement gives an insight into that other persons' cognition and it has this effect whether the movement is copied or not. If we want our learners to understand what we are saying, gesture should not be overlooked.

What kinds of gestures should a teacher use? NcNeill (1992) gives us four types of gesture: beat, deictic, iconic and metaphoric. The first two types of gesture are used to emphasise speech and direct attention (such as by pointing) respectively. The last two are known as representational gestures, as they convey semantic content. It is these representational gestures that we are particularly interested in here.

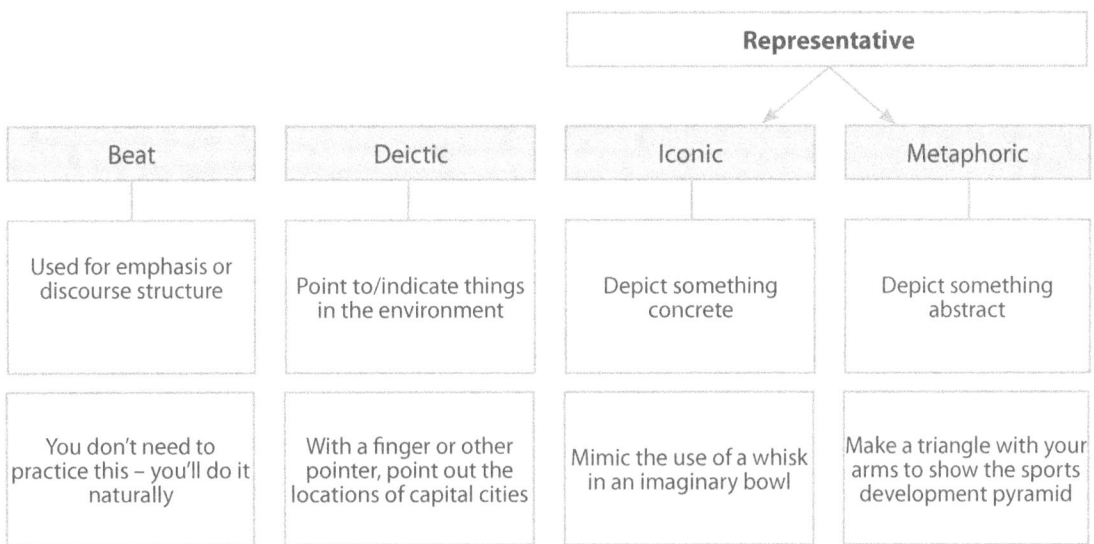

Figure 6.21 *McNeill's types of gesture*

Iconic gestures are those that represent real physical items. You could use an iconic gesture to represent the subduction zone at a plate boundary in A-level geography by holding your arms parallel to the ground in front of you and sliding one arm underneath the other while you explain the process. In catering, you could demonstrate the difference between whipping and folding by using an imaginary whisk in one hand and an imaginary bowl in the other. While a gesture is not always better than using the real tool, it can help to isolate key features of the use of the tool that may otherwise be lost due to the complexity of the context. In this way, it is equivalent to the computational efficiency of a diagram over a photograph.

> **Tip for Teaching**
>
> **Pair gesture with narration**
>
> Be deliberate about introducing your gestures to your learners. Demonstrate and narrate your gesture first, then ask learners to copy the gesture as you do it. Now ask them to turn and talk to a partner repeating both the gesture and the narration.

Have you ever said to a learner 'can you build on that idea?', or 'that's nearly right – you're getting closer', or 'let's dig a bit deeper'? These are all metaphors for cognitive processes borrowed from the material world and revealed in the language we use (Lakoff and Johnson, 1980).

From our earliest days, our cognition develops from our engagement with the material world. As babies we grasp and let go, we push and pull, we build and knock down, we put smaller objects inside larger ones, we learn about stability, solidity, cause and effect, higher and lower, more and less and so on. Thus, our internal cognitive structures come to correlate with the external concrete world and become the basic categories and patterns of cognition for all our thinking, including our abstract thinking. Consequently, we struggle to speak of conceptual or theoretical matters without borrowing language from the physical: objects, paths and containers (Caviglioli, 2019). Tversky (2019) puts it this way: 'the mind regards ideas as objects.'

> **REFLECT**
>
> Say each of the following phrases and, without overthinking it, see if you can provide a gesture that matches what you're saying.
>
> - Can you push that idea a bit further?
> - How does that build idea on this one?
> - This concept is central and that one is peripheral.
> - What is the other side of that argument?
>
> It's easily done, isn't it? The gestures feel almost as if they are already in the words themselves.

Metaphoric gestures are those that represent abstract concepts. If we recognise that much of our language is metaphorically related to movement and space, it gives us a head start in designing our gestures, identifying the spatial metaphors and recreating them for our learners using gestures. For example, if you were preparing your learners to write up a discussion about the pros and cons of fighting in ice hockey, you could hold out your hands palms up to represent the two sides of the argument, allowing one to rise and the other to sink down to represent the 'weightier' side of the argument.

In much the same way that a useful diagram needs to closely match the spoken explanation and not have irrelevant or superfluous information, an effective representational gesture is one that has conceptual salience (Rau and Herder, 2021) and semantic congruence (Hughes-Berheim et al, 2020). Conceptual salience means that the gesture surfaces the important aspects of the learning and doesn't include additional, irrelevant or misleading information. Metaphoric gestures need to have semantic congruence, where the gesture and the spoken words both portray the same central meanings.

It is essential then that any gestures being used as an instructional tool are carefully planned and executed otherwise learners are at risk of making incorrect inferences.

> **Tip for Teaching**
>
> **Devising instructional gestures**
>
> Some gestures seem to appear as you try to explain things, but there may be some benefit to developing a set of subject-relevant gestures and teaching them to your learners to help them remember what they are learning. Here are some thoughts on how you could do this:
>
> - **Select** – Choose a type of gesture that best fits the concept to be taught. Iconic gesture is using your hands to 'draw' the thing itself, while metaphoric gesture is 'drawing' some more abstract aspect or feature of the concept.
> - **Dissect** – If using metaphoric gesture, look for spatial metaphors, analogies, logical relationships and semantic structures in the content you are teaching. What underlying features of the content could be represented by gesture?
> - **Match** – Try to achieve conceptual salience (a clear match between the concept and the gesture) and semantic congruence (a clear match between the movement and the words for which it stands).
> - **Beware** – Avoid Mayer's redundancy principle; over-the-top gestures with unnecessary extraneous features will contribute to confusion. Keep them slick.
>
> Iconic gestures could be devised for subject-specific actions (like your arms representing plate margins or warm and cold fronts in A-level geography) and metaphoric gestures could be devised for more general concepts like hierarchies, comparisons, processes, timelines and graphs, each of which appear in most subjects.

Not only does gesture help with learner understanding, but it also helps with recall. Material learned with the aid of gesture can be more effectively retrieved through exhibiting or enacting that gesture (Kang et al, 2013). This is another example of the encoding specificity principle that was discussed in the section on retrieval practice (see page 165).

As for FES, a meta-analysis by Dargue et al (2019) established that 'gesture robustly facilitates comprehension across the lifespan' (Clough and Duff, 2020), so we are given the green light to try some of these strategies with our post-14 learners.

Teaching with whole-body movements

Besides gesture, how else could we get our learners to embody the concepts they are learning about? Whole-body movements afford further possibilities.

In the mid-2000s, the internet (our little corner, at least) was buzzing about the living graphs of Hans Rosling, a Swedish professor and brilliant data visualiser. His TED talks went viral not merely because of the pressing matters he was discussing but also because of the quality of his visual representations, his use of moving data points and his own movements on the stage. The further the presentation technology improved, the more embodied Rosling's presentations became, until by the end of the decade he was wandering around inside the graphs and manoeuvring the models he was describing, inhabiting and indwelling them as he explained them to his audience.

This captivating approach tells us something about the power of embodied teaching. While gesture can be seen as a relatively accessible entry to embodied teaching, whole-body movements shift the dial further from what we and our learners are accustomed to.

A former colleague used coloured duct tape to mark out a very large human heart diagram on the floor of the sports hall before getting learners to walk through the chambers and blood vessels as if they were blood cells. We used to tell our anatomy and physiology classes, 'in this lesson, your body is your best resource' before asking the learners to demonstrate joint movements as they were called out from the front of the classroom.

Two further concepts are pertinent: simulation and enactment. Simulations are learning experiences designed to mimic the 'real thing' as closely as possible. Often, discussion of simulation implies expensive high-tech equipment such as flight simulators but low-tech simulation through simple role-plays provides many similar benefits. Often these low-cost, low-tech approaches are most practicable in FES for time, cost and safety reasons.

One key strength of simulation (whether high- or low-tech) is that it allows learners to adopt multiple vantage points and experience their learning from those perspectives, encouraging them to 'see the other side' of issues and experience 'fictional emotions' (Medina, 2013). For example, in a criminology lesson, you could simulate trials in a mock courtroom and have learners play different roles each time. More simply, travel learners practicing their trolley skills in an aeroplane cabin could get to experience being both cabin crew and customer. As with experiential learning, the opportunities for reflection become key in making the most of simulations.

Enactment is a broader term that describes what your learners will do during a simulation (such as the roles they are to embody along with expected actions and behaviours), but it is more than this. Enactment encompasses any activities where a learner 'acts out' some of their learning in an embodied fashion. In English and ESOL classrooms, or wherever stories are being told, it may benefit learners to act out or role-play the key moments of the text being studied. This could also be used to aid learning and recall of psychology or criminology case studies and historical events. We have already suggested, with encouragement from Shimamura (2018), that storytelling is a valuable activity. When stories are coupled with enactment, the value is even greater.

> **REFLECT**
>
> How else could you include whole-body movements in your teaching? Of course, you will need to do your own cost-benefit analysis on whether these strategies give more than they cost and whether they are suitable for your learners in your context.

Teaching with physical activity

The difference between physical activity and the previous two categories is the level of intensity of movement. Gesture and whole-body movements are low intensity, but physical activity is high intensity. There is plenty of research evidencing positive impacts of physical activity on learners' executive function, focus, and motivation for learning (Richter et al, 2025), and so there is likely to be a wide range of benefits in incorporating physical activity into the FES curriculum. With that said, our focus here is on learning through physical activity.

When teaching with physical activity it is important that the design of the task is closely related to what you want your learners to learn, and this can pose a design challenge. Rather unsurprisingly, Schmidt et al (2019) report that task-relevant physical activity produces better learning than task-irrelevant physical activity. Such activities can include:

- ESOL learners may benefit from playing cricket to learn English words related to cricket.
- Geographers could learn map reading skills through taking part in an orienteering competition.
- Dancers could experience different dance styles by mirroring the movement of the dance teacher.

Mavilidi et al (2022) argue that to derive both learning gains and improved cognitive function through high intensity gross motor activity, 'a blended approach involving task-relevant and integrated physical and learning tasks' is appropriate. In summary, making use of embodied techniques can be shown to:

- Reduce cognitive load.
- Increase richness of cognitive representations.
- Increase engagement and effort.
- Increase comprehension and inference generation.

Situated and distributed cognition

Other types of cognition suggested by the EMT include situated and distributed cognition, both of which derive their pedagogic utility from the cognitive offloading available (Medrano and Miller-Cotto, 2025). Cognitive offloading is what happens when a leaner's cognition is assisted by something (or someone) other than their own working and long-term memories.

Situated cognition accounts for the impact of environment on learner learning, by including the cultural, social and physical features of that environment. Cognitively offloading to the environment can be done in various ways, and here we will restrict ourselves to how a learner in an FES classroom may offload their thinking onto their environment.

Perhaps the best example of situated cognition is the use of manipulatives, which in this context are things you can move around to help you think. Manipulatives are already widely used in maths education from the early years up. Learners are given blocks or items to group, click together, and move around to represent mathematical concepts of addition, subtraction, sets, and so on. This has direct relevance to some FES contexts such as foundation learning and GCSE resit classes; it will require a little more thought to translate the use of manipulatives into most other subjects.

> **REFLECT**
>
> What abstract concepts in your subject could be represented by physical items, which your learners could then organise in physical space?

Have you ever had to write a long essay? One of the best ways you can plan for this is to use sticky notes or index cards. Write one key idea on each sticky note and now they are moveable in the environment, and therefore easier to move around in your mind. The space in which you work (the desk, a whiteboard, the classroom wall) functions as an external memory field (EMF), allowing to you to make visible to yourself (and others) the organisation and interrelationships of your abstract thought.

Using physical models (such as a replica knee joint, a hairdresser's dummy or an engine part) and allowing learners to handle them, move them around and manipulate them provides a layer of learning that – for vocational subjects in particular – is indispensable. Of course, all the usual caveats apply when selecting and using manipulatives and models in your classroom – think carefully about learner prior knowledge, chunking, scaffolding and checking for understanding.

Finally, if the spatial arrangement is well planned, there may be some benefit in activities in which learners move around the room or from table to table to complete tasks. This could be where the tables are lined up in a straight line to represent stages in a process, and on each table there is an activity to help learners get to grips with that stage of the process. For example, in developing a plan for a tennis coaching session, table one could include tasks around devising coaching points for the session, table two warm up activities, table three isolated skills and so on. Importantly, the spatial (in this case sequential) arrangement of the tables is meaningful and not just the activities being undertaken (classroom layout is explored in more detail in chapter 3).

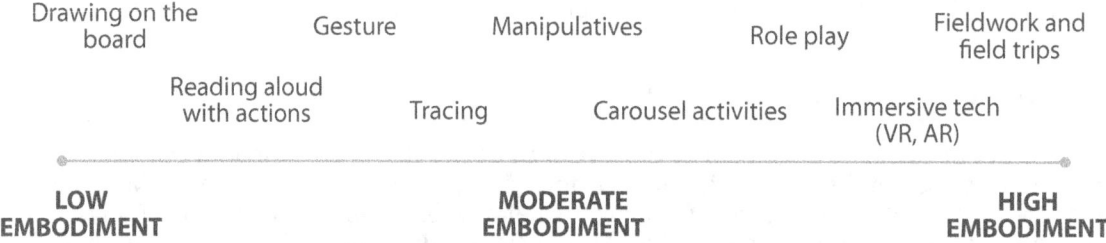

Figure 6.22 *Embodiment scale*

Distributed cognition is when a complex task or problem is distributed between learners working in collaboration. Their combined mental resources – their working and long-term memories, along with their embodied and situated cognitions – can then be leveraged in the search for a solution. When cognition is outsourced to other learners, this alleviates the cognitive load for any one individual, instantiating what has been called a 'collective working memory' (Kirschner et al, 2011). This in turn has given rise to 'collaborative cognitive load theory' (Kirschner et al, 2018).

Gallotti and Frith (2013) have argued that cognition has a 'we-mode' and so immediately we can see implications for structuring the classroom environment (or laboratory, workshop or studio) to allow for dialogue, interaction, and co-operation. In acknowledging the 'we-mode', we are immediately linked back to the social and affective theories of teaching and learning that we have already considered. The more we dig the more we uncover interconnections between our three overarching domains.

We have acknowledged that this area of research is still in its relative infancy, and much of what has been done has focused on children in the early years rather than learners in FES. It remains to be seen how these ideas are refined in the coming decades and how this refinement may shift the implications for our pedagogical practice. For now, the promise of embodied cognition and EMT-associated approaches is, in our estimation, huge.

> **REFLECT**
>
> How can I make the most of group work?
>
> Let's face it, group work is fraught! Lots of learners do not like it, and lots of learners like it for the wrong reasons. Poorly constructed group work can mean some learners do all the work, while others enjoy a break. The famous meme reminds us that the one thing most people learn from group work is 'trust no one'!
>
> - What parameters need to be set to make group work effective?
> - What things should you avoid?
> - How can you maximise the learning impact, and minimise off-task behaviour?

Apprenticeship, connoisseurship and tacit knowledge

To conclude the psychomotor theories section, we come almost full circle back to social theories of learning as we discuss the concept of apprenticeship. In FES, we readily use the language of apprenticeship for obvious reasons, but let's now consider the value of thinking about all teaching and learning in FES from this perspective. Apprenticeships of past eras involved the close entwining of an apprentice and a master. Observing a master engaged in their craft was a crucial part of an apprentice's learning, and practice, replication and imitation were embedded in the process of becoming an expert.

Under the paradigm of apprenticeship, expertise is understood to be something more than the mere ability to give a verbal explanation of explicit knowledge; it is 'something felt and beyond the coherent conceptual description of the expert themselves' (Jackson, 2023) Where the overarching intended learning outcome is the development of a craft – hairdresser, plumber, coach, chef – then the ability to provide a set of clear propositional statements about that craft can be easily recognised as insufficient. Declarative 'know-that' knowledge is only a small part of the whole and cannot on its own bridge the troublesome 'knowing-doing' gap.

Michael Polanyi's (1966) concept of tacit knowledge can help us make sense of why close engagement with the work of a skilled practitioner is so critical to vocational and technical education. Polanyi's famous adage is that 'we can know more than we can tell', by which he means that those unspecifiable elements required for true expertise can indeed be known but only at an embodied, tacit level.

Explicit knowledge relates to tacit knowledge the same way learning about the colour wheel relates to painting a picture or understanding momentum and balance relates to riding a bike. Some of those things may be helpful to know if you are learning to paint or ride a bike, but they are well short of the integrated and embodied 'know-how' of the expert. An expert, then, is a person skilled at relying upon a host of subsidiary particulars into a greater-than-the-sum-of-its-parts integration. This semi-articulable expertise Polanyi (1962) calls 'connoisseurship'.

This gives us a problem to solve: if most of an expert's expertise is held tacitly and is unspecifiable in terms of propositions, how can it ever be transferred to another knower? Polanyi's answer is his concept of 'indwelling'.

Polanyi argues that we can develop our expertise through relying upon what he calls an 'authoritative guide'. Here, Polanyi does not mean authoritative in the sense of authoritarian but rather in the sense of someone (either a person or a tradition) whose expertise is real and whose guidance can be depended upon – embodied, indwelled – by a learner who is feeling their way towards new understanding or a discovery. By copying their movements, watching their form and studying their approach to various tasks, the learner is seeking to indwell the expertise of their teacher and by extension the whole domain of their learning. Like Hans Rosling walking around inside his data, the expert (teacher) invites a novice (learner) to get inside the domain – to embody it – and guides them though their experience of it through demonstration, illustration, exemplification and – yes – verbal explanation.

> **REFLECT**
>
> How could you as an FES practitioner become a connoisseur of teaching?

To conclude, there is 'much we can tell' about being a personal trainer, an electrician or a pastry chef – and we should be telling it – but there is plenty more that we cannot tell; this is what is learned through apprenticeship. We can use the insights of psychomotor theories to support the embodied, experiential, apprenticeship approach while still incorporating the extensive and valuable findings of cognitive science.

6.8 Subject specialist and 'signature' pedagogies

Without writing a subject-specific version of this textbook for each FES subject, we have had to satisfy ourselves so far with generic pedagogical concepts. Throughout this chapter, we have consistently reminded you to take your understanding of these concepts back to your subject specialism to develop your own PCK and see what could work for you. As we conclude this chapter, however, it is important to note that subjects do have their own 'signature' pedagogies that are unique to that discipline.

A 'signature pedagogy' (Shulman, 2005) is the set of pedagogical practices that enable a learner to be prepared for a professional occupation. Each profession has its own fundamental characteristics which teach a learner 'to think, to perform and to act with integrity'.

While Hanley and Thompson (2021) rightly remind us that 'generic pedagogy is not enough', there are both pragmatic and pedagogical benefits to the generic discussion presented in this chapter. The value of generic interdisciplinary discussion lies in the fact that it is exceedingly difficult to transfer pedagogical practices across subject boundaries and apply them without amendment or nuance. This difficulty is a blessing in disguise as it makes necessary the development of a shared pedagogical language that can be shared by peers, mentors, tutors, leadership teams and teachers of other subjects (Lawy and Tedder, 2012). The challenge of converting something that works in the sports hall across to a kitchen or salon means we must become comfortable speaking at a conceptual level if the profession is to cross-fertilise good practice from subject to subject.

Chapter summary

In this chapter, we have considered:

- What is pedagogy?
- The three domains of pedagogy:
    * Heart – the affective and social domain

* Head – the cognitive domain
  * Hands – the psychomotor domain
- The importance of subject-specific and 'signature' pedagogy.

Traditional conceptual boundaries are constantly being blurred, erased and redrawn. In this chapter, you will have seen that the boundaries of Bloom's affective, cognitive and psychomotor domains are rather porous. Embodied cognition collapses much of the distinction between the cognitive and the psychomotor, Shimamura's MARGE cuts a line right through the affective and cognitive domains and the overload theorised by CLT shows up in the affective domain. This ought not to trouble us; in fact, it should serve to remind us that our learners are integrated human beings and each one is completely unique – just like everyone else!

References

Agarwal, P. K. (2019) Retrieval Practice and Bloom's Taxonomy: Do Students Need Fact Knowledge Before Higher Order Learning? Journal of educational psychology, 111 (2), 189–209.

Agarwal, P.K., Roediger, H.L., III, McDaniel, M.A., and McDermott, K.B., (2020). How to use retrieval practice to improve learning. www.retrievalpractice.org

Ahmadi, A., Noetel, M., Parker, P., Ryan, R.M., Ntoumanis, N., Reeve, J., Beauchamp, M., Dicke, T., Yeung, A., Ahmadi, M., Bartholomew, K., Chiu, T.K.F., Curran, T., Erturan, G., Flunger, B., Frederick, C., Froiland, J.M., González-Cutre, D., Haerens, L., Jeno, L.M., Koka, A., Krijgsman, C., Langdon, J., White, R.L., Litalien, D., Lubans, D., Mahoney, J., Nalipay, M.J.N., Patall, E., Perlman, D., Quested, E., Schneider, S., Standage, M., Stroet, K., Tessier, D., Thogersen-Ntoumani, C., Tilga, H., Vasconcellos, D., and Lonsdale, C., (2022) A Classification System for Teachers' Motivational Behaviors Recommended in Self-Determination Theory Interventions. Journal of Educational Psychology, 115(8), pp.1158-1176.

Alexander, R. (2004) Still no pedagogy? Principle, pragmatism and compliance in primary education. Cambridge Journal of Education, 34(1), 7–34.

Atkinson, A.L., Allen, R.J. and Waterman, A.H. (2021) 'Exploring the understanding and experience of working memory in teaching professionals: A large-sample questionnaire study', Teaching and Teacher Education, 103, 103343. DOI: 10.1016/j.tate.2021.103343.

Ausubel, D.P. (1968). Educational Psychology: A Cognitive View. New York: Holt, Rinehart and Winston.

Baddeley, A. D., & Hitch, G. (1974). Working memory. In G.H. Bower (Ed.), The psychology of learning and motivation: Advances in research and theory (Vol. 8, pp. 47–89). New York: Academic Press.

Bandura, A. (1977). Self-efficacy: toward a unifying theory of behavioral change. Psychological Review, 84(2), 191. https://psycnet.apa.org/journals/rev/84/2/191

Bandura, A. (1986). Social foundations of thought and action: A social cognitive theory. Englewood Cliffs, NJ: Prentice Hall.

Barrouillet, P., & Camos, V. (2012). As time goes by: Temporal constraints in working memory. Current Directions in Psychological Science, 21(6), 413–419. https://doi.org/10.1177/0963721412459513

Barsalou, L. W. (2008). Cognitive and Neural Contributions to Understanding the Conceptual System. Current Directions in Psychological Science, 17(2), 91-95. https://doi.org/10.1111/j.1467-8721.2008.00555.x

Bernstein, B. (2000). Pedagogy, Symbolic Control and Identity: Theory, Research, Critique (Revised Edition). Oxford: Rowman & Littlefield.

Bjork, E. L., and Bjork, R. A. (2011). Making things hard on yourself, but in a good way: Creating desirable difficulties to enhance learning. In M. A. Gernsbacher, R. W. Pew, L. M. Hough, and J. R. Pomerantz (Eds.), Psychology and the real world: Essays illustrating fundamental contributions to society (pp. 56–64). Worth Publishers.

Bloom, B.S. (1956) Taxonomy of Educational Objectives, Handbook: The Cognitive Domain. David McKay, New York.

Borton, T. (1970). Reach, Touch and Teach. London: Hutchinson.

Brod, G. (2021) 'Generative learning: Which strategies for what age?', Educational Psychology Review, 33(4), pp. 1295-1318. DOI: 10.25656/01:23704.

Bruner, J. (1978) 'The role of dialogue in language acquisition' In A. Sinclair, R., J. Jarvelle, and W. J. M. Levelt (eds.) The Child's Concept of Language. New York: Springer-Verlag

Buzan, T., and Buzan, B. (1993). The mind map book: How to use radiant thinking to maximize your brain's untapped potential. Plume.

Calvo-Merino, B., Glaser, D.E., Grèzes, J., Passingham, R.E., Haggard, P. (2005) Action Observation and Acquired Motor Skills: An fMRI Study with Expert Dancers, Cerebral Cortex, 15 (8), 1243–1249, https://doi.org/10.1093/cercor/bhi007

Caviglioli, O. (2019) Dual Coding with Teachers. John Catt Educational Ltd.

Caviglioli, O. and Goodwin, D., (2021). Organise Ideas: Thinking by Hand, Extending the Mind. John Catt Educational Ltd.

Cents-Boonstra, M., Lichtwarck-Aschoff, A., Denessen, E., Aelterman, N., and Haerens, L. (2020) 'Fostering learner engagement with motivating teaching: an observation study of teacher and learner behaviours', Research Papers in Education, 36(6), pp. 754–779. doi: 10.1080/02671522.2020.1767184.

Cents-Boonstra, M., Lichtwarck-Aschoff, A., Denessen, E., Haerens, L., and Aelterman, N. (2018) 'Identifying motivational profiles among VET learners: differences in self-efficacy, test anxiety and perceived motivating teaching', Journal of Vocational Education and Training, 71(4), pp. 600–622. doi: 10.1080/13636820.2018.1549092.

Chen, Ssu-Kuang & Yeh, Yu-Chen & Hwang, Fang-Ming & Lin, Sunny. (2013). The relationship between academic self-concept and achievement: A multicohort–multioccasion study. Learning and Individual Differences. 23. 172-178. 10.1016/j.lindif.2012.07.021.

Chen, O., Castro-Alonso, J.C., Paas, F. et al. (2018) Extending Cognitive Load Theory to Incorporate Working Memory Resource Depletion: Evidence from the Spacing Effect. Educ Psychol Rev 30, 483–501. https://doi.org/10.1007/s10648-017-9426-2

Chen, O., Paas, F. and Sweller, J. (2023) A Cognitive Load Theory Approach to Defining and Measuring Task Complexity Through Element Interactivity. Educational Psychology Review 35, 63 https://doi.org/10.1007/s10648-023-09782-w

Clark, A., & Chalmers, D. (1998). The Extended Mind. Analysis, 58(1), 7–19. http://www.jstor.org/stable/3328150

Claxton, G. (2015). Intelligence in the flesh: Why your mind needs your body much more than it thinks. Yale University Press. https://doi.org/10.12987/9780300215977

Clough, S., and Duff, M. C. (2020). The role of gesture in communication and cognition: Implications for understanding and treating neurogenic communication disorders. Frontiers in Human Neuroscience, 14, Article 323. https://doi.org/10.3389/fnhum.2020.00323

Clughen, L. (2023) ''Embodiment is the future': What is embodiment and is it the future paradigm for learning and teaching in higher education?', Innovations in Education and Teaching International, 61(4), pp. 735–747. doi: 10.1080/14703297.2023.2215226.

Coe, R., Aloisi, C., Higgins, S., and Elliot Major, L. (2014) What makes great teaching? Review of the underpinning research. Sutton Trust.

Coffield, F, Moseley, D, Hall, E and Ecclestone, K, (2004), Learning styles and pedagogy in post-16 learning: a systematic and critical review, London, Learning and Skills Research Centre, Learning and Skills Development Agency

Cosman, J. D., and Vecera, S. P. (2010). Attention Affects Visual Perceptual Processing Near the Hand. Psychological Science, 21(9), 1254-1258. https://doi-org.apollo.worc.ac.uk/10.1177/0956797610380697

Cowan, N. (2005). Working Memory Capacity (1st ed.). Psychology Press. https://doi.org/10.4324/9780203342398

Dargue, N., Sweller, N., and Jones, M. P. (2019). When our hands help us understand: a meta-analysis into the effects of gesture on comprehension. Psychological Bulletin. 145, 765–784. doi: 10.1037/bul0000202

Dubeau, A., Plante, I. and Frenay, M. (2017) Achievement Profiles of Learners in High School Vocational Training Programs. Vocations and Learning 10, 101–120. https://doi.org/10.1007/s12186-016-9163-6

Education Endowment Foundation (2021) Feedback. Retrieved December 18, 2024, from https://educationendowmentfoundation.org.uk/education-evidence/teaching-learning-toolkit/feedback

Education Endowment Foundation (2022) Working with worked examples – Simple techniques to enhance their effectiveness. Retrieved September 09, 2025, from https://educationendowmentfoundation.org.uk/news/eef-blog-working-with-worked-examples-simple-techniques-to-enhance-their-effectiveness

Escandell, S., and Chu, T. L. (Alan). (2023). Implementing Relatedness-Supportive Teaching Strategies to Promote Learning in the College Classroom. Teaching of Psychology, 50(4), 441-447. https://doi.org/10.1177/00986283211046873

Fiorella, L. (2023) Making Sense of Generative Learning. Educational Psychology Review 35, 50 https://doi.org/10.1007/s10648-023-09769-7

Fiorella, L., and Mayer, R. E. (2015a). Learning as a generative activity: Eight learning strategies that promote understanding. Cambridge University Press. https://doi.org/10.1017/CBO9781107707085

Fiorella, L., and Mayer, R. E. (2015b). Eight ways to promote generative learning. Educational Psychology Review, 27(3), pp.427-443.

Flavell, J. H. (1976). Metacognitive aspects of problem solving. In L. B. Resnick (Ed.), The nature of intelligence (pp. 231-236). Hillsdale, NJ: Erlbaum.

Frome, P. M., & Eccles, J. S. (1998). Parents' influence on children's achievement-related perceptions. Journal of personality and social psychology, 74(2), 435–452. https://doi.org/10.1037//0022-3514.74.2.435

Gallotti, M., and C. Frith. (2013). Social cognition in the we-mode. Trends in Cognitive Sciences 17: 160–165.

Gathercole, S. E., Pickering, S. J., Ambridge, B., and Wearing, H. (2004). The Structure of Working Memory From 4 to 15 Years of Age. Developmental Psychology, 40(2), 177–190. https://doi.org/10.1037/0012-1649.40.2.177

Geary, D. (2005). The origin of mind: Evolution of brain, cognition, and general intelligence. American Psychological Association.

Geurten, M., Meulemans, T., and Lemaire, P. (2018). From domain-specific to domain-general? The developmental path of metacognition for strategy selection. Cognitive Development, 48, pp. 62-81. Available at: https://doi.org/10.1016/j.cogdev.2018.08.002 [Accessed 20 March 2025].

Gibbs, G. (1988) Learning by Doing: A guide to teaching and learning methods. Oxford: Further Education Unit, Oxford Polytechnic.

Goldin-Meadow (2004) Gesture's Role in the Learning Process, Theory Into Practice, 43 (4), 314-321, DOI: 10.1207/s15430421tip4304_10

Grosse, C. S., & Renkl, A. (2006). Effects of multiple solution methods in mathematics learning. Learning and Instruction, 16(2), 122 –138

Hanley, P. and Thompson, R. (2021). 'Generic pedagogy is not enough': Teacher educators and subject-specialist pedagogy in the Further Education and Skills sector in England. Teaching and Teacher Education, 98. https://doi.org/10.1016/j.tate.2020.103233

Hanley, P., Hepworth J., Orr K., Thompson R. (2018). Literature Review of Subject-Specialist Pedagogy London, Gatsby

Herbert, J., & Stipek, D. (2005). The emergence of gender differences in children's perceptions of their academic competence. Journal of Applied Developmental Psychology, 26(3), 276–295. https://doi.org/10.1016/j.appdev.2005.02.007

Hmelo-Silver, C. and Duncan, R and Chinn, C. (2007). Scaffolding and Achievement in Problem-Based and Inquiry Learning: A Response to Kirschner, Sweller, and Clark (2006). Educational Psychologist. 42. 99-107. 10.1080/00461520701263368.

hooks, b. (1994). Teaching to transgress: Education as the practice of freedom. New York: Routledge.

Hrach, S (2021). Minding Bodies: How Physical Space, Sensation, and Movement Affect Learning. Morgantown: West Virginia University Press.

Hughes-Berheim, Sarah S et al. "Semantic Relationships Between Representational Gestures and Their Lexical Affiliates Are Evaluated Similarly for Speech and Text." Frontiers in psychology vol. 11 575991. 22 Oct. 2020, doi:10.3389/fpsyg.2020.575991

Hyatt, K. J. (2007). Brain Gym®: Building Stronger Brains or Wishful Thinking? Remedial and Special Education, 28(2), 117-124. https://doi.org/10.1177/07419325070280020201

Iverson, J. M., Tencer, H. L., Lany, J., and Goldin-Meadow, S. (2000). The relation between gesture and speech in congenitally blind and sighted language-learners. Journal of Nonverbal Behavior, 24(2), 105–130. https://doi.org/10.1023/A:1006605912965

Jackson, P. (2023) 'Theorising embodied interaction in coaching: A Merleau-Pontian perspective on embodied practice', Theory & Psychology, 33(1), pp. 78–98. https://doi.org/10.1177/09593543221123970

Jacobs, J. E., & Paris, S. G. (1987). Children's metacognition about reading: Issues in definition, measurement, and instruction. Educational Psychologist, 22(3-4), 255–278.

Jerrim, J., Sims, S. and Oliver, M. (2023) 'Teacher self-efficacy and pupil achievement: much ado about nothing? International evidence from TIMSS', Teachers and Teaching, 29(2), pp. 220–240. doi: 10.1080/13540602.2022.2159365.

Jonsson, B., Wiklund-Hörnqvist, C., Stenlund, T., Andersson, M., and Nyberg, L. (2020). A Learning Method for All: The Testing Effect Is Independent of Cognitive Ability. Journal of Educational Psychology.

Kang, S. H. K., McDermott, K. B., and Roediger, H. L., III. (2007). Test format and corrective feedback modify the effect of testing on long-term retention. European Journal of

Cognitive Psychology, 19(4–5), 528–558. doi:10.1080/09541440601056620.

Kang, S., Hallman G.L., Son, L.K., & Black, J.B. (2013). The Different Benefits from Different Gestures in Understanding a Concept. Journal of Science Education and Technology, 22 (6), 825-837

Kirschner, F., Paas, F., and Kirschner, P. A. (2011). Task complexity as a driver for collaborative learning efficiency: The collective working-memory effect. Applied Cognitive Psychology, 25, 615–624. https://doi.org/10.1002/acp.1730.

Kirschner, P.A., Sweller, J., Kirschner, F. et al. From Cognitive Load Theory to Collaborative Cognitive Load Theory. Intern. J. Comput.-Support. Collab. Learn 13, 213–233 (2018). https://doi.org/10.1007/s11412-018-9277-y

Kirschner, P. A., Sweller, J. and Clark, R. E. (2006) 'Why Minimal Guidance During Instruction Does Not Work: An Analysis of the Failure of Constructivist, Discovery, Problem-Based, Experiential, and Inquiry-Based Teaching', Educational Psychologist, 41(2), pp. 75–86. doi: 10.1207/s15326985ep4102.

Kolb, D.A. (2014). Experiential learning: experience as the source of learning and development. (2nd edition) Englewood Cliffs, NJ: Prentice Hall.

Lakoff, G., & Johnson, M. (1980). Johnson Metaphors We Live by. Chicago: University of Chicago Press.

Lawy, R., and Tedder, M. (2012). Beyond compliance: Teacher education practice in a performative framework. Research Papers in Education, 27(3)

Lindgren, R., Morphew, J. W., Kang, J., Planey, J., and Mestre, J. P. (2022). Learning and transfer effects of embodied simulations targeting crosscutting concepts in science. Journal of Educational Psychology, 114(3), 462–481. https://doi.org/10.1037/edu0000697

Loibl, K., Roll, I. and Rummel, N. Towards a Theory of When and How Problem Solving Followed by Instruction Supports Learning. Educ Psychol Rev 29, 693–715 (2017). https://doi.org/10.1007/s10648-016-9379-x

Loibl, K. and Leukel, C., (2023). Problem-solving prior to instruction in learning motor skills - Initial self-determined practice improves javelin throwing performance. Learning and Instruction, 88, p.101828. Available at: https://doi.org/10.1016/j.learninstruc.2023.101828.

Lucas, B., Spencer, E. and Claxton, G. (2012) How to teach vocational education: A theory of vocational pedagogy. London: City & Guilds Centre for Skills Development. Available at: https://www.researchgate.net/publication/296449831 (Accessed 8 September 2025)

Macrine, S.L. and Fugate, J.M.B. (2022) Movement Matters: How Embodied Cognition Informs Teaching and Learning. 1st edn. Edited by S.L. Macrine and J.M.B. Fugate. Cambridge: The MIT Press.

Mahdavi, M. (2014). An Overview: Metacognition in Education. International Journal of Multidisciplinary and Current Research, 2(May/June), pp. 529-534.

Mansworth, M. (2021). Teach to the Top: Aiming High for Every Learner.

Marshall P. J. (2016). Embodiment and Human Development. Child development perspectives, 10(4), 245–250. https://doi.org/10.1111/cdep.12190

Mavilidi, M. F., Ouwehand, K., Schmidt, M., Pesce, C., Tomporowski, P. D., Okely, A. and Paas, F. (2022). 'Embodiment as a pedagogical tool to enhance learning'. In S. A. Stolz (Ed.), The Body, Embodiment, and Education: An Interdisciplinary Approach (pp. 183-203). London, United Kingdom: Routledge.

Mayer, R. E., & Anderson, R. B. (1992). The instructive animation: Helping students build connections between words and pictures in multimedia learning. Journal of Educational Psychology, 84(4), 444–452. https://doi.org/10.1037/0022-0663.84.4.444

Mayer, R. E. (2005). Cognitive Theory of Multimedia Learning. In R. E. Mayer (Ed.), The Cambridge handbook of multimedia learning (pp. 31–48). Cambridge University Press. https://doi.org/10.1017/CBO9780511816819.004

McNeill, D. (1992). Hand and Mind: What Gestures Reveal about Thought. Chicago: University of Chicago Press. pp. 10, 23-24.

Medina, J. (2013). An enactivist approach to the imagination: embodied enactments and "fictional emotions." American Philosophical Quarterly, 50(3), 317–335. http://www.jstor.org/stable/24475354

Medrano, J., and Miller-Cotto, D. (2025). Understanding working memory as a facilitator of math problem-solving: Offloading as a potential strategy. British Journal of Educational Psychology, 00, 1–17. https://doi.org/10.1111/bjep.12767

Miettinen, R. (2000) The concept of experiential learning and John Dewey's theory of reflective thought and action, International Journal of Lifelong Education, 19:1, 54-72, DOI: 10.1080/026013700293458

Mok, M. M. C. and Moore, P. J. (2019) 'Teachers and self-efficacy', Educational Psychology, 39(1), pp. 1–3. doi: 10.1080/01443410.2019.1567070.

Morris, T.H. (2020) Experiential learning – a systematic review and revision of Kolb's model, Interactive Learning Environments, 28:8, 1064-1077, DOI:10.1080/10494820.2019.1570279

Neary, M. (2002) Curriculum Studies in Post-Compulsory and Adult Education: A teacher's and learner teacher's study guide. Cheltenham: Nelson Thornes.

Nelson, T. and Narens, L. (1990). Metamemory: A theoretical framework and new findings. Psychology of Learning and Motivation, 26, 125–173.

Niemiec, C.P. and Ryan, R.M., (2009). Autonomy, competence, and relatedness in the classroom: Applying self-determination theory to educational practice. Theory and Research in Education, 7(2), pp.133-144. Available at: https://doi.org/10.1177/1477878509104318.

Orr D. (1992). Ecological Literacy: Education for a Postmodern World. Albany, NY: State University of New York.

Paivio, A. (1971). Imagery and Verbal Processes. New York: Holt, Rinehart and Winston.

Perkins, D. (1992). Smart Schools: Better Thinking and Learning for Every Child. New York: Free Press.

Perry, J., Lundie, D. and Golder, G. (2018) 'Metacognition in schools: what does the literature suggest about the effectiveness of teaching metacognition in schools?', Educational Review, 71(4), pp. 483–500. doi: 10.1080/00131911.2018.1441127.

Pierre, E., & Oughton, J.M. (2007). The Affective Domain: Undiscovered Country. The College Quarterly, 10, 1-7.

Polanyi, M. (1962). Personal knowledge: Towards a post-critical philosophy. Chicago, IL: University of Chicago.

Polanyi, M. (1966). The Tacit Dimension. London: Routledge & Kegan Paul.

Ranken, E., Manyukhina, Y., Wyse, D., and Bradbury, A. (2023). Experiential Learning for Children Aged 4-14: A Rapid Evidence Assessment. IOE - Faculty of Education and Society, UCL.

Rathunde, K. (2009). Montessori and Embodied Education. In: Woods, P.A., Woods, G.J. (eds) Alternative Education for the 21st Century. Palgrave Macmillan, New York. https://doi.org/10.1057/9780230618367_11

Rau, M.A. and Herder, T. (2021) 'Under Which Conditions Are Physical versus Virtual Representations Effective? Contrasting Conceptual and Embodied Mechanisms of Learning', Journal of educational psychology, 113(8), pp. 1565–1586.

Reif, F. (2010) Applying Cognitive Science to Education. Thinking and Learning in Scientific and Other Complex Domains. Cambridge, MA, MIT Press.

Renkl, A. (2013), Toward an Instructionally Oriented Theory of Example-Based Learning. Cognitive Science, 38: 1-37. https://doi.org/10.1111/cogs.12086

Richter, M. J., Ali, H., and Immink, M. A. (2025). Enhancing Executive Function in Children and Adolescents Through Motor Learning: A Systematic Review. Journal of Motor Learning and Development 13, 1, 59-108, https://doi.org/10.1123/jmld.2024-0038

Rizzolatti, G., Fadiga, L., Gallese, V., & Fogassi, L. (1996). Premotor cortex and the recognition of motor actions. Brain research. Cognitive brain research, 3(2), 131–141. https://doi.org/10.1016/0926-6410(95)00038-0

Roediger, H. L., and Karpicke, J. D. (2006). Test-enhanced learning: taking memory tests improves long-term retention. Psychological Science, 17(3), 249–255

Rosenshine, B. (2012) Principles of Instruction: Research-Based Strategies That All Teachers Should Know. American Educator, 36(1), p12-39.

Rosenshine, B. and Stevens, R. (1986) Teaching Functions. In Witrock, M.C. (Ed). Handbook of research on teaching, 3rd ed., pp376-391. New York; MacMillan.

Schilhab, T. and Groth, C. (eds.) (2024) Embodied Learning and Teaching Using the 4E Cognition Approach: Exploring Perspectives in

Teaching Practices. 1st edn. London: Routledge. https://doi.org/10.4324/9781003341604

Schmidt, M., Benzing, V., Wallman-Jones, A., Mavilidi, M. F., Lubans, D. R., and Paas, F. (2019). Embodied learning in the classroom: Effects on primary school children's attention and foreign language vocabulary learning. Psychology of Sport and Exercise, 43, 45-54

Schön, D. (1983). The Reflective Practitioner: How Professionals Think in Action. London: Temple Smith.

Schweder, S. and Raufelder, D., 2022. Adolescents' enjoyment and effort in class: Influenced by self-directed learning intervals. Journal of School Psychology, 95, pp.72-89. Available at: https://doi.org/10.1016/j.jsp.2022.09.002.

Sherrington, T. (2018) Mode A, Mode B: Effective teaching and a rich enacted curriculum. Teacherhead [Blog]. 22 April. Available at: https://teacherhead.com/2018/04/22/mode-a-mode-b-effective-teaching-and-a-rich-enacted-curriculum/ (Accessed 8 September 2025).

Shimamura, A; (2018) MARGE A Whole-Brain Learning Approach for Students and Teachers accessed at https://shimamurapubs.files.wordpress.com/2018/09/marge_shimamura.pdf

Shulman, L. S. (2005). Signature pedagogies in the professions. Daedalus, 134(3), 52–59. https://doi.org/10.1162/0011526054622015

Sipos Y., Battisti B., Grimm K. (2008). Achieving transformative sustainability learning: Engaging head, hands and heart. International Journal of Sustainability in Higher Education. 9, 68–86. https://doi.org/10.1108/14676370810842193

Spaulding, Lucinda S.; Mostert, Mark P.; and Beam, Andrea, "Is Brain Gym an Effective Educational Intervention?" (2010). Faculty Publications and Presentations. 148. https://digitalcommons.liberty.edu/educ_fac_pubs/148

Stanciu D. (2023). Consciousness, 4E cognition and Aristotle: a few conceptual and historical aspects. Frontiers in computational neuroscience, 17, 1204602. https://doi.org/10.3389/fncom.2023.1204602

Sullivan, J.V., (2018). Learning and Embodied Cognition: A Review and Proposal. Psychology Learning and Teaching, 17(2), pp.128-143.

Sweller, J. (2006). The worked example effect and human cognition. Learning and Instruction, 16(2), 165–169. https://doi.org/10.1016/j.learninstruc.2006.02.005

Sweller, J., Ayres, P., and Kalyuga, S. (2011). Cognitive Load Theory. New York City, NY: Springer.

Sweller, J., van Merrienboer, J. J. G. and Paas, F. (2019). Cognitive Architecture and Instructional Design: 20 Years Later. Educational Psychology Review, 31 (2), 261-292.

ter Bekke, M., Drijvers, L. and Holler, J. (2024), Hand Gestures Have Predictive Potential During Conversation: An Investigation of the Timing of Gestures in Relation to Speech. Cognitive Science, 48: e13407. https://doi.org/10.1111/cogs.13407

Thorburn, M. (2020) 'Embodied experiences: Critical insights from Dewey for contemporary education', Educational Research, 62(1), pp. 35–45. doi: 10.1080/00131881.2019.1711437.

Tulving, E., and Thomson, D. M. (1973). Encoding specificity and retrieval processes in episodic memory. Psychological Review, 80(5), 352–373. https://doi.org/10.1037/h0020071

Tversky, B. (2019). Mind in Motion: How Action Shapes Thought. NY: Basic Books.

Veenman, M. V. J., Wilhelm, P. and Beishuizen, J. J. (2004). The relation between intellectual and metacognitive skills from a developmental perspective. Learning and Instruction, 14, 89–109.

Vygotsky, L.S. (1978). Mind in society: The development of higher psychological processes. Massachusetts: Harvard University Press.

Watson, A.G., and Kelso, G.L. (2014). The Effect of Brain Gym® on Academic Engagement for Children with Developmental Disabilities. International journal of special education, 29, 75-83.

Webb, M., Tracey, M., Harwin, W. et al. Haptic-enabled collaborative learning in virtual reality for schools. Educ Inf Technol 27, 937–960 (2022). https://doi.org/10.1007/s10639-021-10639-4

Wenger, E. (1998). Communities of practice: Learning, meaning, and identity. Cambridge University Press. https://doi.org/10.1017/CBO9780511803932

Wenger-Trayner, E. and Wenger-Trayner, B. (2015) Introduction to communities of practice. Available at: https://www.wenger-trayner.

com/introduction-to-communities-of-practice/ (Accessed 8 September 2025)

Wesenberg, L., Krieglstein, F., Jansen, S., Rey, G.D., Schneider, S., (2024) Teaching with worked examples – Why the selection of problems for exemplification is critical, Contemporary Educational Psychology, doi: https://doi.org/10.1016/j.cedpsych.2024.102328

Wilding, L. (2015) The application of self-determination theory to support learners experiencing disaffection, Educational Psychology in Practice, 31:2, 137-149, DOI: 10.1080/02667363.2014.995154

Wiliam, D. (2017) [Twitter] tweet 26 January. Available at: https://x.com/dylanwiliam/status/824682504602943489?lang=en (Accessed 17 June 2025)

Willingham, D.T. (2009) Why Don't Students Like School? A Cognitive Scientist Answers Questions about How the Mind Works and What It Means for the Classroom. San Francisco, CA: John Wiley and Sons.

Willingham, D. T. (2018). Does tailoring instruction to "learning styles" help students learn? Ask the cognitive scientist. American Educator, 28–43.

Winch, C. (2010). Dimensions of Expertise: A Conceptual Exploration of Vocational Knowledge. Vancouver, CA: Continuum

Wong, M., Castro-Alonso, J. C., Ayres, P., and Paas, F. (2020). The effects of transient information and element interactivity on learning from instructional animations. In S. Tindall-Ford, S. Agostinho, and J. Sweller (Eds.), Advances in cognitive load theory: Rethinking teaching (pp. 80–88). Routledge/Taylor and Francis Group. https://doi.org/10.4324/9780429283895-7

Zaromb, F.M. and Roediger, H.L., III, (2010). The testing effect in free recall is associated with enhanced organizational processes. Memory and Cognition, 38(8), pp.995-1008.

Zhu, X. and Simon, H. A. (1987) 'Learning Mathematics From Examples and by Doing', Cognition and Instruction, 4(3), pp. 137–166. doi: 10.1207/s1532690xci0403_1.

Chapter 7 Assessment

Maintain a focus on outcomes, for all students, so that they recognise the value of their learning and the future opportunities available to them. (Duty 2)

Assessment derives from the Latin assidere, meaning 'to sit beside or with'.
Wiggins (1993)

7.1 Introduction

While it is challenging to sit with every learner in our classroom, the above quote does highlight something important about the process of assessment. Firstly, sitting with each learner emphasises inclusion and equality of opportunity for all, and secondly, it allows for a focus on outcomes where we can work with the learners to identify what they know, understand and can do. This increases both our learners' and our own understanding – and recognition of – their learning journey. Thinking about learning as a journey is a useful metaphor to maintain throughout this chapter, as we engage in an exploration of assessment and think about why we assess and how to enact assessment effectively to support learning.

There are three key questions that we should ask ourselves when undertaking a journey:

1. What is the starting point? (Initial assessment)
2. How well am I progressing towards the destination? (Formative assessment)
3. Did I make it to the intended destination? (Summative assessment)

These questions align to three core principles of assessment that will form the basis for this chapter, along with a range of practical, evidence-informed examples to support understanding and application to a series of reflective activities.

We begin by looking at the first principle, initial assessment, and consider this in two ways to ensure that we have a strong understanding of our learners' starting points. Following this, we examine the second principle, formative assessment, an approach that is often less formal but is ongoing throughout the learning process, enabling us to effectively monitor progress towards the intended outcomes. Finally, we explore the third principle, summative assessment, which is a more formal type of assessment (such as examinations or observation of performance) that sums up the learning that has taken place.

7.2 Methods of assessment

Within each of the core principles of assessment, there are a wide range of assessment methods that can be used, including:

- **Teacher questioning** – The teacher poses questions to individuals or groups to ascertain their knowledge and understanding of a topic.

- **Multiple choice quizzes** – Learners respond to multiple choice questions based on the topic, either through an online tool (e.g. Menti), written responses (e.g. paper-based) or visual responses (e.g. mini whiteboards), revealing their knowledge and understanding of a topic.

- **Essays** – Learners respond to a given task in written form either in exam conditions or at their own pace.

- **Observations of performance** – The teacher observes the learners undertaking an activity to determine what they know, understand or can do, such as a presentation or practical demonstration.

- **Self-assessment** – The learners take responsibility for judging their own knowledge or skills using teacher-set criteria.

- **Peer assessment** – The learners take responsibility for judging one another's knowledge or skills using teacher-set criteria.

These methods can be used at any stage of the journey (the initial, the ongoing or the end), and each have their advantages and disadvantages, which shall be explored as we progress through the chapter.

> **REFLECT**
>
> Can you think of any other assessment methods that can be used across the three core principles of assessment?

> **Take it further...**
>
> Identify some of the advantages and disadvantages of each method under each principle of assessment. For example, what are the advantages of essays at each of the stages of the learning journey?

As noted by Christodoulou (2018), before selecting the assessment method it is important to think carefully about the purpose of your assessment. In other words, we need to be clear about exactly what it is we want to assess, whether that's the starting point, the ongoing progress or the end point of the learning, and select the method that is most suitable in achieving this purpose. Once we have the purpose in mind, we should also consider the following VARCS guidelines in how we enact the chosen method, as adapted from Gravells (2017).

Guideline	What does it mean?	Example
Valid	We should select assessment methods that offer a high validity. This refers to whether the assessment method will measure what it intends to measure.	You want to determine whether your Hospitality learners are accurately able to set a dinner table. Because it is a skill that you are assessing, the most valid method of assessment would be to observe them physically setting a dinner table. A less valid approach would be to ask them to write an essay on how to set a table as this assesses their knowledge and understanding, not the skill.

Guideline	What does it mean?	Example
Authentic	We should select methods that allow for authenticity. This refers to whether the assessment method ensures that the knowledge or skills belong to the learner being assessed.	You want to assess that the learner has written their own essay, and this may be evidenced through their referencing to sources used, or through a signed authenticity statement. Alternatively, a bad example of authenticity is attempting to assess a learner's understanding of a topic which they are presenting to the class in a group of four. This makes it difficult to determine if all four learners have contributed equally to the presentation. In order to authentically assess all learners, all should contribute equally or should be asked follow-up questions to ensure that their knowledge and understanding can be assessed.
Reliable	We should select methods that are reliable. This refers to whether the learner will achieve the same outcome with different assessors, or if the method will assess all learners fairly.	You want to assess all learners' understanding of how to convert fractions to decimals. A more reliable approach would be to ask learners to complete standardised tasks with clear marking criteria. For example, matching fractions with their decimal equivalents, or using a multiple-choice quiz to identify the correct decimal form of fractions. The idea of reliability is to ensure consistency and objectivity.
Current	We should select methods that allow learners to provide current evidence of their knowledge, skills and behaviours. This refers to whether the assessment is accurately measuring the most up-to-date knowledge or skills as per the curriculum guidance.	You ask learners that are undertaking a first aid course to perform CPR using up-to-date breath to compression ratios.
Sufficient	We should select methods that allow learners to provide sufficient evidence of their knowledge, skills and behaviours. This refers to whether the volume of work is sufficient to demonstrate their understanding or meet set criteria.	You ask your travel and tourism learners to demonstrate that they know how to provide customer support to a diverse range of customers by performing a 5-minute role-play to another learner. If you were to only ask them to take part in a role-play with a single customer, this would be insufficient to demonstrate support to a 'diverse range' of customers. For summative assessments, awarding organisations usually indicate what is expected for sufficiency, but for other assessment methods, you need to keep in mind what you feel is enough.

Adapted from Gravells (2017)

Regardless of purpose or the method of assessment, consideration of the VARCS guidelines ultimately helps to ensure fairness for your learners, helping them to recognise the value of their learning. The following sections of this chapter explore the three principles of assessment in detail; you should bear the VARCS guidelines in mind throughout.

7.3 Initial assessment

The most important single factor influencing learning is what the learner already knows. Ascertain this and teach [them] accordingly. (Ausubel, 1968)

An initial assessment has the clear goal of identifying the learners' starting points. While this may relate to a wide range of aspects such as their learning needs, preferences or previous qualifications and experiences, during this chapter we will focus on initial assessment of the learners' knowledge and skills for the subject area they are learning. There are two ways we can consider initial assessment: as an assessment of the learners' starting points upon beginning the programme of study and as an assessment of the learners' starting points at the beginning of teaching sessions.

> **REFLECT**
>
> What are the benefits of identifying learners' starting points? How does this help you as a teacher?

Initial assessment at the beginning of a programme

Initial assessment that is undertaken right at the beginning of a learning programme refers to the judgement of a learners' knowledge and skills upon entry. This can cover a wide range of areas including, but not limited to, their prior qualifications and an English and maths assessment. In some cases, these assessments are supplemented by a diagnostic assessment that identifies specific gaps in knowledge and 'fault finds' the areas preventing a learner from achieving a particular standard. Take the metaphor of a car mechanic who undertakes an MOT to determine the car's safety and general health – where there is a failure (such as an oil leak), they may diagnose the specific fault by carrying out tests to identify the problem areas. This is essentially what a diagnostic assessment does.

As mentioned in chapter 3 (see page 73), many institutions require their teachers to create a group profile or individual learning plan based on the information gathered from initial and diagnostic assessments. These are important, but they are only really worth doing if the information is used to plan future learning. In our experience, the group profile can often become an unwieldy, unusable document that is used to satisfy other stakeholders in the institution rather than as a meaningful, working document that is used to inform planning.

In chapter 5 (see page 124), we explored the planning and sequencing of learning and considered Binder's theory of cumulative dysfluency, which is the idea that if you have gaps in foundational knowledge then these will impact all future learning. Of course, a pass in their level 2 course does not mean that the learner comes equipped with all knowledge and skills from that level of learning. Each learner will have different strengths and weaknesses and, while it may seem a challenging task, identifying the subject specific knowledge and skills that your learners come to your programme with is essential to supporting future learning. This is because doing so allows you to fill any gaps before teaching the higher-level content. So how can you assess this in a way that provides you with validity (measuring what you want it to measure) and reliability (measuring in the same way for different learners)?

> **REFLECT**
>
> Below are examples of two initial assessment activities. Which do you think will be more effective at identifying the key information you need to help you to plan for future learning, and why?

Grace – A-level biology teacher	Jonty – Beauty therapy teacher
Grace, an A-level (level 3) biology teacher uses the GCSE (level 2) biology specification to create a large multiple-choice quiz based on the content of all that should have been learned prior to starting the programme. The quiz is undertaken during the first science lesson, with learners' results analysed to determine common strengths and weaknesses in learners' prior knowledge. For common areas of weakness, Grace plans intervention sessions before introducing new content.	At the start of the level 3 beauty therapy course, Jonty provides learners with a handout which lists the topics they will learn and asks them to rate their level of confidence on a scale of 1–5 (unconfident– very confident) in relation to each topic. For those areas where learners lack confidence, Jonty plans extra time to cover these topics.

Example questions	Topic	Rating
1. Which of the following structures is found in plant cells but not in animal cells? A) Nucleus B) Cell membrane C) Chloroplast D) Mitochondria 2. Which part of the cell is responsible for controlling what enters and leaves the cell? A) Nucleus B) Cell wall C) Cell membrane D) Cytoplasm 3. What is the role of enzymes in biological reactions? A) Increase temperature B) Lower activation energy C) Change pH levels D) Create energy	Health safety and hygiene	
	Consultation techniques and client care	
	Manicure treatments	
	Pedicure treatments	
	Waxing services	
	Facial treatments	
	Skin type analysis	
	Eyebrow shaping services	
	Eyelash and eyebrow tinting services	
	Make-up applications	
	Anatomy and physiology for beauty therapists	
	Health and safety in the salon	
	Client care and consultation	
	Body analysis	
	Skin analysis	
	Swedish massage therapy	
	Body electrical treatment	
	Facial electrical treatment	
	Electrical science	
	Mechanical massage	
	Anatomy and physiology for the face and body systems	

Of course, there are criticisms of multiple-choice questioning, which we shall discuss later in this chapter, but Grace's approach ensures that she is assessing knowledge of her learners with higher validity and reliability compared to Jonty's approach. Asking learners to provide a confidence rating is extremely subjective and unreliable, as what one learner thinks is confident may be another learner's unconfident. Take the Dunning-Kruger effect – this is the idea that individuals with low ability or knowledge in a specific area overestimate their competence, while those with higher ability may underestimate their expertise (Kruger and Dunning, 1999). This is a highly dangerous cognitive bias that may present the teacher with misleading information about what the learners actually know and can do; for this reason, confidence ratings should generally be avoided.

> **Tip for Teaching**
>
> Think carefully about how you structure your initial assessments and consider how you could increase the validity and reliability in the planning of these.

> **REFLECT**
>
> How are learners' starting points assessed at your institution? Take a moment to discuss the impact of these initial assessment activities with a mentor or colleague. Are the findings useful in supporting your planning? In what ways could you improve these methods to provide more useful information to support planning?

> **Take it further...**
>
> How could you use the examples in the table above to inform your planning for initial assessment at the beginning of the programme? How does this relate to cumulative dysfluency as discussed in chapter 5 (see page 124)?

Initial assessment at the beginning of a lesson

The other way in which one can refer to initial assessment is the assessment that takes place at the beginning of a lesson or period of learning, such as a starter quiz. At this point it is worth recognising the multiple benefits of any form of assessment at the start of a lesson (see figure 7.1). In chapter 6 (see page 165), the benefits of retrieval practice were highlighted as a way to strengthen the long-term memory and activate prior knowledge. In addition to this, so long as there are new elements being assessed in the initial assessment at the beginning of the lesson, the teachers and learners also benefit from identifying specific gaps in the knowledge and skills that learners already have about the learning.

Once we identify the starting points of our learners, then we can teach or adapt the planned lesson accordingly. Here, the Goldilocks principle applies – just like the perfect temperature of porridge, there is a perfect amount of new learning we want our learners to face without finding it too easy or difficult.

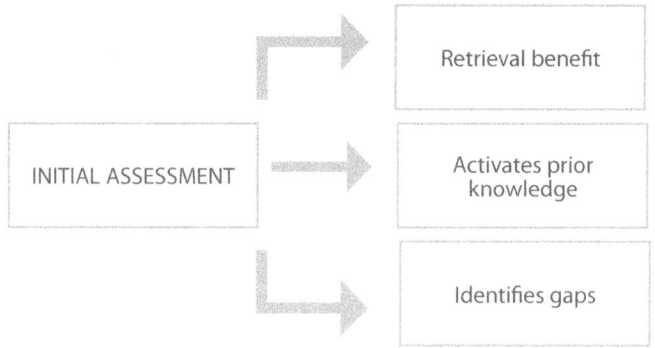

Figure 7.1 *Benefits of initial assessment*

If, during initial assessment, there are too many gaps in learners' knowledge and skills, then any new content is unlikely to stick. Instead, we should ensure pre-requisite prior knowledge is taught instead (see chapter 5, page 124 for the discussion about cumulative dysfluency). If there are too few gaps in learners' knowledge and skills, this will mean that the learners may need to be challenged beyond our planned learning so they do not become disengaged or demotivated.

While it is not an exact science about how much we want our learners to already know and be able to do at the beginning of their learning, we should aim to use our initial assessment to provide learners with the perfect amount of new learning and challenge to support their progress. There is the added challenge here for us as teachers to meet all learners' needs, as they will all know and be able to do different things to a greater or lesser extent. This is why it is essential that our initial assessment considers the previously mentioned VARCS principles (Gravells, 2017) during the design stage in order to accurately determine the starting points of all learners.

7.4 Formative assessment

> *The teacher's job is not to transmit knowledge, nor to facilitate learning. It is to engineer effective learning environments for the students. The key features of effective learning environments are that they create student engagement and allow teachers, learners, and their peers to ensure that the learning is proceeding in the intended direction. The only way we can do this is through assessment. That is why assessment is, indeed, the bridge between teaching and learning. (Wiliam 2018)*

The above quote makes clear that, no matter what teaching style you subscribe to, your role as a teacher is to ensure that learning is moving in the intended direction. To ensure that learners are proceeding in the intended direction and not leaving things to chance, formative assessment must be taking place throughout the teaching. We live and breathe this form of assessment, and all interactions and observations involve us making a judgement on whether our learners are progressing towards the intended destination. As Wiliam points out, formative assessment is the bridge between teaching and learning.

There are three key features of the formative assessment process that we wish to identify and examine throughout this section:

- **Clarify** – How formative assessment clarifies the expectations for learning and this consists of sharing the expected goals.

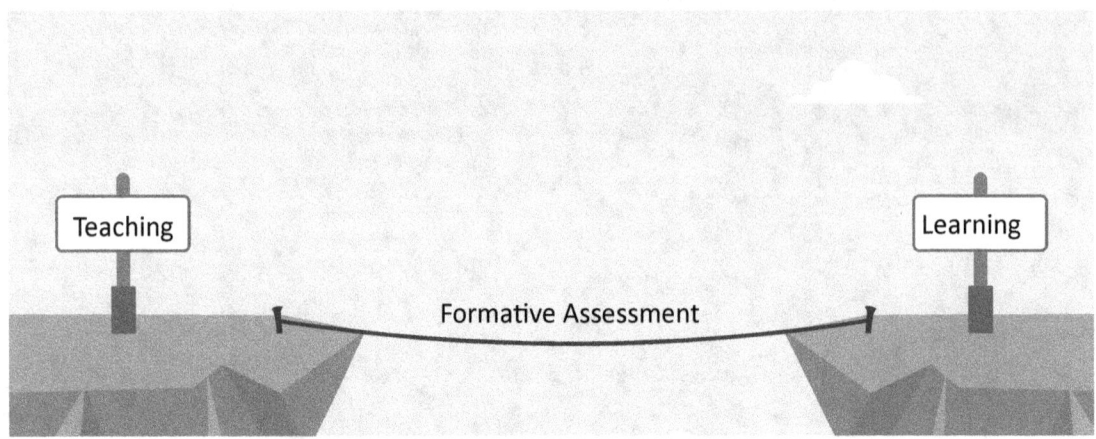

Figure 7.2 *Formative assessment*

- **Check** – The various methods that may be used to check the progress of the learners towards the goals.

- **Correct** – How the learners acquire and act upon feedback.

In this section, we take you through each of these features and, drawing on a range of research, unpack them to explore how we can ensure that formative assessment is used to successfully bridge the teaching and learning.

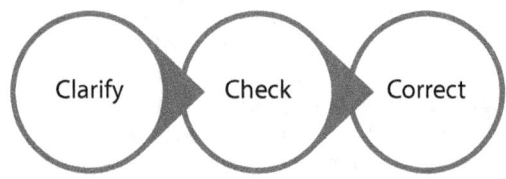

Figure 7.3 *Clarify, check and correct*

Clarify – provide clear goals for the lesson

Without a clear goal, what is the purpose of an assessment? Firstly, the end goal for the lesson is like a 'hook' from which you can hang your assessment to. In other words, you start with the end goal in mind and all your teaching, learning and assessment strategies direct the learners towards this goal.

Let us return to the learning journey metaphor and add a little more detail. If I wish to travel to London St Pancras and be there by 5pm for a 5:10pm train to Paris, I have a clear goal and now know exactly what it is I am expecting to achieve on the first part of the journey – this enables me to assess my progress. However, if I just set out on a journey without a destination in mind, I would have very little information to use in an assessment of my progress.

So, the basic premise of clarifying the goals for a lesson is that the learners have the same idea as their teacher about what is going on in the classroom and what they should be learning. However, before we go any further, and to ensure that there is no confusion with the language we use, we want to differentiate between some of the terminology associated with what is shared with learners at the beginning of a lesson, as different institutions refer to these notions in a variety of ways (sometimes even as synonyms for one another). However, there are slight nuances between the following terms:

- **Aims** – articulate the intentions of the lesson (e.g. to improve apostrophe use).
- **Learning intentions/objectives** – brief statements that outline the steps to achieving the aim (e.g. explore different types of apostrophe use, apply correct use to examples).
- **Outcomes** – the expected results or consequences of what was learned (e.g. be able to use apostrophes correctly).
- **Success criteria** – the specific things that make it a success (e.g. apostrophe use for contractions, before the 's' for singular ownership and after the 's' for plural ownership).

> **REFLECT**
>
> What language does your institution use in relation to these? Is there a requirement to use specific terms?

While some may argue that it does not really matter what you use, Hattie (2023) argues that a key finding in the evidence for the power of learning intentions and success criteria is that, in many instances, both are needed. Hattie goes on to suggest that learning intentions without success criteria give learners little to no concept of what the teachers consider to be successful in this learning (other than completion and compliance). For example, if a learning intention is to learn to write an essay, this leaves the learners wondering what a good essay looks like, something that success criteria set out.

By providing success criteria, this not only helps the teacher with their assessment of progress but learners can also be supported to monitor their own and one another's progress toward these standards. This is an important aspect to consider in the clarify phase of formative assessment as it helps to provide validity in the assessment; in other words, whatever method is selected for the assessment, the teacher and learners are using it to measure progress towards the specific outcome, not a vague destination.

The table below includes some examples of learning intentions and success criteria to support your understanding.

Aim: To develop learners' understanding of Piaget's schema and cognitive development theories.

Learning intention	Success criteria
To explore the key principles of 'schema', 'assimilation' and 'accommodation'.	Define the terms schema, assimilation and accommodation using key words: 'cognitive structures', 'integration', and 'disequilibrium'.
	Recognise the differences between assimilation and accommodation by providing an example of each.
To examine and critique Piaget's four stages of cognitive development.	Describe the four stages (sensorimotor, pre-operational, concrete operational and formal operational), including the name, age range and main features (including terminology above).
	Explain at least two strengths and two limitations of the theory including reference to its empirical evidence base and individual differences.

> **Tip for Teaching**
>
> When writing your learning intentions (whether you call that an 'aim', an 'objective' or an 'outcome'), try to write a few clear success criteria that you will share with your learners too. What are you expecting from them as a minimum to show they have achieved the intention?

Check – monitor learners' progress towards the lesson goal

Rosenshine (2012) draws upon research to suggest that more effective teachers engineer a high success rate of around 80% in their class before moving on with the learning. To ensure that 80% of our class knows and understands a topic, we need to measure progress, but it is important to remember that this is not an exact science; indeed, an 80% success rate would look completely different in making a pastry compared to a maths quiz. However, there are things we can be doing to improve our awareness of how learners are progressing, and the greater insight we have the better we can form judgements about our learners' progression.

The 'check' phase of formative assessment draws on the success criteria and uses a variety of methods to determine how learners are progressing towards it. Thinking back to our journey to London St Pancras, the checks will be regular, involving seeing various signs, listening to various information pieces and regularly checking the time to ensure that progression towards the intended goal is on track. In a teaching context, we reflected on the advantages and disadvantages of different forms of assessment at the beginning of the chapter. As we go through each assessment method in this section, we hope to highlight ways that each can be enhanced to mitigate against the disadvantages and create meaningful, valid and reliable assessment of the learners' progress.

Check phase method 1 – observation

Observation of learners' performance requires the teacher to monitor learners while delivering exposition or while learners are working independent of the teacher. Observation can allow teachers to gather real-time insights into learners' progress. This may sometimes involve the simple monitoring of learners' facial expressions as you provide instruction – this will not reveal much about their understanding, but there are telltale signs that a learner is not comprehending something. Signs of confusion such as frowns, lack of eye contact or hesitant body language may suggest a need for clarification or rephrasing. Conversely, signs of comprehension such as nodding, engaged eye contact or note-taking indicate learners may be following the material. These immediate cues allow teachers to adapt their delivery in the moment to better meet learners' needs.

Hall and Simerai (2015) suggest that observation as a form of assessment is not quite as easy as one may think. For this reason, they propose a more intentional process of noticing things in your class and having clear success criteria, observational rubrics or checklists in mind to make the assessment more objective and reliable. For example, while learners are working on a group task, you could actively monitor discussions with clear criteria in mind for what you are looking to observe, such as signs of engagement or the quantity and quality of the contributions of learners. Similarly, if observing learners completing a maths worksheet, you could intentionally look out for their responses to a particular step in a mathematical problem, which could reveal whether they have a misconception or not. If this is found to be the case, you can then address this widespread misunderstanding with the whole class.

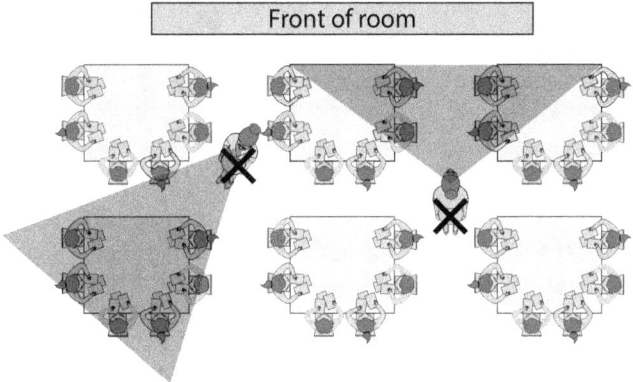

Figure 7.4a *Poor positioning for observational assessment*

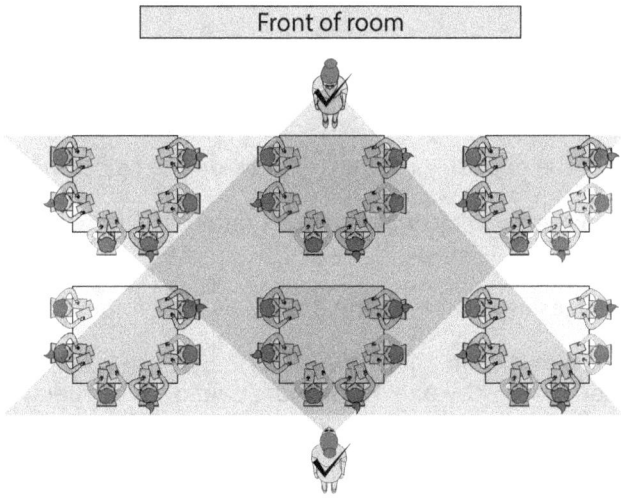

Figure 7.4b *Good positioning for observational assessment*

When thinking about implementing observation, it is also helpful to think about your positioning in the learning environment and consider how best to increase the number of learners being monitored. The first image, figure 7.4a, shows how your position may limit your observation assessment of group work in a typical classroom. In the second image, figure 7.4b, the teacher's position is on the periphery, allowing for a bigger picture of the room to be seen.

Reflect

Do you think about your positioning when you are observing your learners' progress? How could this work in your learning environment?

> **Tip for Teaching**
>
> When observing your learners, keep in mind an objective checklist of what you are looking for from them. Consider combining observation with other assessment strategies such as questioning to increase the reliability of the method.

Check phase method 2 – teacher questioning

Research suggests that teachers ask their learners around 300 questions per day (Almeida and Neri de Souza, 2010), yet too often these questions tend not to be of benefit to either the teacher or the learner. Questioning can be a very useful way to discern how well your learners are progressing towards the intended outcomes and success criteria; aside from this, questioning offers other benefits such as retrieval practice (as mentioned in chapter 6, page 165) and the opportunity to challenge learners' perspectives and encourage alternative ways of thinking. For the purpose of this chapter, we will focus on questioning as an assessment method to monitor understanding and improve the quality of teacher questioning. We will start by thinking about their use in two ways: for breadth of assessment and depth of assessment.

Questioning for breadth

What do we mean by this? When teaching, it is easy to throw out a question to the class that requires a voluntary response from the learners. For example:

- Can anybody tell me the opposing colour to yellow on the colour wheel?

- Do we multiply both the numerator and denominator or just the numerator when multiplying fractions?

- What does Marx suggest is the role of the Bourgeoise in capitalist society?

Posing questions like these results in one of two things: either the teacher accepts the first response that is provided (usually by one of the more confident learners) before clarifying or correcting it, or the teacher answers the question themselves because the room goes silent. Of course, this is hugely limiting as when we ask questions like this, we can only really discern the understanding of the one learner that responds, or in the case where we answer our own question, none of the learners get to showcase their understanding. Furthermore, Howe and Abedin's (2013) research suggests that learners' gender, ethnicity and prior attainment significantly affect the likelihood that they volunteer to contribute, rendering this approach as inherently excluding.

When considering breadth, we are aiming to increase the number of learners that respond to our questions so we get an idea of what most (if not all) of the room know and understand, making it more valid and reliable as a form of assessment. Let us consider the following questioning strategies and the breadth they provide.

Cold calling

Lemov's (2015) concept of cold calling, also known as 'targeted questioning' in some circles, is an inclusive approach to questioning where any learner can be called upon to respond to a question. Aside from some feeling uncomfortable with the notion of cold calling because it puts learners on the spot and may be challenging for some learners (particularly those with additional needs), if it is carefully built into the culture of your classroom – where a supportive and inclusive environment is established – it really does support a broader assessment of the learners. Indeed, Dallimore, Hertenstein and Platt (2012) found that in classes with high cold calling, learners' comfort with participating in class discussions increases, while in classes with low cold calling, learners' comfort with participating does not change. They also found that high cold calling resulted in learners being more willing to respond voluntarily.

The key to getting this right is to set the expectations clearly to the learners by stating that you will be asking for an individual to respond, so you do not want any shouting out or hands up. An example of this is: 'I'm going to ask an important question now and I will be selecting an individual to respond, so I do not want hands up or shouting out, please.' These expectations become the norm over time, so once expectations have been established it may be that you are no longer required to set the scene in this manner. The next step would be to pose the question you wish to be answered.

To support the inclusive nature of this approach, it is important to provide sufficient 'thinking time' to the learners by holding back the name of the learner you intend to ask the question to (as soon as you say the name, you are, in effect, ending the thinking for anyone else in your class). Figure 7.5 below is adapted from the work of Lemov and Taylor (2021); as you can see, once you ask the question, the sooner a name is provided, the sooner the remainder of the class can stop thinking about a response.

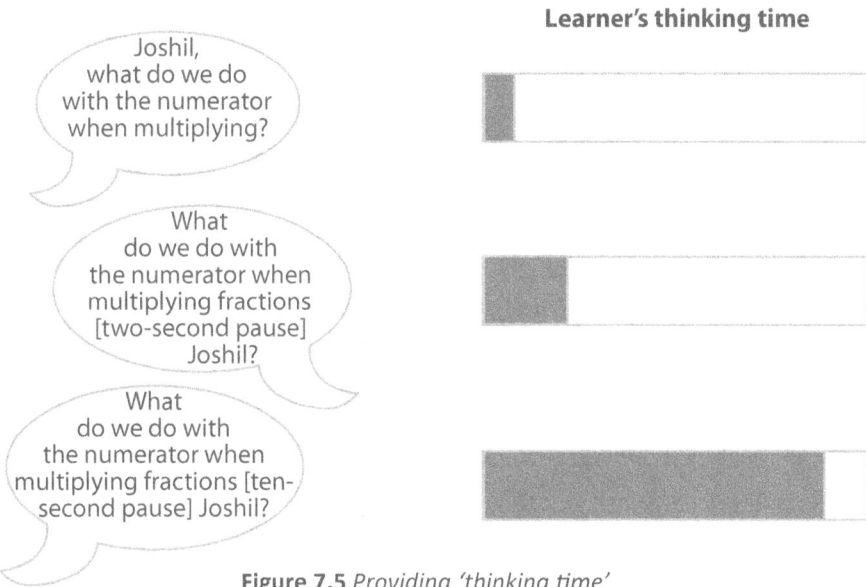

Figure 7.5 *Providing 'thinking time'*

However, you may be thinking that increasing the thinking time for the learners does not add breadth to the assessment. In other words, the teacher still knows as much as they would by asking the 'volunteer response' question. You would be right, though it does allow for more targeted assessment as there is a choice in who responds, rather than the first person that shouts or puts their hand up.

We can enhance this approach further by drawing on Petty's (2018) 'thank you' response, which is a great way of adding breadth to your assessment of learners because it does not reveal the correct answer immediately, leaving learners with a different answer the opportunity to attempt a response. Not only this, but it shows the learners appreciation for their responses, which helps establish a respectful and participatory learning environment.

Let us look at an example:

- **Teacher:** Without any shouting out or putting hands up, what does Marx suggest is the role of the bourgeoise in capitalist society? [10-second pause] Ifra?
- **Ifra:** That the bourgeoise owns the means of production
- **Teacher:** Thank you, Ifra. Callum, what do you think?
- **Callum:** I think they are the class that is oppressed.
- **Teacher:** Thank you, Callum. And Niamh, what about you?
- **Niamh:** I think the same as Ifra, that the bourgeoise owns the means of production and it's the proletariat class that is oppressed.
- **Teacher:** Thank you. Yes, the bourgeoise are the ones that own the means of production, and the proletariats are the oppressed class, so let's make sure we have those names the right way around everyone.

This example shows how a simple 'thank you' in response to the first answer meant that the teacher could also determine what other learners in the class thought. Had the teacher acknowledged that Ifra responded with the correct answer initially, then they would not know that Callum had a misconception or that Niamh knew the answer. So here we are starting to build a bigger picture of who knows and understands what in the class.

This line of questioning could continue, but it may get a bit tedious for everyone if the teacher keeps asking every learner individually and saying thank you. However, there is a further tweak that can be made to this to enhance the breadth of assessment. Continuing to use 'thank you' to acknowledge the learners' responses the teacher can build an even bigger picture of the learners' understanding by using the 'agree or disagree' approach.

- **Teacher:** Without any shouting out or putting hands up, what does Marx suggest is the role of the Bourgeoise in capitalist society? [10-second pause] Ifra?
- **Ifra**: That the bourgeoise owns the means of production.
- **Teacher:** Thank you, Ifra. Callum, what do you think?
- **Callum:** I think they are the class that is oppressed"
- **Teacher:** Thank you, Callum. Put your hand up if you agree with Callum. [Waits for response and observes who else has misconception] Thank you. Now put your hand up if you agree with Ifra. [Waits for response and observes who else understands] Thank you. The correct answer is that the bourgeoise owns the means of production, and it is the proletariat that are the oppressed class.

Of course, there is always the risk that learners just put their hand up to agree or disagree without knowing the correct answer, but we are moving closer to finding out what more of our learners know and understand, which is the whole purpose of the check phase for formative assessment. Remember, if we just asked the open 'voluntary response' question, it is only the one confident learner that has revealed their understanding, so we simply cannot make a judgement of all learners' understanding on the basis of a single learner.

> **REFLECT**
>
> What approach to questioning do you usually adopt in the classroom? Does it offer breadth?

> **Take it further...**
>
> Can you think of any issues with your approach to questioning? How could you mitigate against these?

Cold calling does bring about an issue when thinking about reliability of assessment, as it is easy for the teacher to fall into the trap of only asking a few learners the same question. The result is that throughout the course of a lesson learners are asked different questions that require entirely different answers. One way to manage this, and the issue of increasing breadth, is to give all learners the opportunity to respond to the same questions.

Think, pair, share

This method of questioning affords learners many benefits but does increase the number of learners involved in the question. As with cold calling, a culture must be established that supports learners to prepare a response and have an opportunity to respond. After beginning with independent thinking time, learners have an opportunity to give a response to their partner. In pairs, they can then share initial thoughts, identify gaps and misconceptions, agree on the paired response and rehearse it before sharing with the group (Sherrington, 2019). The teacher is then able to draw upon a number of responses to build a clearer picture of all learners' knowledge and understanding (such as in the following example).

- **Teacher:** I'm going to ask a question, and I'd like you to think about the answer for about 10 seconds, I'll then prompt you to speak to your partner and reach an agreement on your answer, before I select some of you to share with the whole group.

- **Teacher:** What is the opposing colour to yellow on the colour wheel and why do we need to know this? [10-second pause] Right, now share your answers with a partner and decide on a final answer to share with the group. [one-minute pause] Sid, what did you and Mikaela respond with?

- **Sid:** We said it's purple and that we would need to know it when bleaching hair because it may go yellow, and we would use purple toner to make it look less yellow.

- **Teacher:** Thank you, Sid. What about your pair, Meg?

- **Meg:** Isabelle and I said that it's violet, and using a toner with this colour helps to neutralise the yellow colour on bleached hair.

- **Teacher:** Thank you, Meg. Put your hands up if you said similar to Meg and Sid's pairs? [Pause to see who raises their hand] Hafza, your hand is down, what did your pair respond?

- **Hafza:** We said green, but we aren't very sure about it. We know it's important for hair colouring though.

- **Teacher:** Thank you. Yes, you are correct that it's important for when we are working with colours on hair and the correct answer for the opposite colour to yellow is violet and a violet toner would help to neutralise the yellows following a bleach.

As we can see in this example, the teacher can start to gauge the knowledge and understanding of a much larger number of learners by combining the paired element with the questioning, and crucially, more learners are responding to the same questions, which helps with the reliability of this style of questioning.

Whole class responses

While there are several ways a teacher can gain a response from the whole class (such as writing a short answer on a whiteboard), multiple choice questions (MCQs) can reliably be used as whole class response questions to support the teacher in identifying the gaps in learners' knowledge and understanding. MCQs also benefit from learners being able to respond in a wide variety of ways, for example:

- A handout quiz that learners complete individually and swap with a partner for marking.

- A simple set of questions on the board or slides where learners respond with mini whiteboards, 'ABCD' card sets or hands to provide a response. When the learners answer these questions, we need to be able to see the responses of all individuals and make a judgement quickly to determine whether to move on or revisit information accordingly.

- A wealth of online tools allow for MCQs to be administered to all, and automated marking can generate clear analytics quickly. Examples include an online quiz that learners complete individually using an electronic device (e.g. Kahoot) or a Plickers quiz that only requires the teacher to have a device and learners to show a graphic to reveal their answer to questions.

If we think back to Rosenshine's suggestion that we should obtain high success rates of at least 80% before moving on, then a well-planned whole class response activity may provide us with more usable data to determine success rates and whether the class is ready to move on. Wiliam (2018) attests to this approach, suggesting that at key 'hinge' points in the lesson MCQs can be used as a marker as to whether to re-teach or progress with the lesson material.

While there is always the argument that learners can simply guess answers to MCQs, if we increase the number of questions to respond to, this increases the reliability of the assessment. For example, an assessment with 10 questions and four choices per question gives learners a 1-in-285 probability of getting seven of the answers correct by simply guessing. In this case, 70% would still be less than the suggested 80% success rate we would like to attain.

Another way to increase validity and reliability is through careful crafting and design of the question stem and optional answers, though this can be challenging and time-consuming. The table below includes some considerations that may help when planning your MCQs.

Considerations when designing MCQs

Consideration	Example
The stem for the question should be meaningful by itself and should include the main idea. Basically, this means that the main thing you're trying to find out about should be in the stem.	What chamber does deoxygenated blood enter in the heart? *(I am trying to find out if they know about chambers of the heart)*
The stem should not contain irrelevant material. The questions need to get to the point and avoid any confusion.	In the body there are a number of organs which function together to keep us alive. The heart is one of them, but which chamber does deoxygenated blood enter it?

Consideration	Example
Avoid a negatively written stem. Negatives can cause ambiguity in what is being asked and, just because a learner knows an incorrect answer, this doesn't mean that they know the correct one.	Which of the following elements is NOT one of the four Ps of the marketing mix? a) Product b) Price c) Promotion d) Partnership
Rodriguez (2005) informs us that it is not the number of distractors but the quality of distractors that are important when designing answers for MCQs. Essentially, each incorrect answer should be plausible. In the example, there is clearly one implausible response.	In what year was Winston Churchill first chosen as Prime Minister? a) 1700 b) 1940 c) 1941 d) 1942
There should not be more than one answer that can be defended as a correct response by using correct reasoning. In the example, the two starred responses could be defended as correct.	How long does an annual plant generally live? a) It dies after the first year. b) It lives for many years. c) It lives for more than one year. d) It needs to be replanted each year.
Avoid including a word from the stem in the answers. This can provide a clue to the answer, and for some, they may think of it as a trick question, thus go with an alternative answer.	What muscle is the agonist on a biceps curl? a) Biceps b) Deltoid c) Hamstring d) Triceps
Avoid 'all of the above' and 'none of the above' as, more often than not, this option is the correct answer in MCQs.	Which of the following are branches of engineering? a) Mechanical engineering b) Civil engineering c) Electrical engineering d) All of the above
The choices should be presented in a logical order (e.g. numerical or alphabetical) to avoid any clues as to which is the correct response. Avoid having the starting letters of each answer show an obviously different response. For example, in the first set of answers, Hungary clearly stands out and this may lead learners to respond with that, whereas in the second set of responses, each starting letter is different and leaves no clues.	Which country was part of the Central Powers during World War I? a) Greece a) France b) Ghana b) Hungary c) Greenland c) Russia d) Hungary d) Spain

As we can see, writing MCQs is not something you can throw together a few minutes before a lesson. Writing them effectively requires time and a number of elements need to be considered.

> **Tip for Teaching**
>
> To save you some time generating MCQs, try using an AI platform such as Chat GPT to generate your questions, but do make sure you critique what is produced and amend accordingly. The better your prompts, the better the questions. It may also help to work with your colleagues to build a bank of questions that can be used in your subject.

Questioning for depth

Where breadth refers to broad coverage of the learners in your class, depth refers to how much detail you garner from the learners. For example, if you involve all the learners in the response to an MCQ, you may have a lot of useful information, but this is limited to a single response and may not reveal the extent to which the learners understand or have misconceptions. Depth requires us to probe learners' understanding by using 'how' and 'why' questions; not only does this better reveal their understanding, but it also allows the teacher to challenge and support deeper and critical thinking.

The 'agree, build, challenge' (ABC) method is a great way to enhance the breadth – we can see an example of it below:

- **Teacher:** Without any shouting out or putting hands up, what does Marx suggest is the role of the bourgeoise in capitalist society? [10-second pause] Ifra?
- **Ifra:** That the bourgeoise owns the means of production.
- **Teacher:** Thank you, Ifra. Put your hand up if you **agree** with Ifra. [Waits for response and observes who else agrees] Niamh, your hand is up, **build** upon Ifra's answer by explaining why you agree.
- **Niamh:** I agree that the bourgeoisie own the means of production, and their role is actually to control what is produced, how it is produced, and for whom it is produced which enables them to control the labour process.
- **Teacher:** Thank you, Niamh. Callum, your hand was down, **challenge** Ifra and Niamh by saying why you disagree.
- **Callum:** I disagree because I think the bourgeoise are the class that is oppressed by the proletariat, and it is the proletariats that own the means of production.
- **Teacher:** Thank you, Callum. I can see by your answer that you understand the key principles here, but I think you have confused the two groups. Now that we know it is the bourgeoise that owns the means to production, can you build on Niamh's point and explain how they can control the labour process?

This approach to questioning aligns with Bloom's taxonomy (Anderson and Krathwohl, 2001), which, while being imperfect as a classification of knowledge and skills, does help us think about the difference between lower- and higher-order thinking (regurgitation of facts versus a deeper understanding of the connection between facts and processes). The development of learners' higher-order learning is critical in education, and Bloom's taxonomy has been used as a template for teachers to frame questions that progresses learners from lower-order thinking to higher-order thinking (Farmer et al, 2021).

For example, a lower-order question could be, 'What is the capital of France?' This requires simple factual knowledge. On the other hand, a higher-order question could be, 'How could France's economic model both limit and leverage its potential for technological innovation and global economic competitiveness in the rapidly changing global marketplace?' This is a much more challenging question that requires the learners to analyse economic structure, synthesise and then think critically about their knowledge of economics, technology and policy. The table below provides examples to help you build these higher-order questions.

LOW → HIGH						
Question	Is...?	Did...?	Can...?	Would...?	Will...?	May...?
What						
Where						
When						
Who						
Why						
How						

(LOW ↓ HIGH on vertical axis)

In Argarwal's (2019) study, learners engaged in retrieval practice with lower-order (fact-based) questions, higher-order questions or a mix of the two to examine the optimal type of retrieval practice for enhancing higher-order learning. The study demonstrated that higher-order learning increases most from higher-order retrieval practice, and though fact-based quizzes were beneficial for factual learning, they did not facilitate higher-order learning contrary to popular intuition based on Bloom's taxonomy.

Tip for Teaching

Consider how you build your questioning towards those that promote higher-order thinking in your subject specialism. Use the questioning grid in figure 7.6 above to support.

Peer assessment

Within a typical class, there is a ratio of one teacher to 25–30 learners, which means that the resource to determine learners' progress towards the lesson goal is very limited. As a teacher, it is challenging to monitor the progress and identify the strengths and areas for development of all learners through questioning and observation alone, so it is important to create more resource in the classroom to monitor and support progression for the learners. We can do this by getting the learners to check and support one another's work or performance.

Wiliam (2018) advocates using learners as resources for one another as a vital strategy in formative assessment as it empowers learners to learn with and from one another. The peer assessment method requires learners to provide feedback to their peers based on the quality of their work or performance. This can not only improve the learning of those gaining feedback about their strengths and areas for development, but it also improves the learning of those carrying out the assessment and feedback as they acquire a better understanding of performance expectations and how to improve themselves, akin to metacognition (as discussed in chapter 6, see page 172).

However, despite the potential benefits of encouraging peer assessment and feedback, there are problems that may arise that can impact the validity and reliability of this method. For example, Nuthall's (2007) comprehensive, longitudinal classroom research in middle schools in New Zealand found that much of what learners learn in classrooms comes from peers anyway, rather than teachers. His findings suggest that as much as 80% of feedback in a typical classroom is between peers, yet around 80% of that feedback is inaccurate. It is important for us to consider how we could mitigate against some of the issues in the planning process to increase the validity and reliability of the method.

Problem	Potential mitigation
Learners are not aware of how to assess or give feedback	Provide suitable structures and ensure that clear success criteria are provided (what good 'looks like'). It is helpful to provide a writing frame for this feedback to support verbal comments.
Bias or inaccuracies in peer feedback	As far as possible, you should share success criteria, which allows for objectivity. In other words, the peer must be factual about the degree to which a performance or piece of work meets the success criteria.
Reluctance to critique peers due to social dynamics	Establishing a supportive environment is crucial to enable learners to take part in honest and respectful exchanges. Feedback should focus on constructive, actionable insights.

Tip for Teaching

When planning opportunities for peer assessment and feedback, ensure that you foster a supportive environment with clear success criteria and guidance for giving feedback.

Self-assessment

Self-assessment is one of the most powerful forms of formative assessment according to Wiliam (2018) as it helps learners to take ownership of their learning and promotes independence. Indeed, Hattie's (2023) large-scale meta-analysis emphasises the significant role that self-assessment has in fostering learners' ability to reflect and regulate their own learning, suggesting a moderate positive impact on learner achievement.

Self-assessment requires learners to evaluate their performance or work against clearly established success criteria, identifying strengths and areas for improvement. This goes some way to helping learners to value their learning and build confidence and motivation. However, like all of the strategies discussed so far, self-assessment is not without its problems. The table below includes some of these issues along with potential mitigations to increase the reliability and validity of the method.

Problem	Potential mitigation
Learners may lack the skills to assess themselves accurately	You should explicitly train your learners how to carry out assessment using a clearly structured framework for the assessment and feedback. By modelling how to perform the assessment, you can set the expected standards.
Learners may over- or underestimate their own performance or work quality	As with removing bias from peer assessment, as far as possible, you should share success criteria which allows for objectivity. In other words, the learner must be factual about the degree to which their performance or piece of work meets the success criteria. It is helpful to include a checklist or rubric here.

Tip for Teaching

You should model effective self-assessment and provide clear success criteria, using checklists, rubrics or reflective journals to guide learners.

In this 'check' section, we have looked at four strategies that you could use to monitor learners' progress towards learning goals. We have considered various ways to enhance the reliability and validity of these strategies to maximise our (and the learners') ability to identify strengths and areas for development. In the 'correct' section, we delve further into the principles of feedback to ensure that learners are given the best opportunity to action any areas for development and progress towards the learning goals.

Correct – provide feedback to move learning forward

Feedback, on average, is powerful, but some feedback is more powerful.
(Wisniewski, Zierer and Hattie, 2020)

A fundamental component of 'correct' requires feedback that shows whether learners have met the learning goals or success criteria and to what extent. I will know if I made it to St Pancras by seeing a sign for the station, but if I did not get there for 5pm, I would need to know the extent to which I missed the time frame and what I can do to ensure I make it on time in the future. In the context of teaching, feedback is information provided either by the teacher to learners or one learner to another regarding aspects of the learners' performance or understanding (Hattie and Timperley, 2007).

In their **meta-analysis** of feedback, Wisniewski, Zierer and Hattie (2020) found that feedback overall has a positive effect on learning. However, there are certain ways that feedback can be delivered, whether written or verbally, to enhance learning further.

(**Meta-analysis** is where researchers examine the data from a number of separate studies in the same subject to find trends.)

Feedback with grades

There is an adage when it comes to assessment that 'you don't fatten a pig by weighing it'. In essence, if we just measure our learners' progress (weighing them) and do not provide feedback (or food in the case of the pig) to move them forward, they will not grow.

Indeed, this idea stems from the research of Butler (1988), where she found the following outcomes from different types of evaluation for learners.

Type of feedback	Low achievers	High achievers
Grade-only feedback	Low interest and performance	High interest and no impact on performance
Comment-only feedback	High interest and performance	High interest and performance
Grade and comment feedback	Low interest and performance	High interest and low performance

Figure 7.6 *Feedback to ensure progress*

What is interesting from this study is that 'grade-only' had no impact on performance for both low and high achievers, but high achievers quite liked the fact that they were getting higher grades. This makes a lot of sense as there will not be much improvement in subsequent performances if there is no information about how to improve. The comments only group had high interest and performance from both low and high achievers, so we would probably expect the same for grades with comments, would we not? Well, it turns out that the grading is the problem and, again, while interest was increased for high achievers, both groups failed to benefit from the comments.

> **REFLECT**
>
> Have you ever been handed back an essay or exam paper with the grade and feedback on? What is it you were most interested in when you got it back? Did you pay any attention to the feedback comments? No? Us neither!

Feedback on the task

In an earlier study by Butler (1987), she provided different types of feedback to a different group of learners following a lesson and examined the difference in the quality of work produced in the next lesson. The different types of feedback included comments only, grades only, praise only and no feedback.

In addition to this, the learners completed a questionnaire to identify what factors influenced their work, such as whether their effort and success or failure was attributed to themselves (ego-focused) or the work they were doing (task-focused). Examples of each can be found in the table below.

Attribution to...	Ego-focused	Task-focused
Effort	To do better than others	Interest
	To avoid doing worse than others	To improve performance
Success or failure	Ability	Interest
	Performance of other	Effort
		Experience of previous learning

Type of feedback	Task focus	Ego focus
Comment-only feedback	High	Low
Grade-only feedback	Low	High
Praise-only feedback	Low	High
No feedback	Low	Low

Adapted from Wiliam (2018)

The table above shows that learners in receipt of 'comment-only' feedback on their performance had high levels of task involvement with the same level of ego involvement as the control group, whereas those given praise and those in receipt of 'grade-only' had comparably high levels of ego involvement and low task. In other words, getting grades or praise in feedback only serves the ego and results in comparisons to others or one's view of their natural ability.

Findings from this seminal research suggests that 'comment-only' feedback is more beneficial to supporting learner's interest and focusing on improving their learning compared to 'grade-only' or 'praise-only' feedback.

Tip for Teaching

Where possible, try to remove any talk of grades and praise in feedback given to your learners. Focus on the effort they make and the task (success criteria), not the learners' abilities or performances against one another.

Feed forward

Feedback is more effective the more information it contains, particularly about where-to-next.

(Hattie and Clarke, 2019)

There is no doubt that feedback is an essential ingredient for assessment – only by giving feedback can we 'fatten the pig'. However, a word of caution: Kluger and DeNisi's (1996) review of 3,000 feedback studies found that, on average, feedback increases achievement with an effect size of 0.81. This is great, and suggests that feedback can support a significant improvement in achievement. However, the research found that around one third of the studies reviewed, feedback had a negative impact. This led Kluger and DeNisi to dig a little deeper to find out why some feedback has a negative impact while other feedback is positive, and they found two things of note.

First, like Butler, they found that feedback that was task-focused was more impactful than feedback that was ego-focused. Ego-focused feedback comments on the individual's self-perception, emotions and identity (for example, 'you're not very good at this task'), whereas task-focused feedback comments on specific actions, behaviours and performance related to a task (for example, 'this report lacks the detailed explanation needed to pass').

Second, feedback that looked forward rather than focusing on the past was deemed to be more effective. However, many readers have probably undertaken some form of training where feedback models focus on the past. One such example is the 'feedback sandwich', whereby something negative is packaged between two positive comments about the performance or quality of work.

Even if feedback is task-focused, this is problematic as the learner may not know how to move forward with their work. When we drive, for example, we acknowledge what is behind us (in the past) by looking in the mirrors but give most of our attention to what is ahead of us.

Figure 7.8 *Driving as a metaphor for feedback*

There are many different strategies you that may have come across to support feedback in this manner. For example, Petty's (2018) 'medal and mission' suggests that you award learners a medal for the positive aspects of the task before setting them a task-based mission to improve their work for future. Let us look at an example of this:

*Jamal, you have clearly fit-up the plates accurately and your weld indicates that the distance to the joint was good, as the arc is the correct depth (**medal**). If you look at the model example, the bead size is slightly larger. To increase the size of the bead, you need to decrease the speed that you move along the joint. In your next attempt, continue in the same manner as before, but with a slightly slower speed (**mission**).*

Similar approaches in education circles include the 'what went well' (WWW) and 'even better if (EBI)' method and the 'two stars and a wish' model. Regardless of the name, what all of these have in common is a forward-looking focus.

Tip for Teaching

With clear success criteria and a framework for giving feedback (such as 'medal and mission'), your learners will benefit from contributing more to their own and their peer's learning.

Wiliam (2018) argues that 'the first fundamental principle of effective classroom feedback is that [it] should be more work for the recipient than the donor.' In other words, the effectiveness of feedback – whether that is from the teacher, peers or the learner – can only be understood if learners are provided with the opportunity to act upon it and improve their performance. It is essential, therefore, that learners are given the opportunity to redress any misconceptions or errors with their work and that further checks are made to determine success towards the learning goals. This is arguably a feature of formative assessment that is often overlooked.

> **Tip for Teaching**
>
> Plan time into your lessons to allow for remedial work.

Case study

Now that you have been introduced to the key features of effective formative assessment, below are a series of case studies demonstrating – to varying degrees of quality – some of these features from different contexts within FES.

General FE college

BTEC level 3 sport, Unit 9: Sports coaching

Dexter is teaching his learners about adapting sports coaching sessions for participants from different backgrounds.

He provides learners with some key principles for adapting coaching sessions to different participants, using questions to check understanding and provides feedback to clarify and/or correct this. He then explains that learners will use the key principles to adapt their previously completed coaching plans for three different scenarios. An example of the expected standard of work is provided to learners for reference.

Learners are asked to work in pairs on different challenging scenarios which they have to adapt their session plans to. Dexter monitors progress throughout the task, constantly observing and where necessary, encouraging, prompting and probing. When each pair has completed the task, Dexter gets the pairs to join another pair to peer assess each other's work and offer suggestions for improvement using the key principles as success criteria. Each pair then has time to consider this feedback, and, if necessary, use it to improve their work. When this is complete, each pair takes turns in presenting their final plan to the rest of the group.

Independent training provider

Level 2 diploma in hairdressing – washing and drying

Nichola's hairdressing learners are working in the salon learning to wash and dry their clients' hair. Nichola explains the purpose of the lesson and models how to perform the washing and drying techniques, breaking each down with clear steps (success criteria) to follow which are written on the board.

Nichola then sets the learners off to work independently, and she circulates the room as learners are working. As she circulates, she asks questions which are closely linked to the success criteria, such as:

- Why is it important to test the water temperature?
- What is important to check before putting shampoo onto the hair?
- What would you do if the client had an allergy to something in the shampoo?

She then confirms or clarifies the correct answer before moving on to another learner.

Technical college
T Level in onsite construction – carpentry (basic wood joints)

Sandra is teaching her T Level learners how to construct a basic mortise and tenon joint.

She begins the lesson with a demonstration on proper tool use and techniques to construct the joint before asking learners to work in pairs to construct a small frame using provided blueprints. As the learners are working, she circulates to offer guidance.

At the end of the lesson, the learners present their work for feedback from peers.

Adult community learning centre
Functional skills level 1 maths – converting fractions and decimals

Yulia is teaching her learners how to convert fractions to decimals in functional skills maths.

She knows that most are anxious about this, having struggled in their previous education experiences, so provides many examples on the board to show how to do the conversions, before putting learners into groups of three to complete different worksheets.

Every 10 minutes, she asks each group to review and evaluate their progress by sharing correct answers on the board which they use to check their progress against.

After the first review, she identified the learners with the higher scores and mixed them up with learners with lower scores into new groups of three, explaining that they need to work together on the next worksheet to make sure that everybody's learning is as good as the best.

She repeats this process a further two times, providing bespoke feedback and support to those that struggled, until everyone is scoring highly. She then moves on to the next segment of the lesson.

> **REFLECT**
>
> Review the scenarios above and, using the key features of effective formative assessment (clarify, check, correct), identify how effective each teacher's formative assessment practices are.

> **Take it further...**
>
> How would you improve the different approaches used to ensure that all of the key features of effective formative assessment (clarify, check, correct) are included.

Summary of formative assessment

In this section, we have focused on formative assessment as the bridge between teaching and learning. It has highlighted the three key features of formative assessment that, if done well, can help you as a teacher to meet the requirements of occupational duty 2 – 'maintain a focus on outcomes, for all learners, so that they recognise the value of their learning and the future opportunities available to them.' These key features include:

- **Clarify** the learning intentions and success criteria with learners. This helps you and the learners to maintain a focus on outcomes.

- **Check** the progress learners are making through methods that allow for breadth and depth (observation, questioning, self-assessment and peer assessment). This helps you and the learners to recognise the value of their learning.

- **Correct** through high-quality feedback that is task-based and being focused on how to improve and redress areas for development. This helps you and the learners to be mindful of the opportunities for development they have throughout the programme of study.

Where formative assessment is the bridge between teaching and learning, the next section will focus on assessing the learning that has taken place after a period of study, also known as summative assessment.

7.5 Summative assessment

The goal of instruction is to facilitate learning, which must be inferred at some point after instruction. Learning, however, must be distinguished from performance, which is what can be observed and measured during instruction or training.

(Soderstrom and Bjork, 2015)

This quote makes a strong distinction between learning – that which is a relatively permanent change in long-term memory (see chapter 6 for more information) – and performance – the knowledge, understanding and skills that we assess through formative assessment methods during the teaching. What is the difference between the two?

Case study: The difference between learning and performance

I'm going to teach you a new concept, scrying, which you've likely never heard of but will no doubt be able to understand based on your prior knowledge.

Scrying involves gazing into a reflective surface such as water or glass to receive visions or insights. It has historically been used in different cultures from ancient Egypt to medieval Europe and was often associated with mystics. Many believe it taps into the subconscious, offering insights that aren't immediately apparent.

Having provided a basic overview, I'm now going to formatively assess by asking you to respond aloud to the following questions without looking back at the above paragraph.

- What is the name for gazing into a reflective surface to receive visions or insights?

- What do people believe that the process taps into?

For those of you that responded correctly to the above questions, you have just 'performed'. You can't be certain that you've learned the information because it's not clear that you've integrated the information into your schema and secured a permanent change in your long-term memory. Only when you're able to return to these questions in a few days or weeks can a better judgement about whether you have learned it be made.

In this case study, there should be assessment of the learning once the teaching has taken place. The purpose of summative assessment is to summarise the learning that took place, and unlike formative assessment (which is embedded within teaching), summative assessment is separate from teaching. Summative assessment can take many forms, but for most study programmes it will likely take the form of a written exam or observation or a piece of coursework that is either written or presented.

> **REFLECT**
>
> How are the learners on your programme of study summatively assessed? Do you think this assessment comes after an appropriate period of learning to summarise what has been learned?

External summative assessments

For formal examinations, awarding organisations usually produce external summative assessments and the requirements for them; when learners undertake the assessment, exam conditions apply. The assessment is usually externally assessed by trained individuals on behalf of the awarding organisation; for example, an end-point assessor (EPA) from the awarding organisation may visit your centre to observe and have a professional discussion with a learner to assess them against their apprenticeship standard. Another approach involves all learners' papers being sent to the awarding organisation for marking and grading following a formal written assessment under exam conditions.

Details about how the logistics of an exam, past examination papers and grading criteria can be found on the awarding bodies' websites; it is your responsibility to be aware of any requirements well in advance of your learners undertaking them. In addition to the core learning on the programme, it is worth supporting your learners with techniques that can help with exam conditions so that it is not overwhelming for them. For example, you could plan to integrate exam questions and self-marking into some lessons as part of your formative assessment, teach them how to read the meaning of exam questions and how to answer them succinctly or plan for them to undertake a practice exam under exam conditions.

Internal summative assessments

For programmes of study that have flexibility in the assessment design, it is important to follow the programme specification guidance to ensure that all requirements of the awarding body are met. This information provides detail in relation to the validity, authenticity, reliability, currency and sufficiency (VARCS) principles discussed earlier in this chapter (see page 200). These assessments are usually internally assessed, meaning that you will be required to mark and feed back to the learners against the assessment criteria.

To ensure all learners studying these programmes across the country are assessed reliably and fairly, institutions are required to appoint an internal verifier or moderator who undertakes specific training. Their role is to randomly sample your marking and feedback and confirm that the awarding organisations' standards have been maintained. The awarding organisation also appoints an individual who acts on their behalf to externally confirm that the standards have been maintained. This may involve sampling a small number of pieces of work remotely, an in-person visit to sample a larger body of work or both.

Awarding organisations often provide example assessment briefs that can be used, but there is flexibility to allow you to adapt these to your context and the learners you are working with. For example, if you are teaching a BTEC sport and are based near a coastal area, the assessment brief scenario may refer to water sports, which would be more applicable to those that are more likely to gain employment in the industry compared to learners on the same programme located far from a coastline.

Whether creating your own internally assessed summative assessment in line with awarding organisation requirements (or following an example they provide), it is crucial that you keep the VARCS principles in mind to ensure that the assessment is fair and robust.

> **REFLECT**
>
> Based on the VARCS model, reflect on the two scenarios in the table below and determine whether they are suitable to assess learning in relation to the assessment criteria.

Scenario 1: BTEC Level 1/Level 2 First Award in Health and Social Care – Unit 2: Health and Social Care Values	Scenario 2: BTEC Level 3 National Diploma in Business – Unit 3: Business Finance
The assessment criteria in the unit specification are: P1: Describe the care values that underpin current practice in health and social care. P2: Explain the importance of applying care values in health and social care settings. **The teacher uses this assessment criteria to create the following assessment task:** You are preparing a presentation for new staff at a local health and social care organisation, 'care2you'. The presentation aims to help new employees understand the care values that underpin good practice and the importance of applying these values in their day-to-day roles. Working in groups of three, you should create a poster on A3 paper that identifies three care values required for high-quality care and support. Your poster should contain appropriate images. Once you have completed your poster, take a photograph of it and upload it to the MS Teams site.	**The assessment criteria in the unit specification are:** P1: Explain the importance of costs, revenue, and profit for a business organisation. M1: Analyse how changes in costs and revenue affect profitability in a business. **The teacher uses this assessment criteria to create the following assessment task:** Roy's Cycles is a local bicycle shop that sells bikes, accessories, and provides repair services. As the financial consultant for Roy's Cycles, your task is to explore and explain the various costs that the business incurs in order to help the owners understand the financial implications of running their business. The company is interested in better managing its finances to ensure long-term sustainability and profitability. You have been asked to produce a detailed report that covers the following: An explanation of the different types of costs Roy's Cycles may face, such as fixed, variable, direct and indirect. Examples of costs for Roy's Cycles (e.g. parts, salaries and marketing). A calculation of the break-even point using the formula and a break-even chart to visually represent this calculation. An explanation for the significance of the break-even point and how it helps Roy's Cycles understand the minimum level of sales needed to cover costs. An analysis of how the break-even will help Roy's Cycles in making important decisions. Submit your report to the virtual learning environment using your learner account, including the college's declaration statement confirming that it is your own work.

Thoughts on scenario 1

- This assessment task is poor and fails to address the VARCS principles.

- The assessment task asks the learners to identify three care values, whereas the assessment criteria require them to 'describe' and then 'explain'.

- By identifying values on a poster and then not presenting this information, it is not a valid way to assess the learners against the criteria; they need to be given the opportunity to describe and explain as per the criteria.

- The task asks for learners to work in groups of three to create a poster. If we consider authenticity, it would be extremely difficult to discern what each learner did on the poster. Furthermore, by only identifying three values, the learners are only able to realistically identify one each, which brings into question the sufficiency of the work.

Thoughts on scenario 2

- This assessment task appropriately addresses the VARCS principles.

- It provides the learners with a real-world scenario that has a valid form of assessment for meeting the criteria (writing a report that includes 'explanation' and 'analysis' – the verbs in the criteria).

- While it is limited in detail as to the sufficiency expected to pass, the checklist of items to include provides a minimum expectation for the learners.

- By submitting the report using their own account and with a declaration that it is their own work, this provides some evidence of authenticity.

> **Take it further...**
>
> How would you change the assessment task for scenario 1 to ensure that it better addresses the VARCS principles?

Problems with summative assessment

Atkins (2019) suggests that there are difficulties with reliability and validity when examining assessment through a social justice lens. Social justice is about fairness, but Atkins argues that no assessment process can be completely fair or objective; for example, a learner with dyslexia may be better suited to presenting their learning rather than writing an essay about it because of the inherent challenges they face putting words to paper. However, awarding organisations do tend to offer flexibility with the method of assessment that can be used for internal summative assessments, and for external summative assessments, learners may be provided with a scribe or reader depending on their disability.

Christodoulou (2018) also outlines several limitations of summative assessments, including a similar view to Atkins where she suggests that the results can be influenced by factors unrelated to a learner's actual understanding, such as exam anxiety, timing or familiarity with the test format that make summative assessments a flawed reflection of true learning. Because summative assessments are retrospective rather than proactive (as they occurring at set times of the term or year), Christodoulou argues that this means they do not provide continuous feedback to learners during the learning process or provide detailed insights into why a learner may have performed poorly or where specific misunderstandings lie. This makes it difficult to plan targeted interventions for learners. More significantly, summative assessments place an emphasis on final outcomes that can encourage 'teaching to the test', whereby teaching and learning strategies that support short-term performance rather than sustained learning are selected.

AI and assessment validity – challenges and opportunities

The integration of generative AI into educational contexts has prompted a critical re-examination of assessment validity and reliability (Eaton, 2022). While initial reactions often focused on prevention and prohibition of AI due to challenges with the authenticity of learners' work and unreliable output from the AI (particularly for written methods of assessment), emerging research suggests a more nuanced approach that embraces AI as a transformative tool in educational assessment (Cotton et al, 2023; Sullivan et al, 2023).

As FES teachers, we cannot bury our heads in the sand with this one. We need to consider how our assessments are 'AI proofed' to enable us to make valid and reliable judgements of our learners' progress. While traditional examinations will unlikely be affected by AI, programmes of study that require coursework completion or other forms of summative assessment are potentially at risk of being impacted.

> **REFLECT**
>
> Are there any assessments in your current programme of study that are particularly vulnerable to AI?

If we are trying to avoid AI as part of a summative assessment task, our take is simple. Given that many of you will be teaching FES programmes designed to support advancement towards the workplace, assessment tasks should be designed to incorporate personal reflection and application to specific contexts. This allows learners to demonstrate their understanding in relation to their own circumstances, which would prove a challenge to produce using AI and therefore increase the validity of assessment.

AI proofing is not simply avoiding AI altogether. As suggested by the research by Eaton, Cotton and Sullivan above, given that AI is a tool that is only going to advance and be increasingly utilised in and beyond the workplace, we really ought to consider how we support our learners to use it ethically. If you want to integrate AI into assessment, consider using it as a collaborative tool where, as part of their submission, learners submit a transcript of their discussion with AI to demonstrate how they engaged with it to develop the work. (This requires careful consideration of what the output or product may look like and is perhaps more process-focused by its nature.) Alternatively, assessment design may require learners to critically evaluate and refine AI generated content, where they use AI to generate an output and use their learning to critically evaluate or analyse what was produced. While this somewhat improves the validity of the assessment, care should be taken in respect to authenticity as generative AI could be used to critically evaluate the product it created.

> **Tip for Teaching**
>
> Consider a multi-stage assessment approach:
> - Learners receive an initial prompt or problem.
> - They engage in an AI-mediated dialogue to explore potential solutions.
> - They then critically analyse the AI-generated responses.
> - They produce a final submission that demonstrates:
>   * original thinking
>   * critical evaluation of AI-generated content
>   * metacognitive reflection on the problem-solving process.

There is value in the learning

Reflect on occupational duty 2, to which this chapter is aligned: 'maintain a focus on outcomes, for all learners, so that they recognise the value of their learning and the future opportunities available to them.' While we can support learners through their learning journey to recognise the value of it, like our St Pancras journey metaphor, it is only once we get to the destination that we can properly look back at how far we have come, how successful our journey was and where we want to go next.

In summarising the learning at the end of their study programme, learners are provided with a transportable and comparable output, such as a qualification or grade, that can be compared between a group and nationally (Christodoulou, 2018). The value of this learning can then be found in the opportunities that the qualification and grade afford.

For some learners, their attainment opens up a range of options, whether that be progression the next level of qualification or employment. We must also recognise that, for some, the doors to these options may be well and truly slammed shut. This may result in demotivation and disengagement, so it is important as teachers that we are mindful of this further limitation of summative assessment and consider how we support learners to recognise their successes, no matter how small, and maintain a growth mindset.

It is also important for us to recognise the value of summative assessment for our future planning. While this may not always benefit the learners that undertake the assessment, it may benefit future learners were we able to recognise patterns in the strengths and weaknesses of the work and plan to address these accordingly.

Chapter summary

In this chapter, we started out by considering the purpose of assessment and examined three core principles of assessment with a range of practical, research-informed examples to support understanding and application to a series of reflective activities. These principles included:

- What does the learner already know or can do? (Initial assessment)

- How well is the learner progressing towards the intended outcome? (Formative assessment)
- What has the learner learned during their journey? (Summative assessment)

For the first principle, two forms of initial assessment were discussed. The initial assessment that takes place at the start of the programme of study can be used to support planning towards desired outcomes, while the initial assessment that takes place at the beginning of each session plays an important role in activating prior learning and adapting the lesson to meet learners' needs.

For the second principle, three key features of formative assessment – clarify, check and correct – were examined as a way to bridge the gap between the teaching and learning. The 'clarify' phase involves establishing clear learning goals for your learners, and to enhance the learning, sharing measurable success criteria with learners was shown to be an important addition to the learning intentions. The 'check' phase explored four methods that can be used to monitor the progress of all learners, along with some potential risks and mitigations. We started by examining observation as a form of assessment. Here, the focus should be on purposeful observation using the success criteria and consideration should also be given to your position in the learning environment. Next, we looked at ways to increase the breadth and depth of our questioning to include more of the learners and find out more about what they know and can do. We then explored ways to activate learners as resources for themselves and one another through clearly structured tasks aligned to the success criteria. Finally, the 'correct' phase emphasised the importance of high-quality feedback which is task-focused with clear steps for improvement provided, with learners provided opportunities to act upon the feedback to support their progress.

For the third principle, we explored summative assessment as a way to evaluate the learning that has taken place, considering the difference between learning and performance and ways to enhance the validity and reliability of summative assessment practices. Due consideration was also given to the limitations of summative assessment and recognition for value of having a transportable and comparable output that can be used to support progression. We started this chapter by identifying the Latin for assessment – assidere, meaning 'to sit with'. Throughout we have made clear that learner involvement is crucial to the assessment process and can aid us in supporting learners to recognise the value of their learning and future learning opportunities.

References

Agarwal, P. K. (2019) Retrieval Practice and Bloom's Taxonomy: Do Students Need Fact Knowledge Before Higher Order Learning? Journal of educational psychology, 111 (2), 189–209.

Almeida, P., and Neri de Souza, F. (2010). Questioning Profiles in Secondary Science Classrooms. International Journal of Learning and Change, 4(3), 237-251.

Anderson, L.W., and Krathwohl, D.R.(2001). A Taxonomy for Learning, Teaching, and Assessing: A Revision of Bloom's Taxonomy of Educational Objectives. Complete Edition. New York: Longman.

Atkins, L. (2019). Social Justice and Education in J. Tummons (ed) PCET: Learning and teaching in the post-compulsory sector. London: SAGE.

Ausubel, D.P. (1968). Educational Psychology: A Cognitive View. New York: Holt, Rinehart and Winston.

Burton, S.J., Sudweeks, R.R., Merrill, P.F. and Wood, B. (1991). How to Prepare Better Multiple-Choice Test Items: Guidelines for University Faculty. Provo, UT: Brigham Young University Testing Services and the Department of Instructional Science.

Butler, R. (1987). Task-involving and ego-involving properties of evaluation: Effects of different feedback conditions on motivational perceptions, interest, and performance. Journal of Educational Psychology, 79(4), 474-482.

Butler, R. (1988). Enhancing and undermining intrinsic motivation: The effects of task-involving and ego-involving evaluation on interest and performance. British Journal of Educational Psychology, 58(1), 1-14.

Christodoulou, D. (2018). Making Good Progress? The Future of Assessment for Learning. Oxford: Oxford University Press.

Cotton, D.R., Cotton, P.A. and Shipway, J.R., 2023. 'Chatting and cheating: Ensuring academic integrity in the era of ChatGPT'. Innovations in Education and Teaching International, 60(3), 376-386.

Dallimore, E. J., Hertenstein, J. H., and Platt, M. B. (2013). Impact of Cold-Calling on Student Voluntary Participation. Journal of Management Education, 37(3), 305-341.

Eaton, S.E., 2022. 'Academic integrity in the age of artificial intelligence: Fundamental research and assessment approaches'. International Journal of Educational Integrity, 18(1), 1-14.

Farmer, R.W., Saner, S., Weingartner, L.A. and Rabalais, G. (2021). Questioning Aid for Rich, Real-Time Discussion (QARRD): A Tool to Improve Critical Thinking in Clinical Settings. MedEdPORTAL, 17, 11132.

Gravells, A. (2017). Principles and practices of teaching and training : a guide for teachers and trainers in the FE and skills sector. London: Learning Matters.

Hall, P. and Simeral, A. (2015). Teach, Reflect, Learn: Building Your Capacity for Success in the Classroom. Alexandria. VA: ASCD.

Hattie, J. (2023). Teaching with intent. Visible Learning: The Sequel: A Synthesis of Over 2,100 Meta-Analyses Relating to Achievement. London: Routledge.

Hattie, J. and Clarke, S. (2019). Visible Learning: Feedback. London: Routledge.

Hattie, J., and Timperley, H. (2007). The power of feedback. Review of Educational Research, 77(1), 81–112

Howe, C. and Abedin, M. (2013). Classroom dialogue: A systematic review across four decades of research. Cambridge Journal of Education, 43(3), 325-356.

Kluger, A.N. and DiNisi, A. (1996). The effects of feedback interventions on performance: A historical review, a meta-analysis and a preliminary feedback intervention theory. Psychological Bulletin, 119 (2), 254-284.

Kruger, J., and Dunning, D. (1999). Unskilled and unaware of it: how difficulties in recognizing one's own incompetence lead to inflated self-assessments. Journal of Personality and Social Psychology, 77 (6), 1121.

Lemov, D. (2015) Teach like a champion 2.0: 62 techniques that put students on the path to college. 2nd edn. San Francisco: Jossey-Bass.

Lemov, D. and Taylor, L. (2021). Teach Like a Champion 3.0: 63 Techniques that Put Students on the Path to College. San Francisco, CA: Jossey-Bass.

Nuthall, G. (2007). The Hidden Lives of Learners. Wellington, NZ: NZCER Press.

Petty, G. (2018). How to Teach Even Better: an evidence based approach. Oxford University Press.

Rosenshine, B. (2012). Principles of Instruction: Research-Based Strategies That All Teachers Should Know. American Educator, 36(1), 12-19.

Sherrington, T. (2019). Rosenshine's Principles in Action. Melton, Woodbridge: John Catt Educational.

Soderstrom, N.C. and Bjork, R.A. (2015). Learning versus performance: An integrative review. Perspectives on Psychological Science, 10(2),176-199.

Sullivan, M., Kelly, A. and McLaughlan, P., 2023. 'Negotiating AI in assessment: A critical review of tools, techniques, and theoretical frameworks'. Assessment and Evaluation in Higher Education, 48(6), 723-742.

Wiggins, G. (1993). Assessing student performance: Exploring the purpose and limits of testing. San Francisco: Jossey-Bass

Wiliam, D. (2018). Embedded formative assessment. Second edition. Bloomington, Indiana: Solution Tree Press.

Wisniewski, B., Zierer, K. and Hattie, J. (2020). The Power of Feedback Revisited: A Meta-Analysis of Educational Feedback Research. Frontiers in Psychology, 10, 3087.

Chapter 8 Collaborating in FES

Model professional relationships with students, colleagues and stakeholders that support the highest quality education and training. (Duty 6)

When the trust account is high, communication is easy, instant and effective.

Stephen R. Covey (1989)

8.1 Introduction

The purpose of this chapter is to explore what it means to model professional relationships with different stakeholders. As the quote above suggests, the key to doing so arguably lies in the way we communicate.

In chapter 2, we explored what it means to be a 'dual professional', a concept that suggests that occupational expertise is combined with excellent teaching and learning practices (CAVTL, 2014; ETF, 2022). We used Millerson's (1964) list of requirements to consider how the ITE programme contributes to this, along with sector bodies such as the Education and Training Foundation (ETF) and their membership body the Society for Education and Training (SET), whose code of practice its members must adhere to.

Professional responsibility

As a member of SET, you agree to:

- Uphold the reputation of the profession – you must not act in a manner that is likely to undermine the public's faith and confidence in you and your profession.

- Uphold your responsibilities as a Further Education and Training professional towards stakeholders and the wider community.

- Ensure appropriate access to inclusive activities and services for the Further Education and Training sector.

- Support others in their development and be an advocate for the profession.

- Behave in a suitable way to safeguard young people, adults at risk and, where relevant, children within your care.

- Not engage in any online behaviour that you would not be acceptable in your workplace, that puts your profession into discredit, or that is illegal.

This SET Code of Ethics and Conduct is as of September 2025 and © Education and Training Foundation Please check www.et-foundation.co.uk for any future changes or updates.

Professional behaviour

As a member of SET, you agree to:

- Act ethically, honestly and with integrity in the educational setting, without compromising or abusing your position.

- Act in a way that exhibits and fosters respect for other people's customs, habits, culture and personal beliefs, recognising difference as a strength.

- Act in a way which demonstrates and promotes sustainable development and respects human rights standards.

- Comply with all reasonable requests for information from SET (including all reasonable requests that you consent to the disclosure of information held by third parties about you).

- Co-operate with any investigation in your capacity as a Further Education and Training professional and in accordance with the law.

- Not seek to stop any person from raising a concern or from whistleblowing, nor to act unfairly towards them if they were to do so.

- Act in accordance and adhere to the Terms and Conditions of Membership and inform SET within 15 working days of any information which may have a bearing on your suitability for membership.

Professional competency

As a member of SET, you agree to:

- Uphold and demonstrate commitment to the ETF Professional Standards.

- Use reasonable professional judgement when it comes to your responsibilities and obligations to learners, colleagues, institutions and the profession as a whole.

- Take care to ensure the safety and welfare of learners and comply with relevant statutory provisions to support their well-being and development.

- Respect the rights of learners and colleagues in line with relevant legislation and organisation requirements.

- Maintain professional knowledge and competence through continuing professional development in both teaching and subject specialism.

> **REFLECT**
>
> Identify some of the themes from this code of practice that relates directly to Duty 6.

What are professional relationships?

In chapter 1, we concerned ourselves with professional relationships for maintaining boundaries with learners and other stakeholders, such as in the case of safeguarding. We looked at professional relationships in chapter 3, where we explored the importance of developing relationships with learners as a way to mitigate against any behavioural issues. In addition to learners, FES teachers interact with a wide range of colleagues and stakeholders in the learning process, including fellow teachers and support staff, leadership and management, employers and parents or carers. In this chapter, we want you to think about professional relationships through the lens of communicating with others and the way this communication may be impacted by our previous experiences. This has direct relevance to the professional responsibilities and behaviours set out in the ETF's code of practice on page 234.

> **REFLECT**
>
> Make a list of all of the stakeholders that you interact with in your role. Who are they and why do they have a stake in the learning process at your institution?

To better understand how professional relationships function in FES, we can draw on Wenger's (2011) concept of 'communities of practice' to illuminate the dynamics of collaboration and communication in educational settings. Communities of practice are groups of people who share a concern or passion for something they do and learn how to do it better as they interact regularly. In FES, these communities include subject-specific teaching teams, cross-institutional networks and professional learning communities.

According to Tummons (2023), communities of practice are characterised by:

- A joint enterprise or shared domain of interest.
- Mutual engagement (otherwise known as community interactions), where members learn from each other.
- A shared practice, resulting in a repertoire of resources, tools and experiences.

Research by Hodkinson and Hodkinson (2005) and Tummons (2023) demonstrates that FES teachers who actively participate in professional communities develop more innovative and authentic practices and experience greater job satisfaction than those who work in isolation.

> **REFLECT**
>
> Using Tummons' communities of practice framework, identify one professional community you belong to. How does this community support your professional development and enhance your relationships with your colleagues and stakeholders?

> **Take it further...**
>
> Tummons shows us how communities of practice have been used in FES and adult education, both drawing and building upon Lave and Wenger's initial theorisation. Have a look at some of Tummons' suggestions for opportunities and challenges in this sector (which can be found in chapter 8 of his book) and see if you agree.

Within communities of practice, relationships require different boundaries and approaches and may be impacted by legislative factors; for example, when interacting with colleagues, professional boundaries may include respecting the confidentiality of learners' data in accordance with GDPR. Effective boundary management in these relationships requires a clear understanding of professional roles and responsibilities (as discussed in chapters 1 and 2) and strong communication skills and emotional intelligence, which we will explore later in this chapter.

8.2 Communication

According to Signore et al (2021), communication permeates the life of individuals from birth to death, allowing them to create new shared meanings, relationships and networks. The process of communication is considered to be ongoing and ever moving forward, and virtually impossible to determine when it starts and stops (Gamble and Gamble, 2020). In other words, communication is happening continuously, some of which we may be aware of and much of which may be subconscious. To explore this further, we will consider communication through two forms: verbal and non-verbal.

Verbal communication

In a teaching context, effective verbal communication is the cornerstone of great teaching, helping us to minimise conflict, motivate and lead learners and facilitate high-quality learning (White, 2016). White argues that two functions of verbal communication are relevant to teaching: the command function and the relational function.

'Command' refers to any message that influences others, whether that be the learners or other stakeholders in an institution, to accept a particular idea or set of ideas. This may be in the form of an order but may also involve statements or questions. For example:

- **Order** – 'Azaan, please remove your coat in the workshop.'

- **Statement** – 'It's not safe to wear a coat in the workshop with this machinery, Azaan.'

- **Question** – 'Azaan, do you think it's appropriate to wear your coat while working with the workshop machinery?'

Each of the above may be used to influence Azaan to accept the idea that wearing a coat around machinery is unsafe. However, in selecting the approach to make such a command, we should consider how the message is given and received.

There are numerous communication models that offer similar ideas about communication, but one that makes a lot of sense to us is based on the early work of Shannon and Weaver (1963). This model suggests that there are a series of steps in communication that may result in miscommunication or misunderstanding (see figure 8.1 below):

- **The encoding phase** – when a thought or idea is put into a verbal or non-verbal code to be transmitted.

- **The transmitting phase** – the physical act of sending a message by vocal cords, mouth or non-verbal means (e.g. clapping).

- **The receiving phase** – the physical act of hearing a verbal or non-verbal message.

- **The decoding phase** – the process of perceiving and making sense of a verbal or non-verbal message.

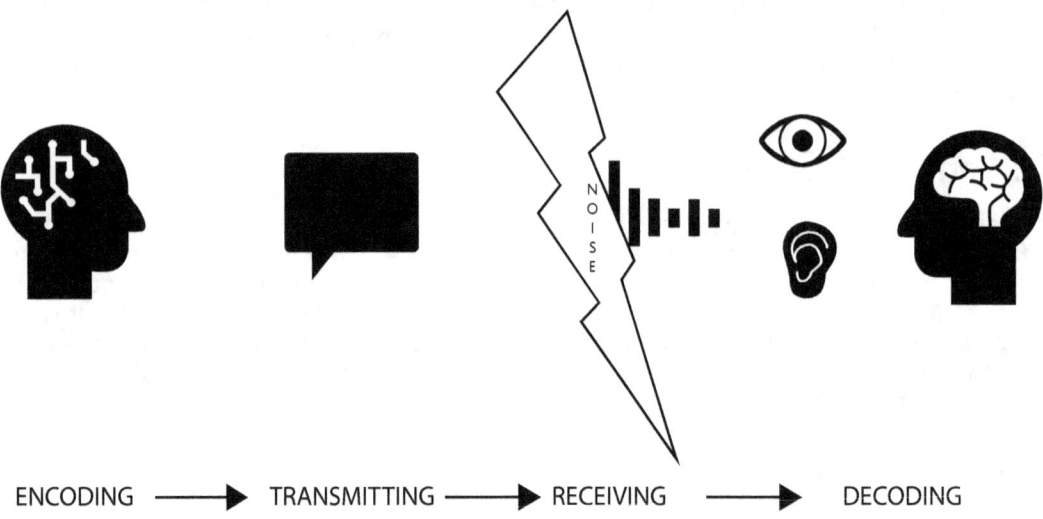

ENCODING ⟶ TRANSMITTING ⟶ RECEIVING ⟶ DECODING

Figure 8.1 *Shannon and Weaver's model*

Given the nature of this model and the multiple steps involved in communication, there are various points at which misunderstanding can occur. Misunderstanding is often a result of the challenges communicators face in acknowledging one another's prejudices and personal feelings, and White (2016) suggests that these factors must be addressed to mitigate against the misunderstanding. Therefore, it is important for a teacher to acknowledge the following aspects in the process of communication:

- The horizons of experience, which relates to the fact that a teacher is limited to how far they can determine whether the learner can see or understand a point they are making.

- The prejudices you and others have that relate to the perceptions, values, biases, attitudes, experiences and opinions that filter a person's meaning of verbal and non-verbal messages.

When considering prejudices, it is important to reflect on the way we express our views on what we consider to be 'normal' or 'natural'. Society – sometimes overtly but at other times covertly – shapes the views, attitudes and opinions we have about a wide range of topics, and the social environments we grew up and immerse ourselves in have played a key role in what our values and beliefs are today (Gamble and Gamble, 2020).

In chapter 4, we discussed some of these factors in relation to learners' needs; for example, gendering is still a problem in many FES subject areas such as hair and beauty and construction, which are dominated by certain genders. It is important that we recognise this in the way we communicate, for example when using the pronouns 'she' and 'her' when referring to workers in hair and beauty.

In addition to the various steps where an individual's perception can influence what is communicated and understood, there is also external noise to factor in. In the classroom, this noise may be other learners having conversations while the teacher is trying to convey a message, or it could be staffroom conversations that are taking place in the background while the teacher is on the phone to a parent. Each example would contribute interference (or noise) in the communication.

> **REFLECT**
>
> Take a moment to reflect on a communication you have had with a learner or colleague that resulted in a misunderstanding. Can you recognise at which point this miscommunication may have arisen? What 'noise' may have led to this?

Non-verbal communication

Non-verbal communication comprises a significant portion of our overall communication, with some research suggesting it accounts for 65–93% of the total meaning conveyed in interpersonal interactions (Bambaeeroo and Shokrpour, 2017). Whether communicating with learners or other stakeholders, effective non-verbal communication can enhance credibility and build rapport. There are many forms of non-verbal communication, including those in the table below.

Non-verbal communication	Explained
Facial expressions and eye contact	Research by Babad (2009) found that teachers communicate their expectations of learners through unconscious facial expressions, which can significantly impact learners' performance and self-concept. Maintaining appropriate eye contact with whoever you are communicating with demonstrates attentiveness and builds trust, though cultural variations in eye contact norms should be respected. Eye rolling, frowning and lack of eye contact send a poor message to the individual you are communicating with.
Body language and posture	Open posture, facing the individual you are communicating with directly and using confident gestures convey authority and approachability. On the contrary, defensive body language (e.g. folded arms) or facing away from the individual can suggest you are not interested in the individual's thoughts.
Paralanguage	Voice qualities such as tone, pitch, volume and rate affect how messages are received, so you should consider these and the appropriateness of each as you relay messages in different contexts. For example, raising the volume of your voice may be necessary to demonstrate confidence and assertiveness in a classroom, though this could also be perceived as aggressive in certain situations.
Use of space	How you position yourself in relation to who you communicate with can send important messages about power, accessibility and relationship. As discussed in chapter 3, your positioning in the classroom can increase engagement and reduce behavioural issues, though standing over individuals that are seated can be overbearing and intimidating.
Use of time	How we allocate time to different stakeholders sends messages about their perceived importance. Being punctual for meetings with external partners, responding promptly to emails and giving full attention during interactions all demonstrate professional respect.

It is important to recognise that non-verbal communication norms vary across cultures. What may be appropriate in one context could be considered rude or inappropriate in another; therefore, knowing the individuals that you are communicating with and their values and culture is essential to ensuring successful and effective communication.

> **REFLECT**
>
> Record yourself teaching a short segment or attending a meeting with colleagues (5–10 minutes) and analyse your non-verbal communication. What messages could your body language, facial expressions and use of space be sending to your learners or colleagues? Identify one aspect of your non-verbal communication you could develop to enhance your professional relationships.

Online communication

In modern society, online communication may often occur more than face-to-face, whether that be through email, social media or online video calls such as on Teams or Zoom. This presents a different set of 'noises' that can impact communication. The added challenge we face as professionals is that when something goes online it often becomes logged and can be traced back to you, so it is important to bear in mind the way in which messages are sent as well as the tone of these messages.

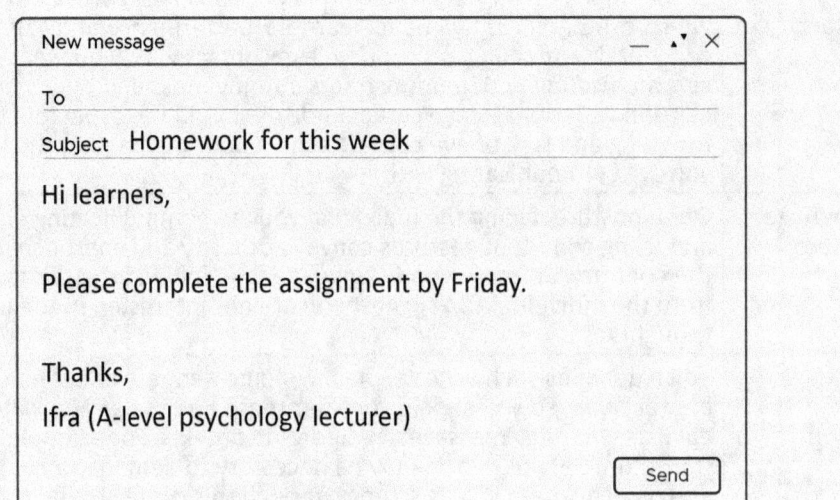

Possible misunderstandings from this email:

- **Details** – What is the specific assignment?
- **Format** – How should the assignment be submitted (online or in person)?
- **Deadline** – Is the deadline at the start or end of the day on Friday?

In addition to a lack of clarity, the tone of some messages may be well-intended but come across as passive aggressive or confusing. For example:

> *Hello Mr Smith,*
>
> *Let me clarify the situation again. Your son was involved in an altercation with another learner and this meant that he missed the lesson due to being interviewed by a member of the senior leadership team as part of their investigation.*

REFLECT

How did you perceive the message to Mr Smith?

While 'let me clarify' could mean 'you read what I wrote wrong, stupid', it could also mean 'sorry, I actually meant to say this'.

Professional boundaries with stakeholders

In chapter 1, we considered a range of examples in relation to our professional boundaries when it comes to working with learners. Our boundaries do not just apply to learners; occasionally, colleagues or other stakeholders may demonstrate inappropriate behaviours, and as professionals we have a duty to challenge these.

For example, you may have heard a fellow colleague speaking negatively about a learner or group of learners in the staffroom. While the staffroom should always be a safe space and place to vent after a challenging day, we should all take caution in how we communicate about our learners.

REFLECT

How would you challenge the following inappropriate behaviours?

- You overhear colleagues gossiping about a safeguarding incident in the corridor.
- A parent uses profanities in an email exchange with you.
- A learner tells you that a colleague was making comments about another colleague's incompetence.
- An employer diminishes a learner's hobbies and interests in conversation with you.

Managing digital professional identity

As we discussed in chapter 2, the boundaries between professional and personal identities have become increasingly blurred in digital spaces. Digital technologies have created new forms of visibility and scrutiny for educators, requiring more conscious management of professional boundaries by maintaining appropriate content in digital communications, respecting confidentiality across platforms and understanding the permanence and public nature of digital communications. Research by Andersson and Hedstrom (2024) on effective digital communication in educational settings suggests the following guidance:

- **Clarity and conciseness** – Structure emails with clear subject lines, greetings, body text and signatures. Break information into digestible chunks using paragraphs, bullets or numbered lists.

- **Appropriate formality** – Match your tone to your audience and purpose. Communications with learners' parents or guardians typically require more formality than messages to immediate colleagues.

- **Response timeliness** – Set reasonable expectations for email response times (e.g. within 24–48 hours on workdays) and communicate these to stakeholders.

- **Platform appropriateness** – Consider which platform best suits your message. Use email for formal communications, messaging apps for urgent but brief exchanges and video calls for complex discussions requiring visual cues.

- **Digital accessibility** – Ensure communications are accessible to all recipients, including those with disabilities. Use alt text for images, provide transcripts for audio and ensure documents are screen reader compatible.

> **REFLECT**
>
> Review your most recent professional email exchanges. How could you apply the principles of effective digital communication best practices to enhance these interactions?

Conflict resolution

It is inevitable that there will occasionally be conflict in your professional environment as people have different opinions, perspectives and ways of working. As we alluded to earlier, there are various ways that your communication with others can trigger misunderstandings, sometimes without you even realising. Achinstein (2002) argues that conflict is central to the development and growth of educational communities by challenging groupthink and surfacing important issues. However, when conflict does occur, it is important to have some methods for navigating it to ensure positive outcomes rather than letting it escalate into untenable situations.

According to Jennings and Greenberg (2009), those that demonstrate higher levels of emotional intelligence are more able to navigate conflict. This includes having a good awareness of your emotional triggers and being able to regulate yourself during challenging conversations. In addition to self-control, it also includes the ability to be open to, aware of and willing to listen to other people's perspectives and opinions.

Fisher and Ury's (1981) 'getting to yes' is a conflict resolution method that considers these factors in helping to manage conflict, as outlined below in the following table.

Traditional conflict resolution	'Getting to yes'
Each side takes a position – Your perspective and opinions shape the side you are on in the conflict. **Each side argues for that position** – You defend your position by arguing why you are right, and the other side is wrong. **Each side makes concessions to reach a compromise** – One side has to concede ground to reach a compromise or agreement.	**Separate the people from the problem** – Try to understand where the other person is coming from and respect their position by actively listening and acknowledging what is being said. **Focus on interests, not positions** – Although you may have opposite positions, beneath these lie shared interests and you should write these down to make them concrete. **Invent options that both parties gain from** – With the shared interests in mind, map out several alternative solutions that benefit both sides and are acceptable to you. Give the other side a choice. **Insist on using objective criteria** – Base the agreement on fair standards and objective benchmarks rather than on the will or power of either party. This ensures that the solution is justifiable and acceptable to both sides.
This traditional way is problematic because once you take a position, you are generally wedded to it and changing your mind becomes difficult. When one person wins the other loses by conceding, with the latter leaving the conflict feeling as though they have lost.	The 'getting to yes' negotiating model helps to generate as satisfying an agreement as possible without damaging the relationship further.

Case study

A sociology teacher recently handed back marked essays and grades to their learners. One learner approached the teacher quite upset and angry about getting a grade D.

The teacher listened to and acknowledged the learner's frustrations, taking note of why it was important for the learner to achieve a higher grade in readiness for a university interview.

Instead of focusing on the learner's feelings or their own subjective opinion, the teacher suggested – and the learner agreed – that together they revisit the assessment rubric with clear, predefined criteria to evaluate the essay. The rubric included aspects such as clarity of argument, use of evidence, organisation and grammar.

By referring to the rubric, both the teacher and learner could objectively assess the essay based on specific standards. This approach helped the learner to understand the areas they needed to improve and ensured that the grading was accurate, fair and transparent.

> **REFLECT**
>
> Have you had any conflict recently that would benefit from adopting an approach such as the 'getting to yes' method? If so, how could it have helped?

Working with stakeholders to enhance Education and Training

To ensure the highest quality education and training, we all have a responsibility to engage with a range of stakeholders in quality assurance and improvement processes. Quality in FES is a contested concept with multiple dimensions. Research by O'Leary (2018) suggests moving beyond narrow metrics to consider the following qualities:

- **Transformative quality** – how education changes learners' capabilities and self-perceptions.
- **Process quality** – how teaching and support are delivered.
- **Outcome quality** – what learners achieve and progress to.
- **Value-added quality** – the distance travelled by learners relative to starting points.

Quality assurance frameworks and processes in FES typically involves several interconnected processes, such as those outlined in the table below.

Process	Explanation
Internal verification and standardisation	These processes ensure assessment decisions are consistent, valid and reliable and are usually undertaken by an experienced assessor or individual qualified as an internal quality assurer.
Self-assessment and quality improvement planning	Providers typically engage in annual self-assessment against national frameworks and use the findings to create an action plan for improvement. These should: • focus on impact rather than compliance • lead to specific, measurable improvement actions • be ongoing rather than once-yearly events.
Observation processes	O'Leary and Wood (2019) argue for moving away from graded lesson observations toward developmental models focused on collaborative professional learning. Their research demonstrated that developmental observation models led to more sustained improvement in teaching quality compared to performance management approaches. Many providers now adopt developmental approaches to observation, though there are hybrid versions that some providers use that continue to grade lessons.

Process	Explanation
External quality assurance	In England, this typically includes Ofsted inspections, awarding organisation verification and sampling of work to ensure accuracy and fairness in assessment processes.
Learner voice	Gathering and responding to learner feedback is a crucial element of quality improvement. However, research by Hall (2017) suggests that many FES providers struggle to move beyond tokenistic approaches to learner voice. Learner voice can be gathered through various means, including surveys and course representative meetings.

Case study: Developmental teaching observation

An FE college in the south of England replaced graded observations with peer learning conversations. Leaning on O'Leary's (2018) principles, their new model featured:

- pre-observation professional dialogue to identify focus areas
- non-judgmental peer observation
- post-observation reflective discussion using video evidence
- collaborative action planning
- follow-up activities to support implementation.

This approach led to increased teacher engagement with observation, more sustainable changes in practice and ultimately improved learner experiences and outcomes.

REFLECT

How does quality assurance operate in your organisation? To what extent does it focus on compliance versus improvement?

Identify one way you could enhance your engagement with quality processes and, in doing so, improve your professional relationships with colleagues or stakeholders.

Take it further...

Imagine your institution has just received a call from Ofsted informing them of an inspection due to take place next week. What could you need to do in preparation for this and who can help you to understand more?

(It is important to note that you should not change any of your usual practices because of Ofsted. They want to inspect the provision in a way that reflects the day-to-day experience of the learners. While you are undertaking your ITE, Ofsted will not usually observe you teach but they may wish to discuss your practice and see some of your learners' work.)

Chapter summary

In this chapter, in accordance with Duty 6 we explored the significance of modelling professional relationships with learners, colleagues and stakeholders to ensure high-quality education and training. We emphasised the importance of effective communication, both verbal and non-verbal, in building trust and fostering collaboration.

We highlighted the role of professional responsibility and behaviour as outlined by the ETF's code of practice and examined the concept of communities of practice to understand the dynamics of professional relationships and collaboration in educational settings. We acknowledged that conflict may occur in complex professional settings and that this may present opportunities for growth – if managed well. We explored strategies for resolving conflict, with opportunities for you to reflect on this in your own practice.

Finally, we reviewed quality assurance processes in FES, emphasising the importance of collaborative engagement with stakeholders and the need for continuous improvement.

References

Achinstein, B. (2002). Conflict amid community: The micropolitics teacher collaboration. Teachers College Record, 104(3), 421–455.

Andersson, A. & Hedstrom, K., 2024. How education professionals manage personal and professional boundaries when using social technologies. New Technology, Work and Employment, 39(3), pp.382–401

Babad, E. (2009). The Social Psychology of the Classroom (1st ed.). New York: Routledge.

Bambaeeroo, F., and Shokrpour, N. (2017). The impact of the teachers' non-verbal communication on success in teaching. Journal of Advances in Medical Education and Professionalism, 5(2), 51-59.

CAVTL. (2014). Commission on Adult Vocational Teaching and Learning: one year on review. Learning and Skills Improvement Service, Coventry, England.

Education and Training Foundation (ETF). (2022). Professional Standards for Teachers and Trainers. Available at: https://www.et-foundation.co.uk/professional-standards/teachers/ (Accessed 31 March 2025).

Fisher, R. and Ury, W. (1981). Getting to Yes: Negotiating Agreement Without Giving In. Houghton Mifflin.

Gamble, TK., and Gamble, M.W. (2020). The Gender Communication Connection, Taylor and Francis Group.

Hall, V. (2017). Student Voice: Time for a Conversation. Chartered College of Teaching.

Hodkinson, H., and Hodkinson, P. (2005). Improving schoolteachers' workplace learning. Research Papers in Education, 20(2), 109-131.

Jennings, P. A., and Greenberg, M. T. (2009). The prosocial classroom: Teacher social and emotional competence in relation to student and classroom outcomes. Review of Educational Research, 79(1), 491–525.

Millerson, G. (1964). The Qualifying Associations. London: Routledge and Kegan Paul.

O'Leary, M. (2018). Classroom Observation: A Guide to the Effective Observation of Teaching and Learning. Routledge.

O'Leary, M. and Wood, P. (2019). Reimagining Teaching Excellence: Why Collaboration, Rather than Competition, Holds the Key to Improving Teaching and Learning in Higher Education. Educational Review, 71(1), 122-139.

Shannon, C. E. and Weaver, W. (1963). The Mathematical Theory of Communication. Illinois: University of Illinois Press.

Signore, F., Pasca, P., Valente, W., Ciavolino, E. and Ingusci, E. (2021). Social Resources and Emotional Exhaustion: The Role of Communication in Professional Relationships. Intellectual Economics 15(2), 205-220.

Tummons, J. (2023). Exploring communities of practice in further and adult education : apprenticeship, expertise and belonging. Routledge, Taylor and Francis Group.

Wenger, E. (2011). Communities of practice: A brief introduction. STEP Leadership Workshop, University of Oregon.

White, K. (2016). Teacher Communication: A Guide to Relational, Organizational, and Classroom Communication, Rowman and Littlefield Publishers, Incorporated.

Chapter 9 Supporting learners' progression

Support students with their next steps for progression and learning by providing appropriate information, advice, and guidance. (Duty 9)

Effective careers guidance is crucial for all young people, whatever their background. It helps young people achieve better outcomes, leading to huge benefits for society and the economy. (Gatsby, 2024: 1)

9.1 Introduction

While greater participation in career guidance activities has been shown to significantly increase career readiness (Dodd et al, 2021), particularly for learners from disadvantaged backgrounds who may not have access to the same levels of social capital as their peers (Hunt et al, 2021), the nature of this guidance can vary. In FES, careers guidance often takes more traditional forms such as a separate careers programme or through appointments with specialist careers advisors. However, given that most technical and vocational programmes of study are designed with employability in mind, including practice placements, it could be argued that the curriculum also serves as a careers guidance activity. This blurring of the lines between curriculum and career guidance practices may need further separation and clarity though, as research in some fields has identified very low conversion rates between education and employment, suggesting ineffective support for learners' progression. For example, in the 2015–16 academic year, alarmingly only 28% of learners on construction courses progressed to the construction workforce (Pye, McGillan and Watson-Harper, 2020).

The purpose of this chapter is to consider the many ways in which FES teachers can support their learners with their progression – wherever that may be – through and beyond the curriculum they are teaching. Through purposeful curriculum design, collaborating with stakeholders and working in accordance with legislative and regulatory requirements such as those set by Ofsted, the focus of this chapter will be on creating a holistic approach to support learners' development beyond the classroom and into their future careers and educational pursuits.

9.2 Purposeful curriculum design

According to Ofsted (2025), careers guidance works best when it is not an isolated aspect of college provision but is integrated into a course of study. Therefore, the curriculum can play an important role in supporting learners' progression, and, for maximal efficacy, it is imperative that the curriculum is designed to sequence the learning towards the intended learning goals, as discussed in chapter 5. The formulation of these goals will depend on the nature of the programme of study and its purpose. For example, for a programme intending to support progression to employment, it should arguably be designed in such a way that it aligns with the respective industry requirements or occupational standards (Huddleston and Unwin, 2013). This means that the transition from the FES provider to employment is smoother, with fewer skills and less new knowledge needed by the learner to make the transition.

If a programme is not aligned with industry requirements, the learner will need to bridge the knowledge and skills gap before transitioning to employment. On the other hand, programmes of study designed for progression to higher education require the curriculum to be less focused on the needs of industry and more on the broader knowledge and skills associated with different subject disciplines. Some curricula in FES support a more flexible progression pathway, accommodating learners with diverse goals and abilities. This may include learners with SEND or those from disadvantaged backgrounds where the development of personal and life skills, such as independent living, is the goal. As this chapter progresses, we shall consider each of these in turn, taking a critical position on the

> **REFLECT**
>
> How does your curriculum ensure that it is aligned with the most appropriate progression route for learners? What are the destinations of your learners from the current programme of study and does this reflect the overarching intention of the programme?

purpose and value of each along with covering the stakeholders that you may engage with in developing the curriculum to best support learners' progression.

9.3 Legislative and regulatory requirements

As we discussed in chapters 1, 2 and 4, FES teachers must be aware of, and adhere to, various legislative and regulatory requirements that impact learners and their progression. Aside from legislative requirements such as ensuring that progression support is inclusive and accessible to all learners (in line with the Equality Act 2010), there are also regulatory expectations that affect us in FES.

Ofsted

The Office for Standards in Education, Children's Services and Skills (Ofsted) is the main regulatory body in FES; they inspect services providing education and skills for learners of all ages. At the time of writing, Ofsted are consulting on a new inspection methodology with some changes to the evaluation criteria, though fundamentally their scrutiny of providers' support for learners' progression remains unchanged.

Within their inspection of the curriculum, Ofsted seek to determine the extent to which the intent and design prepares and enables learners to make their next steps, whether that is further study, employment or independent living. When inspecting the teaching and learning of the curriculum, they are looking at the ways in which teachers deliver the curriculum to support progression and the expertise they have in providing effective support and guidance to learners.

Finally, Ofsted scrutinise the extent to which learners develop the knowledge, skills and behaviours to achieve their learning goals and progress to positive destinations. Within their inspection, as part of their broader institutional focus, Ofsted will scrutinise the careers information, education, advice, guidance and how leadership supports staff development and partnership working with employers and other stakeholders in support of learners' progression.

> **REFLECT**
>
> Go to reports.ofsted.gov.uk and search for your institution's latest Ofsted inspection report. What are the strengths and weaknesses in terms of supporting the learners' progression, including working with employers and other stakeholders?

Gatsby benchmarks

In 2014, the Gatsby Foundation established eight benchmarks in an attempt to ensure that all young people receive careers guidance that fulfils their ambitions and aspirations, whatever their background. These benchmarks contribute towards high-quality careers guidance in education and, despite being updated in 2024 to reflect contemporary society and the labour market, they largely remain unchanged (Gatsby, 2024). FES teachers can support learner progression by incorporating these benchmarks into their practice.

Benchmark	Explained
1. A stable careers programme	Collaborate with career services to develop a comprehensive careers education programme that is integrated into the curriculum.
2. Learning from career and labour market information	Provide learners with access to up-to-date labour market information and guidance on how to use it.
3. Addressing the needs of each young person	Offer personalised career guidance that takes into account individual learner aspirations, abilities and circumstances.
4. Linking curriculum learning to careers	Demonstrate the relevance of subject learning to future career paths across all curriculum areas.
5. Encounters with employers and employees	Organise regular interactions with employers through workplace visits, career fairs and guest speakers.
6. Experiences of workplaces	Facilitate work experience placements and job shadowing opportunities for learners.
7. Encounters with further and higher education	Arrange visits to universities and other FES providers to explore further study options.
8. Personal guidance	Ensure that every learner has access to one-to-one career guidance from a qualified professional.

> **REFLECT**
>
> In your opinion, does your current institution meet the benchmarks?
>
> If you are not aware of any aspects of the benchmarks, discuss them with a mentor, colleague or manager to find out more.

While each of these benchmarks is of equal importance, the following section will only focus on the benchmarks that we as FES teachers have most jurisdiction with, as the broader institution has a key role to play in establishing some of the wider reaching benchmarks (such as 'A stable careers programme').

9.4 Progression pathways

In chapter 1, we looked at figure 9.1 below, which highlights many of the progression pathways within FES. A wider range of qualifications exist in each space, but broadly speaking these fall under the categories of: a) 'academic' routes that support progression to higher education, b) Technical Vocational Education and Training (TVET) routes that support progression to the workplace and c) foundation learning routes that support progression to further study and the development of life skills.

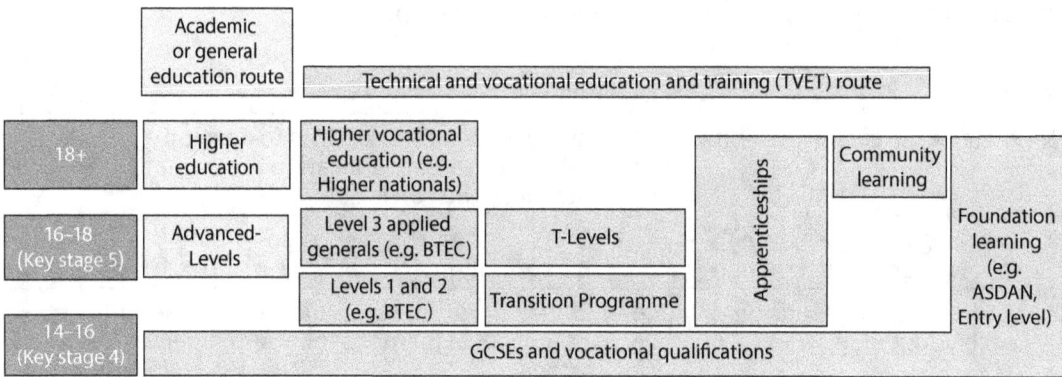

Figure 9.1 *Progression pathways in FES*

TVET curricula

These curricula are designed with the intention of supporting progression to the workplace and should have clear links between the learning and careers. If you work as an FES teacher of a TVET curriculum, you may have the opportunity to support benchmarks 4, 5 and 6 through your curriculum decisions. The need for strong partnerships between educational institutions and employers has been central to a lot of TVET curriculum research (Huddleston and Unwin, 2013; Guile and Unwin, 2018), ensuring that the education and training provided aligns with industry needs. While there are a wide range of TVET qualifications available including national vocational qualifications (NVQs) and higher national certificates and diplomas (HNCs/HNDs), in this section we will primarily focus on apprenticeships, applied general qualifications (including BTECs) and T Levels.

Apprenticeship pathways

Apprenticeships represent a significant progression pathway in the TVET landscape and offer learners the opportunity to earn while they learn and develop industry-specific skills. Recent reforms have expanded apprenticeship opportunities across levels 2–7, creating clear progression routes from intermediate to degree-level qualifications. The table below outlines the current apprenticeship framework.

Level	Equivalent educational level	Typical duration	Example roles
2	GCSE	12–18 months	Adult care worker, customer service, practitioner
3	A-level or T Level	18–24 months	Team leader, teaching assistant, digital marketer
4	First year of degree	18–24 months	Software developer, associate project manager
5	Foundation degree	24–36 months	Operations manager, nursing associate
6	Bachelor's degree	36–48 months	Digital and technology solutions professional, teacher
7	Master's degree	24–36 months	Senior leader, academic professional, supporting progression to (and through) apprenticeships

Following a consultation on post-16 qualifications in 2021, the Conservative government at the time wanted clearly defined academic and technical routes for post-16 progression that sat alongside apprenticeships (Lewis, 2024).

T Levels

The Conservative government were clear that A-levels were to remain central to the 'academic route' for general subjects such as psychology, history and English, but they saw a gap in TVET qualifications that held parity with A-Levels. Introduced in 2020 as an alternative to A-levels and apprenticeships, T Levels are two-year technical programs studied within colleges with the equivalence to three A-levels (level 3) (DfE/DBEIS, 2016). They are distinguished by the inclusion of a large industry work placement and alignment to employer-led occupational standards.

It was proposed that T Levels would become the main qualification option for the technical route and be intended to support progression into skilled employment, further technical study or apprenticeships. Other level 3 qualifications such as applied general qualifications (AGQs) would have a place alongside apprenticeships and T Levels so long as they could demonstrate their quality and distinct purpose. The government proposed that any AGQ qualifications overlapping with T Level subjects (and those that do not meet quality criteria) would be defunded. However, upon taking power in 2024 and following pressure from sector leaders, the Labour government paused these proposals, leaving a question mark over the purpose and value of the current level 3 offer.

Applied General Qualifications (AGQs)

AGQs are vocational qualifications designed for learners who want to continue their education through applied learning related to a general employment area rather than a specific occupation or pure academic study. These qualifications are primarily offered at level 3 (though some are at level 2 and below), considered equivalent to A-levels and designed to support progression to higher education or further technical training (Allan, 2017).

Designing your TVET curricula

In designing schemes of work and lessons for your respective curricula, you have an opportunity to consider the links between the content and the career. For example, if teaching hairdressing, you are not only teaching the learners the technique of cutting hair but also how to interact with their clients in the same professional manner that they would in a working salon. You also should consider drawing on the expertise of employers and the workplaces; for example, in the case of the hairdressing learners, they may visit a working salon or have a guest speaker teach them an innovative colour technique.

Below is an example of a scheme of work for a hairdressing that considers employer engagement and links to the career.

Week	Technical content	Professional skills	Industry connection	Assessment
1–2	Basic cutting techniques review	Client consultation, professional communication	Video interviews with salon owners discussing expectations of new stylists	Role-play consultations with peer feedback
3–4	Advanced cutting techniques	Time management, client care during lengthy procedures	Visit to a professional salon to observe workflow	Practical cutting assessment with timing constraints
5–6	Styling and finishing techniques	Managing client expectations, receiving feedback	Guest stylist demonstration of current trends	Complete client service (consultation to styling) in salon environment

In addition to integrating links to the career and engaging employers, it is important to consider how you could provide work experience. During a work experience placement, it is essential that adequate support and structured learning opportunities are provided (Huddleston and Unwin, 2013) so that it does not simply become a 'tick-box' exercise. It can be a challenge to do this however; for example, in a gym learners under the age of 18 may be prohibited from showing clients how to use the fitness equipment due to health and safety regulations. Therefore, the context of the workplace in relation to the curriculum and the learners' needs should be carefully considered to ensure that the work experience is meaningful, benefiting both the learner and the employer.

Ofsted (2025) found that a key challenge is finding enough work placements for all learners, which has become particularly difficult now that virtual working has become more common since the Covid-19 pandemic. This may result in the available placements being allocated more frequently to the higher-level programmes of study; as a result, lower-level qualifications where work experience is not a requirement but a valued experience to develop knowledge of the vocation suffer.

> **REFLECT**
>
> What opportunities are there in your curriculum to engage with employers? Are there any barriers that prevent you from engaging more with employers? What can you put in place to overcome those barriers? Are there digital opportunities?

Tip for Teaching

In your planning documentation, consider adding a space for consideration of industry connections.

Critical discussion of TVET

The effectiveness of TVET curricula evidently depends on the quality of interactions between the those working in the education and the employment systems (Bolli et al, 2018). While many FES institutions recognise the importance of engaging employers in working groups to determine the skills they need and help in curriculum design, what is sometimes forgotten is that these employers are not a homogenous group. Not only do employers differ in the focus of their work (which involves entirely different skills), but they also differ in size, which means that they may not always be able to identify their skills needs.

Take the Midlands, for example, where Rolls Royce are a large employer in the field of STEM whose work focuses on nuclear submarines and aircraft engines, among other things. The difference in the skills needed within Rolls Royce is vast; then there's the supply chain, where smaller employers may only prepare a very small component for the company. Then, within the same STEM field, there are other large employers such as Alstom (formerly Bombardier) who specialise in the rail industry and therefore require another set of skills.

Larger industries tend to have big HR teams with learning and development capacity to perform skills audits that identify the specific needs of the organisation. Smaller- and medium-sized businesses with fewer than 250 people may not have this resource, meaning they have less capacity to identify specific gaps in their workforce. So, when an FES provider draws upon a range of employer groups to identify the skills needed in the region, it is difficult for them to identify specific competencies; instead, they form lists of skills based on broader generic attributes. These attributes may include communication, teamwork, leadership, adaptability and problem solving, for example.

All of these attributes and skills are valuable in their own right, but when they are disassociated from the context in which they are exercised (such as the workplace) and taught in a generic manner (such as outside the workplace and in a classroom), it becomes problematic for the effective learning of such skills (Winch, 2010; Williams, 2024).

Firstly, these generic skills are highly context dependent; for example, communication skills in a healthcare setting differ significantly from those needed in engineering or retail contexts. Problem solving in a creative industry operates differently from problem solving in a procedural environment. When taught generically, these skills may not transfer effectively to specific workplace contexts (Winch, 2010). Secondly, the focus on generic employability skills may inadvertently reinforce class-based inequalities in education. Esmond and Atkins (2022) argue that recent reforms to technical education have led to a division in TVET where those able to access T Levels at level 3 are viewed as part of the 'technical elite' – a privileged and valued group who, due to their higher-level skills, have more perceived value to the economy. They engage in longer work placements, have strong links to the future careers through the employer-led qualifications and occupational standards and meet the requirements of the benchmarks (4, 5 and 6). While more advantaged learners have access to more specialised and contextually embedded skill development, programmes that are heavily focused on generic employability skills often target learners from lower socioeconomic backgrounds who engage with broad, vocational, classroom-based programmes of study at level 2 and below and find that their qualifications have little to no exchange in the labour market (Atkins, 2009; 2013). This dynamic can further fuel social inequalities rather than address them.

> **REFLECT**
>
> Do you agree with Esmond and Atkin's idea of a divide in the TVET system? How do you think this affects the learners and their aspirations for progression in these programmes?

> **Take it further...**
>
> Do you agree with this discussion about employability skills?

9.5 Lower-level vocational and foundation learning

While lower-level vocational programmes (at level 1 and 2) should also consider benchmarks 4, 5 and 6, it is perhaps more pertinent to consider benchmark 3 ('addressing the needs of each learner') given the diverse nature of the learners that study these programmes and their trajectories through FES and beyond.

According to the Social Mobility Commission (2020), the most effective programmes in FES appear to be those that offer comprehensive support and integrate course curricula with broader development (for example, embedding basic skills provision within a vocational pathway). However, Atkins (2013) has raised concerns about lower-level vocational courses and their lack of aspiration for young people, with the system inherently adopting a deficit view of the young people it serves, as evidenced in the language used to describe these young people such as 'disaffected', 'disadvantaged' and 'non-academic' with 'low aspirations'. Atkins suggests that this is because the majority of young people undertaking vocational education programmes are drawn from lower socioeconomic groups, often with a history of low achievement in school alongside additional characteristics associated with social exclusion such as learning difficulties and disabilities.

Aronowitz (2002) also notes that these pathways disproportionately cater for 'young people whose patterns of speech or behaviour position them outside of the norms of the middle class and have marked them out for low skilled and low status roles.' Only 36% of young people from a disadvantaged background (those eligible for free school meals (FSM)) who enter education post-16 progress to a level 3 qualification by the time they are 19, compared to 60% of non-FSM learners (Lenon, 2018). According to Wolf (2011), as many as 20% of Key stage 4 completers are not able to start a level 2 course, with 17% of school leavers at 16 functionally illiterate and 22% functionally innumerate.

Atkins (2013) argues that the generic vocational and employability programmes have little value in the labour market and only serve to disadvantage the already disadvantaged. Those who are more likely to follow broad, low-level vocational qualifications are not seen to be sufficiently equipped for entry to the labour market, or can only access low-skilled work. This marginalisation of these groups is no more evident than in the Conservative government's 'Skills plan' (DfE/DBEIS, 2016), where very little coverage or detail was provided on a 'transition pathway' that catered for those below level 3. The transition programme, now named the T Level foundation year, was established to support learners who did not have the prerequisite entry qualifications for level 3 to be supported with relevant preparation for what they would experience on T Levels. However, just 8% of the 2021–22 cohort actually progressed to a T Level, emphasising the attainment gap (Maris, Khandekar and Robinson, 2024).

As we have argued, the system is inherently exclusive, and although there will be a range of barriers faced by learners, whatever curricula you are working with in FES those on lower-level vocational or SEND programmes will undoubtedly face more barriers to progression than those on other routes. The table below includes some of these barriers, how they impact the learner and strategies you may use to support.

Barrier	Explained	Strategies that FES teachers can take for inclusive progression support
Aspirations	Learners on these lower-level programmes may be hindered by the aspirations of the programme or indeed have little aspiration themselves through feeling trapped and unable to progress. Though Ofsted (2025) found that young people from lower socioeconomic backgrounds are more likely to be claiming out-of-work benefits by the time they are 27 compared to their peers, yet they have similar levels of aspiration. It is often the expectations of teachers and parents that limit the careers options considered by learners from disadvantaged backgrounds.	Support learners' foundation skills that enable future progression such as English, maths and digital.

Develop learners' learning confidence and positive educational identities through experiencing meaningful workplace learning opportunities.

Creating meaningful connections to potential progression routes so that learners can aspire to progress to the next phase.

Supporting informed decision-making about next steps through challenging limited aspirations while remaining realistic about future opportunities. |
| Physical disabilities | Disabled learners may face physical accessibility issues, attitudinal barriers, limited work experience opportunities and concerns about reasonable adjustments. | Provide disability-specific work experience programs and connect learners with mentors who have similar disabilities.

Educate employers you work with about the value of diverse workforces and reasonable accommodation requirements.

Focus on strengths-based approaches that highlight learners' capabilities. |

Barrier	Explained	Strategies that FES teachers can take for inclusive progression support
Learning disabilities	Neurodiverse learners may require adjustments to traditional career guidance approaches and benefit from specialised support with workplace transitions.	Offer structured, clear career information with visual supports. Provide explicit coaching to your learners on workplace social norms and communication expectations. Guide learners on if, when and how to disclose their condition to potential employers. Help identify careers and pathways that align with specific neurological strengths and interests.
Socioeconomic background	Socioeconomically disadvantaged learners may lack social capital, role models in aspirational careers, financial resources for higher education and may face pressure to earn immediately rather than invest in further qualifications.	Create opportunities to develop professional connections through mentoring programmes. Provide comprehensive information about available financial support, scholarships and paid internships. Highlight part-time study options and apprenticeships so they can earn while they learn. Connect learners with professionals from similar backgrounds who have succeeded in various fields.
Ethnic background	Learners from certain ethnic backgrounds may encounter structural barriers including bias in recruitment processes, lack of representation in certain industries and cultural expectations about suitable careers.	Learn and support your colleagues' understanding of diverse cultural values and expectations. Partner with employers committed to diverse hiring practices. Involve families and community leaders in career education programmes. Showcase successful professionals from diverse backgrounds across various industries.
Gender	Female learners remain underrepresented in STEM careers and apprenticeships, while male learners are underrepresented in care and education sectors.	Use gender-neutral language and diverse imagery in career materials. Provide early exposure to non-traditional career paths through workshops and site visits. Create gender-specific networking groups and mentoring opportunities.

> **REFLECT**
>
> Are there any practices in the table above that you are currently implementing? Which areas will you explore further to promote an inclusive approach to support learners' progression?

Tip for Teaching

Focus on a strengths-based approach regardless of the barriers that learners may face. Always centre your conversations on what the learners can do and never set a bar for their aspirations.

9.6 General education (or 'academic' programmes that support progression to higher education)

The programmes of study that typically support progression to higher education are A-levels (which are usually studied in a sixth form college), Access to Higher Education programmes (which are for learners over the age of 18 looking to return to education), and, increasingly, AGQs such as BTEC Nationals (Allen, 2017).

A-levels are subject-based qualifications including sciences, humanities and the arts that learners in the UK typically take after completing their GCSEs. They are usually studied over two years, assessed through a combination of coursework and examinations and are a key pathway to higher education institutions who hold them in high regard.

Access to Higher Education programmes are designed to prepare individuals without traditional qualifications for study at university. These programmes cover a range of subjects including social sciences, business, law and nursing. They typically last one year, are assessed through coursework and examinations and are aimed at adults who have been out of education for some time and wish to pursue higher education.

While widening participation has been high on the agenda in higher education since the late 1990s, enabling learners from disadvantaged backgrounds to gain access, succeed and progress, this step towards equity may not address deeper systemic issues such as the quality of education and support learners receive. According to Jones (2021), non-traditional learners – those from diverse backgrounds – often face barriers such as inadequate preparation, financial constraints and lack of support, which can affect their academic performance and retention rates. Indeed, despite the Office for Students (OfS) being established by the Conservative government in 2018 as the regulator of higher education in England to promote fair access to high education, research by Bolton and Lewis (2024) highlights that the background and prior attainment of learners has a significant impact on their ability to succeed in higher education.

For example, Bolton and Lewis found that females are more likely to go to university and successfully complete their studies than males. However, males have better progression to higher-skilled employment after graduating. White learners are less likely to go to university but are less likely to drop out and more likely to achieve upper second-class degrees than other ethnic groups. Black learners are more likely to drop out from higher education than other ethnic groups and less likely to achieve a first- or upper second-class degree. Learners with a disability are more likely to drop out from HE and less likely to achieve a first or upper second-class degree than other learners. Finally, those eligible for free school meals are less likely than others to go into higher education, particularly to more prestigious universities. Graduates who were eligible for FSM earn around 10% less than other graduates.

Bolton and Lewis suggest that these stark statistics may be impacted by insufficient advice and support both before and during university. For curricula that are designed for progression to higher education (typically A-levels, Access to Higher Education and some AGQs), the Gatsby benchmark 7 applies, and as such, FES teachers can provide support through the following approaches:

- Offering workshops and individual support with the university application process, including personal statement writing and course selection.

- Equipping learners with the academic skills necessary for success in higher education, such as research methods, critical thinking and academic writing.

- Developing relationships with local universities to provide taster sessions, campus visits and guest lectures from university staff.

- Creating transition courses or modules that prepare learners for the demands of higher education study.

- Connecting current learners with past learners who have progressed to higher education to share experiences and advice.

9.7 Collaborating with other stakeholders to support progression

Successful progression support relies on collaborative relationships with a range of stakeholders who can offer different perspectives, opportunities and expertise. Ofsted's (2025) research found that the stronger FES providers tended to have an 'overarching strategy in place that allowed for collaborative working between curriculum staff, careers advisers and employers.' These strategies ensure that the links between aspirations, curriculum and their progression are meaningful. Developing these partnerships requires intentional effort but can significantly enhance the quality and impact of progression support. In addition to employers and higher education institutions, the following should be considered as stakeholders that can work with you to support your learners' progression.

Stakeholder	What they offer	How you can collaborate
Parents and guardians For learners under the age of 18, parents and guardians may be involved in supporting you in your role.	They may provide regular updates to you on your learners' progress outside of your institution. Their own experiences and networks may influence learners' aspirations and perceptions of available options.	Regular communication through parent/guardian evenings, newsletters, and digital platforms. Clear information about progression pathways and requirements in your sector. Support to explore their own assumptions about appropriate progression routes.

Stakeholder	What they offer	How you can collaborate
Careers advisors	Provide specialised expertise in career development theory and practice. Offer up-to-date knowledge of labour market trends and requirements. Facilitate impartial guidance complementing curriculum-based progression support. Have access to specialised resources and assessment tools.	Regular information sharing about curriculum developments and learner needs. Joint planning of progression activities and interventions. Clear referral processes for learners requiring specialised guidance. Shared CPD opportunities to enhance mutual understanding.
Awarding bodies	Define assessment requirements that may impact progression readiness. Provide frameworks that structure curriculum delivery and progression pathways. Offer resources and support for progression-focused teaching and learning.	Regular engagement with awarding body updates and guidance. Participation in networks and forums to share good practice. Feedback on qualification design and assessment to enhance progression value.
Community organisations and support services	Offer specialised expertise in areas such as mental health, housing, and finance. Create additional networks and opportunities for learners. May support transitions into independence.	Establish referral pathways for learners requiring additional support. Information sharing (within appropriate data protection guidelines). Joint case management for learners with complex needs. Collaborative funding bids for progression-focused initiatives.
Local schools	May provide information on the learners and their needs. Can advise on prior learning, curriculum content and careers advice.	Engage with schools to learn more about the curriculum and careers support offered. Attend school progression activities to promote the subject and career opportunities.

REFLECT

Which stakeholder relationships are strongest in your current practice? Which could be developed further to enhance progression support? What barriers exist to effective stakeholder collaboration in your context?

9.8 Digital tools for career guidance and progression planning

Digital tools have significantly enhanced the capacity of FES teachers to provide personalised progression support. These resources can expand learners' horizons, provide up-to-date information and enable independent exploration of options. The table below involves a range of tools and how they could be considered as part of your practice.

Digital tool type	Examples	Benefits	Considerations
Career exploration platforms	National Careers Service Prospects iCould Interactive job profiles	Labour market information Personality assessments	Requires digital literacy May need facilitated use
Skills assessment tools	Skills Builder SkillsCheck	Self-awareness development Targeted skill development Progress tracking	Should be integrated with curriculum, not stand-alone
Virtual work experience	Speakers for Schools Forage Virtual and augmented reality	Access to employers otherwise inaccessible Flexible engagement Reduced geographic barriers	Cannot fully replace in-person experiences Quality varies
E-portfolio systems	OneFile Smart Assessor	Evidence collection Reflection prompts Progress visualisation	Requires teacher and learner training Infrastructure needs
Social media for career research	LinkedIn Professional Facebook communities	Current industry insights Networking opportunities Role models	Requires guidance on professional digital identity

> **REFLECT**
>
> How could you integrate digital tools into your progression support while ensuring that all learners benefit equally, regardless of digital access or confidence?

Tip for Teaching

- Schedule regular 'digital exploration' sessions where learners can investigate progression options.
- Create structured worksheets to guide learners' use of digital tools.
- Use collaborative digital spaces for peer sharing of progression research.
- Incorporate digital tools into individual learning plans.
- Develop learners' critical digital literacy to evaluate online career information.

9.9 The role of personal tutoring in supporting progression

Personal tutoring represents a crucial opportunity for individualised progression support in line with benchmark 3 ('addressing the needs of each student'). The personal tutor role allows for ongoing dialogue about learners' developing aspirations, personalised guidance and targeted support for progression challenges.

> **REFLECT**
>
> How often do you organise individual tutorials with your learners to discuss their progress? What approach do you take in these meetings? What are the focus areas in the meetings?

Stork and Walker (2015) outline the difference between personal tutoring and coaching, emphasising the nurturing and longer-term benefit to regular personal tutorials.

	Personal tutoring	**Coaching**
Approach	Can be directive (you take more of a lead and offer advice and guidance) and non-directive (you encourage the learner to take more of the lead), stretching intellectual or academic needs or nurturing wellbeing.	Can be directive or non-directive. Usually focuses on stretching the intellectual or academic need.
Core Focus	Follow an educational or learning agenda. Developing a longer-term relationship	Affect an immediate improvement in skills or knowledge.
Context	More relationships based between the tutor and learner.	More of a functional process designed to be immediately practical and useful
How it helps learners	Helps learners to acquire new knowledge and skills and nurture their emotional wellbeing through regular communication.	Helps to improve learner performance and skills through one-to-one coaching conversations.

Adapted from Stork and Walker (2015)

Despite the clear differences between the two approaches, we think the coaching approach can be adapted to suit the model of personal tutoring. The GROW model adapted by Whitmore (2017) from a coaching approach could arguably be effective in supporting learners to develop broader knowledge and skills and for nurturing positive wellbeing.

GROW definitions	Explained
Goal – Establish goals for the session and long-term aspirations.	Review and discuss progress against previously set actions and goals and establish the intent for the session in line with long-term aspirations.
Reality – Explore the current situation, challenges, and context, reflecting on recent experiences and their implications for progression.	Encourage aspirational dialogue, challenging limited thinking and encouraging ambition. This is particularly important when considering learners who may ordinarily have low expectations imposed on them.
Options – Identify possible strategies, resources, and approaches.	Work with the learner to research and identify information needs and sources that are tailored to their individual circumstances, strengths and development needs. Adopting a strengths-based approach during this phase could add real value to learners who may face barriers.
Way forward – Develop concrete action plans and commitments.	Plan and agree specific, time-bound actions to support progression. In doing so, connect learners with specialist support beyond your professional boundary (careers advisors, learning support etc.) and document discussions and commitments while supporting learners to take responsibility for their progression planning.

> **REFLECT**
>
> How do you think the GROW model would work in your context? Are there any changes you would make to better meet the needs of your context and learners?

Case study: Applying the GROW model in a digital apprenticeship programme

Teacher: Saima

Learner: Alex, a young professional who is enrolled in a digital marketing apprenticeship.

Goal – Saima reviewed Alex's progress on previously set actions, such as completing foundational modules and participating in team projects. Alex demonstrated good progress with each of these and is still on track to achieve his long-term aspiration of becoming a certified digital marketing specialist within the next 18 months, which Saima confirmed was still appropriate, specific, measurable and time bound.

Saima established the session goal: to support Alex's ambition for mastering digital marketing tools.

Reality – Saima encouraged Alex to reflect on his recent experiences and how they impact his progression. Alex outlined that he has a basic understanding of digital marketing concepts but struggles with advanced analytics and SEO techniques. One of the challenges outlined was balancing apprenticeship tasks with personal commitments, limited practical experience and occasional self-doubt.

Saima challenged Alex's thinking by highlighting his strengths and past successes, particularly in relation to mentor feedback. Though Alex has received positive feedback from mentors, they did acknowledge the difficulty he has in applying theoretical knowledge to practical scenarios.

Options – Saima questioned Alex to identify the most relevant resources and strategies tailored to his needs. They came up with the following suggestions together which align with his strengths and development needs:

- Enrol on supplementary workshops focused on analytics and SEO techniques.
- Pair with a mentor who specialises in digital marketing analytics.
- Utilise online resources and forums for additional support.
- Schedule regular check-ins with his mentor to track progress.

Way forward – Saima and Alex collectively planned and agreed on specific, time-bound actions to support Alex's progression:

- **Short term** – Complete a supplementary workshop on digital marketing analytics within the next month.
- **Medium term** – Schedule bi-weekly mentoring sessions for the next three months.
- **Long term** – Apply for internships or volunteer opportunities in digital marketing within six months. Alex was also asked to connect with the career advisors to support this.

All conversations were documented to support Alex and his progression.

9.10 Measuring progression outcomes

Effective progression support requires systematic monitoring and evaluation. By tracking learners' destinations and measuring the impact of interventions, FES teachers and institutions can continuously improve their approach. Progression data can be gathered through both quantitative and qualitative measures.

Quantitative measures	Qualitative measures
Destination data (e.g. employment, further study, apprenticeships).	Learner satisfaction with progression support.
Salary levels of graduates.	Relevance of employment to qualification.
Progression rates to higher level qualifications.	Development of career management skills.
Retention in employment or further study (3, 6, 12 months).	Learner confidence in career decision making.
Time to secure relevant employment.	Employer feedback on preparedness.

What constitutes successful progress for each curriculum should be established before gathering data, with clear intervals outlined for this to be collected. Following this, evaluation should be used to drive improvements in the curriculum so that learners are able to progress to their respective destinations regardless of their background. Furthermore, having an awareness of the Gatsby benchmarks and evaluating your curriculum design with these in mind can help to ensure that the approach to evaluation is evidence-informed while also being compliant with the expectations of regulatory bodies.

Chapter summary

Supporting learner progression in FES requires a multifaceted approach that extends beyond the classroom. By designing curricula that align with industry needs and embedding opportunities for learners to engage with employers through their curriculum and work placements, FES teachers can lay a strong foundation for learner success. Collaboration with stakeholders such as employers and higher education institutions provides learners with valuable insights and opportunities for their future paths.

Adherence to legislative and regulatory requirements ensures that progression support is inclusive and of high quality. The Gatsby benchmarks offer a comprehensive framework for career guidance, helping learners make informed decisions about their future progression. Ultimately, effective support for learner progression involves creating a holistic learning environment that not only imparts knowledge and skills but also nurtures ambition, resilience and adaptability. By implementing some of the strategies outlined in this chapter, you can play a crucial role in empowering learners to achieve their full potential and make successful transitions to their chosen careers or further study, wherever they may be.

References

Allan, T. (2017). Applied General user research. Office of Qualifications and Examinations Regulation. Available at: https://www.gov.uk/government/publications/applied-general-user-research (Accessed 9 April 2025).

Aronowitz, S., and Bratsis, P. (2002). Paradigm Lost: State Theory Reconsidered. (First edition). Minneapolis: University of Minnesota Press

Association of Colleges. (2019). Careers Guidance in Colleges: Increasing Impact through Partnerships. London: AoC.

Atkins, L. (2009). Invisible Students, Impossible Dreams: Experiencing Vocational Education 14-19. Stoke-on-Trent: Trentham Books.

Atkins, L. (2013). 'From Marginal Learning to Marginal Employment? The Real Impact of 'Learning' Employability Skills'. Power and Education, 5 (1): 28-37.

Bolli, T., Caves, K. M., Renold, U., and Buergi, J. (2018). Beyond employer engagement: measuring education-employment linkage in vocational education and training programmes. Journal of Vocational Education and Training, 70(4), 524–563.

Bolton, P. and Lewis, J. (2024). Equality of access and outcomes in higher education in England. House of Commons Library. Available at: https://commonslibrary.parliament.uk/research-briefings/cbp-9195/ [Accessed 1 April 2025].

Department for Education. (2018). Careers guidance and access for education and training providers. London: DfE.

Department for Education. (2021). Skills for Jobs: Lifelong Learning for Opportunity and Growth. London: DfE.

Department for Education/Department for Business, Energy and Industrial Strategy (DfE/DBEIS). (2016). The Post 16 Skills Plan. Available at: https://assets.publishing.service.gov.uk/media/5a80d94ded915d74e6230cbe/Post-16_Skills_Plan.pdf (Accessed 18 May 2025)

Dodd, V., Hanson, J., and Hooley, T. (2021). Increasing students' career readiness through career guidance: measuring the impact with a validated measure. British Journal of Guidance and Counselling, 50(2), 260–272.

Education and Training Foundation. (2020). Teaching for Distinction in Further Education. London: ETF.

Esmond, B. and Atkins, L. (2022). Education, Skills and Social Justice in a Polarising World. Between Technical Elites and Welfare Vocationalism. London: Routledge.

Equality and Human Rights Commission. (2014). What equality law means for you as an education provider – further and higher education. Manchester: EHRC.

Gatsby Charitable Foundation. (2014). Good Career Guidance. London: Gatsby Charitable Foundation.

Guile, D. and Unwin, L. (eds.) (2019). The Wiley handbook of vocational education and training. 1st ed. Hoboken, New Jersey: Wiley Blackwell.

Huddleston, P., and Unwin, L. (2013). Teaching and Learning in Further Education: Diversity and Change. 4th ed. Routledge.

Hunt, J., Atherton, K., Collerton, E. and Wilkinson, N. (2021). 'Effective careers interventions for disadvantaged young people: a report by the behavioural insights team', The Careers and Enterprise Company.

Information Commissioner's Office. (2018). Guide to the General Data Protection Regulation (GDPR). Wilmslow: ICO.

Jones, I. (2021) 'Reconceptualizing the "problem" of widening participation in higher education in England'. London Review of Education, 19 (1), 2, 1–14

Lenon, B. (2018). Other People's Children: What happens to those in the bottom 50% academically? Woodbridge: John Catt Publishers.

Lewis, J. (2024). The reform of level 3 qualifications in England. Commons Library Research Briefing, 15 November. Available at: commonslibrary.parliament.uk (Accessed 8 April 2025).

Maris, R., Khandekar, S., and Robinson, D. (2024). A quantitative analysis of T-level access and progression. Education Policy Institute. Available at: https://epi.org.uk/publications-and-research/a-quantitative-analysis-of-t-level-access-and-progression/ (Accessed 9 April 2025).

Ofsted. (2019). Education Inspection Framework. Manchester: Ofsted.

Ofsted. (2025). Navigating post-16 careers guidance: supporting learners from lower socioeconomic backgrounds. Available at: https://www.gov.uk/government/publications/navigating-post-16-careers-guidance-supporting-learners-from-lower-socioeconomic-backgrounds/navigating-post-16-careers-guidance-supporting-learners-from-lower-socioeconomic-backgrounds (Accessed 7 April 2025)

Pye, M., McGillan, J., and Watson-Harper, A. (2020). Further Education Learners into the Construction Workforce. CITB. Available at: https://www.citb.co.uk/media/curmt35z/citb_fe_learners.pdf [Accessed 19 March 2025].

Social Mobility Commission. (2020). Improving attainment among disadvantaged students in the FE and adult learning sector: evidence review. GOV.UK. Available at: https://www.gov.uk/government/publications/improving-attainment-in-the-fe-and-adult-learning-sector/improving-attainment-among-disadvantaged-students-in-the-fe-and-adult-learning-sector-evidence-review-html [Accessed 19 March 2025].

Stork, A., and Walker, B. (2015). Becoming an outstanding personal tutor supporting learners through personal tutoring and coaching. Critical Publishing.

UCAS. (2021). Progression Pathways. Cheltenham: UCAS.

Whitmore, J. (2017). Coaching for Performance: The Principles and Practice of Coaching and Leadership (5th ed.). Nicholas Brealey Publishing.

Williams, D. (2024). What's in a word? An Interdisciplinary Critical Discourse Analysis of 'Skill' in Technical and Vocational Education and Training in England. College of Arts, Humanities and Education, University of Derby.

Winch, C. (2010). Dimensions of Expertise: A Conceptual Exploration of Vocational Knowledge. Vancouver, CA: Continuum.

Wolf, A. (2011). Review of Vocational Education – The Wolf Report. Available at: https://www.gov.uk/government/publications/review-of-vocational-education-the-wolf-report (Accessed 17 April 2025)

Chapter 10 Success in your initial teacher education programme

10.1 Introduction

This chapter pulls together key insights from previous chapters to equip you with a comprehensive toolkit for success in your FES ITE programme. Whether you are pursuing a level 5 learning and skills teacher apprenticeship, a level 5 diploma in teaching or a higher education validated certificate in education, PGCE or PGDE, the guidance provided in this chapter will support your journey toward becoming an effective and reflective FES practitioner. While your ITE programme is fundamentally designed to develop the knowledge, skills and behaviours expected of FES teachers in accordance with the occupational standards, it should also provide opportunities to foster critical reflection and support your professional identity formation.

We will guide you through the following themes to enable your success on your ITE programme:

- Understanding the requirements of FES ITE programmes
- Developing effective reflective practice to support your teaching
- Preparing for observations and models for supporting your planning
- Building a strong portfolio of evidence and preparing for your professional discussions
- Maximising work or placement opportunities
- Working effectively with mentors
- Engaging in meaningful continuing professional development
- Developing academic writing skills

By the end of this chapter, you will have a clear roadmap for navigating the complexities of your ITE programme and laying the foundations for a successful teaching career in FES.

10.2 Requirements of your ITE programme

The following table details the distinct assessment requirements across different ITE routes at level 5 and above. While these vary in structure, all align with the occupational standards for the learning and skills teacher apprenticeship, ensuring consistency in professional expectations regardless of your chosen pathway.

	Level 5 learning and skills teacher	Level 5 diploma in teaching	Higher education validated Cert Ed, PGCE or PGDE
Length of programme	Approximately 1,800 hours across a typical 18-month apprenticeship (around 100 hours per month)	Usually, 2 academic years part-time and 1 academic year for full-time.	
Credits (This refers to the size of the programme. 10 credits typically refers to 100 learning hours.)	Complete on-programme training to meet the KSBs as outlined in the occupational standard for a minimum of 12 months. Complete the required amount of off-the-job training specified by the apprenticeship funding rules and as arranged by the employer and training provider.	120 credits, 360 guided learning hours, and a minimum of 1200 hours total qualification time.	
Teaching practice requirements	Undefined	At least 250 hours in duration. At least 150 hours of this should be teaching practice with at least 100 hours in the trainee's subject area.	
Portfolio of evidence requirements	Must ensure that a portfolio is developed during the programme which evidences progress towards the occupational standards but this cannot be used as evidence in the end point assessment (EPA).	Should include a professional practice portfolio which evidences progression towards the occupational standards. This should evidence all practice hours	
Observed practice requirements	Undefined	10 developmental observations to establish whether the trainee is teaching at the level expected in the occupational standards.	

10.2 Requirements of your ITE programme

	Level 5 learning and skills teacher	Level 5 diploma in teaching	Higher education validated Cert Ed, PGCE or PGDE
Summative assessment	EPA must be conducted by an approved end point assessment organisation (EPAO) This EPA consists of two discrete assessment methods: observation of teaching practice and a professional discussion, both of which are assessed as fail, pass or distinction towards the apprenticeship standard.	Awarding organisation determined in accordance with the Diploma in Teaching (Further Education and Skills) qualification framework. The assessment model used for this qualification requires all trainees to pass all modules through assessment, except the Professional Practice modules. This will be used to participate in a final assessment involving a 30-minute oral discussion relating to any aspect of professional practice.	Higher education provider determined based on modules and assessments in line with the higher education Quality Assurance Agency (QAA) requirements and the DiT Framework. All will include a portfolio of evidence, including the 10 observations, and a professional discussion.
Quality assurance	EPA internal moderation.	Internal and external verification.	Internal moderation and external examination.
External regulation	Awarding organisation and Ofsted regulated.	Awarding organisation regulated.	Ofsted regulated.
English and maths (A level 2 qualification in English and maths should be considered the minimum level to show communication, literacy and numeracy skills.)	Trainees undertaking the LST apprenticeship will need to achieve level 2 in English and maths if they have not already* *This requirement has recently been revoked since the wholesale removal of English and maths from apprenticeships, but providers should still ensure that they are supporting trainees to be working at level 2.	A pass at level 2 in both English and maths as an entry requirement.	A pass at level 2 in both English and maths as an entry requirement.

While each of these requirements are subject to change, the table above represents the typical requirements and format for the different ITE pathways for FES at level 5 and above.

Should you want further information, you can access the DfE's 'Expectations for the delivery of initial teacher education for FE' (DfE, 2025).

While summative assessment is crucial to ensure that a programme has rigour, all ITE programmes will also provide regular formative opportunities for growth through the collation of a range of portfolio reflections in line with occupational standards and observations of your teaching practice from tutors, mentors or managers. Throughout your journey, you will come to value the opportunity to draw upon a variety of feedback from a range of individuals to reflect on your practice and identify ways to improve. Reflective practice is a crucial exercise for all FES teachers to undertake; in the next section we explore some ideas for structuring your reflections to maximise their impact.

10.3 Reflective practice

What is reflective practice?

As we established in the introduction to this book (see page 2), as 'evidence-informed' practitioners in FES we need to reflect on our experiences if we are going to improve our teaching skills and move from being an experienced teacher to an expert teacher. Reflection is more than simply thinking about your teaching – it is a structured process of critically examining your practice to refine and develop your approach. As Brookfield (2017) defines it:

> *Reflective practice is the process of interrogating our actions, decisions and judgments so that we can draw conclusions about how to act, decide and judge in the future.*

For FES teachers, this means critically analysing teaching experiences, questioning assumptions, exploring alternative approaches and using these insights to inform future practice.

Why is reflective practice important?

Research consistently demonstrates the importance of reflection in teacher development. Thompson and Pascal's (2012) longitudinal study found that teachers who engaged in regular structured reflection showed greater adaptability in their practice and higher levels of learner satisfaction. Reflecting can help us to make sense of – and bridge – the gap between theory and practice. This enables us as FES teachers to respond more effectively to our learners' needs and navigate complex institutional demands.

As Marshall and colleagues (2022) argue, reflective practice is both a personal and relational process. In other words, it happens privately within people (in our heads) and publicly between people (in discussions with colleagues). They found that newer teachers in particular struggle to construct their reflections and often feel uncertain and worried about sharing them with colleagues.

With this in mind, it is essential that a safe and supportive space is established, where more experienced colleagues can enrich the knowledge and perspectives from the reflections; this is where mentorship comes in. A safe and supportive space also helps to deconstruct the process of reflection to enable more meaningful reflections to take place both privately and with others. This is where reflective models may help trainee teachers to learn how to reflect meaningfully on their practice.

Reflective models

There are numerous models that can be used to support and structure reflective practice and conversations (some of which we shared in chapter 6, see page 178 figure 6.19). In this section, we will cover a few of the more popular ones that can support your reflections. You will have the opportunity to consider if any of these work for you or whether a combination of models may better serve your reflective practice.

Borton's model (1970)

This is a simple three-stage model that asks:

Figure 10.1 *Borton's model*

The 'what?' stage of reflection requires you to outline a description of the event. For example, you may describe a behavioural issue you experienced in one of your classes, such as a learner getting angry at you and leaving the room.

The 'so what?' stage of reflection requires you to analyse and interpret the event. This is probably the most challenging stage but equally the most important aspect of the reflection. Here, you will need to think deeply about the event and make sense of it. In the case of the behavioural issue mentioned above, it may be a reflection on the sequence of events that led to the anger manifesting. Had the learner had a bad day? Were they their usual self prior to their angry outburst? Did you communicate in a positive or negative manner with them? Were they confused or finding the work difficult? It is important to ask yourself (or your colleagues) a lot of probing questions here (see chapter 3 for more specific ideas on this).

The 'now what?' stage of this reflection requires you to think about the next steps and set appropriate actions for improvement. If it was the way you communicated with the learner that led to their angry outburst, how will you improve in future interactions?

Gibbs' reflective cycle (1988)

This six-stage model provides a more detailed framework compared to Borton's, though some of the steps may get confused and overlap slightly:

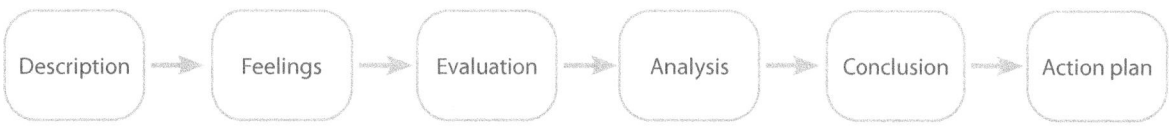

Figure 10.2 *Gibbs' reflective cycle*

Like Borton's model, the initial stage of reflection requires a description of what happened. Next, the model requires you to reflect on what you were thinking and how you felt at the time of the event. Following this, the evaluation stage requires you to explain what was good and bad about the experience, and the analysis stage requires you to make sense of this: what did this mean? Why did it happen? The conclusion stage requires you to consider alternatives that may have been taken before using these to plan actions for the future.

Brookfield's four lenses (2017)

Unlike the previous models, which structure the thinking process into clear stages, this model suggests viewing your practice through four different perspectives:

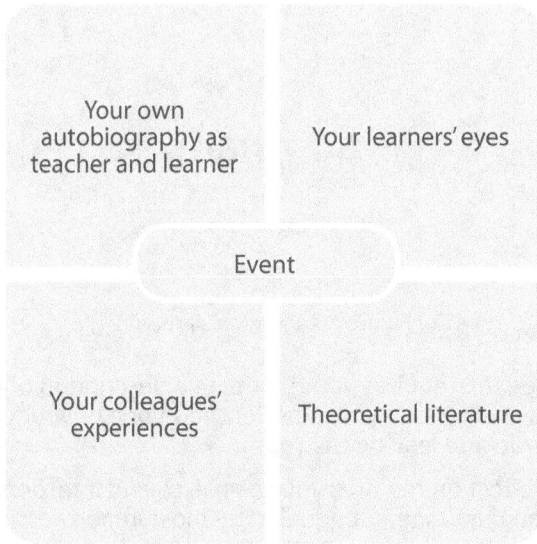

Figure 10.3 *Brookfield's four lenses*

In some ways, Brookfield's model reminds us of the evidence-informed practice model (Scutt, 2018) that we identified in the introduction to this book (see page 2). According to Scutt, in order to become evidence-informed, we must consider the best available evidence from the research (theoretical literature), the context of the system we are working in (learners and colleagues) and teacher expertise and judgement (our own autobiography). In a similar manner, Brookfield asks us to reflect on each perspective and draw conclusions based on these perspectives. Where evidence-informed practice clearly has a focus on improving practice, Brookfield's lenses seem to focus more attention on what happened, with less emphasis on future changes of practice. However, these detailed reflections should allow us to create actionable areas for improvement.

> **REFLECT**
>
> Is there a particular model that you think could support your reflective practice? Do any of the approaches match the way you already reflect on your practice? Do you see value in combining the approaches?

> **Take it further...**
>
> Consider the following scenario:
>
> You delivered a lesson on workplace communications to a group of apprentices. While most learners engaged well, you noticed several struggling to connect the content to their specific workplace contexts.
>
> Use each of the reflective models described above and apply it to this scenario. Once you have completed this, consider:
>
> - Which model felt the most natural to use?
> - Which aspects of your practice did this model help you examine?
> - What insights did you gain that may not have emerged without using this structured approach?

Digital reflection tools

Contemporary reflective practice increasingly incorporates digital tools, and your ITE programme may integrate these in order to support your reflections, whether that is through visual mapping or audio and video logs. The research in this field is varied though; where Collet (2024) found that blogging providing a structure for trainee teachers to consider past and future practice, Dalgarno and colleagues (2015) found that the quality of trainee teachers' blogging while on professional placement was substantially different, with some trainees highlighting the value of collaborative learning and reflection on practice while others questioned its value and were less interested in providing feedback to their peers. Our position is that reflection should take the form that best meets your needs in terms of the structure and format.

As mentioned at the outset of this section, reflection done well should involve safe, open conversations with colleagues. Individual, private reflection may take place prior to this, but more contemporary research by Arefian et al (2024) found that teachers' individual reflection in conversation with generative AI software served as a complementary preparatory step for contributing insightful perspectives to a community of practice. Therefore, having a reflective discussion with AI (where you pose various questions to a chatbot) prior to conversations with colleagues may support the structuring of ideas and give you more confidence to share your reflections with colleagues.

Technology not only affords us the opportunity to reflect, but it can also be a tool to prompt reflections. For example, reflecting on something that happened in a lesson after the event took place requires us to recall the events, which may lead to misinterpretation. On the other hand, watching a recording of a lesson we taught and reflecting as we watch requires less need to recall the event, which arguably provides more space to reflect and therefore a more accurate picture of what happened. This is supported by Hamel and Viau-Guay's (2019) literature review on the use of recorded lesson observations, which showed that video-based training mechanisms lead to significant learning.

> **Tip for Teaching**
>
> Record one of your teaching sessions and see if you notice more about your practice compared to your usual reflections.

10.4 Successful observation practice

Teaching observations are pivotal assessment components across all ITE routes and, as seen in the table on page 268, all require observations of your teaching practice from either your ITE tutor or mentor. The aim of these observations is to provide authentic assessment of your ability to apply theoretical knowledge in practical contexts (Lahiff, 2015).

According to Maxwell (2010), trainee teachers place high value on observations during their ITE programme, with many feeling that this was one of the greatest learning opportunities on their programme. The current DiT Framework (ETF, 2024) requires 10 formal observations during ITE programmes and suggests that the earlier observations should be mostly developmental, which is encouraging, though there does need to be some judgement made to determine progress towards the occupational standards. It has been suggested that there is greater receptiveness to feedback and more rapid improvement from trainees who see observations as developmental opportunities rather than evaluative judgements (Lahiff, 2015). It is important, therefore, that you see the observations during your ITE programme as opportunities for improvement and development (and not to be judged).

Contemporary observation frameworks tend to emphasise the impact of teaching practice on the learning and progress of the learners rather than simply focusing on the performative aspects of your teaching practice. For example, feedback may be structured in a way that foregrounds the learners:

> *All learners benefit from very clear explanations and modelling of the X technique, which enabled them to implement it in practice with high levels of accuracy.*

We believe it is important that you adopt this perspective too so that your focus is primarily on the impact on the learners and not just what you do in the learning environment. This focus should be through the planning, delivery and reflections of your practice.

Prior to the observation – planning and justifying your choices

You should be able to explain not just what you do but why you do it – observers will expect you to be able to articulate the reasoning behind your teaching decisions. For each key element of your observed session, be prepared to discuss:

- How this session connects to the 'bigger picture', i.e. what the learners have learned before, how it will be built upon and how it prepares them for future learning.

- Why you selected particular teaching approaches and how these approaches align with the content being taught and the needs of the learners.

- How your choices demonstrate evidence-informed practice, i.e. drawing on research and your previous experiences.

- The alternatives you considered and why you rejected them.

Several models and principles can support you to build a coherent and well-sequenced lesson or series of lessons. While some of these are quite prescriptive in nature and may not suit your context or subject area, they are underpinned by a strong body of research to support your evidence-informed practice.

Receive-apply-reuse (RAR) model (Petty, 2018)	Nine events of instruction (Gagne, 1985)	Principles of instruction (Rosenshine, 2012)
Receive – the purpose of this stage is to orientate learners: • Establish prior learning. • Summarise what you are going to teach. • Set goals for the lesson. **Apply** – learners complete a range of learning activities by: • Reproducing the new information. • Applying reasoning to questions on the information. • Addressing challenging, 'open' tasks, using the new information. **Reuse** – the purpose is to consolidate the learning: • Through a quiz or other formative assessment method.	• Gain attention of the learners with a starter 'do now' activity. • Inform learners of the objectives. • Stimulate recall of prior learning. • Present the new content in the most appropriate form. • Provide learning guidance while learners apply their new learning. • Elicit performance through formative assessment methods. • Provide feedback based on the formative assessment. • Assess performance to determine overall understanding. • Enhance retention and transfer with a real-world application task.	• Begin a lesson with a short review. • Present new material in small steps. • Ask a large number of questions. • Provide models. • Guide learner practice. • Check for learner understanding. • Obtain a high success rate. • Provide scaffolds for difficult tasks. • Require and monitor independent practice. • Engage learners in weekly and monthly review.

> **REFLECT**
>
> Do you follow any of the principles above in your lesson planning? Which of the models would best fit your subject and context? Create a lesson plan for your next lesson using the chosen model.

Tip for Teaching

Planning workshop and practical teaching lessons

The planning models above may not be conducive to your context, particularly if working in a practical or workshop environment. You can draw upon some of the key principles, but we recommend you also consider the following in your plan:

- **Safety first** – Begin planning with risk assessment and safety protocols. This is a non-negotiable in the practical setting and aligns to the professional responsibility of adhering to health and safety legislation (for more information, see chapter 1).
- **Demonstration staging** – Plan strategic viewing angles and repetition points. Can all learners see your demonstration of a practical technique, and does that position enable them to understand the requirements of the technique?
- **Individual practice** – Practical learning may require more opportunities for the learners to practise independently, so schedule adequate time with appropriate supervision ratios.
- **Digital enhancement** – Consider how video demonstrations and digital resources can support practical learning and formative assessment. For example, learners could film themselves performing a technique and watch it back for peer or self-assessment.
- **Assessment milestones** – Incorporate clear checkpoints to assess practical skill development.

Tip for Teaching

Planning for online teaching

While many of the principles above are equally applicable to the online learning environment as suggested by Nilson and Goodson (2021) and Scott (2022), there are some practices that benefit live, online teaching, and these should be considered in the planning:

- **Setting the scene** – Ensure that the online 'netiquette' is considered to reinforce learning expectations, e.g. cameras on, microphones off, how and when to contribute.
- **Chunk content** – Break learning into smaller segments than in face-to-face teaching to manage the cognitive load.
- **Build in interaction** – Plan specific activities that require learner engagement every 5–10 minutes to maintain focus and engagement.
- **Build in time off-screen** – Provide opportunities off-screen for learners (and you) to rest your eyes.
- **Technological redundancy** – Have backup plans for technical failures to avoid lost learning time.
- **Cognitive presence** – Design learning activities that make thinking visible, such as collaborative notetaking or breakout discussions.
- **Social presence** – Include community-building elements that allow learners to gain confidence in an online environment.

Generative AI tools can offer opportunities for planning support but require critical engagement. Research by Lammert and colleagues (2024) found that while AI-generated lesson plans are useful for teachers in their early years of teaching, they do not always align well with evidence-informed approaches and require modifications to successfully support learners with diverse needs. It is therefore essential that where AI is used to plan lessons, the prompts should be very specific and thoughtful and a critical eye is cast over the content to ensure that it aligns with research and your learners' needs. Therefore, start with clear parameters and context for the lesson when using AI for planning, for example:

I am planning a lesson for a group of BTEC level 3 national diploma learners who are studying module A: exploring and developing creative media skills.

I would like a lesson plan that addresses the lesson learning outcomes: identify a range of factors which constrain or challenge creative media practices and analyse at least four factors and their implications for a given media practice.

The lesson is three hours in length, and I would like the plan to be presented in a table with a column for teacher activities, learner activities, formative assessment activities and resources.

Include aspects of Rosenshine's principles of instruction to sequence the lesson.

Once the plan has been generated, you should critically review the suggested activities and resources and either customise it for your learners and their specific needs or ask questions of the AI to refine the lesson plan further. You may even ask the AI to create the suggested resources for you (such as teaching slides or a worksheet) to give you a starting point.

> **REFLECT**
>
> Using a generative AI platform, try planning a lesson for one of your classes by using prompts such as the example above. Critique what was generated – is structured appropriately? Does it consider the context in which you are teaching?

During the observation – some pointers

It is important that the observer sees your daily practice, not a one-off, all-singing-all-dancing lesson that does not represent what the learners experience day-to-day with you. This will ensure that feedback is representative of your practice.

The observation itself can be quite daunting, and having an observer in the room may impact how you and the learners behave (known as the Hawthorne effect). With this in mind, try to prepare somewhere for your observer to sit where they will be the least intrusive. It is helpful to imagine the observer is not there; it is very important that you do not try to integrate them into the lesson activities, no matter how helpful you think that may be, as it is a distraction from what they are there for.

Usually, observations will last 45–60 minutes but, if your lesson is longer than an hour, observers may decide to stay for the whole lesson or drop in and out of appropriate times. They will usually determine the logistics with you prior to the observation so you know what to expect. Ensure that the observer has a copy of your lesson plan and any other information pertinent to the lesson (either printed or accessible digitally). It may also be helpful to provide a brief justification so they can understand why you are teaching in your chosen way and consider the impact of this on the learners. Observers may decide to discreetly talk to learners at appropriate points in the lesson in order to build a better understanding of how well learners are progressing within the lesson and over time, so do not be alarmed if you see this happening.

After the observation

Your observer will usually provide you with some written and verbal feedback. As we explored in chapter 7, good feedback adopts an approach that looks forward (for example, medal and mission). As with your planning, it is important that the feedback is based on not only what you did as a teacher but the impact you had on the learners. This feedback should be dialogic and collegiate, where you have an opportunity to provide your perspective; it is helpful for feedback to be aligned with the occupational standards to enable focused reflections (try using one of the models on pages 271-2 for this), which can support the co-development of targets with your tutor or mentor for your future development.

10.5 Successful professional development portfolios and discussions

Professional discussions, whether as part of your EPA or ongoing programme assessment, require careful preparation and practice. These discussions will be informed by your professional development portfolio.

Professional development portfolios are dynamic, reflective tools that capture a teacher's professional growth, critical thinking and pedagogical development (Klenowski, 2002). Darling-Hammond et al (2023) emphasise the importance of these portfolios as critical mechanisms for demonstrating competence against the occupational standards. Therefore, building a portfolio can showcase your journey during your ITE and support you to articulate your progression during the summative professional discussion.

As evidence-informed practitioners, there is an expectation that you make reference throughout your portfolio to the best available research evidence, in addition to your own reflections and experiences in relation to the specific subject and context of your practice (Scutt, 2018). It is also helpful if the work within your portfolio is clearly signposted to the relevant occupational standards.

Each institution will have their own format and approach for this. Some may have more prescriptive reflections aligned to specific standards, whereas others may give more flexibility in the reflections and evidence collected to demonstrate progress towards the occupational standards. A typical portfolio may consist of the following:

Typical section	Typical content
Professional background	Personal teaching philosophy
	Career aspirations
	Professional goals
Evidence to aligned to standards	Lesson plans
	Learner work samples
	Classroom observation feedback
	Professional development certificates
	Action research projects
Reflective narratives	Critical incident analyses
	Professional learning reflections
	Personal growth commentaries
Professional development records	Training attendance
	Workshop participation
	CPD logs
Log of practice hours	Independent and team-teaching hours
	Meetings
	Open days or recruitment events
	Assessment and feedback

Tip for Teaching

Portfolio building

Below are some quick wins you should consider whether you are studying an ITE programme or simply building a portfolio of professional development.

- **Start early** – Collect evidence from the beginning of your programme.

- **Be selective** – Quality matters more than quantity. You do not need a lot of examples brief reflections, or lesson plans. It is better to focus on fewer things in greater detail, always thinking about the impact on you and your learners.

- **Provide context** – Explain why each piece of evidence matters and how it relates to the occupational standards.

- **Show development** – Include earlier and later examples to demonstrate growth.

- **Incorporate diverse evidence** – Including examples of annotated lesson plans and resources, feedback from mentors or learners, and your own critical reflections.

- **Use multimedia** – Your portfolio does not have to only be written. Feel free to include video, audio, and visual evidence to accompany the written work.

> **Take it further...**
>
> **Portfolio analytics**
>
> For those interested in a more systematic approach to portfolio development, analysing the content in greater detail may help you to demonstrate a stronger body of evidence:
>
> - Map each piece of evidence against the specific Occupational Standards
> - Track the distribution of evidence across different standards
> - Identify areas with strong evidence and gaps requiring attention
> - Analyse the depth of your reflections using a rubric (descriptive, analytical, critical) or RAG (red, amber, green) rating.

Preparing for your professional discussion

The professional discussion is a summative assessment method designed to give you an opportunity to showcase your professional accomplishments and detail how you meet the occupational standards. Drawing on your portfolio, you should have a strong understanding of the progress you have made and where and how the evidence supports this. Try to avoid broad and generic descriptive comments that do not demonstrate your progression clearly, as these will make it difficult for you when responding to questions during the professional discussion.

Professional discussions typically include questions that:

- **Probe decision-making** – Why did you choose that particular approach for this lesson?
- **Explore theoretical understanding** – How does your assessment strategy reflect principles of formative assessment?
- **Examine professional values** – How have you ensured inclusivity in your teaching practice?
- **Address challenges** – Describe a challenging teaching situation and how you addressed it.
- **Focus on impact** – What evidence do you have that your approach improved learner outcomes?
- **Explore professional development** – How have you developed your subject knowledge during your programme?

It is important that you prepare well to articulate responses for these sorts of questions. We recommend that you organise a mock professional discussion with your tutor or peers to help you practise your responses and receive feedback in readiness for the real thing.

Case study: Construction teacher trainee

Sarah was preparing for her EPA professional discussion for her level 5 learning and skills teacher apprenticeship. She initially struggled with articulating the rationale behind her teaching approaches. Her mentor suggested she practice 'thinking aloud' when planning lessons and reviewing her teaching.

Sarah began audio-recording her reflections immediately after teaching and then transcribing key insights. This helped her develop the language to express her reasoning behind her teaching practice. During her professional discussion, Sarah was able to clearly explain how her understanding of scaffolding techniques had evolved through her apprenticeship and how this had improved engagement among her construction learners.

The assessor commended Sarah's ability to connect theoretical concepts to specific examples from her practice and her clear explanation of how she had modified her approaches based on learners' feedback.

10.6 Getting the most from placements or workplace experiences

Workplace or practice placements provide essential contextual experience that will help you to connect theory to practice in the broad roles and responsibilities you have as an FES teacher. In this section, we explore some of the opportunities you have in the workplace and what you can do to make the most of them.

While those of you working as full-time teachers will meet the requirements for 150 teaching practice hours, remember that in addition to these hours there is a requirement of the DiT framework (ETF, 2024) to undertake 100 hours of additional practice in relation to the broader role. Whichever ITE route you are on, the table below outlines ways you can participate and develop your knowledge and skills in this regard.

Role and responsibilities	Ways to increase your knowledge and skills
Assessment and internal verification	Understanding assessment processes within your placement setting is crucial. Key activities include: Shadowing experienced assessors Participating in standardisation meetings Understanding quality assurance processes Developing assessment materials under supervision Receiving feedback on your assessment decisions
Working with others	Collaborative practice enhances placement learning. Consider the following: Team teaching opportunities Curriculum development projects Curriculum planning meetings Cross-departmental initiatives External partnership activities

Role and responsibilities	Ways to increase your knowledge and skills
External stakeholder engagement	Seek opportunities beyond direct teaching, including: Open days and recruitment events Parent or employer evenings

> **Case study: Maximising placement experience**
>
> Jamal was completing his PGCE while placed in a college business department. Rather than limiting himself to his assigned BTEC level 2 classes, he proactively sought broader experiences:
>
> - He arranged to observe sessions in the college's T Level programme to understand the new qualification.
> - He volunteered to help with the department's employer advisory board meetings.
> - He participated in the college's internal verification process for business BTEC level 3 assignments.
> - He spent a day with the careers team to understand progression pathways.
> - He collaborated with the learning support team to develop inclusive resources.
>
> By the end of his placement, Jamal had developed a comprehensive understanding of the business education ecosystem beyond his immediate teaching responsibilities. This broader perspective enhanced his employability and informed his approach to curriculum planning.

Alternative context experience

In chapter 1, we covered the wide range of FES contexts that you may be employed within, and gaining experience in these different contexts will enhance your versatility as a practitioner. The ETF's DiT framework (2024) requires all trainee teachers undertake a minimum of 20 hours experience in another context; in doing so, you should seek opportunities to observe teaching in different subject areas, experience different levels of provision, engage with different learner demographics and experience different organisational cultures. Doing this will support your broader understanding of the FES sector, which may be crucial for your future career progression.

10.7 Getting the most from your mentors

The adage that 'it takes a village to raise a child' suggests that there is a community that is responsible for the development of one individual. By the same token, we believe that it takes a whole institution to support and develop a new teacher, and key to this is mentoring.

Tummons and Ingleby's (2012) research on the mentoring of trainee teachers in FES found that mentoring is more complex than some may think due to the power dynamics in the mentoring and trainee relationship and the institutional contexts that may impact the quality of the professional learning experience. In terms of power dynamics, your relationship with a mentor can either help you to thrive or hinder your development, so it is crucial that care is undertaken to ensure the right person undertakes this crucial role. As the DfE (2024) states in their expectations for FES ITE:

Trainees should not be expected to find their own mentor as part of a recruitment process. In employment based ITE, employers should be part of the process of agreeing an appropriate mentor from their organisation, if one is available. For pre-service programmes, the responsibility rests with the ITE provider.

Under the current DiT framework (ETF, 2024), trainees are expected to have two mentors: subject specialists and those who provide pastoral support.

A subject specialist mentor provides expertise in a specific discipline. They should be able to model excellent subject teaching practices, give you feedback and advice related to subject specialist teaching and guide you on where to access subject knowledge and industry currency.

REFLECT

1. Identify one subject-specific area where you need development.
2. Identify one broader professional area where you need growth.

Answer the following questions for each area:

- What specific support will you request from your mentor?
- What preparation will make mentor meetings more productive?
- What evidence will demonstrate your development in this area?

Schedule a discussion with your mentor about these development priorities.

Due to the nature of many ITE programmes (which tend to have a range of subjects being taught collectively), subject specialist teaching input comes mainly from the trainees' placement or workplace experiences, so having a subject specialist mentor is essential. These individuals should also be qualified teachers and have sufficient experience and expertise in the role to enable them to support you effectively while enacting the taught elements of your ITE curriculum.

However, it is important to recognise that some institutions simply have no suitable individuals for undertaking the role, whether this is due to a lack of qualified staff or the size of the team in which you are working. Therefore, other mechanisms may need to be put in place to ensure adequate support is provided, such as a subject specialist buddy from another institution.

The mentor may need to be a line manager, though this can sometimes blur the line between what is intended as a developmental process (ITE) and the performative nature of the teaching role. For this reason, we suggest avoiding manager-mentor relationship as far as possible.

The second mentor in the DfE guidance is one who provides pastoral support. Pastoral mentors support your broader professional development, including your professional progress, academic progress, work-life balance and wellbeing. It can be challenging enough for some institutions to provide one appropriate mentor, so sometimes this role may fall under the remit of the FES ITE provision, such as a personal tutor.

10.8 Continuing Professional Development CPD

Dreer-Goethe's (2025) research emphasises that teaching is a social profession and that teacher development involves social interaction not just with formal mentors but also with those outside of the mentoring relationship. The findings from their study suggest that high-quality connections with colleagues can improve engagement and psychological safety; in other words, teachers feel more comfortable taking risks, sharing their successes and failures and learning with and from others. With this in mind, it is important that FES teachers, particularly when new to an organisation, are thoroughly inducted and that opportunities are provided to work with others in the organisation.

In chapter 2, we outlined some of the key features of effective professional development from the work of Darling-Hammond and colleagues (2017) (see page 36), though each institution will have their own priorities and approaches to this depending on their values and beliefs. Therefore, sometimes you may need to take matters into your own hands to ensure high-quality professional development. In the table below, we summarise some of the ways in which you may collaborate with others to advance your professional knowledge and skills during and beyond your ITE.

Professional development	Examples
Membership at the Education and Training Foundation (ETF) (formerly Society for Education and Training [SET]) As trainee teachers, you benefit from free membership of the professional membership body, providing credibility and recognition for your skills and abilities and opportunities to further enhance your practice.	• Professional standards frameworks to support your career development. • Webinars and conferences to learn with and from others in the sector. • Journal access to provide research and opinions of best practice in FES.
Subject networks Joining subject specialist network opportunities to enhance subject or industry knowledge or how to teach the subject.	• Subject associations, a number of which can be found on the following Padlet page: rb.gy/k72j6b • Online communities of practice on social media. • Industry connections or industry days. • Subject-specific research groups.
Scholarship and research As part of our evidence-informed practice, engagement with scholarship as both a consumer (i.e. reading the research) and producer (i.e. participating in new knowledge creation) is crucial.	• Action research projects • Journal clubs • Research conferences such as LSRN and TVET • Collaborative inquiry groups • Higher level study (e.g. undergraduate degree, master's degree, PhD)

Professional development	Examples
Professional status Within the FES sector, professional status is voluntary but, as part of a career pathway, there are different statuses which can be acquired.	Qualified teacher learning and skills (QTLS) status is a post-qualification professional status for early career teachers in FES that requires demonstration of your commitment to your professional development via successful completion of a six-month period of professional formation. Advanced teacher status (ATS) is a progression route from QTLS aimed at experienced teachers who have held their ITE qualification for a minimum of four years and who are in a position to formally coach or mentor others and influence the organisation at a strategic level.

> **REFLECT**
>
> What professional development opportunities will you undertake outside of the organisation you work? What benefit do you think this will bring to your practice?

10.9 Academic writing

For many ITE routes, academic writing is a core assessment component. Given the nature of FES ITE programmes, which can be rooted in both professional practice and academia, it can be a tough to balance the two elements.

The DfE (2024) expectations for FES ITE outline that teachers in the sector should have the skills such as critical analysis to determine what works and how to assess new knowledge or theory and integrate it into their own practice. For this reason, you will be introduced to a range of evidence during your ITE such as randomised control trials (RCTs) and peer-reviewed journals and be expected to critically analyse them to determine their utility in your own practice.

Critical writing

Critical writing moves beyond description to analysis and evaluation. Key elements include questioning and challenging assumptions, examining multiple perspectives and determining their credibility and building your own arguments based on the findings.

On the left-hand side of the table below are some light-hearted extracts of text about cake written for demonstration purposes, and on the right-hand side we outline the strengths and weaknesses of each extract. You will see that the further down the table we go, the better the critical writing becomes; you should seek to follow this guidance in your own written work.

Example of written work	Strengths and weaknesses
The best type of cake is a cherry bakewell.	This is very limited as it is simply the writer's opinion with no justification for their choice.
Smith (2021) argues that a cherry bakewell is the best cake due to the combination of strawberry jam and a rich almond filling.	This extract shares a researcher's justification for the best type of cake, but it is unclear if the author agrees or disagrees.
Smith (2021) argues that a cherry bakewell is the best cake due to the combination of strawberry jam and a rich almond filling, however Jones (2021) points out that carrot cake is a much healthier option.	This enhances the above extract by drawing on a contrasting argument for the best type of cake. This is an important step in building an argument because we should always consider different perspectives.
Smith (2021) argues that a cherry bakewell is the best cake due to the combination of strawberry jam and a rich almond filling, however Jones (2021) points out that carrot cake is a much healthier option. I concur with Smith's view, as many of my learners hate carrots, which is supported by Grealish (2023), who demonstrates that 75% of FES learners despise carrots.	This is developing into a much better piece of work, with multiple sources and perspectives used to build an argument. The author has also contextualised it to their learners, which is what you will need to do in your academic writing to demonstrate your understanding and application of theory or research.

Chapter summary

As we come to the end of this textbook, it seems fitting to bring together some of the key themes we discussed.

We set out to write a textbook that was accessible and easily digestible yet challenging and supportive to enable you to connect key evidence-informed concepts to your FES classrooms and subject specialist teaching practice. We align each chapter with an occupational duty set out in the Learning and Skills Teacher Occupational Standards. In the earlier chapters, we considered duties 7 and 8, elaborating on the broad roles and responsibilities you have in FES and how these are informed by broader policy and legislation, supporting you to work within your professional boundaries. We then examined the principles that underpin duties 1 and 5, where we considered the learners that study within the FES sector and how to meet their very diverse needs through inclusive practices both within and beyond the classroom. Setting expectations and maintaining a warm but demanding approach with learners is deemed to be the most effective way to promote positive learning behaviours within FES environments.

Our attention then turned to duties 3 and 4 with an evidence-informed approach to curriculum planning, providing you with a theoretical understanding of the different models and philosophies that underpin your practice. This was then considered at the micro level through a focus on a wide range of evidence-informed teaching practices under the themes of head, heart and hand, which supports you to contextualise them based on your subject specialist teaching.

The deep dive into assessment practices allowed us to focus on duty 2 in order to emphasise learner outcomes. Here, we interrogated a range of literature to consider the most valid and reliable methods that we can use to formatively and summatively assess learners to support them to become owners of their learning journey.

Finally, duties 6 and 9 were the focus of attention. Here, we explored ways to develop professional relationships and support learners' progression through and beyond the FES sector. The core themes of the textbook were then pulled together for this chapter, enabling you to understand how to be successful in your FES ITE programme.

We would like to thank you for using this textbook and wish you well in your studies and beyond into your teaching career!

References

Arefian, M. H. Çomoğlu, I. and Dikilitaş, K. (2024). 'Understanding EFL teachers' experiences of ChatGPT-driven collaborative reflective practice through a community of practice lens.' Innovation in language learning and teaching, 1–16.

Borton, T. (1970). Reach, Touch and Teach. London: Hutchinson.

Brookfield, S.D., 2017. Becoming a Critically Reflective Teacher. 2nd ed. San Francisco, CA: Jossey-Bass.

Collet, V. S. (2024). 'The Selfie Project: Blogging as Online Reflection During Student Teaching.' Teacher education quarterly, 51 (2), 32–51.

Department for Education (DfE). (2024). Expectations for the delivery of initial teacher education for FE. Available at: Expectations for the delivery of initial teacher education for FE - GOV.UK [Accessed 26 March 2025.]

Dalgarno, B., Reupert, A. and Bishop, A. (2015). 'Blogging while on professional placement: explaining the diversity in student attitudes and engagement.' Technology, pedagogy and education, 24 (2), 189–209.

Darling-Hammond, L., Hyler, M. E., Gardner, M. (2017). Effective Teacher Professional Development. Palo Alto, CA: Learning Policy Institute.

Darling-Hammond, L., Hyler, M.E. and Gardner, M., (2023). 'Effective teacher professional development: Key principles and innovative approaches'. Journal of Teacher Education, 74(2), 135-156.

Dreer-Goethe, B. (2025). 'The impact of mentor support and high-quality connections on student teachers' psychological safety and engagement during practicum'. Frontiers in Education, 10.

Education and Training Foundation (ETF). (2024). Diploma in Teaching (Further Education and Skills) qualification framework. Available at: https://www.gov.uk/government/publications/further-education-initial-teacher-education/diploma-in-teaching-further-education-and-skills-qualification-framework [Accessed 26 March 2025.

Gagné, R.M. (1985). The Conditions of Learning. 4th ed. New York: Holt, Rinehart and Winston.

Gibbs, G. (1988). Learning by Doing: A Guide to Teaching and Learning Methods. Oxford: Further Education Unit, Oxford Polytechnic.

Hamel, C. and Viau-Guay, A. (2019). 'Using video to support teachers' reflective practice: A literature review'. Cogent education, 6 (1).

Klenowski, V. (2002). Developing Portfolios for Learning and Assessment: Processes and Principles (1st ed.). London: Routledge.

Lahiff, A. (2015). 'Maximising vocational teachers' learning: The feedback discussion in the observation of teaching for initial teacher training in further education'. London review of education, 13 (1).

Lammert, C., DeJulio, S., Grote- Garcia, S., and Fraga, L. M. (2024). 'Better than Nothing? An Analysis of AI-Generated Lesson Plans Using the Universal Design for Learning and Transition Frameworks.' The Clearing House: A Journal of Educational Strategies, Issues and Ideas, 97(5), 168–175.

Marshall, T., Keville, S. ; Cain, A. ; Adler, J. R. (2022). 'Facilitating reflection: a review and synthesis of the factors enabling effective facilitation of reflective practice.' Reflective practice, 23 (4), 483–496.

Nilson, L.B. and Goodson, L.A. (2021). Online Teaching at Its Best: Merging Instructional Design with Teaching and Learning Research. John Wiley and Sons, Incorporated, Newark.

O'Leary, M. (2020) Classroom observation : a guide to the effective observation of teaching and learning. Second edition. London ; Routledge Falmer.

Petty, G. (2018). How to Teach Even Better: An Evidence-Based Approach. 2nd ed. Oxford: Oxford University Press.

Rosenshine, B. (2012). Principles of instruction: Research-based strategies that all teachers should know. American Educator, 36(1), 12-19.

Scutt C., (2018) Is engaging with and in research a worthwhile investment for teachers? In: Carden C (ed) Primary Teaching: Learning and Teaching in Primary Schools Today. London: SAGE, pp. 595–610

Scott, D. (2022). Digital learning, teaching and assessment for HE and FE practitioners. St Albans: Critical Publishing.

Thompson, N. and Pascal, J. (2012). 'Developing critically reflective practice'. Reflective Practice, 13(2), 311–325.

Tummons, J., and Ingleby, E. (2012). 'The problematics of mentoring, and the professional learning of trainee teachers in the English further education sector.' International Journal of Adult Vocational Education and Technology, 3(1), 29-39.

Index

The page number followed by *f* indicates figures.

A

Abedin, M., 210
Abie, S., 130
academic programmes (A-level), 8, 10, 14, 16–17, 30, 107, 183, 185, 203, 251–252, 257–258
academic self-concept, 142, 147
academic writing, 285
access arrangements, 72
Achinstein, B., 242
active listening, 65
active processing assumption, 161
Acts of Parliament, 10–11
adaptive teaching, 89–90, 91f, 92f, 144
    PCK and learner needs, 93–94
    resources, 91–92
    trauma-informed practices, 95–96, 97f
ADHD see Attention deficit hyperactivity disorder
adult skills fund (ASF), 8
advance organiser, 139
Advanced teacher status (ATS), 284
'affect' domain, 137–138, 145
Agarwal, P. K., 217
AGQs see applied general qualifications
'agree, build, challenge' (ABC) method, 216
Ahmadi, A., 141–142
Alexander, R., 133
Allan, T., 252
'all, most, some' objectives, 89, 90f
Anderson, A., 242
Anderson, R.B.,159
andragogy, 134
anxiety, 59, 79
applied general qualifications (AGQs), 250–252
apprenticeships, 15–16, 30, 70, 107, 189–190, 251
Arefian, M. H., 273
Aronowitz, S., 254
arthritis, 80
ASF see adult skills fund
Ashbee, R., 115–116
assertive teachers, 53–54
assessment, 27, 32, 114, 121, 199, 252, 269, 276, 281
    AI and validity of, 229
    design, 121
    formative, 114, 129, 165, 168, 205–225, 276
    of individual needs, 72–73
    initial, 72–73, 84, 154, 202–205, 231
    methods of, 199–202
    observation as, 208–209, 209f
    ongoing, 88, 114
    peer, 217–218
    risk, 12, 83, 276
    self-assessment see self-assessment
    summative see summative assessment
Atkins, L., 16, 33–34, 86, 228, 253–254
ATS see Advanced teacher status
attention deficit hyperactivity disorder (ADHD), 77
Ausubel, D. P., 153
authentic curriculum, 117
autism, 78
autonomy, 140–141
Avis, J., 33–34
Avola, P., 39–40
awarding organisations (awarding bodies), 13, 152, 201, 226–227, 269
awareness, metacognitive, 174, 174f

B

Babad, E., 239
Baddeley, A 150, 158
Bandura, A., 147–148
Bandura's social learning theory, 147–148, 147f
Barrouillet, P., 150
Barrow, R., 110
Barsalou, L., 182
Beadle, P., 66
Beck, J., 108
behaviour iceberg, 88–89, 88f
behaviour management, 39, 44–54, 60, 64–67, 107, 126, 141, 143, 148
behaviourism, 46, 135, 147
belonging, learners, 55–57, 65
Bennett, T., 44–45, 48
Bernstein, B., 104, 108, 116, 133
best endeavours, 71
big questions, 138
Biggs, J., 120–121
Bigg's taxonomies, 120, 120f

Bilge, N., 83
Binder, C., 124–125
Bjork, E. L., 128, 144, 157
Bjork, R. A., 125–126, 128, 144, 157, 225
blocked/massed practice, 128, 128f
Bloom, B., 6, 120, 137, 176, 191
Bloom's taxonomy, 120–121, 120f, 137, 216–217
Bolton, P., 257–258
Borton's reflective model (1970), 271, 271f
Brookfield, S. D., 270
Brookfield's four lenses (2017), 272, 272f
Bromfield, C., 47
Bruner, J., 116, 144
BTEC, 15–16, 106, 223, 227, 257, 282
Butler, R., 220–221

C
Camos, V., 150
Canter, L., 53
Canter, M., 53
Caviglioli, O., 67, 164, 171
CAYP see safeguarding children, adolescents and young people
CEDEFOP see European Centre for the Development of Vocational Training
Chalmers, D., 181
Chase, W., 123
Chen, O., 150
Chen, S-K., 142
Chesterton, G. K., 111
Children and Families Act (2014), 11, 14
Christodoulou, D., 200, 228–229
chronic fatigue syndrome, 80
Chu, T. L., 57, 142
chunking, 77, 117, 152, 170
Clark, A., 181
Clarke, R., 179
Clarke, S., 221
classroom layout, 61, 61f
Claxton, G., 176, 182
CLT see cognitive load theory
Clughen, L., 176
code of conduct, 31, 33, 49–50
codes of practice, 10–11, 33
Coe, R., 93, 118, 140
cognition see neurodiversity
cognitive constructivism, 135
cognitive load theory (CLT), 150–158, 153f, 171, 182

cognitive offloading, 187
cognitive theory multimedia learning (CTML), 158, 161–165, 162f
    generative learning, 168–170
    metacognitive approaches, 172–176
    retrieval practice, 165–168
    Shimamura's MARGE, 170–172
    twelve instructional principles, 162–163, 163f
coherence principle, 163, 163f
cold calling, 55, 60, 210–213
Collet, V. S., 273
command function, 237
comment-only feedback, 220–221
communication, 110, 237, 253
    channels, 23
    non-verbal, 239–240
    online, 240–241
    verbal, 237–239
communities of practice, 236–237
competence, 15, 32, 142–145, 278
conflict resolution, 242–243
connoisseurship, 189–190
Conservative governments, 11, 251, 255, 257
    in 1980s and 1990s, 15
    in 2010s and 2020s, 16
contemporary observation frameworks, 274
Cotton, D. R., 229
Counter-Terrorism and Security Act (2015), 11
Covid-19 pandemic, 16, 252
CPD, 35, 259, 283–284
Crawley, J., 32, 107
Crenshaw, K., 87
critical pedagogies, 135
critical writing, 285
CTML see cognitive theory multimedia learning
cued recall, 166–167, 170
cumulative dysfluency, 124–125, 124f, 202
curriculum/curricula
    considerations for designing, 122–130
    construction, 111
    definition, 104–105
    development, 27
    diversify, 84, 97–98, 111
    explicit vs. implicit, 112
    linear, spiral, network and web models, 115–117, 115f
    objectives, establishing, 120–121
    process vs. product model of, 113–115

purposeful design, 247–248
TVET, 250–252

D
Dalgarno, B., 273
Dallimore, E. J., 211
Dargue, N., 185
Darling-Hammond, L., 35, 278, 284
Data Protection Act (2018), 11, 23
DCT see dual coding theory
decoding phase, 238
DeNisi, A., 221
Department for Education (DfE), 12, 32, 80, 282, 285
depression, 78–79
DfE see Department for Education
diabetes, 80
differentiation, 89–91
digital boundaries, 23
digital tools, 135, 260, 273
DiT framework, 274, 281–283
drawing, 108, 169, 280
Dreer-Goethe, B., 283
dual coding theory (DCT), 158–161, 159f, 182
dual professionalism, 30–31, 117–119, 234
    closure of profession by restrictive organisations, 31–33
    code of conduct, 31, 33
    intellectual training and education, 30–32
    skill based on theoretical knowledge, 31–32
    testing of competence, 31–32
Dubeau, A., 148
dyscalculia, 76
dysfluency, 124–125, 125f
dysgraphia, 80
dyslexia, 76, 228
dyspraxia, 77

E
EAL see English as an additional language learners
Eaton, S. E., 229
Ebbinghaus, H., 130
Ebbinghaus's forgetting curve, 126–130, 127f
Eccles, J., 144
Education and Skills Funding Agency (ESFA), 8
Education and Training Foundation (ETF), 6–7, 13, 17, 26, 28, 32–34, 37, 40, 234–235, 284
education for sustainable development (ESD), 34, 36–37, 41

educational health care plan (EHCP), 8, 71, 73
effective coping strategies, 39–40, 124, 148
ego-focused feedback, 220–221
EHCP see educational health care plan
ELT see experiential learning theory
embodied cognition, 137, 177, 181–185, 191
embodiment scale, 188f
emergent curriculum, 117
EMF see external memory field
emotional arousal, 147–148, 191
emotional boundary, 18–19
EMT see extended mind thesis
enacting, 168–169
enactivism, 135
encoding and retrieval, 122
encoding phase, 237
encoding specificity principle, 167, 185
end-point assessor (EPA), 226, 268–269, 278, 281
English and maths initial assessments, 72–73, 202, 269
English as an additional language (EAL) learners, 85–86, 87f
English speakers of other languages (ESOL) learners, 85–86, 117, 186–187
EPA see end-point assessor
epilepsy, 80
Equality Act 2010, 11–12, 14, 21, 63, 71, 74–75, 99
Escandell, S., 57, 142
ESD see education for sustainable development
ESFA see Education and Skills Funding Agency
Esmond, B., 16, 253
ESOL learners see English speakers of other languages learners
ETF see Education and Training Foundation
ethnic minority, 84
European Centre for the Development of Vocational Training (CEDEFOP), 37
evaluation, 104, 248, 264, 272
Evens, M., 119
experiential learning theory (ELT), 177–181
expert learning, 123, 153–154
expertise reversal effect, 155, 157
explaining, GLA, 168
explicit curriculum, 112
extended mind thesis (EMT), 177, 181, 187–188
external memory field (EMF), 188
extraneous load, 150–152, 151f
extrinsic motivation, 47, 49

F

false views, teaching, 119
FAME approach, 157
FE and skills teachers
    balancing teaching and responsibilities, 28–29
    core responsibilities of, 26–27
    data gathering, learners, 73–74
    difficult conversations, handling, 64–65
    dual professional, 30–34, 30f
    education for sustainable development (ESD), 36–39
    flexibility and resilience, 39–41
    learning names of learners, 55–56
    mentoring, 282–283
    navigate online spaces, 23
    positioning, 51–53
    professional boundaries, 18–20
    roles of, 26
    standards, professional, 34–36
    subject specialist, 93
    support networks and resources, 40–41
    types of, 53–54
    value diversity, 70–71
feedback, 27, 36, 218–219, 259, 274, 278
    formative, 90, 144
    forward, 221–223
    with grades, 219–220
    on task, 220–221
    types of, 220–221
fibromyalgia, 80
Fiorella, L., 163, 168–169, 171
Fisher, R., 242
Flavell, J., 173
fluency, 124, 127
footprint, digital, 23
formal learning, 112, 113f
formative assessment, 114, 129, 168, 199, 205–206, 206f
    check phase of, 208–219
    clarifying the goals, 205–207
    correct through feedback, 219–224
    summary of, 224–225
free recall, 166
Frenay, M., 148
Frith, C., 188
Frome, P., 144
Fugate, J. M. B., 182
further education and skills (FE and Skills) sector, 8–10, 9f, 14
    analogy for, 17–18
    history of, 15
    learners see learners
    learning environment, 44–45
    progression pathways in, 250, 250f
    quality assurance frameworks and processes, 244–245
    relevance to, 11–14
    teachers see FE and skills teachers
Further Education Teachers' Qualifications (England) Regulations 2007, 31

G

GAD see generalised anxiety disorder
Gallagher, E., 124
Gallotti, M., 188
Gatsby benchmarks, 249–250, 258, 264
GDPR see General Data Protection Regulations
Geary, D., 149
gender reassignment, 81–82
General Data Protection Regulations (GDPR), 11–12, 23, 73, 237
general education, 15, 31, 257–258
generalised anxiety disorder (GAD), 79
generative AI, 90, 216, 229–230, 273, 277
generative learning activities (GLA), 168–170
gestures, 182–186, 183f
'Getting to yes' conflict resolution, 242–243
Gibbs' reflective cycle (1988), 271–272, 271f
GLA see generative learning activities
goal-free effect, 155
Goodson, L. A., 276
grade and comment feedback, 220
grade-only feedback, 220–221
Gravells, A., 200–201
green construction skills, 37–38
green papers, 10–12
Greenberg, M. T., 242
Grosse, C., 157
Groth, C., 182
group profile, 73–74, 202
grouped tables, 61, 61f
GROW model, 262–263
Gutman, L. M., 84

H

Haapanen, L., 37
Hall, P., 208
Hall, V., 245
Hamel, C., 273
Hanley, P., 117, 133, 190
Hattie, J., 219
haptic modality, 182–185
HASAWA see Health and Safety at Work etc. Act 1974
Hattie, J., 207, 218, 219
head of sixth form (HoS), 55
Health and Safety at Work etc. Act 1974 (HASAWA), 11–12
hearing impairment, 80
Hedstrom, K., 242
HEIs see higher education institutions
Herbet, J., 144
Hertenstein, J. H., 211
'hidden' or 'covert' curriculum, 112
higher education institutions (HEIs), 10, 32, 257–258, 264
Hitch, G., 150, 158
Hitchcock, 51–52
Hodkinson, H., 236
Hodkinson, P., 236
hooks, b., 97, 135, 176, 182
Hordern, J., 108
horizontal discourse, 108, 116
HoS see head of sixth form
Howe, C., 210
Hrach, S., 182
Hughes-Berheim, S., 184

I

IDEA framework, 99–100
IfL see Institute for Learning
ILOs see intended learning outcomes
ILP see individualised learning plan
imagining, 168–169
implicit curriculum, 112
independent learning providers, 8
individualised learning plan (ILP), 73–74
informal learning, 112, 113f
Ingleby, E., 282
initial assessment, 73, 88, 154, 202
    at beginning of lesson, 204–205
    at beginning of programme, 202–204
    benefits of, 205f

initial teacher education (ITE) programmes, 31–32, 34, 234, 267–270, 273–274, 279, 282–286
Institute for Apprenticeships and Technical Education (IfATE) see Skills England
Institute for Learning (IfL), 32
intended learning outcomes (ILOs), 120–121, 189
interleaving approach, 129–130, 129f
intrinsic load, 150–152, 151f
intrinsic motivations, 47, 49
ITE programmes see initial teacher education programmes

J

Jackson, P., 189
Jacobs, J., 173
JCQ see Joint Council for Qualifications
Jennings, P. A., 242
Johnson, S., 109
Joint Council for Qualifications (JCQ), 71–72
Jones, I, 257, 285

K

Kang, S., 185
Karpicke, J. D., 165
Keenan, M., 124
Keep, E., 109
Kemp, B., 97
Kerr, K. P., 124
Kirschner, P, 179, 188
Kluger, A. N., 221
knowing-doing gap, 176–177, 189
knowledge, skill and behaviour (KSB), 10, 32, 105–108, 117, 126, 146, 150, 152, 201, 248, 267
knowledge boundary, 19–20
Koedinger, K., 127
Kolb, D. A., 177–178, 181
Kolb's learning cycle, 177–178, 177f
Kounin, J., 51
KSB see knowledge, skill and behaviour

L

Labour governments
    in 1960s and 1970s, 15
    in 1990s and 2000s, 16
    in 2020s, 16–17
Lammert, C., 277
Land, R., 118

Index

learner needs
    age impacts, 74
    assessments of individual, 72–73
    PCK and, 93–94
    physical disability, 79–81
    planning for, 74–85
    pregnancy and maternity, 83
    reducing disability barriers, 75–81
    social and emotional, 78–79
learners
    adaptation of resources, 91
    age, 74
    assessment see assessment
    attendance and punctuality, 66–67
    background of, 85–86
    behaviourism, 46–47
    career guidance, 247
    cohort in FES, 70
    compliance, assuming, 66
    consistency and routines, 58–61
    develop knowledge, skills and behaviours, 106–107
    disability, 75–81
    expectations, 61–64, 63f
    generative learning, 168–169
    grouping, 60–61
    intersectionality, 87
    in learning environment, 44–45
    learning names of, 55–56
    LGBTQ+, 81
    long term memory, 162, 168
    metacognitive strategies, 175–176
    needs see learners needs
    observing performance, 208–209
    one-on-one discussions with, 66
    positioning in learning space, 61
    religions, cultures and beliefs of, 84, 85f
    self-efficacy, 148
    teacher questioning, 199, 210
    teacher relationships with, 53–54
    think, pair, share, 213
    thinking time, 211, 211f
    tone and volume with, 66
    voice, 245
    whole class responses, 211
    working memory of, 151
learning
    vs. performance, 125–126, 225
    activities, 121
    affective domain, 137–145
    assessment for see assessment
    cognitive theories of, 149–161
    definition, 125
    environment see learning environment
    formal, non-formal and informal, 112, 113f
    generative, 168–170
    names, 55–56
    planning and delivering, 27
    psychomotor theories of, 176–180
    social theories of, 145–148
    style, 158, 181
    theories and application, 136–137
    value in, 230
Learning and Skills Research Network (LSRN), 40
learning environment
    creating positive, 57–61
    expectations, establishing, 62–64, 63f
    in FE and skills sector, 44
    institutional culture and policy, 45–50
    maintaining expectations, 64–66
    policy return, 66–67
    professional relationships, establishing, 53–57
    teacher positioning, 51–53
LEAs see local education authorities
legislation and policy, 10–11
legislative and regulatory requirements, 21–23, 247–250
Lenon, B., 254
Lemov, D., 57, 210
Lewis, J., 257–258
LGBTQ+, 81
local education authorities (LEAs), 15
Loibl, K., 179
long-term memory, 122–123, 128, 150, 153, 153f, 159, 162, 165, 166f, 168, 204, 225
lower-level vocational programmes, 254–256
LSRN see Learning and Skills Research Network

M

Macrine, S. L., 182
Mansworth, M., 144
manthanology, 115–116
mapping, 168–169
MARGE (motivate, attend, relate, generate and evaluate), 138–140, 170–172
marriage and civil partnership, 81–82
Marshall, P., 176

Marshall, T., 270
Mavilidi, M. F., 182, 187
Maxwell, 274
Mayer, R., 159, 161–163, 162f, 169, 171
McDowell, C., 124
MCQs see multiple choice questions
McTighe, J., 121
Melton, A. W., 122
meta-analysis, 185, 218–219
metacognition, 172–176, 172f
metacognitive knowledge, 173
metaphoric gestures, 184–185
Meyer, J. H. F., 118
microaggressions, 100
Millerson, G., 30–31, 33, 234
MKO see 'more knowledgeable other'
modality effect, 155
'mode A' teaching, 141
'mode B' teaching, 141
'more knowledgeable other' (MKO), 144
Muller, J., 108
multimedia theories, 150, 158, 161
multiple choice questions (MCQs), 199, 214–216
Murphy, J., 66

N
narcolepsy, 80
Narens, L., 172, 172f
National Education Union (NEU), principles, 95–96, 97f
national vocational qualifications (NVQs), 15–16, 106–107, 250
NcNeill, 183
Nelson, T., 172, 172f
Nelson and Naren's model of metacognition, 172–173, 172f
NEU see National Education Union
neurodiversity, 75–78
neurotypical, neudiversity, 75
Niemiec, C. P., 148
Nilson, L. B., 276
nine events of instruction, 275
non-assertive teachers, 53–54
non-formal learning, 112, 113f
novice learning, 123, 153–154
null curriculum, 117
Nunn, L., 56
Nuthall, G., 127, 218
NVQs see national vocational qualifications

O
observation practice
during, 277–278
after, 278
prior to, 274–277
obsessive compulsive disorder (OCD), 75
OCD see obsessive compulsive disorder
Office for Students (OfS), 257
OfS see Office for Students
Ofsted, 13–14, 245, 247–248, 252, 255, 258
O'Leary, M., 244–245
Oliver, M., 75
online teaching, 23, 163, 276
Oughton, J., 138, 145
overarching frameworks, 138–139

P
Paas, F., 153–154
Paivio, A., 158
Paivio's dual coding theory (DCT), 158–161, 182
Paris, S., 173
Pascal, J., 270
pastoral mentors support, 283
PCK see pedagogical content knowledge
pedagogical content knowledge (PCK), 93–94, 117–119, 175, 190
pedagogy, 104, 133–134
Bloom's domains, 137f
four dimensions, 134f
philosophies, 135–136
practice, 125
signature, 190
three domains of, 137–190
peer assessment, 200, 217–219
performance accomplishments, 147–148, 191
Perkins, D., 174
Perry, J., 172, 175
personal protective equipment (PPE), 12
personal tutoring vs. coaching, 261
personalised curriculum, 117
Petty, G., 211, 222
physical activity, 177, 186–187
physical boundary, 18–19
Piaget, J., 135, 176, 207
Piaget's schema and cognitive development, 207
Pierce, C., 100
Pierre, E., 138, 145
planning workshop & practical learning, 276
Plante, I., 148

Platt, M. B., 211
Polanyi, M., 189
policies, 10–11, 71
    on behaviour procedures, 45f, 46–47, 46f
    legislation and, 10–12
    post-pandemic, 16
    restorative practice, 45f, 47–48, 47f
    return, 66–67
portfolio building, 114, 278–279
Post-16 Education Bill (2021), 16
Post-16 Skills Plan, 11–12, 16, 255
power and powerful knowledge, 108
PPE see personal protective equipment
praise-only feedback, 221
Prevent duty, 11, 22
prior knowledge, 154, 157, 163, 165, 169, 171, 175, 179–180, 188, 204–205
prior learning, 16, 127, 150, 161, 165–166, 231
problem solving skill, 109, 156, 159, 179, 253
professional boundaries, 241
    effective signposting and referral, 20–21, 20f
    legislative and regulatory frameworks that impact, 21–23
    in online spaces, 23
    with stakeholders, 241
    types of, 18–20
    working within, 18–20
profession/professional
    behaviour, 235
    boundaries see professional boundaries
    competency, 235
    development portfolios, 278–281
    digital identity, managing, 241–242
    digital professional identity, managing, 241–242
    discussion, 280
    relationships, 236–237
    responsibility, 234
psychomotor domain, 114–115, 133, 137, 176–177
purposeful curriculum design, 247–248

Q

QTLS status see Qualified teacher learning and skills status
QTS see qualified teacher status
Qualified teacher learning and skills (QTLS) status, 33, 284
qualified teacher status (QTS), 33

R

race and ethnicity, 83–84
Ranken, E., 179
RAR model see receive-apply-reuse model
Rathunde, K., 176
reasonable adjustments, 71, 75, 79, 88–89
receive-apply-reuse (RAR) model, 275
receiving phase, 237
redundancy effect, 155
reflective models, 178, 178f, 180, 271–273
reflective practice, 270–273
regulation, metacognitive, 173–174, 173f
regulatory bodies, 13, 248
relatedness, 57, 142–143
Renkl, A., 153, 157
restorative practices, 45, 47–48, 66
Rizollatti, G., 183
Roberts, H., 53–54, 62
Rodriguez, 215
Roediger, H. L., 165
Roll, I., 179
Rosenshine, B., 127, 144, 208, 214, 277
Rosenshine's Principles of instruction, 127, 275
Rosling, H., 185, 190
Rummel, N., 179
Russell, D, 17
Ryan, R. M., 148

S

safeguarding children, adolescents and young people (CAYP), 22
Safeguarding Children and Young People Act (2023), 11
SAMHSA see Substance Abuse and Mental Health Services Administration
scaffolding, 90, 123, 144, 157, 162
schemas/schemata, 122–123, 165–166, 170
    theory, 122, 122f
    using, 123
scheme of work/learning, 105, 252
Schilhab, T., 182
Schmidt, M., 187
Scott, D., 276
Scutt, C., 272
SDT see self-determination theory
seating plan, 51, 51f, 60
select, organise and integrate (SOI) framework, 161–162

selective interference effect, 161
self-assessment, 200, 218–219, 244
self-determination theory (SDT), 140–145
self-efficacy, 147–148, 147f, 190–191
self-explaining, 169
self-explanation effect, 155
self-testing, 169
SEND code of practice: 0 to 25 years (2014), 11, 14, 22, 71, 80
SEND review: right support, right place, right time (2022), 11
senior leadership team (SLT), 45
sense of 'fit', 56
sense of 'valued involvement', 56
sentimentalist teacher, 54
SET see Society for Education and Training
sex and sexual orientation, 81–82
Shannon, C. E., 237, 238f
Shannon and Weaver's model, 237–238, 238f
Sherrington, T., 141
Shimamura, A., 138-140, 170-172, 186, 191
Shulman, L. S., 93–94, 117
Siegal, H., 109
signalling principle, 163, 163f
signature pedagogy, 190
Signore, F., 237
Simerai, A., 208
Simon, H., 123, 153
simulation and enactment, 186
Singer, J., 75
situated and distributed cognition, 181, 187–188
Skills England, 13, 16, 107
Skills for jobs: lifelong learning for opportunity and growth (2021), 11
Skills Plan (2016), 255
SLT see senior leadership team
Smedley, A., 83
Smedley, B. D., 83
social boundary, 18–19
social constructivism, 135
social media, 23, 114, 260
Social Mobility Commission, 254
social skills, 110
Society for Education and Training (SET), 32, 284
socioeconomic status, 85–86
Soderstrom, N. C., 125–126, 225
SOI framework see select, organise and integrate framework
sophisticate teacher, 54

spaced practice, 128–129, 129f
spatial contiguity principle, 163, 163f
specification, 105, 226–227
split-attention effect, 155
Stanciu, D., 181
stakeholders, 34, 39–40, 73, 236–237, 281
    to enhance education and training, 244–245
    professional boundaries with, 241
    to support progression, 258–259
Stenhouse, L., 104–105
Stipek, D., 144
storage, memory, 122
Stork, A., 261
storytelling, 138–139, 186
subject or occupational expertise, 30, 33
subject specialism, 30, 32, 93, 117–119, 190
subject specialist, 32, 40, 82, 91, 93, 117, 190, 283, 286
Substance Abuse and Mental Health Services Administration (SAMHSA), 95
Sullivan, J. V., 182
Sullivan, M., 229
summarising, 168–169, 230
summative assessment, 72, 114, 199, 201, 225–226, 269–270
    external, 226
    internal, 226–228
    problems with, 228–229
support progression, 44, 217, 247–248, 250–252, 257–258
    digital tools helps, 260
    measuring outcomes, 264
    role of personal tutoring, 261–263
    stakeholders, collaborating, 258–259
Swain, R. B., 37
Sweller, J., 150–151, 153–154, 156, 179, 182
syllabus, 105

T
tacit knowledge, 177, 189–190
targeted questioning see cold calling
task-focused feedback, 220–222
Taylor, L., 211
teacher motivational behaviours (TMBs), 141
teacher questioning, 199, 210
teacher self-efficacy (TSE), 148, 190–191
temporal boundary, 18–19
temporal contiguity principle, 163, 163f
temporal dimension, 104

testing effect, 165–166, 166f
Thompson, N., 270
Thompson, R., 14, 117, 190
Thorburn, M., 176
Timperley, H., 219
T Levels, 8, 11–12, 16, 107, 224, 251, 255
TMBs see teacher motivational behaviours
traditional teacher, 54, 63
trainee teachers, 32–33, 44, 51, 92
transient information effect, 155
transition to independence, 136, 136f
transmitting phase, 237
trauma-informed practices, 95–96, 97f
tripartite education system, 15
TSE see teacher self-efficacy
Tummons, J., 236, 282
TVET, 10–11, 14, 17, 82, 107–108, 250
    critical discussion of, 253–254
    curricula, 250–252
    designing, 252
Tyler, M., 113

U

unconscious bias, 99
universal design for learning, 117
unsystematic social processes, 108
Ury, W., 242
U-shaped tables, 61, 61f

V

validity, authenticity, reliability, currency and sufficiency (VARCS) guidelines, 200–202, 205, 226–228
van Merrienboer, J. J. G., 153–154
VARCS guidelines see validity, authenticity, reliability, currency and sufficiency guidelines
Veenman, M. V. J., 172, 175
verbal persuasion, 147–148, 191
vertical discourse, 108
Viau-Guay, A., 273
vicarious experience, 147–148, 191
visual impairment, 80
visualising, GLA, 168
visuospatial sketchpad, 158–159
vocational qualifications, 15–17, 251
Vygotsky, L. S., 135, 142, 143f, 144

W

Walker, B., 261
warm and cold teacher, 54f
warm demander teacher, 54, 63
water cycle, 160
'we' language, use, 65
Weaver, W., 237, 238f
well-structured knowledge domain, 116
we-mode, 188
Wenger, E., 146, 236
Wenger-Traynor, E., 146
Wheelahan, L., 108–109
White, K., 23
white papers, 10–11
Whitmore, J., 262
whole-body movements, 185–186
Wiggins, G., 121
Wiliam, D., 3, 150, 205, 214, 217–218, 222
Williams, D., 32, 253
Willingham, D., 149-150, 158
Willingham's simple memory model, 149–150, 149f
Winch, C., 108–110, 177, 253
Wisniewski, B., 219
Wolf Report (2011), 16
Wolf, A., 16, 254
Wong, M., 151
Wood, P., 244
worked example effect, 155–157
working memory models, 149–150, 149f, 158
workplace or practice placements, 281–282
work-related stress, 39–40

Y

Younas, F., 84
Young, M., 108

Z

Zhu, X., 153
Zierer, K., 219
zone of proximal development (ZPD), 142, 143f, 144
ZPD see zone of proximal development

www.ingramcontent.com/pod-product-compliance
Lightning Source LLC
Chambersburg PA
CBHW051401070526
44584CB00023B/3239